THE GERONTOLOGICAL PRISM:

Developing Interdisciplinary Bridges

Edited by

Jeffrey Michael Clair
and
Richard M. Allman

University of Alabama at Birmingham

Jon Hendricks, Series Editor

Society and Aging Series

Baywood Publishing Company, Inc.
Amityville, New York

Library of Congress Catalog Number: 99-32264
ISBN: 0-89503-201-5 (Cloth)

Library of Congress Cataloging-in-Publication Data

The gerontological prism : developing interdisciplinary bridges /
    edited by Jeffrey Michael Clair and Richard M. Allman.
        p.   cm. - - (Society and aging)
    Includes bibliographical references and index.
    ISBN 0-89503-201-5 (cloth)
    1. Gerontology.   2. Aged- -Medical care.   I. Clair, Jeffrey M.,
1958-   .   II. Allman, Richard M., 1955-   .   III. Series : Society
and aging series.
HQ1061.G416 1999
305.26- -dc21   99-32264
                                                                        CIP

Preface

This book has its origins from a meeting to promote disciplinary cooperation in aging research and practice undertaken by a group of multidisciplinary scholars who came together to discuss their ideas in May of 1996. The enterprise was sponsored by the Boldizar Social Medicine Fund, and by the Department of Sociology, School of Social and Behavioral Sciences, School of Health Related Professions, and the Center for Aging at the University of Alabama at Birmingham. From this conference each participant has produced a chapter for this volume which represents their contributions to the original gathering. We come back together here under the eventual title of our effort: *The Gerontological Prism: Developing Interdisciplinary Bridges.*

Chapters prepared for this book will challenge and stimulate anyone concerned with the human interactions and biopsychosocial processes that constitute aging. The authors come close to representing the almost bewildering number of disciplines currently offering suggestions on improving research and practice strategies in gerontology and geriatrics. They include researchers and practicing physicians, from general medicine, geriatrics, surgery, neurology, OB-GYN, urology, and ophthalmology, as well as the disciplines within the social and behavioral sciences such as sociology, psychology, history, and medical sociology; the health administration professions; nursing; and from the economic and ethical dimensions of public health.

Our intention is to draw distinctions between disciplinary, multidisciplinary, and interdisciplinary studies. Our approach is to provide original manuscripts that are focused and comprehensive, drawing on empirical and applied research, literature reviews, and theoretical and research agenda setting contributions. We come together as contributors with a diverse, yet specifically focused, body of material that should encourage concentrated efforts to develop bridges for integrating the disparate parts of the gerontological literature.

Although the strength of disciplinary perspectives is apparent, the issues raised, when combined, cut across disciplinary boundaries. We codify a host of literature in gerontology and geriatrics and generate new questions in a language meant to be discipline-friendly. This is another purpose of our union: to put together a body of work that can be used in the varied gerontology and geriatric education programs. We have found that no matter where a course offering is housed, today's student body is diverse and the topics addressed here will make up the stuff of many class discussions. We have tried to make the issues here accessible to scholars and students in many disciplines, especially those outside the specialized backgrounds of the authors.

To some extent, each chapter explores a unified objective, that of generating a disciplinary-blind gerontology. The fundamental assumption throughout this book is that the aging individual and society can be enhanced by an understanding of the correlates of basic social, behavioral, demographic, economic, political, ethical, and biomedical processes involving aging. Each author touches on issues that have both social psychological and practical policy significance. We aim toward sensitizing the reader to the possibilities of a properly informed interdisciplinary approach to gerontology.

Our perspective promises movement toward an eventual rapprochement between opposing disciplinary perspectives, although we identify many significant issues still unresolved. First, while virtually all disciplines offer perspectives on how much the overall environment of aging has changed, training and research in gerontology and geriatrics remains enmeshed in traditional perspectives and methods. Second, disciplinary jargon is a major obstacle to shared information. We need to deal with differences in our conceptual languages before we can identify promising ideas, and distinguish them from dead-ends. Third, most professional journals typically publish only a single discipline's research. Since the cited research shows almost no overlap across disciplines, the result is the failure to promote broad based information on aging. The themes of interdisciplinary bridges and research priorities epitomize the need for, and provide the substantive basis of, a gerontological dialogue across disciplines.

The idea for putting prism in our title was borrowed from our co-authors in this volume, Stanford and Stanford. They describe the cultural diversity in society as a prism. We like the primary essence of the analogy, and agree that one of the colors in the spectrum of diversity is gerontology. The prism represents a perspective generated from a variety of sources all weaved together, casting light, and drawing light from each other. In academia, gerontological boundaries are usually demarcated, even as we speak of diffusion and generality. Like the color spectrum of a prism, these boundaries should blend and merge with the agenda and concerns of race, ethnicity, gender, socioeconomic status, social support, religion, personal preferences, aspirations, and co-morbid health trajectories. Even the fluctuant quality of the life course itself relates to the metaphorical prism. Each person, like the crystal slant, varies in complexity and capacity. We can see a mosaic of people taking this fluctuant reality and, like art, forging something more permanent to house personhood and the rhythm of life. Viewing our lives like a prism makes us recognize that we do not exist in a homogeneous world. We have our identities, habits, personal presentations of self, group affiliations, and our special way of living. These examples, too, identify another reason for our cooperation here, to generate integrative efforts, to focus on becoming leaders toward helping our institutions grow into seamless organizations, molding and merging seemingly isolated gerontological research agendas. To accomplish this, we have to understand that we cannot continue to perpetuate narrow disciplinary agenda that fail to focus on the breadth and depth of the prism before us.

This book is timely in that social change has placed new demands on our aging society, thereby altering almost every aspect of the individual aging process.

Mandates toward changing aging programs and practices are abundant. Just as medicine was encouraged to embrace the biological sciences some 100 years ago, recent directives are now suggesting the importance of bridging or blending the gerontological disciplines and professions, developing a broader view of the gerontological spectrum. This book is an attempt to contribute to that dialogue by producing questions and evidence concerning the appropriate goals and objectives of gerontology in the context of a changing environment.

The turn of this century will prove to be a pivotal period for the politics of aging. Social policies for older persons are undergoing a scrutiny unlike anything seen since existing programs and laws benefiting older persons were enacted in the 1930s and 1960s. Torres-Gil, in many of his writings, has informed us that our near future should prove to be a "watershed" in the transition from the modern aging period to a new aging era "where generational claims, diversity and longevity" will be hallmarks of the politics of aging and social policy. This transition is observable by the growing public awareness about aging and gerontological and geriatric concerns. Aging no longer is just the domain of gerontology and geriatrics, but cuts across disciplines and policy agenda. We are all becoming aware that the aging of America has implications for the economic, political, and social conditions of our nation. Our responses will shape what this country looks like in the next century.

Many issues raised within the following pages are only now receiving proper attention from multiple perspectives. The current lack of convergence among gerontological and geriatric scientific perspectives needs to be replaced with interdisciplinary collaborative efforts. Such efforts are rare for many reasons, but conceptual language differences across disciplines remain the most formidable obstacle. This edited collection represents a beginning effort to bring together within one volume the gerontological prism.

In producing a collection which builds toward an interdisciplinary gerontology, we provide observations that influence and challenge health care professionals, social, behavioral, and basic scientists, those in the various schools of medicine, nursing, and public health, and others concerned about the present problems and future direction of our aging population and society. We fully expect this book to have an impact on generating additional thinking about interdisciplinary gerontology, thereby transforming general theoretical debate and permeating empirical practice.

Acknowledgments

We would like to thank Joe Hendricks for his support of this project. We also would like to thank Bill Ershler, William Hazzard, John Mountz, and Fernando Torres-Gil for their early contributions and participation. Our appreciation to Bill Cockerham, Mark La Gory, Toshio Sei, and Michael Wrigley for reviewing various parts of this collection, and to the anonymous external reviewers. Also, our gratitude to Freddie Thomas for preparing all the manuscripts for this publication, and, most important, her giving spirit.

Jeffrey Michael Clair
Richard M. Allman

Table of Contents

Introduction

SOME NOTES ON ORGANIZATION AND CONTENT

In varying degrees, each chapter: 1) addresses the psychosocial content of gerontology as a venue for thinking through theoretical issues of general interest to various sciences and professions; 2) presents variables and findings to gain new insights or make important observations about the possibility of interdisciplinary gerontological research and practice; 3) asks new questions and opens up new areas of inquiry; and 4) suggests new approaches to practice, education, and research.

The first section of this book deals with laying out "Core Disciplinary Perspectives." Cutler, a sociologist, focuses on the reciprocal relationships between aging and social change. Individual and population aging are viewed as forces fostering social change. In turn, the presence or absence of social change is seen as having implications for the process of aging. These reciprocal relationships are illustrated using selected dimensions of demographic aging and selected dimensions of social change. Distinctions are then drawn between disciplinary, multidisciplinary, and interdisciplinary studies, and it is argued that work in the area of aging and social change has been dominated by disciplinary and multidisciplinary approaches. Examples of interdisciplinary studies that have the potential to illuminate the connections between aging and social change are cited. Particular attention is given to the possibility of bringing together researchers from the biomedical sciences, the social and behavioral sciences, and the humanities to examine issues associated with aging and rapid advances in biomedical technology.

In chapter 2, a group of psychologists lead by Carstensen selectively review contributions that the field of psychology has made to the understanding of human aging. The chapter focuses on recent and reliable findings in the subdomains of personality, cognition, and social relationships. They maintain that a major thrust of research in the psychology of aging has been to identify both potentials and constraints that are associated with the aging process and subsequently organize their comments around these themes in each of the subsections. They conclude that psychology's emphasis on the mechanisms that underlie age changes makes it especially well-suited to go beyond the documentation of outcomes and point the way to optimal aging.

In chapter 3, Clair, Yoels, and Karp focus on the subjective implications of current policy issues that impact us all. They connect such issues as intergenerational

1

conflict, multiracial integration, child care, and long-term care with the *subjective, personal responses* persons make when dealing with these issues and their own aging in the course of their daily lives. While they highlight what they feel are the most pressing age-related policy issues in need of interdisciplinary attention, the description of such issues alone is not their sole purpose. They strive to make a *theoretical statement* as well. They infuse a social psychological *point of view,* an organized framework for thinking about these life cycle policy issues. Their emphasis throughout is on persons' continual efforts to give meaning and significance to their lives. They do this realizing that any focus on the *meanings* of aging throughout the life cycle also must remain sensitive to the dynamic interplay between face-to-face relations and the world "behind our backs," the macro domain of history, demography, and social.

Allman, a geriatrician, Baker, a medical sociologist, and Maisiak, a psychologist, provide the reader with an understanding of the importance of clinical and health services delivery research among older adults. Examples of some of the research progress made in the last decade, as well as within the broad categories of clinical and health services delivery research are discussed. Throughout the chapter, the importance of an interdisciplinary approach to clinical and health care delivery research is highlighted. They discuss medical research of aging ranging from the biological, molecular level to clinical research. Their focus of clinical and health care delivery research is on the patient. They contrast this to basic biomedical research with a focus on the cellular or tissue level of organisms. They stress that clinical and health services delivery research addresses the interaction of normal aging and disease in individual humans with the preventive, therapeutic, and palliative interventions of medicine as well as the process through which these procedures are obtained. Clinical research includes the broad categories of the investigation of the pathophysiology of aging, the identification of at-risk and special populations, the classification and diagnosis of specific conditions and diseases, and the evaluation of preventive and therapeutic interventions. Health services delivery research investigates the process and consequences of distributing health care to patients, including cost, access, health care settings, and delivery systems. The efficacy of health care services are evaluated in terms of universality, effectiveness, quality improvement, and quality of life. Thus, variables of interest for clinical and health services research may include biological, psychological, social, and the spiritual aspects of the patient.

The second section of this book highlights "Key Substantive Issues." Stanford and Stanford argue that diversity has emerged as a leading social concept of the century. Scholars and lay persons must seriously question the traditional articulation of diversity. It no longer connotes simple differences. The insurgence of diversity causes major rethinking about how older persons' lives are ordered. As a major social force, diversity requires one to think flexibly about the concept. As society is viewed as less homogeneous, the focus is more on common natural differences. The Diverse Life Patterns concept suggests that individuals and groups flow from varying life situations that make them who they are. They argue that to be effective, scholars must re-examine the nature of the nongeneric universe in which they work. Diversity as a major catalyst for change will influence intra-disciplinary directions in gerontology, and will affect older persons as consumers in all facets of life. Diversity, aging, and social change are seemingly at once dissimilar, but yet have numerous common elements. They are concepts that aid in explaining the status of highly visible social conditions. Diversity as a more recent social concept has not been easy to sort out. Therefore, diversity has emerged as a way of not only assisting in explaining similarities and differences among population groups, but has also begun to be accepted as a way of justifying social, political, and economic actions.

Bengtson and colleagues' chapter examines trends in families, aging, and social change, looking toward intergenerational relationships in the future. It has been suggested that the American family is declining in importance and function; yet they see evidence of strong kinship ties between adult generations despite the presence of intergenerational conflict. They share data they have been collecting from over 300 multigenerational families for more than two decades as part of the Longitudinal Study of Generations (LSG). These data suggest that extended-generational families' constantly-changing metabolism—as a result of the interplay between solidarity and conflict over time—is an indication of its resiliency. Results from the LSG run contrary to the argument that there is a decline in American family structures and functions. This appears to be true even when intergenerational family relationships are considered within a macrosocial context, looking at solidarity and conflict between age cohorts. They suggest a model for future research on multigenerational families that incorporates society-level, family-level, and individual-level mechanisms. Their conclusion is that, as we look toward the future, the "social optimists" are more likely than the "social pessimists" to be correct concerning intergenerational relationships in the twenty-first century.

Drinka discusses caring for patients with problems that do not lend themselves to simple cures as best embodied in a well-functioning interdisciplinary healthcare team. However, she points out that this type of team has been misunderstood and maligned to the point of a threatened existence. In the past 100 years, numerous factors have coalesced to create the matrix of confusion that represents the United States' healthcare enterprise. In creating a need for collaborative practice these factors have made it almost impossible to carry out. The misunderstandings that health providers and health administrators have about healthcare teams and the lack of a sound science to guide their development has added to the problems with implementation. However, the problems that created the need for teams in health care are becoming more intense. In this chapter, she identifies some of the issues that must be addressed if we are to benefit from efficient and effective interdisciplinary practice.

Aaronson and colleagues discuss the considerable disagreement about the merits of interdisciplinary research in advancing knowledge in the area of aging. However, they argue it is clear than when it comes to environmental issues related to aging, interdisciplinary research is critical. They examine the convergence of behavioral, medical, and organizational research as essential to understanding issues related to chronic care organization, financing, delivery, and policy. The research literature is reviewed and issues related to this convergence are discussed. In particular, the relationship between service need and provider role is considered from the perspective of the convergence in theory.

Morrrisey and Wolinsky point out that nursing homes continue to be one of the major providers of long-term care services. They review the literatures on the utilization of nursing home services, and the nature of the nursing home market. They argue that projected use rates portend substantial increases in the demand for nursing homes, and increased pressure on Medicaid and certificate of need agencies. Because major expansions of Medicaid are not likely to occur, this chapter focuses on the implications of the increased demand for long-term care services on the private long-term care market. They conclude by identifying an urgent research agenda that focuses on: 1) the price sensitivity of long-term care services among the elderly, 2) the extent of both technical and market substitutability alternative types of long-term care services, 3) the effects of restrictions on the number of nursing home beds on price, quality, and the mix of services in the community, and 4) the effects of market distortions arising from Medicaid.

The third section of this book, "Patient Care Concerns" deals with some of the most prominent health issues surrounding the aged. Cohen presents cancer as the second leading cause of death in people over the age of sixty-five, and discusses how this segment of our population is increasing in size rapidly. He argues that progress has been made in our understanding of the biological processes involved, the psychosocial issues, and issues relating to clinical aspects of the interface. He discusses priorities for future research in the context of the Biopsychosocial Model for the interface of aging and cancer treatment. He concludes by espousing that there is tremendous potential for discovery if we pursue the research priorities in the biologic, psychosocial, and clinical aspects of the age-related cancers.

Lou Burgio and his interdisciplinary colleagues have chosen three topics that are of particular current interest to Alzheimer's researchers: problems and interventions for community residing patients; problems and interventions in the nursing home; and the assessment of Alzheimer's patients' abilities to communicate medical consent and advance directives. The authors chose these topics to show the breadth of pertinent issues. Not coincidentally, these also are areas wherein the authors are conducting ongoing research. Consequently, wherever possible, they have provided more detailed descriptions of recently completed and ongoing research. They suggest that the capacity to execute an advance directive is an increasingly important issue for Alzheimer's disease (AD) patients and for older adults generally. At the present time, research work on advance directive capacity remains limited. They identify areas for further research that include instrument development, studies of normal older adult capacity to execute advance directives, identification of neuropsychological predictors of this capacity, and individual differences differentiating those people who choose to execute advance directives from those who do not. They feel such research will lead to the development of interventions to support the advance directive capacity of AD and other dementia patients with decisional impairment. For those individuals without full autonomous decisional capacity and for those choosing not to formally execute advance directives, the roll of surrogate decision makers in the process of medical decision making also must be better understood.

Baker, Clair, Yoels, and Allman focus on the content and context of communication during geriatric encounters. Properties of older patient-physician encounters are considered here in terms of the medical system, physician expectations, and the persons seeking care. In view of the increasing numbers of older patients accompanied by others when they visit physicians, they present transcriptions of actual medical encounters from triads. They conclude with suggestions on how sociologists can contribute to interdisciplinary collection of geriatric patient care data.

Kathy Burgio and her interdisciplinary team of psychologists, nurses, urologists, and sociologists present urinary incontinence as a multi-faceted condition with many causes, presentations, and treatments. As a result, a variety of treatments have been developed to address behavioral, physiological, environmental, medical, and surgical aspects of the problem. In this chapter, they describe the current status of the major approaches to incontinence including behavioral treatments, pharmacologic treatments, electrical stimulation, surgical treatments, periurethral injection, and artificial sphincter devices. They divide older patients with incontinence into two general categories: those who are essentially intact functionally, living independently in the community and able to participate in their own treatment; and those with significant cognitive or physical impairments which make them dependent on caregivers at home or in an institutional setting. In this chapter they address the first group of individuals because their numbers are larger and the treatment modalities are oriented to patients themselves rather than a caregiver or an institutional environment. They point out that most studies have examined the results of treatment in terms of physiological change or reduction in the size or frequency of incontinent episodes. Few have considered the psychosocial impact of incontinence or the effects of treatment, or the quality of the patient's life. Often, incontinence can be cured but treatments may introduce new problems such as intolerable side-effects or new voiding difficulties. A satisfactory outcome for one patient might be considered a treatment failure to another. A reduction of incontinence that gives one person a renewed sense of freedom may have little impact on the restricted lifestyle of another. Therefore, they suggest, future studies could be improved by measuring not only the reduction of urine loss but the patient's satisfaction with treatment and the impact of that treatment on quality of life.

Owsley and her interdisciplinary team develop a theoretical perspective on mobility impairment. They use mobility to refer to a person's purposeful movement through the environment from one place to another and as linked to physical and psychological well-being. Mobility is conceptualized as a functional continuum ranging from no mobility to distant excursions from home, with many cross-cutting dimensions (e.g., frequency of excursions, purpose, satisfaction, assistive device use, and adaptive strategies). They feel the concept of "life-space," or the magnitude of an older person's mobility, may prove useful as an outcome measure in studies evaluating treatments for impaired mobility. Prior research on mobility impairment in the elderly has focused on adverse outcomes or complications of mobility impairment (e.g., falls, hip fractures, vehicle crashes, pressure ulcers) and suggests that these outcomes may share risk factors. Their own preliminary data suggest that falling is linked with vehicle crashing in older adults, suggesting the existence of an "impaired mobility syndrome," implying that a more unified approach to intervention evaluation and treatment is merited.

In the most specific sense, this volume focuses on the need for attention to putting the reader in touch with the possibilities for a properly informed interdisciplinary gerontology. Constructive scholars need to take a new look at the nature of the varied universe in which they work. The diversity of our population and disciplines should be embraced as an incentive for change in order to influence interdisciplinary directions in gerontology. Such a focus will enhance all our research, and thereby ultimately affecting persons' overall well-being throughout the life cycle.

Because of the growing diversity of disciplines studying gerontology, fragmented and divergent viewpoints are manifest. Rather than just going about advancing our particular disciplines with a specific point of view, we need to make an effort to share and learn from each other. Such a shift in focus will require great effort and desire to know more about other areas within gerontology and geriatrics. Here, we have attempted to look past the limited agendas of our own subdisciplines. These chapters call attention to the importance of scholars from diverse backgrounds sharing with one another. We hope the work here stimulates further efforts in this direction.

Jeffrey Michael Clair
Richard M. Allman

SECTION I

Core Disciplinary Perspectives

CHAPTER 1

Aging and Social Change: Toward an Interdisciplinary Research Agenda

Stephen J. Cutler

Even the most casual observer will note that we are living in an era of unprecedented social and technological change. Throughout the world, social, economic, and political structures are in a constant state of flux. Some of these changes are taking place in a slow and evolutionary fashion. Others are occurring rapidly and seemingly disjointed from the past. Structural change has altered family systems, population growth and dispersion have changed the geographic landscape, political and economic systems in several Communist nations have been dismantled in favor of democracy and capitalism, and cartographers are increasingly being challenged by the dissolution of old political entities and the emergence of new ones.

At the same time, the rate of technological change has steadily increased. Public health and other biomedical advances have led to reductions in mortality and increases in life expectancy. Technological developments have fundamentally altered modes of transportation and communications. Journeys that once may have taken days, even weeks, can now be made in a matter of hours, and new modes of communications technology have truly created a "global village."

That social change, in its broadest sense, is pervasive is undeniable. The purpose of this chapter is to examine some of the linkages between social change and aging and the implications of these linkages for interdisciplinary research in gerontology and geriatrics. In particular, I want to point, as others have done, to the reciprocal nature of the relationships between aging and social change. From this perspective, individual and population aging will be viewed as forces fostering social change, while social change in turn will be seen as a force affecting processes of aging. The chapter will also argue that the nexus between aging and social change is ripe for interdisciplinary research, although such efforts have been rare to this time. Examples of research topics that lend themselves to interdisciplinary investigations of aging and social change will be described with a particular focus on the potential for bringing together researchers from the biomedical sciences, the social and behavioral sciences, and the humanities to examine issues associated with aging and rapid advances in biomedical technology.

THE DEMOGRAPHIC BACKDROP

Developed Nations

The dramatic shifts in population age structures, especially during the twentieth century, are well-known and set the stage for any consideration of the effects of aging on social change. In the United States, for example, the number of persons aged sixty-five and over has increased more than tenfold from the turn of the century to the present. As Table 1 indicates, there were just over three million persons sixty-five and over in 1900. By 1995, that figure had grown to well over thirty-three million. Slow, but steady increases in the size of the older population will occur for the next decade and a half when it is projected that there will be some forty million older persons by the year 2010. Between 2010 and 2030, however, the United States will witness unprecedented growth in the size of its older population due to the flow of the baby-boom cohorts into the older age groups. The vanguard of the boomers, born between 1946 and 1964, has now reached fifty years of age. Beginning in the year 2010, when the baby-boom generation reaches old age, the numbers of persons sixty-five and older will rise dramatically—from forty million in 2010 to fifty-three million in 2020 and seventy million in 2030.

Coupled with the numerical growth of the older population in the United States has been an equally significant increase in the percentage of the population sixty-five years of age and older, from 4 percent in 1900 to 12.8 percent in 1995. Again, however, when the baby-boom generation reaches old age, a sharp increase is expected to occur in the percentage of older persons. By the year 2030, it is projected that persons sixty-five years of age and older will comprise one-fifth of the population in the United States.

Table 1. Total Population, Population 65+, and Population 85+ for the United States: 1900-2050 (Numbers in Thousands)[a]

	1900	1995	2000	2010	2020	2030	2050
Total	76,303	262,890	276,241	300,431	325,942	349,993	392,031
Total 65+	3,084	33,544	35,322	40,104	53,348	70,175	80,109
% 65+	4.0	12.8	12.8	13.3	16.4	20.1	20.4
Total 85+	123	3,652	4,333	5,969	6,959	8,843	18,893
% 85+	0.2	1.4	1.6	2.0	2.1	2.5	4.8
85+/65+: %	4.0	10.9	12.3	14.9	13.0	12.6	23.6

[a]Middle series projections for years 2000-2050.
Sources: 1900 data, U.S. Senate Special Committee on Aging, 1991: Table 1-2 [6]; 1995 data, U.S. Bureau of the Census, 1997 [61]; 2000-2050 data, U.S. Bureau of the Census, 1996: Table 2-1 [62].

Two other points should be made about demographic dimensions of aging. First, not only is the size of the older population growing, bringing with it a shift toward the aging of the overall population, but the age composition of the older population itself is shifting owing to gains in life expectancy. Average life expectancy at birth in 1900 stood at 47.3 years (46.3 for males and 48.3 for females). By 1995, overall life expectancy at birth was 75.8 years (72.5 for males and 78.9 for females). Over this same period, life expectancy at age sixty-five increased from 11.9 to 17.4 years [1, 2].

These increases in life expectancy, particularly at the older ages, have led to a pronounced trend toward the "aging of the aged." In particular, the segment of the older population commonly referred to as the "oldest-old"—those ages eighty-five and older—has increased both numerically and proportionately. In 1900, persons 85+ were 4 percent of the total population sixty-five and older (see Table 1). By 1995, the oldest-old represented 10.9 percent of the total older population, and by the year 2030 it is projected that persons eighty-five and older will make up about 12.6 percent of the total older population. Furthermore, current projections suggest that by the year 2050, when the baby-boom cohorts have joined the ranks of the oldest-old, persons eighty-five and over will make up close to one out of every four persons sixty-five and older.[1] This steady shift in the direction of the aging of the older population is especially significant in setting the stage for social change given the greater prevalence of a variety of social, economic, and health problems at these advanced ages.

The second point that needs to be made is that these demographic aging trends are by no means unique to the United States. They are common to all developed nations of the world. Indeed, many Western nations are much further along in the transition to an aging population than is the United States. In 1992, for example, the United States, at 12.6 percent, ranked twentieth among developed nations in the percentage of the population sixty-five years of age and older. Sweden, with 17.9 percent of its population sixty-five and over, had the highest percentage of older persons, and eight other countries (Norway, the United Kingdom, Belgium, Denmark, Austria, Italy, France, and Germany) had older populations that comprised 15 percent or more of their total populations [4]. The median age, life expectancy at birth and at age sixty-five, and the numbers and proportions of people sixty-five and older and eighty-five and older are all increasing throughout the developed nations.

---

[1] Even these projections may understate the future potential growth of the older population. As Guralnik, Yanagishita, and Schneider note, standard Census Bureau projections have typically used mortality assumptions that underestimate declines in death rates [3]. Alternative projections that they present, based on an assumption of a continuation of current trends in mortality, lead to substantially higher estimates of the future size of the older population. For example, Census Bureau middle series projections issued in the mid-1980s indicated that persons eighty-five years of age and older would number 12.8 million in 2040. In contrast, under the assumption that mortality trends of recent decades would continue (i.e., a 2% annual decline in mortality), persons 85+ would number 23.5 million in 2040.

Developing Nations

It is equally important to note, however, that population aging is a worldwide phenomenon. It is not restricted to Western countries, but is occurring in developing nations as well. In some respects, in fact, the population aging taking place outside of Europe and North America is even more dramatic than that which is occurring in the developed regions. Of the fifty nations examined in *An Aging World II* [4], percentage increases in the size of the elderly population between 1990 and 2025 are appreciably higher among the countries in the developing regions of the world. All of the nations in the top twenty-five are in the developing regions, with growth rates ranging from 414 percent in the case of Indonesia to 146 percent in the case of Pakistan. Conversely, of the twenty-five countries with the lowest percentage increases in their elderly populations, twenty are among the developed nations.

While population aging is a global phenomenon, the implications for social change are likely to vary considerably in countries of the different regions of the world. Importantly, population aging in Western nations has been spread out over a much longer period of time. For developing nations, it is anticipated that this process will be vastly telescoped. By way of illustration, it took France 115 years for its older population to increase from 7 percent to 14 percent (1865 to 1980) and Sweden eighty-five years (1890 to 1975). On the other hand, the percentage of China's population sixty-five and older is expected to increase from 7 to 14 percent between 2000 and 2027, a span of only twenty-seven years [4]. Thus, the developed nations have had a considerably longer period of time to adjust to their aging populations, while the pressures brought about by demographic aging will be much more precipitous in the case of the developing countries. Moreover, the numbers of older persons involved will be substantially larger in the developing nations: when persons sixty-five and older comprise approximately 14 percent of the population of the United States shortly after the year 2010, they will number approximately forty million (see Table 1); the 14 percent of China's population in the year 2027 is estimated to be on the order of 220 million older persons [5], a figure which is roughly equivalent to the size of the *total* population of the United States in 1977.

AGING AND SOCIAL CHANGE:
THE RECIPROCAL RELATIONSHIP

A basic premise of this chapter is that aging and social change stand in a potentially reciprocal relationship to each other. As indicated by the two-headed arrows in Figure 1, individual and population aging can be viewed as forces having

Aging <————————————> Social Change

Figure 1.

the potential to affect the rate and nature of social change. Conversely, and construed in its broadest sense, social change has the potential to influence the aging process. In what follows, illustrations of these bi-directional effects will be presented to suggest how these two forces operate.

The effects of aging on society's institutional structures are numerous. Take the realm of political economy, for example. Population aging, the shifting age structure of the United States, and increases in the sheer numbers of older persons have been coupled with low fertility rates since the mid-1960s. The effect of these demographic forces has been to increase the size of the older population relative to that of younger and middle aged segments. Of particular importance in the current context is the ratio of persons sixty-five years of age and older to persons eighteen to sixty-four years of age. In 1900, the "elderly" support ratio stood at seven persons sixty-five and older to every 100 persons eighteen to sixty-four. By 1990, the ratio had nearly tripled to twenty persons 65+ for every 100 persons eighteen to sixty-four. And by the year 2040, it is expected that the ratio will nearly double again, with a projected thirty-nine persons 65+ for every 100 persons eighteen to sixty-four [6].

Although support ratios are relatively crude indicators [7], they do provide some general insights into the implications of shifting age structures. For example, it is clear that the balance between older persons in their retirement years relative to persons in the work force will be fundamentally altered with attendant implications for economic support in old age. Thus, our Social Security system, which depends on the contributions of current workers to provide economic support for retirees, will face continued pressure as the balance between the number of recipients and the number of contributors changes. Such effects have already resulted in two changes regarding retirement and Social Security. On the one hand, mandatory retirement at a prescribed age has been abolished for most categories of workers in the United States. On the other hand, between the years 2000 and 2022, the age at which one is eligible to received full Social Security benefits is slated to rise from sixty-five to sixty-seven. These policy changes in mandatory retirement and in age of eligibility for full Social Security benefits may be viewed as efforts to prolong employment, or to decelerate the flow of cohorts out of the labor force [8], in response to population aging [9].

As another illustration, and as Bengtson notes elsewhere in this volume, increasing life expectancy has had profound effects on family structure and functioning. With the growth of the older population and especially the increase in the numbers of the oldest-old, it is now far more common for families to be composed of four and even five generations of members. One analysis of the effects of changing mortality on family structure over the past century documents the magnitude of these shifts [10]. In 1900, only 21 percent of persons thirty years old had one or more of their grandparents still alive; by the year 2000, it is expected that 76 percent of thirty-year-olds will have living grandparents. Similarly, only 1 percent of persons who were forty years of age in 1900 had one or more living grandparents, a figure expected to increase to 21 percent at the beginning of the next century. Further demonstrating the effects of declining mortality and increasing life expectancy on the structure of the American family are shifts by age in the likelihood of having one or more of one's own parents alive. In 1900, only 39 percent of fifty-year-olds and only 7 percent of sixty-year-olds had one or more living parents; by the year 2000 it is expected that 80 percent of fifty-year-olds and 44 percent of sixty-year-olds will have one or more living parents.

This shift toward increasing longevity along with lowered fertility has led to a "verticalization" of family structure, to a transformation of the intergenerational structure of the family from one resembling a pyramid to one more nearly resembling a beanpole [11]. But, as Clair, Yoels, and Karp discuss elsewhere in this volume, an equally important impact of this shift has been the greater prevalence of caregiving responsibilities thrust upon and assumed by contemporary families. With more parents living for a longer period of time, the likelihood that a family will be called upon to provide informal care to a frail elderly relative has increased. It is well-established that the bulk of this task falls on the shoulders of women who, after raising their own children, may find themselves in the position of providing care to a needy parent, perhaps simultaneously to a frail mother-in-law or father-in-law, and eventually to her spouse. Brody has suggested the notion of "caregiving career" to describe these multiple and sequential caregiving demands placed on family members [12].

At the same time that demographic aging has had profound consequences for family structure and for familial caregiving responsibilities, other currents of social change have been occurring that have affected the abilities of families to assume and perform these age-related, caregiving roles [13]. For instance, the steady increase in the labor force participation of women has placed some in the position of having competing occupational obligations. Although recent evidence suggests that fewer women actually occupy such multiple roles than has typically been assumed [14], those women who do have competing role obligations may be forced to decide between continuing their employment while balancing and juggling caregiving and work commitments, seeking or arranging for a part-time job or one with flexible hours, or dropping out of the labor force entirely to accommodate caregiving responsibilities [15].

LIMITS ON THE EFFECTS OF AGING
ON SOCIAL CHANGE

The examples presented above draw attention to the potential impact of population aging on social change. However, limits on the effects of aging on social change also need to be considered. In this section, two such constraints are considered. The first postulates that characteristics of the process of individual aging may prove to be inimical to the occurrence of social change. The second, suggested by the concept of "structural lag" [16], points to sources of structural inertia that impede aging from inducing social change.

Aging, Sociopolitical Attitude Change, and Social Change

There is a persistent assumption that individual aging is associated with two outcomes of relevance to a consideration of the effects of aging on social change. The first of these is that aging is often seen to be accompanied by a shift toward increasingly conservative social and political attitudes. Presumably associated with aging is growing resistance or opposition to change in general and to change that would benefit disadvantaged segments of the population; a higher valuation of social order; an increasing emphasis on authority and obedience; and the adoption of a generally restrictive, rather than permissive and tolerant, attitude toward human behavior [17].

While this first argument does posit attitude change with aging, albeit in a conservative direction, the second notion holds that persons become rigid and "set in their ways" as they age [18]. Finding its most common expression in the familiar, yet ageist, saying "you can't teach an old dog new tricks," the second assumption suggests that aging results in the cessation of attitude change or in attitudinal rigidity.

Examples of these hypothesized attitudinal accompaniments of aging can be drawn from a wide variety of sources. Sigmund Freud, for instance, commenting on the appropriateness of psychoanalytic treatment for older persons, stated that

> The age of patients has this importance in determining their fitness for psychoanalytic treatment; that, on the one hand, more or less above the fifties, the elasticity of mental processes, on which the treatment depends, is as a rule lacking—*older people are no longer educable*—and on the other hand, the mass of material to be dealt with would prolong the duration of treatment indefinitely (emphasis added) [cited in 19, p. 1].

Demographic speculation about the social consequences of the "graying" of the population exposes similar assumptions. Coale, in an early discussion of how a population ages or grows younger, suggests that

> a population with the age composition of a health resort is a mildly depressing prospect. Such a population would presumably be cautious, conservative, and full of regard for the past [20, p. 57].

Lincoln Day notes that "one well-known economist-demographer has averred that a society with the older age structure of a stationary population 'would not be likely to be receptive to change and indeed would have a strong tendency towards nostalgia and conservatism' " [21 p. 27]. Similarly, the Commission on Population Growth and the American Future speculated that an older age structure will bring with it "a larger proportion of the population who are less adaptable to social and political change, thus suggesting the possibility of 'social stagnation' " [21 p. 69]. Finally, popular images of older persons convey the same impression. Findings from the 1974 NCOA/Harris survey showed that only 19 percent of persons eighteen to sixty-four and only 34 percent of persons sixty-five and older viewed most older people as being very open-minded and adaptable [23]. In short, these notions collectively suggest that individual aging brings with it either rigidity or growing conservatism and that these processes associated with aging will likely prove to impede the occurrence of social change.

Theoretical support for these assumptions about the course of attitude change with aging takes several forms [24-29]. Some contend that successive cohorts are socialized to different attitudes, values, and ideologies as the content of culture changes. Associated with the subsequent movement of individual cohort members through the age strata are psychologically-based, age-related changes in the direction of greater rigidity and cautiousness and increasing resistance to change. Others suggest that parental values rejected in adolescence may be reaffirmed at a later time, and that significant life events and changes, occurring with some frequency during late adolescence and early adulthood, become less dense with the passage of time. Increasing integration into the social system with growing family, occupational, and community involvement is also viewed as leading to a greater stake in the maintenance of the status quo. For these and other reasons, social and political attitudes are assumed to rigidify or become more conservative as persons age.

Empirical studies of the link between aging and attitude change, however, have rather consistently provided little support for these assumptions. A series of cohort analyses using replicated items drawn from nationally representative surveys has shown that attitude change is a common occurrence with aging and that when public opinion at large is shifting in a more liberal, less traditional direction, changes evidenced by older cohorts are routinely in the same direction and often at the same pace as the changes taking place among younger cohorts.

For example, an early study by Cutler and Kaufman looked at cohort changes in tolerance of ideological nonconformity over the period 1954-1972 [30]. The results of that investigation showed that the attitudes of all five of the cohorts examined in the analysis (including those 60 years of age and older in 1954 who were 78 years of age and older in 1972) changed in the direction of greater support for civil liberties. An examination of attitudes about the legalization of abortion using seven nationally representative surveys over the period 1965-1977 again demonstrated attitude change across all cohorts, especially between 1965-1973, and in the direction of more liberal attitudes [31]. A similar analysis of attitudes about race relations, using eighteen national surveys covering the period 1959-1985, showed an overall trend toward increasing liberalism for all cohorts combined, increasingly liberal attitudes concerning most racial issues for each of the four cohorts examined in the analysis, and no tendency for the increase in liberal attitudes of the oldest cohort to be at a slower rate than that of the younger cohorts [32].

An interesting variation on this theme involves attitudes about law and order, an attitudinal domain that was marked by conservative shifts in public opinion in the 1960s through the mid-1980s. If persons are prone to change their attitudes in a conservative direction as they age, it might be expected that conservative shifts in the attitudes of older cohorts would outstrip those of younger cohorts. This hypothesis was examined using three replicated items on law and order issues drawn from eighteen national surveys conducted during the period 1959-1985. Results from these analyses showed that each of the four cohorts participated in the shift toward more conservative opinions on the law and order issues, but that either constant or zero differences characterized the trends in percentage differences between the oldest and the other cohorts. In the absence of differential rates of change, it appeared as if older cohorts were no more likely than younger cohorts to adopt conservative law and order attitudes [33].

The results of these several studies are consistent and have important implications for concerns about the impact of an aging society on social change. To begin, there is no evidence that older cohorts are rigid, set in their ways, and incapable of change. Rather, attitude change occurred across all cohorts examined in the several analyses. If public opinion at large was shifting, change characterized the older cohorts as well. Second, in a number of the attitudinal domains examined, overall shifts were in a liberal direction. If national trends were in the direction of less traditional and less conservative attitudes, so too were the shifts among the older cohorts. In the one area where conservative trends dominated national changes, the older cohorts followed suit, but not at a faster rate than the changes taking place among the younger cohorts. In short, change consistently characterizes the older cohorts, these changes tend to be in the same direction as changes occurring nationally, and these changes are neither necessarily nor inevitably in a conservative direction. If public opinion is becoming more liberal, it is likely that the opinions and attitudes of older cohorts will change in that direction and often at the same rate that attitude change is taking place among younger cohorts.

In general, then, one might interpret these findings to suggest that the "graying" of America (and quite possibly other nations) is not inherently incompatible with social and political change. These studies show clearly that the "aging" of older cohorts has been accompanied by change, at least at the social-psychological level (also see Clair et al. this volume). The aging process, per se, does not lead inevitably to a kind of rigidity that would impede social change from occurring. Then, too, it must be remembered that the period examined by the data—the 1950s and 1960s to the mid-1980s—was one in which there had been a continuous, inexorable increase in the size and proportion of the older population. As noted at the beginning of this chapter, the population of the United States was graying steadily during this time. Few would argue, however, that this was an era bereft of social change. Rather, we have witnessed profound changes in areas such as civil rights, family structure, marital status, patterns of labor force participation, concerns about the environment, and so on, all while the graying of the population was occurring.

Structural Lag

Although concerns that individual and population aging might act to retard social change do not receive support at the social psychological level in the empirical literature, it would be incorrect to assume that aging inevitably and invariably serves as a force leading to social change or that its effect is immediate. Rather, as Riley et al. [16] and others have indicated, there may be a considerable delay before social change catches up with population aging. To capture this disjuncture, they have introduced the concept of "structural lag":

> While the 20th century has experienced a revolution in human development and aging, there has been no comparable revolution in the role structures of

society to keep pace with the changes in the ways people grow up and grow old. The lag involves not only institutional and organizational arrangements but also the many aspects of culture that, in addition to being internalized by people, are built into role expectations and societal mores and laws [34, pp. 16-17].

In other words, they point to the mismatch between the growing numbers of fit and capable older persons and the opportunity structures available to them to perform meaningful roles (see also [35]).

As a general example of the problem of structural lag, Riley and Riley note that opportunity structures are largely age differentiated [34]. That is, major segments of the life course are generally allocated to different pursuits: the early years to education, the middle years to work, and the later years to leisure. Yet, such an age differentiated structure fails to keep pace with changes that have occurred in the surrounding society: the need for continuing education to stay abreast of rapid changes in the work place, a desire on the part of some older workers to extend their employment into what had typically been considered to be the retirement years, and the need to spread leisure out more evenly over the life course, particularly to counter excessive role demands of work and family during mid-life. In other words, the Rileys point to the need for age integrated opportunity structures that are more consistent with current social reality.

Future Directions

It should be clear from the foregoing that population and individual aging can and have been forces for social change. Moreover, future shifts in the age composition of societies will exert continuing pressures on social structures to accommodate the growing numbers of older persons and changes in their characteristics, capabilities, and preferences. At the same time, it is no doubt correct that these structural changes have often lagged behind population and individual aging.

What is called for at this point is a more systematic theoretical consideration of the conditions under which aging is likely to be a force leading to social change [36]. In what structural arenas is aging more likely to effect change? Are there structural areas that are more sensitive and responsive to the occurrence of population and individual aging? Conversely, what are the structures that are more resistant, that are characterized by greater inertia? Further, are there situations in which structural lag might profitably be viewed as a stabilizing force during periods of rapid social change?

A related priority in the future study of the effects of aging on social change should be the development of operational indicators of social change, that is the development of a "metric" that is widely applicable to various structural dimensions and can be used to measure the rate and extent of social change that has occurred in response to aging. One major and promising effort along these lines is the Program on Age and Structural Change, under the direction of Matilda White Riley at the National Institute on Aging, the purpose of which is "to develop conceptual, methodological, and substantive understanding of changes in social institutions and their linkage to people's lives . . ." [16, p. 5].

DISCIPLINARY, MULTIDISCIPLINARY, AND INTERDISCIPLINARY APPROACHES

In keeping with the major purpose of this book—to set out priorities for inter-disciplinary collaboration—it would be well to point briefly to distinctions between disciplinary, multidisciplinary, and interdisciplinary approaches.[2] Although these differences may be reasonably straightforward, it is worth identifying the charac-teristics of each in order 1) to assess the extent to which interdisciplinary efforts have been used in the study of aging and social change, and 2) to suggest topics that might lend themselves to fruitful interdisciplinary collaboration. These are the major tasks for the remainder of this chapter.

Disciplinary research can be viewed as work that is conducted within the confines a single discipline. The focus is on a particular substantive topic, and the theories, concepts, and research design are drawn from the central traditions of that discipline.

Like disciplinary research, *multidisciplinary* research focuses on a particular topic, but it draws on the body of knowledge and the research approaches of two or more disciplines. Typically, it involves a group effort on the part of investigators from several disciplines who are working in parallel on a common topic. It is in this sense, at the most general level, that gerontology is often characterized as a multi-disciplinary field of inquiry. With a common interest in understanding processes of aging, researchers from a variety of scientific disciplines bring the theories, concepts, and tools of their disciplinary background to the examination of a given substantive issue. Thus, in the case of social change, the sociologist may be interested in understanding the demographic antecedents of change in the intergenerational struc-ture of families. The economist might be interested in the effects of labor supply, economic conditions, and the availability of pensions on changes in retirement patterns. The broader issue under consideration is aspects of social change, but the approaches taken by the investigators tend to be those of their own disciplines.

Interdisciplinary research is generally considered to be team research where investigators from two or more disciplines are working *collaboratively* on a single project. In this instance, the theories, concepts, and methods of different disciplines are brought together in the examination of a common topic of mutual interest to the researchers. If the common concern of the investigators is accounting for differences in health in the later years, a sociological component of the research might focus on social support, social networks, and socioeconomic status; input from social psychologists and psychologists might focus on health beliefs and health locus of control; health services researchers might be concerned with insurance coverage and

---

[2] The following section draws on Busse [37] and Harris [38].

the availability and accessibility of health care resources and facilities; and physicians might focus their attention on various biomedical assessments of persons.

These three forms of research, of course, are ideal types. Any actual investigation may depart from them in various ways. Most often, perhaps, is the situation where one or more researchers from one discipline borrow theories, concepts, and indicators from another discipline. Alternatively, a particular model that may be employed within a given investigation may itself have elements that tend toward multidisciplinarity or interdiscipinarity, a notable example being Andersen's health behavior model with its focus on predisposing, enabling, and need variables [39]. For present purposes, the important point is that the hallmark of interdisciplinary work is the extent to which investigators from two or more disciplines actively collaborate in the design and execution of research on a topic of common interest to them.

APPROACHES TO THE
STUDY OF AGING AND SOCIAL CHANGE

Drawing upon the distinctions made in the preceding section, I would argue that much of the work on the topic of aging and social change has been disciplinary and, at best, multidisciplinary. Scholars working in this area have made many notable contributions to our understanding of how population and societal aging have fostered social change or created a kind of societal tension with the potential for bringing about change. However, much of this work has taken place within the confines of traditional disciplines, either singly or in parallel. Interdisciplinary research—as defined above and characterized by the active collaboration of investigators representing multiple disciplines—has been rare.

The contributions to three edited collections broadly dealing with aging and social change point to this pattern [16, 35, 40]. Contributors come from a wide variety of disciplines: sociology, economics, demography, history, anthropology, social psychology, social welfare, and social policy. But aside from editors' introductions and summary overviews, individual chapters tend overwhelmingly to be discipline-specific, even when co-authored. Multidisciplinarity results when viewing the collections as a whole, but interdisciplinary collaborations are virtually absent.

INTERDISCIPLINARY APPROACHES:
A MODEL

What I want to set out in this last section is one model for how interdisciplinary research on aging and social change might proceed. The example draws on advances in testing for the presence of genetically-based diseases and points to the possibility of bringing together investigators from the biomedical sciences, the social and behavioral sciences, and the humanities to examine issues associated with aging and rapid advances in biomedical technology.

Technological Change, Social Change, and Cultural Lag

One need not look very far to find examples of rapid technological changes occurring throughout society. The year 1996 represents the fiftieth anniversary of the use of what is considered to be the first electronic computer—the University of Pennsylvania's Electronic Numerical Integrator and Computer—ENIAC [41]. The computing power of this machine, which took up a large room, weighed over fifty tons, and contained more than 17,000 vacuum tubes is now surpassed by inexpensive, hand-held calculators available at grocery store check-out counters and composed of wafer-thin chips that fit easily on the tip of one's finger. Many of our desktop PCs today have as much, if not more, computing power than mainframes of twenty-five years ago.

This computer revolution has also spawned a variety of related changes. For example, communications technology has been altered in major ways with the advent of e-mail, the Internet, and the World Wide Web. What is equally clear is that the emergence of these new computing and communications technologies has not been accompanied by agreements and understandings about the limits of their appropriate use. Witness the passage in 1996 of the Telecommunications Act and the controversy that parts of that legislation—the Communications Decency Act—have engendered about the bounds of appropriate messages and content that can be disseminated over the Internet.

Conceptually, a similar set of issues has arisen regarding biomedical technology. There can be no doubt that medicine's diagnostic and curative abilities have advanced with great rapidity with the continuing development of new and more refined technologies and procedures. But these technologies also have the ability to keep patients alive, prolong the dying process, and postpone death beyond the point that many persons would see as desirable. The controversies surrounding this situation are readily illustrated by the passage in 1994 of Oregon's physician assisted suicide legislation and subsequent legal challenges to it and by widely publicized cases such as those involving Nancy Cruzan and Dr. Jack Kevorkian. In the context of older patients, these and related end-of-life issues have been explored by Callahan [42], Binstock and Post [43], and many others.

Underlying both of these examples (and numerous others that could be cited) is the concept of "cultural lag." Introduced by sociologist William F. Ogburn [44], this concept draws our attention to the fact that a society's cultural system is composed of two general sets of elements: 1) material elements, representing the stock of technological solutions to problems of human existence, and 2) non-material elements—such as values, norms, and sanctions—which represent "social" solutions to problems of human existence. What Ogburn points to is the possibility, indeed the likelihood, that the rates of change along these two dimensions will differ and that change in the material aspects of culture will outstrip change in the non-material aspects. In other words, the pace of technological change will proceed far faster than the pace of change in the values, norms, and sanctions that are relevant to those technologies. The disjuncture in the rate of change in these two cultural spheres leads to a situation where there are no clear guidelines governing the application and utilization of the technologies. Until norms develop regarding the appropriate application of cutting-edge technologies, the climate is ripe for the kinds of controversies noted above.

Genetic Testing

The point I would like to make here is that a conceptually similar set of circumstances exists in the case of some diseases with a genetic component [45, 46]. In recent years, there have been rapid advances in the field of molecular genetics such that it is now possible to conduct predictive testing to determine whether asymptomatic individuals are at risk of developing particular diseases. The conditions under which such tests should be conducted and how the results of testing should and could be used are topics of considerable debate [47].

In the case of Huntington's disease, for example, children of an afflicted parent have a 50 percent chance of developing the disease. Although no cure is presently available, predictive tests are available that are 95 to 99 percent accurate in indicating whether the individual will develop the disease [48]. In the absence of a cure, however, fundamental questions arise about whether at-risk individuals should be tested, what the consequences are of learning that one's risk of developing the disease is heightened or diminished, and whether various life-course transitions and statuses will be altered as a result of having that information. One longitudinal investigation—the Canadian Collaborative Study of Predictive Testing—compared three groups of persons with a parent afflicted with Huntington's: 1) persons whose test results indicated an increased risk of developing the disease; 2) persons whose results indicated a decreased risk; and 3) persons with no change in their knowledge of risk because they either declined to be tested or because the results of the test were uninformative. Results of the study showed that depression was lower and psychological well-being higher among both the decreased *and* increased risk groups than among the no change group at twelve-month follow-up. These findings were interpreted to indicate the value of being informed and being able to plan for the future, regardless of outcome and regardless of the inability to take steps to cure the disease [48, 49].

A somewhat similar situation appears to be developing in the case of Alzheimer's disease, also a progressive, degenerative, incurable condition. Recent work has pointed to the presence of genetic markers that may be associated with an increased risk of developing late-onset Alzheimer's. Research has shown that the likelihood of developing Alzheimer's is greater and the age of onset lower among persons who have the gene for apoE4 [50], and the risk appears to be even greater among those who have two copies of this gene. Although not everyone with the gene for apoE4 develops the disease and some who do develop the disease do not have the gene, findings from such genetics research have set the stage for debate about whether testing should be available to individuals who wish to be informed about their risk [51, 52].

Thus, a 1995 Conference on Apolipoprotein E Genotyping in Alzheimer's Disease, convened by the Alzheimer's Association and the National Institute on Aging, concluded that the use of currently available genetic tests to predict who might get late-onset Alzheimer's is not recommended [53, 54]. On the other hand, a recent survey conducted by the Long Island Alzheimer's Foundation showed that 66 percent of persons with family members with Alzheimer's would want the test and an additional 19 percent would want such a test but only if counseling systems are in place [55]. Only 13 percent of the respondents indicated they would not want the test.[3] Furthermore, 81 percent of those responding thought that medical personnel should not decide whether an individual can have the test.

This discrepancy between the results of the Long Island survey and expert recommendations about the use of such a test again points to a situation where social and technological changes are occurring rapidly, but a shared set of norms about the application and use of newly emerging diagnostic technologies has not emerged. What I would like to suggest, however, is that the cultural lag surrounding rapid change in diagnostic technology points to a set of fruitful areas for the interdisciplinary investigation of aging and social change. Let me sketch out a partial framework for one such study that potentially draws upon the expertise and contributions of investigators from the biomedical sciences, the social and behavioral sciences, and the humanities.

The Long Island survey of interest in being tested for Alzheimer's disease was largely descriptive. Little was done to determine the characteristics of individuals who were willing or unwilling to be tested. The research to be outlined here is intended to take a more careful look at the predictors of interest in undergoing genetic testing to assess one's possible risk of developing Alzheimer's disease.

The principal outcome variable would be whether an individual wishes to be tested for the presence of a genetic marker potentially indicative of a heightened risk of developing Alzheimer's. In view of the current uncertainties about the diagnostic validity of such tests, this measure would need to be carefully designed by or with input from biomedical scientists in order to accurately reflect what such a test could and could not disclose. Drawing on research on the psychology of preferences [57], the measure itself might take into account degrees of uncertainty by asking persons about their willingness to be tested if the test were 50 percent accurate, 75 percent accurate, 90 percent accurate, and so on [58].

Development of a set of predictors could potentially draw upon the full range of disciplinary expertise represented by the research team. Biomedical scientists would be in a unique position to draw upon their clinical experience to suggest characteristics of individuals who may have expressed an interest in being tested and characteristics of those who have indicated no interest. Given that a person's desire to be tested may tap autonomy as a construct, ethicists would be in a unique position to

---

[3] Similarly high percentages of persons interested in being tested for Huntington's disease are reported by Kessler, Field, Worth, and Mosbarger [56].

contribute to the development of indicators reflecting an individual's disposition to autonomous actions.

A number of other potential hypotheses suggest themselves that would draw upon the expertise of social and behavioral scientists. Interest in being tested may be a reflection of a person's coping styles. Those whose adaptive strategies reflect active mastery as a coping style may be more disposed to testing than those whose strategy more nearly reflects a passive coping style. Similarly, locus of control and efficacy are related concepts that may be of relevance. One might entertain a seemingly reasonable hypothesis that persons with internal locus of control and a higher sense of self-efficacy would be more interested in undergoing testing than persons with an external locus of control and a lower sense of efficacy. Then, too, religiosity may play a role: persons who are more religious and perhaps more inclined to believe that their fate is in the hands of some higher being may be less interested in being tested than persons who along this dimension are not as religious.

Several sociological variables are of potential relevance also. One might argue that a desire to be tested would be associated with level of education attainment, with persons who have higher levels of education being more likely to want to be tested. Marital and family status variables may be pertinent. Given that Alzheimer's disease is known to have a familial dimension in some cases, persons with a relative who has or had Alzheimer's are expected to be more interested in being tested than those from families with no history of dementia. Similarly, persons with children would be expected to be more interested in acquiring information about their genetic predisposition to Alzheimer's than those without children. Theoretical discussions about gender differences in health beliefs and health behavior [59] suggest that women may be more likely than men to want such a test, and there is a substantial empirical literature pointing to a relationship between age and acquiescence to authority figures [60].

In short, advances in molecular genetics and in associated biomedical technology are for the first time providing opportunities for persons to learn whether their genetic makeup predisposes them to certain diseases and to make life course decisions based on those test results. This information can be made available to persons who are asymptomatic and about conditions for which no treatment or cure is presently available. These technological developments, broadly construed as being part of the larger currents of social change occurring within society, may soon be applicable to Alzheimer's disease and suggest a variety of important and intriguing research questions, questions that are best posed and answered through the coordinated efforts of interdisciplinary research.

SUMMARY

This chapter has explored a variety of considerations surrounding the relationship between aging and social change. Surely, population and individual aging will continue to be forces for social change both in the developed and developing regions of the world. How these forces will play out in the different regions may well vary. Countries in the developed regions already have in place extensive infrastructures for social and economic security and for the delivery of health care. Pressure to adapt and refine those systems and to develop new ones to meet the needs of a growing number of older persons will not diminish. In important respects, however, these pressures will be even greater in developing countries. The aging of their populations will take place over a much shorter period of time, the numbers of older persons involved will be far greater than was the case for Western nations, and the infrastructures to support the older segments of their populations are less well developed. Although the dynamics of the relationship between aging and social change may differ from one country to another and from one region to another, it can be said with some certainty that the graying of the globe will be a continuing force for change.

Despite speculation to the contrary, this chapter has also made the point that aging, at the social-psychological level, is not inimical to the occurrence of social change. A body of research has shown that older persons are capable of changing their attitudes about important social and political issues and that these changes are by no means limited to shifts toward more traditional orientations. The fact that major social change has taken place over the past several decades in the presence of an aging population further argues against a presumption that aging and social change are somehow incompatible. Of greater import is structural lag, the inertia built into social systems that prevents them from adjusting as quickly as is desirable to the growing numbers and changing needs and characteristics of older persons. Consequently, the development and monitoring of indicators of social and structural change, examining their relationship to aging, and developing theoretical frameworks to account for variation in the closeness of the linkages between aging and social change is proposed as a high priority item on the agenda of future work in this area.

Finally, it was argued that most of the scholarly efforts on the topic of aging and social change have been disciplinary or, at best, multidisciplinary. Coordinated, collaborative interdisciplinary work is notable by its absence. As an example of one direction such interdisciplinary work might take, it was suggested that rapid technological change resulting in cultural lag might prove to be one fruitful area for interdisciplinary studies, especially as it relates to issues surrounding the life course implications of genetic testing for late-onset diseases such as Alzheimer's.

REFERENCES

1. R. N. Anderson, K. D. Kochanek, and S. L. Murphy, Report of Final Mortality Statistics, 1995, *Monthly Vital Statistics Report, 45*:11(supp. 2), National Center for Health Statistics, Hyattsville, Maryland, 1997.
2. J. Treas, Older Americans in the 1990s and Beyond, *Population Bulletin, 50,* Population Reference Bureau, Inc., Washington, D.C., 1995.
3. J. M. Guralnik, M. Yanagishita, and E. L. Schneider, "Projecting the Older Population of the United States: Lessons from the Past and Prospects for the Future, *The Milbank Quarterly, 66,* pp. 283-308, 1988.
4. U.S. Bureau of the Census, *An Aging World II,* International Population Reports, P25, 92-3, U.S. Government Printing Office, Washington, D.C., 1992.

5. Population Reference Bureau, *1997 World Population Data Sheet*, Washington, D.C., Author, May 1997.

6. U.S. Senate Special Committee on Aging, American Association of Retired Persons, Federal Council on the Aging, and U.S. Administration on Aging, *Aging America: Trends and Projections, 1991 Edition* (DHHS Publication No. [FCoA] 91-28001), U.S. Department of Health and Human Services, Washington, D.C., 1991.

7. J. M. Cornman and E. R. Kingson, Trends, Issues, Perspectives, and Values for the Aging of the Baby Boom Cohorts, *The Gerontologist, 36,* pp. 69-81, 1996.

8. J. M. Waring, Social Replenishment and Social Change, *American Behavioral Scientist, 19,* pp. 237-256, 1975.

9. R. V. Burkhauser and J. F. Quinn, Changing Policy Signals, in *Age and Structural Lag,* M. W. Riley, R. L. Kahn, and A. Foner (eds.), John Wiley & Sons, Inc., New York, pp. 237-262, 1994.

10. P. Uhlenberg, Mortality Decline in the Twentieth Century and Supply of Kin Over the Life Course, *The Gerontologist, 36,* pp. 681-685, 1996.

11. V. L. Bengtson and M. Silverstein, Families, Aging, and Social Change: Seven Agendas for 21st Century Researchers, in *Annual Review of Gerontology and Geriatrics,* Vol. 13, *Focus on Kinship, Aging, and Social Change,* G. L. Maddox and M. P. Lawton (eds.), Springer, New York, pp. 15-38, 1993.

12. E. M. Brody, Parent Care as a Normative Family Stress, *The Gerontologist, 25,* pp. 19-29, 1985.

13. A. Martin-Matthews and C. J. Rosenthal, Balancing Work and Family in an Aging Society: The Canadian Experience, in *Annual Review of Gerontology and Geriatrics,* Vol. 13, *Focus on Kinship, Aging, and Social Change,* G. L. Maddox and M. P. Lawton (eds.), Springer, New York, pp. 96-119, 1993.

14. C. J. Rosenthal, A. Martin-Matthews, and S. H. Matthews, Caught in the Middle? Occupancy in Multiple Roles and Help to Parents in a National Probability Sample of Canadian Adults, *Journal of Gerontology: Social Sciences, 51B,* pp. S274-S283, 1996.

15. E. K. Pavalko and J. E. Artis, Women's Caregiving and Paid Work: Causal Relationships in Late Midlife, *Journal of Gerontology: Social Sciences, 52B,* pp. S170-S179, 1997.

16. M. W. Riley, R. L. Kahn, and A. Foner (eds.), *Age and Structural Lag,* John Wiley & Sons, Inc., New York, 1994.

17. N. D. Glenn, Aging and Conservatism, *Annals of the American Academcy of Political and Social Science, 415,* pp. 176-186, 1974.

18. D. K. Lapsley and R. D. Enright, Cognitive Developmental Model of Rigidity in Senescence, *International Journal of Aging and Human Development, 16,* pp. 81-93, 1983.

19. A. M. Horton, Jr., *Mental Health Interventions for the Aging,* Praeger, New York, 1982.

20. A. J. Coale, How a Population Ages or Grows Younger, in *Population: The Vital Revolution,* R. Freedman (ed.), Anchor Books, Garden City, New York, pp. 47-58, 1964.

21. L. H. Day, What Will a ZPG Society Be Like? *Population Bulletin, 33,* pp. 1-43, 1978.

22. Commission on Population Growth and the American Future, *Population and the American Future,* New American Library, New York, 1972.

23. National Council on the Aging, Inc., *The Myth and Reality of Aging in America,* Author, Washington, D.C., 1975.

24. N. E. Cutler, Demographic, Social-Psychological, and Political Factors in the Politics of Aging: A Foundation for Research in "Political Gerontology," *American Political Science Review, 71,* pp. 1011-1025, 1977.

25. R. J. Dalton, Was There a Revolution? A Note on Generational Versus Life Cycle Explanations of Value Differences, *Comparative Political Studies, 9,* 459-472, 1977.

26. N. D. Glenn, Values, Attitudes, and Beliefs, in *Constancy and Change in Human Development*, O. G. Brim, Jr. and J. Kagan (eds.), Harvard University Press, Cambridge, Massachusetts, pp. 596-640, 1980.

27. J. A. Krosnick and D. F. Alwin, Aging and Susceptibility to Attitude Change, *Journal of Personality and Social Psychology, 57,* pp. 416-425, 1989.

28. C. W. Roberts, Tracing Formative Influences on Event Recall: A Test of Mannheim's Sensitivity Hypothesis, *Social Forces, 65,* pp. 74-86, 1986.

29. D. O. Sears, Life-Stage Effects on Attitude Change, Especially among the Elderly, in *Aging: Social Change,* S. B. Kiesler, J. N. Morgan, and V. Kincade Oppenheimer (eds.), Academic Press, New York, pp. 183-204, 1981.

30. S. J. Cutler and R. L. Kaufman, Cohort Changes in Political Attitudes: Tolerance of Ideological Nonconformity, *Public Opinion Quarterly, 39,* pp. 69-81, 1975.

31. S. J. Cutler, S. A. Lentz, M. J. Muha, and R. N. Riter, Aging and Conservatism: Cohort Changes in Attitudes About Legalized Abortion, *Journal of Gerontology, 35,* pp. 115-123, 1980.

32. N. L. Danigelis and S. J. Cutler, An Inter-Cohort Comparison of Changes in Racial Attitudes, *Research on Aging, 13,* pp. 383-404, 1991.

33. N. L. Danigelis and S. J. Cutler, Cohort Trends in Attitudes About Law and Order: Who's Leading the Conservative Wave? *Public Opinion Quarterly, 55,* pp. 24-49, 1991.

34. M. W. Riley and J. W. Riley, Jr., Structural Lag: Past and Future, in *Age and Structural Lag,* M. W. Riley, R. L. Kahn, and A. Foner (eds.), John Wiley & Sons, Inc., New York, pp. 15-36, 1994.

35. G. L. Maddox, Sociology, Aging, and Guided Social Change: Relating Alternative Organization of Helping Resources to Well-Being, in *Major Social Issues: A Multidisciplinary View,* J. M. Yinger and S. J. Cutler (eds.), The Free Press, New York, pp. 323-337, 1978.

36. A. Foner, Endnote: The Reach of an Idea, in *Age and Structural Lag,* M. W. Riley, R. L. Kahn, and A. Foner (eds.), John Wiley & Sons, New York, pp. 263-280, 1994.

37. E. W. Busse, Administration of the Interdisciplinary Research Team, in *Normal Aging,* E. Palmore (ed.), Duke University Press, Durham, North Carolina, pp. 7-17, 1970.

38. D. K. Harris, *Dictionary of Gerontology,* Greenwood Press, Westport, Connecticut, 1988.

39. R. M. Andersen, *A Behavioral Model of Families' Use of Health Services,* Center for Health Administration Studies, Chicago, 1968.

40. V. L. Bengtson and W. A. Achenbaum (eds.), *The Changing Contract Across Generations,* Aldine de Gruyter, New York, 1993.

41. Associated Press, University Celebrates 50th Year of Computing, *The Burlington Free Press,* p. 2A, February 12, 1996.

42. D. Callahan, *Setting Limits: Medical Goals in an Aging Society,* Simon and Schuster, New York, 1987.

43. R. H. Binstock and S. G. Post (eds.), *Too Old for Health Care?: Controversies in Medicine, Law, Economics, and Ethics,* Johns Hopkins University Press, Baltimore, 1991.

44. W. F. Ogburn, *On Culture and Social Change,* University of Chicago Press, Chicago, 1964.

45. G. J. Annas and S. Elias, The Major Social Policy Issues Raised by the Human Genome Project, in *Gene Mapping: Using Law and Ethics as Guides,* G. J. Annas and S. Elias (eds.), Oxford University Press, New York, pp. 3-17, 1992.

46. M. J. Mehlman and J. R. Botkin, *Access to the Genome: The Challenge to Equality,* Georgetown University Press, Washington, D.C., 1998.

47. E. Masood, Gene Tests: Who Benefits from Risk? *Nature, 379,* pp. 389-392, 1996.

48. J. Brandt, K. A. Quaid, S. E. Folstein, P. Garber, N. E. Maestri, M. H. Abbott, P. R. Slavney, M. L. Franz, L. Kasch, and H. H. Kazazian, Jr., Presymptomatic Diagnosis of Delayed-Onset Disease with Linked DNA Markers: The Experience in Huntington's Disease, *Journal of the American Medical Association, 261,* pp. 3108-3114, 1989.

49. S. Wiggins, P. Whyte, M. Huggins, S. Adam, J. Theilmann, M. Bloch, S. B. Sheps, M. T. Schechter, and M. R. Hayden, The Psychological Consequences of Predictive Testing for Huntington's Disease, *New England Journal of Medicine, 327,* pp. 1401-1405, 1992.

50. National Institute on Aging, *Progress Report on Alzheimer's Disease 1997* (NIH Publication No. 97-4014, Author, Washington, D.C., 1997.

51. H. Karlinsky, A. Lennox, and M. Rossor, Alzheimer's Disease and Genetic Testing, *Alzheimer Disease and Associated Disorders, 8,* pp. 63-65, 1994.

52. S. G. Post, Genetics, Ethics, and Alzheimer Disease, *Journal of the American Geriatrics Society, 42,* pp. 782-786, 1994.

53. National Institute on Aging/Alzheimer's Association Working Group, Apolipoprotein E Genotyping in Alzheimer's Disease, *Lancet, 347,* pp. 1091-1095, 1996.

54. S. G. Post et al., The Clinical Introduction of Genetic Testing for Alzheimer Disease: An Ethical Perspective, *Journal of the American Medical Association, 277,* pp. 832-836, 1997.

55. Long Island Alzheimer's Foundation, Gene Survey Results, *LIAFline* (newsletter). (Available from Long Island Alzheimer's Foundation, 382 Main Street, Port Washington, NY 11050), January 1996.

56. S. Kessler, T. Field, L. Worth, and H. Mosbarger, Attitudes of Persons at Risk for Huntington Disease Toward Predictive Testing, *American Journal of Medical Genetics, 26,* pp. 259-270, 1987.

57. D. Kahneman and A. Tversky, The Psychology of Preferences, *Scientific American, 246,* pp. 160-173, 1982.

58. R. C. Green, V. C. Clark, N. J. Thompson, J. L. Woodward, and R. Letz, Early Detection of Alzheimer's Disease: Methods, Markers, and Misgivings, *Alzheimer Disease and Associated Disorders, 11*(Suppl. 5), pp. 51-55, 1997.

59. L. M. Verbrugge, Gender and Health: An Update on Hypotheses and Evidence, *Journal of Health and Social Behavior, 26,* pp. 156-182, 1985.

60. M. Haug, Doctor Patient Relationships and the Older Patient, *Journal of Gerontology, 34,* pp. 852-860, 1979.

61. U.S. Bureau of the Census, *Resident Population of the United States: Estimates by Age and Sex* [Online]. Available HTTP: http://www.census.gov/population/estimates/nation/intfile2-1.txt [June 1997].

62. U.S. Bureau of the Census, *65+ in the United States,* Current Population Reports, Special Studies, U.S. Government Printing Office, Washington, D.C., P23-190, 1996.

CHAPTER
2

Psychology's Contributio...
Gerontology

Laura L. Carstensen, Jeremy Graff,
and Frieder Lang

The field of psychology aims to describe, predict, explain, and ultimately modify functioning in behavioral, emotional, and cognitive domains. The study of aging within psychology has a relatively short history, undertaken only about forty or fifty years ago. At the onset, the subdiscipline in psychology most interested in the study of aging was clinical psychology, where the focus on frailty and decline made it well-suited to contribute to the study of decline and loss in the second half of life. About twenty-five years ago, however, life-span psychology—a branch of psychology that views development as a lifelong process—was born [1]. This approach broadened research and theory in gerontopsychology such that old age is now viewed as a normal life stage that entails both gains and losses. In part due to this expanded focus and in part due to increasing societal pressures to understand the full spectrum of possibilities and challenges that aging may entail, geropsychology has flourished. Today, many research agendas emphasize optimal aging, recognizing that no life stage is uniformly characterized by problems or pleasures.

Nevertheless, the majority of research in psychological gerontology continues to be organized around the concept of loss. Consideration of healthy aging continues to represent a minority of research in the area. Certainly, the problems associated with old age are sufficiently widespread that research focused on loss is more than justifiable. Research on age-related constraints on human systems shed considerable light on highly reliable, deleterious processes that influence thought and behavior in late life. Because of psychology's focus on experimentation and manipulation of potential causal variables, it has also shed considerable light on the modifiability of the problems and the potentials of aging. Subsequently, in our view, the greatest contribution psychology has made to the study of aging is not its chronicle of loss. Rather, in the quest for deepening the understanding of deleterious phenomena, it has uncovered evidence that "plasticity" is nearly as ubiquitous as loss in old age.

The remainder of our comments address three substantive domains in the field of geropsychology: personality, cognition, and social relationships and emotional

29

each domain, we consider psychology's contributions to understanding the gains and losses of old age.

PERSONALITY AND WELL-BEING

The subdomain of personality psychology is arguably the most ill-defined in psychology because it is the subdomain that attempts to consider the functioning of the whole person within his or her social world. Subsequently, cognitive, social, emotional, and behavioral factors are all relevant. Nearly from its inception, the field has been fueled by debates about the best ways to study and characterize human functioning [2]. Trait theorists have attempted to identify the most encompassing lexical terms that describe individual differences [3], whereas social cognitive theorists have argued instead that people need to be understood in terms of individual goals and within the context of specific tasks [4-7].

In gerontology, these different approaches have yielded different findings about later life which, at first, seemed at odds with one another, but quickly came to be viewed as naturally compatible. Trait theorists have found reliable evidence for stability in personality well into old age [8, 9]. It appears that beyond the age of thirty, extraverts remain extraverts and neurotics remain neurotics. This consistency is found whether researchers ask individuals to describe themselves over time or, alternatively, ask significant others, like spouses, to describe those same individuals [10]. Thus, there is remarkable consistency in the characteristics that distinguish individuals from one another over time. Many scholars believe that a core set of traits or temperaments that differentiate people are genetically based and exert their influence throughout the life course [11, 12].

At the same time, researchers who have taken a goal-focused approach have brought a different set of findings to bare on discussions of personality and aging, showing that beliefs about one's own competencies and personal goals do change with age and influence behavior. One study of memory efficacy, for example, showed that people's adaptive beliefs about memory in old age are associated with relatively good memory performance [13]. McFarland, Ross, and Giltrow [14] have demonstrated that people's implicit theories about aging in general influence perceptions of their own aging process. Frederickson and Carstensen, in a series of studies, have shown that the perception of the future as limited results in an emphasis on emotional goals, best satisfied by contact with emotionally-close social partners [15]. Because aging is inextricably and positively associated with limitations on future time, older people are more likely than their younger counterparts to prefer contact with family and old friends rather than acquaintances or novel social partners. Recently, Lang, Staudinger, and Carstensen showed that selective narrowing of the social network, in which close social partners are maintained and more peripheral social partners are discarded, occurs across different personality "types" [16]. The latter finding offers a union of sorts between the trait and social cognitive literatures on aging: People do maintain considerable consistency in their basic personalities over the years, but their goals, beliefs, and preferences do change and relate to everyday functioning.

One area centrally related to personality is emotion. Here again, it appears that there is both consistency and change over time. Although very early models of adult development viewed aging as a time of emotional flattening and disengagement, empirical research has shown clearly that this is not the case. As indexed by subjective ratings, older people experience emotions as intensely as their younger counterparts [17, 18]. However, relative to younger people, they say that they experience better control over their emotions [19] and, in fact, do seem to experience fewer negative emotions, at the same time maintaining both the frequency and intensity of positive emotions [20]. It may be that certain emotions do dampen with age, but are limited primarily to a reduction in surgency or excitability [21].

Another index of individual differences concerns the degree and type of psychopathological characteristics people display. Again, this is a domain where, for many years, researchers expected to find considerable, negative change with age. However, empirical studies clearly suggest that, with the exception of the dementias, older people experience lower rates of virtually every form of psychopathology [22]. Even major depression, once presumed to be the hallmark of old age, occurs at lower rates in the over fifty-five age group. One important caveat is that depression rates are higher in infirm elderly, just as they are higher in all age groups among people suffering from significant disease. In fact, the increase in the comorbidity of depression and disease is actually lower among the elderly than younger age groups. It is possible that these surprisingly low rates of mental disorders reflects cohort, as opposed to age changes, and will not be found in future generations [23]. Nevertheless, the notion that aging itself causes depression is untenable.

Research findings concerning personality and well-being in old age are considered by many to represent a basic "paradox of aging." Older people experience inevitable losses as they grow older. They lose social roles, social partners, physical health and, eventually, anticipate the loss of life itself. Yet, despite these losses, older adults manage their social worlds and their personal feelings remarkably well.

COGNITION AND AGING

A major influence of psychology on the understanding of aging has come through the study of cognitive aging. The study of cognitive aging entails the examination of how adult cognitive processes such as reasoning, learning, and memory change throughout the life course. Early work on these issues presented a uniformly negative view of the cognitive aging process [24]. Growing out of work in the developmental and biological fields, mental functions through the life course were hypothesized to increase through the first two decades of life and steadily decrease thereafter until death [25, 26]. Furthermore, general measures of intelligence showed steady declines from youth onward, further reinforcing the view that aging has a uniform and negative effect on intellectual functioning [27].

Contrary to this unidimensional view, psychological research since the early 1970s (starting with Horn's extension [28] of findings by Cattell [29] on multidimensional models of intelligence) has shown that a conception of unidimensional decline in mental ability with age is much too simple. There are several reasons why age itself may not explain much of the variance in cognitive performance seen in older people. Many studies of age differences in cognitive performance are cross-sectional, and cannot account for differences due to cohort effects [30, 31]. Research has also shown that training can slow or reverse the effects of aging on intelligence, suggesting that plasticity is a hallmark of cognitive processes throughout life [32]. In sum, the central task of cognitive psychology with regard to aging has been mapping both the constraints as well as the potentials of the aging mind.

Multidimensionality and Multidirectionality

In psychology, intelligence has been conceptualized broadly rather than as a single unidimensional concept. In early work by Cattell [29] and Horn [28], fluid and crystallized intelligence were conceptualized as two factors of cognitive performance that accounted for different dimensions of intelligence. Fluid intelligence concerns the mechanics of intelligence such as the speed of processing, spatial ability, sensory discrimination, and categorization [24, 33-35]. The mechanics of intelligence are based on biologically determined intellectual processes that aid an individual in learning, remembering, and making sense out of new information [33, 34]. In contrast, the pragmatics of intelligence refer to cognitive processes that entail meaningfulness, such as stores of factual and procedural knowledge that allow individuals to act according to their desires and the dictates of particular situations [33, 34]. The pragmatics of intelligence are believed to derive from patterns of cultural meaning and action as well as individual experience.

The developmental course of the mechanics and pragmatics of intelligence differs quite remarkably from a general unidimensional decline model. The mechanics of intelligence are hypothesized to increase over the first few decades of life, and then to decline quite rapidly after middle age. Pragmatic intelligence, however, is hypothesized to increase steadily throughout life, showing little or no decrement even after fluid abilities begin to decline [28, 33, 34]. Certain abilities, such as processing speed and memory for novel events (which are associated with mechanics of intelligence), are commonly thought to decline as people get older, as such deficits may be linked to the decline in certain biological systems related to such abilities [24]. Other abilities, linked to crystallized intelligence, such as wisdom and knowing how to act in culturally defined situations, are believed to remain unchanged, if not improved, with age [33].

Empirical studies of this two-factor model generally support the distinction between mechanics and pragmatics in intelligence [33-35]. However, there are important ability-by-age and ability-by-cohort interactions that suggest a more complex interpretation of the theory. Schaie and Labouvie-Vief compared cross-sectional and longitudinal data, finding that within cohorts patterns of ability in domains such as verbal meaning, reasoning, number abilities, and word fluency remained quite stable over periods as long as fourteen years [30]. Yet, because younger subjects scored higher on these abilities than older subjects did when they were the same age as the younger subjects, the cross-sectional differences suggested a more rapid decline in intellectual ability than was actually taking place. In other words, rapid changes in sociocultural patterns of education, job training, and career selection may have accounted for much of the variance in cognitive ability when comparing different cohorts in cross-sectional samples [24, 34]. More recent analyses of Schaie's data set suggest further changes in cohorts as younger groups from the baby-boom generation are found to have lower scores on tests taken at a given age than their older counterparts [31]. Although the general picture given by longitudinal research is that fluid intelligence declines earlier than crystallized abilities, perhaps the final word on such research is that "there is no uniform pattern of age-related changes across all intellectual abilities" [31]. Hence, cognitive ability is both multi-dimensional and multidirectional in nature.

A good example of the flexibility that results from such multidimensionality and multidirectionality in the domain of cognitive aging has been demonstrated in the work of Salthouse on older and younger typists [36]. He found that, although younger typists are able to type faster on average than older typists, older typists were still as effective overall as younger typists with respect to their overall speed of work. Salthouse found that the older typists were more sensitive to characters farther in advance of the currently typed work than younger typists. Older typists where thus relying on their pragmatic expertise and knowledge and thus compensated for the loss in mechanic skills.

In sum, psychology has in the last thirty or so years been able to expand the concept of cognitive ability and how it changes over the life course. Intelligence is not unidimensional, and it does not simply decline with age as was once thought. Rather, intelligence is multidimensional, and the causes of change in intellectual functioning with age are necessarily over-determined. Horn's work has shown that different types of cognitive abilities can change at different rates with age [28]. Furthermore, Schaie [31] and Schaie and Willis' [37] longitudinal studies have provided further evidence that intellectual decline occurs rather late in the life course, if at all, and that many different factors besides chronological age play into how an individual's abilities change with age. Therefore, the story of cognitive aging, as told by psychology, is one of flexibility, where multiple facets of intelligence can decline or grow according to environmental, biological, and individual influences. This flexibility also relates to the question of plasticity of cognitive functioning. Can intervention and training enhance cognitive performance in late life?

Plasticity

In addition to the evidence for complex patterns of age-related decline, there has also been considerable research on the reversibility of age declines and developmental reserve capacities for learning. Because age differences in ability seem to appear late in life, and individual differences in ability are high, psychologists began to try to explain sources of variance in intellectual functioning [24, 34]. Descriptive work gave way to more experimentally based research that focused on identifying factors that may affect intellectual functioning over the life course, explaining them, and then manipulating them to determine if some observed decrements in intellectual functioning could actually be improved or even reversed through training or practice [32, 34].

Many of these "training experiments" were based on the notion that disuse was a major factor associated with decrements in intellectual functioning. Exercise and intellectual stimulation were found to have highly beneficial effects on physiology, from the heart to the nervous system [25]. Adverse lifestyles that accentuated physical declines were found to contribute to declines in intellectual functioning while lifestyles that included environmental stimulation (e.g., continuing one's education) were associated with the maintenance of higher levels of functioning [38, 39]. Such findings encouraged researchers in their belief that some of the variance in intellectual functioning in old age may be related to the extent to which individuals actively used various cognitive abilities. Early studies were exciting, for they showed that many cognitive abilities improved with training, and in some cases training actually reversed the effects of aging [37, 40].

The general procedure for such studies, as described by Schaie and Willis [37], would be to assign subjects to a number of training sessions that would teach subjects concepts or rules that could be used to solve different tests of intellectual ability as well as give subjects practice on solving problems relating to the ability being trained. For example, subjects being trained in reasoning abilities would be taught pattern description rules that could be used to solve pattern recognition problems. Subjects would then solve various pattern recognition problems in a variety of domains that were different from what they would actually be tested on (for example, patterns of musical notes or travel schedules would be devised and solved to help subjects solve patterns of letters in the ability test).

Subjects would then be tested on a battery of mental ability scores. Results from the training study could then be compared to the subjects' abilities in the past to determine if subjects were returning to past levels of ability or were learning new information that they previously didn't have. Results suggested that, indeed, cognitive training can reverse documented decline in the mechanics of intelligence [37]. Training effects also enhanced the performance of adults who had not experienced declines, and these effects were not related to age, education, or income. These results are similar to the results found by many other studies [32, 34, 40] which suggest that the intellectual abilities of adulthood, besides being multidimensional, are also quite plastic. Such plasticity gave great hope that measured decline in mental ability linked to aging could be reversed through experience.

Another contribution in this domain concerned whether or not plasticity in ability could change over the life course. Paul Baltes and his colleagues began to test the limits of training to determine what the practical limits of the training paradigms were, and to see if the decrements found in cognition really could be reversed through exposure to the right environmental experiences [32, 33, 41-43]. The main element in these experiments was to train young people as well as old people to see whether there were age differences in how much training improved an individual's score on a cognitive test with regard to their own age group and an older or younger group. For example, young and old subjects would be given many training sessions teaching them how to use the method of loci [44] to remember lists of words. At pretest, neither group of subjects were very good at this task, and people remembered an average of five to seven words from a list of thirty words. The results of this training looked very similar to the results of the earlier training experiments: both young and old subjects improved quite a bit and were able to remember many words more than they could before. The findings suggest that, indeed, there is a reserve capacity for learning, and that decrements associated with aging can be overcome with the right training. However, when one examines the results in terms of which group showed the maximum benefit from training, one finds that the younger subjects got a lot more out of training than the older subjects. By increasing the speed of word presentation, the peak performances of young and old subjects no longer overlapped: older subjects clearly had some limit to their ability to benefit from training when compared to younger subjects. This has also been demonstrated in cognitive training experiments with young and older adults [43].

As can be seen in the Figure 1, after having gone through extensive training and intervention, differences in cognitive performance between old and young subjects even increased as compared to pre-training.

This research shows that, although there exists quite a large developmental reserve capacity for learning or maintaining cognitive ability through life, this capacity is limited, and is likely to become more so with age. Research has shown that, at the limits of ability and training, younger subjects still retain an advantage over older subjects on tasks that reflect cognitive mechanics [34, 42]. Furthermore, investing time and energy into improving or maintaining a particular ability may preclude one's ability to keep up in other domains. By investing energy into maintaining one's ability to play the piano, for example, a person may limit their ability to maintain their ability to solve crossword puzzles or use the Internet.

There are gains and losses inherent in every stage of a person's life. With age, the amount of losses in one's life begins to overtake the amount of gains. Yet, this process is very plastic and is influenced by the individual's choices and sociocultural environment. Although plasticity is an important hallmark of the cognitive aging process, psychological theory of the past few years has focused on explaining how individuals adapt or cope with the myriad gains and losses they experience through life [33, 41, 45].

In sum we see that psychology has illuminated several important processes in cognitive aging. We have learned that intellectual change over the life course is not unidimensional or unidirectional. We have found that there are many different domains of intelligence that change in different ways over the life course. We have also learned that there is a certain amount of plasticity in one's abilities, and such developmental reserves can be tapped by young and old alike to increase performance. Yet, there are limits to such reserves. The illumination of mechanisms, such as selective optimization with compensation, that help us understand the course of gains and losses over the life course, is one of the great contributions of psychology to the study of aging.

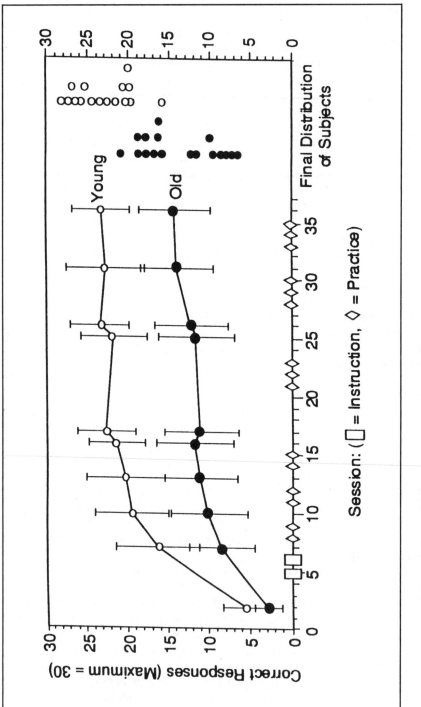

Figure 1. Testing the limits of a cognitive retraining program aimed to improve memory [43].

SOCIAL RELATIONSHIPS AND EMOTIONAL NEEDS

A third, major realm of psychological research on aging pertains to the social and emotional lives of older people. Much of this research has been couched in the negative terms of reduced social interactions, social loss, loneliness, and loss of autonomy. Are such concepts accurate descriptors of the social and emotional lives of older people? Empirical evidence shows that the rate of social contact as well as the number of social relationships does decrease in old age [46]. Such an overall reduction of social interaction in late life, despite a seeming increased need of social support, has inspired much empirical work in the field of social aging over the past fifty years and has stimulated much controversial discussion about the psychological reasons of such age changes [47, 48].

For example, disengagement theory has proposed that social withdrawal in old age reflects the older individual's reduced need and capacity for emotional involvement with others [49]. Older people have been assumed to be less capable of flexibly adjusting their emotional and social worlds to their age-specific life situation. Therefore, disengaging from social ties would be a natural consequence of this reduced flexibility. More recently, though, psychological work on the emotional and motivational processes that regulate social behavior and social relationships in late life suggests that there is indeed some flexibility and potential in the social functioning of older individuals, although there are also clear age-specific constraints on the social and emotional lives of older people.

Evidence for Flexibility and Potentials in Social Functioning

Over the last fifty years of research in social gerontology, evidence for an age-related decrease of social activity, social contact, and social integration has been found in numerous studies. Indeed, the oldest-old have smaller networks than younger-old people, a finding confirmed in our own research and shown in Figure 2 [16, 46].

Building on these findings, recent theoretical reasoning has stressed the individual's capacity to flexibly adapt to differing social contexts in later life [50-52].

Obviously, while many changes in the social networks of older people follow a more or less predictable pattern, such as the loss of professional contact or the loss of one's spouse, relatives, or friends, other age-related changes in the structure and function of personal networks might be characterized by the old person's idiosyncratic and goal-oriented efforts and interaction behaviors [51, 53, 54]. Research has therefore emphasized the adaptive and motivational mechanisms by which older people select and regulate their social partners such that their emotional needs and preferences can be satisfied and optimized [16, 45, 46, 51, 55]. This perspective is paradigmatically reflected in socioemotional selectivity theory that was recently proposed by Laura Carstensen [47, 51, 56, 57]. According to socioemotional selectivity theory, three basic functions of social interaction—acquiring information, developing the self, and regulating emotions—operate in different constellations

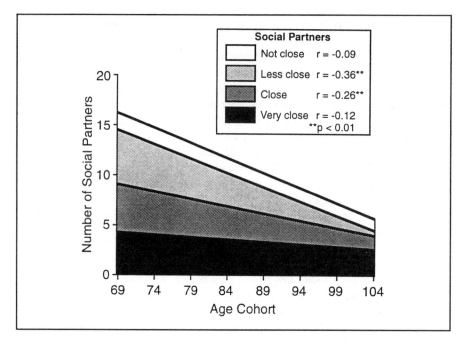

Figure 2. The negative relationship between number of social
partners in one's network and age [16].

across the life span. Carstensen argues that when individuals perceive close future
endings, long-term future goals become less important resulting in reduced interest
in informational or identity-related functions of social interactions [51]. Consequently, emotion regulation becomes more important in old age because the reduced
future perspective makes it seem more promising to seek and obtain benefits
and gratifications in the older individual's immediate relational context. Thus,
socioemotional selectivity theory has integrated some of the seemingly contra-
dictory psychological assumptions of activity theory and disengagement theory.
Old people narrow down the width of their social life and their social participation
in order to intensify their engagement in a selected range of social functions and
close emotional relationships that seem to give the most meaning for the remaining
life-time.

Perhaps because passive selection due to personal and social losses is ubiquitous
in late life, very little attention has been paid to proactive processes that may also
operate on the management of social relationships toward the end of life. In particular, we have been exploring the idea—grounded in socioemotional selectivity—
that older people engage in the regulation of social networks such that they comprise
a disproportionate number of emotionally close social partners [16, 46]. We reasoned
that if networks are reduced primarily through deaths of network members, this
reduction should occur on a relatively random basis throughout the social network

regardless of how close social partners are to target individuals. If, instead, reductions are motivated, reflecting a diminished desire for contact with social partners who do not offer emotional rewards, there should be a selective reduction in social networks that operates increasingly with the emotional distance of network members. Thus, we hypothesized that the number of emotionally close social partners would be highly comparable for younger and older people, whereas the number of less close social partners should drop significantly with age.

In order to address these questions, we examined data from the Berlin Aging Study (BASE), a large multidisciplinary research project based on a representative sample of old and very old people aged 70 to 104 years [58]. The social network measure used in the project was the German version of the circle diagram developed by Kahn and Antonucci [59]. We considered social partners classified in different concentric circles to be qualitatively different from one another along the dimension of emotional closeness, i.e., persons named in the first circle were considered extremely close and persons named in the outer circles (or not named in the circles at all) were considered increasingly less close emotionally (see Figure 3).

While there were differences in overall network size between younger and older subjects, differences were not distributed evenly across levels of emotional closeness as one would expect if morbidity and mortality alone accounted for differences in network size. Rather, reductions in more peripheral relationships accounted for most of the observed age differences. Perhaps even more importantly, we found evidence for the adaptiveness of the reduction in network size [16, 46]. When there are fewer peripheral social relationships but more very close ones available, the overall density of emotionally close relationships in an individual's social network increases. In our first study, we found that this emotional density was positively related to feelings of social embeddedness [46].

In an extension and replication of these findings, Lang, Staudinger, and Carstensen confirmed these patterns of selection in social networks in late life and differentiated more closely between the quantitative (i.e., size) and qualitative (i.e., emotional density) aspects of social networks [16]. In addition, we considered possible personality dimensions that might explain age-related differences in social networks such as extraversion, openness, and neuroticism. We found that qualitative aspects of social networks, such as the degree of emotional closeness with network partners, contributed above and beyond network size and personality differences to social embeddedness. Irrespective of individual differences in personality characteristics, older people appear to profit from a distilling of the social network such that the proportion of emotionally meaningful social partners increases. If the reduction in networks was due to mortality alone, older people would not profit from feelings of social and emotional satisfaction with networks. We contend that networks are not just "dying out," but that to some extent people engage in goal-oriented construction of social relationships. Thus, reduced social interactions and personal relationships in late life might reflect the older individual's changed needs and motivations. It is not the frequency of social interaction or the number of network partners but rather the quality, emotional meaningfulness, and functional adequacy of enduring close ties that contribute to well-being in late life [60-64]. This also pertains to the

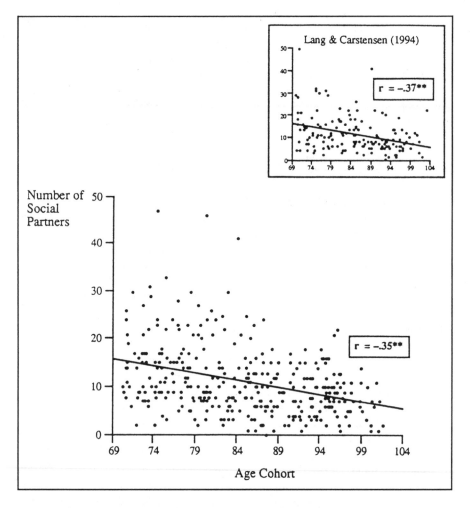

Figure 3. The selective reduction in the number of social partners,
illustrating that emotionally close social partners are
maintained into very old age [16].

well-established finding that the absence of close confidants and intimate relationships is associated with increased vulnerability and mortality in old age [65-70].

However, personal relationships and social networks of older people are not
exclusively providing gratification and resources but do also involve unpleasant sides
of social interactions [64, 67, 71]. Personal relationships are often a major source of
daily stressors [71, 72]. For example, most personal relationships go through times of
conflict or periods of relational crises that need to be mastered if the social partners
are willing to maintain their relationship [73, 74]. Successfully managing the stable
and varying, positive and negative aspects of family ties or friendships might be

fundamental for high levels of social adaptivity throughout adulthood and late life [45, 75, 76].

To summarize, age-related changes in personal relationships are explained by the older individual's changed social motivations and needs that result from having a limited future. However, there are also inevitable constraints in the social worlds of older people as defined by the structure and provisions of family and friend relationships.

Contextual Constraints of Social Relationships in Late Life

In general, family relations prove to be reliable and stable ties in old and very old age, even if no special efforts are made to keep in touch or maintain the relationship [77, 78]. This seems to be equally valid for parent-child relationships in late life [57] and for sibling relationships [79]. Moreover, the most often named source of instrumental and emotional social support in old age is the close family [80, 81].

Surprisingly, though, friendship relationships are associated with higher social satisfaction than relationships with family members who are not living in the same household [82, 83]. A possible explanation for this could be that friends are often discharged from tasks that are related to instrumental support exchange. Thus, they are less burdened with instrumental care tasks than family members. Friends are often named as confidants of old people [84, 85] or are associated with pleasant interactions such as social companionship [77, 86]. In this respect, friends might play a moderating role in older people's social networks by functioning as a counter-balance to the family [87] and by providing opportunities for various social activities in the community [88].

Another fundamental challenge in late life is related to the experience of becoming increasingly dependent on other people's willingness and capacity to provide adequate social support. While the individual during middle adulthood typically was used to master daily routines and tasks easily and autonomously, in late life the same activities of everyday life may become strenuous and require additional efforts. Thus, old people find themselves confronted with the developmental task of having to accept being dependent on others in some behavioral domains and simultaneously maintain autonomy in some selected domains that are important to their self and well-being [89].

Empirical evidence in nursing homes revealed that dependent behaviors of old residents were more often reinforced by responsiveness and contact of social partners than independent behaviors of residents. Further research demonstrated that independent behaviors of residents increased when social partners were trained to be responsive to independent behaviors [90]. When initiating such dependence-support and independence-ignore scripts, individuals who live in nursing homes regulate and optimize the available resources in their social environment [91, 92]. Bandura has proposed the concept "proxy control" for such processes, when the individual assigns control in particular domains of functioning to other persons and thus exerts an indirect influence over the environment [93]. Through use of proxy control in interpersonal contexts the older individual can compensate for the loss of direct control.

Finally, life-span developmental psychology has offered another explanation for the specific structural facets of older people's social relationships. Kahn proposed the convoy model of social relationships and the concept of the support bank as metaphors for lifelong and long-term social bonding [59, 94, 95]. According to the social convoy model, close relationships created at earlier phases of the life course have a strong influence on structural and functional properties of the social network in later life phases [59, 90]. Just like a convoy in traffic, a person is accompanied by a convoy of social ties throughout the life span. An individual's convoy changes though and has particular characteristics at different life phases.

The concept of the support bank assumes that within an individual's convoy there is long-term reciprocal exchange; that is, any help one receives can be reciprocated later when there is an opportunity. The concept of the support bank is not limited to age-specific exchange rules but broadens the perspective to a consideration of lifelong processes. It is an open question whether the support bank and particular exchange rules in old age are complementary or not and how they may be combined [96]. It seems plausible that both age-specific exchange rules and long-term support exchange influence the process of exchange in old age depending on the kind of relationship and the object of exchange.

In sum, social relationships and social contact in old age provide both potentials and constraints to adaptivity in everyday life. Relational resources contribute to the old person's adaptive potentials to regulate, select, and construct, close emotional relationships and supportive exchanges while, at the same time, social contexts in later life also place constraints on the older individual.

A FINAL THEORETICAL NOTE

In psychology, there has been some effort to bring together diverse evidence for flexibility, constraints, and limits in the different domains of functioning within one broader theoretical model that describes how people successfully manage the potentials and constraints in the experience of aging [33, 45]. One such attempt to explain the dynamic interchange of potentials and constraints through life has been undertaken with the model of selective optimization with compensation [33, 41, 45]. Selective optimization with compensation is a metamodel of successful development that explains how individuals make adaptations in the face of change brought about by the aging process. The model conceptualizes three broad processes by which people can modify their thinking, feelings, behaviors, or environments to attain desired goals throughout development.

Selection refers to the narrowing developmental options throughout the life span [33, 41, 45]. Such a narrowing of functional domains or developmental goals as reflected in an individual's choices of where to invest energy are influenced by contexts such as perceived future time or the sociocultural environment. Selection helps individuals gain new knowledge and experience as well as maintain valued knowledge and skills over time.

Compensation refers to the use of different means for achieving the same goal [45]. For example, with regard to intellectual functioning in older age, one finds that losses in the fluid mechanics of intellectual ability are often offset by compensatory mechanisms that maintain high levels of functioning in pragmatic domains that are important to the individual.

Optimization reflects a view that development is regulated so as to strive toward higher and more desirable levels of functioning [45]. Some examples of optimization include training, practice, or education.

This metamodel of positive or healthy aging represents a general framework that helps to organize the profile of gains and losses that are observed in old age. We expect that the next fifty years of research will yield additional evidence for stability and change in the latter half of the human life span.

REFERENCES

1. P. B. Baltes and L. R. Goulet, Status and Issues of Life-Span Developmental Psychology, in *Life-Span Developmental Psychology: Research and Theory,* L. R. Goulet and P. B. Baltes (eds.), Academic Press, New York, pp. 4-21, 1970.
2. J. Hilgard, Personality and the Self, in *Psychology in America: A Historical Survey,* Harcourt, Brace, Jovanovich, New York, Chapter 14, pp. 490-523, 1987.
3. O. John, The Big-five Factor Taxonomy: Dimensions of Personality in the Natural Language and Questionnaires, in *Handbook of Personality: Theory and Research,* L.A. Pervin (ed.), pp. 66-100, Guilford Press, New York, 1990.
4. A. Bandura, Human Agency in Social Cognitive Theory, *American Psychologist, 44,* pp. 1175-1184, 1989.
5. A. Bandura, Self-regulation of Motivation and Action Through Internal Standards and Goal Systems, in *Goal Concepts in Personality and Social Psychology,* L. A. Pervin (ed.), pp. 19-85, Erlbaum, Hillsdale, New Jersey, 1989.
6. N. Cantor, J. K. Norem, P. M. Niedenthal, C. A. Langston, and A. M. Brower, Life Tasks, Self-Concept Ideals, and Cognitive Strategies in a Life Transition, *Journal of Personality and Social Psychology, 53,* pp. 1178-1191, 1987.
7. W. Mischel, Toward a Cognitive Social Learning Reconceptualization of Personality, *Psychological Review, 80,* pp. 252-283, 1973.
8. P. Costa, Still Stable after All These Years: Personality as a Key to Some Issues of Adulthood and Old Age, in *Life-Span Development and Behavior* (Vol. 3), P. B. Baltes and O. G. Brim, Jr. (eds.), Academic Press, New York, 1980.
9. R. McRae and P. Costa, Validation of the Five-Factor Model of Personality Across Instruments and Observers, *Journal of Personality and Social Psychology, 52,* pp. 81-90, 1987.
10. P. Costa and R. McRae, Personality in Adulthood: A Six-year Longitudinal Study of Self-Reports and Spouse Rating in the Neo Personality Inventory, *Journal of Personality and Social Psychology 54,* pp. 853-863, 1988.
11. M. Gatz, N. L. Pederson, R. Plomin, and J. R. Nesselroade, Importance of Shared Genes and Shared Environments for Symptoms of Depression in Older Adults, *Journal of Abnormal Psychology, 101,* pp. 701-708, 1992.
12. R. Plomin, N. L. Pederson, P. Lichtenstein, and G.E. McClearn, Variability and Stability in Cognitive Abilities, *Behavior Genetics, 24,* pp. 207-215, 1994.

13. M. E. Lachman, S. L. Weaver, M. Bandura, E. Elliot, and C. J. Lewkowicz, Improving Memory and Control Beliefs Through Cognitive Restructuring and Self-Generated Strategies, *Journal of Gerontology: Psychological Sciences, 47,* pp. 293-299, 1992.
14. C. McFarland, M. Ross, and M. Giltrow, Biased Recollections in Older Adults: The Role of Implicit Theories of Aging, *Journal of Personality and Social Psychology, 62,* pp. 837-850, 1992.
15. B. L. Frederickson and L. L. Carstensen, Choosing Social Partners: How Old Age and Anticipated Endings Make People More Selective, *Psychology of Aging, 5*:3, pp. 335-347, 1990.
16. F. R. Lang, U. M. Staudinger, and L. L. Carstensen, Socioemotional Selectivity in Late Life: How Personality Does (And Does Not) Make a Difference, *Journal of Gerontology: Psychological Sciences, 53,* pp. P21-P30, 1998.
17. C. Z. Malatesta and M. Kalnok, Emotional Experience in Younger and Older Adults, *Journal of Gerontology, 39*:3, pp. 301-308, 1984.
18. R. W. Levenson, L. L. Carstensen, W. V. Friesen, and P. Ekman, Emotion, Physiology, and Expression in Old Age, *Psychology and Aging, 6*:1, pp. 28-35, 1991.
19. J. Gross, L. L. Carstensen, M. Pasupathi, K. Gottestam, J. Tsai, and A. Hus, A., Emotion and Aging: Experience, Expression and Control, *Pyschology of Aging, 12,* 590-599, 1997.
20. L. L. Carstensen, M. Pasupathi, and U. Mayr, *Emotional Experience in the Daily Lives of Older and Younger Adults,* paper presented at the meetings of the American Psychological Society, San Francisco, California, 1996.
21. M. P. Lawton, M. H. Kleban, D. Rajagopal, and J. Dean, Dimensions of Affective Experience in Three Age Groups, *Psychology and Aging, 7,* pp. 171-184, 1992.
22. L. K. George, D. F. Blazer, I. Winfield-Laird, P. J. Leaf, and R. L. Fischback, Psychiatric Disorders and Mental Health Service Use in Later Life: Evidence from the Epidemiologic Catchment Area Program, in *Epidemiology and Aging,* J. Brody and G. Maddox (eds.), Springer, New York, pp. 189-219, 1988.
23. M. Weissman, P. J. Leaf, M. L. Bruce, and L. P. Florio, The Epidemiology of Dysthyia in Five Communities: Rates, Risks, Comorbidity and Treatment, *American Journal of Psychiatry, 145,* pp. 815-819, 1988.
24. G. Labouvie-Vief, Intelligence and Cognition, in *Handbook of the Psychology of Aging,* J. E. Birren and K. W. Schaie (eds.), Van Nostrand Reinhold, New York, 1985.
25. W. M. Bortz, Disuse and Aging, *Journal of the American Medical Association, 248,* pp. 1203-1208, 1982.
26. H. E. Jones, Intelligence and Problem Solving, in *Handbook of Aging and the Individual,* J. E. Birren (ed.), University of Chicago Press, Chicago, pp. 700-738, 1959.
27. H. E. Jones and O. J. Kaplan, Psychological Aspects of Mental Disorders in Later Life, in *Mental Disorders in Later Life,* O. J. Kaplan (ed.), Stanford University Press, Stanford, California, pp. 69-115, 1945.
28. J. L. Horn, Organization of Data on Life-Span Development of Human Abilities, in *Life-Span Developmental Psychology: Research and Theory,* L. R. Goulet and P. B. Baltes (eds.), Academic Press, New York, 1970.
29. R. B. Cattell, Theory of Fluid and Crystallized Intelligence: A Critical Experiment, *Journal of Educational Psychology, 54,* pp. 1-22, 1963.
30. K. W. Schaie and G. Labouvie-Vief, Generational Versus Ontogenetic Components of Change in Adult Cognitive Behavior: A Fourteen Year Cross- Sequential Study, *Developmental Psychology, 13,* pp. 649-653, 1974.
31. K. W. Schaie, The Seattle Longitudinal Studies of Adult Intelligence, *Current Directions in Psychological Science, 2,* pp. 171-175, 1993.

32. P. B. Baltes and U. Lindenberger, On the Range of Cognitive Plasticity in Old Age as a Function of Experience: Fifteen Years of Intervention Research, *Behavior Therapy, 19*, pp. 283-300, 1988.
33. P. B. Baltes, The Aging Mind: Potentials and Limits, *Gerontologist, 33*, pp. 580-594, 1993.
34. P. B. Baltes, F. Dittmann-Kohli, and R. A. Dixon, New Perspectives on the Development of Intelligence in Adulthood: Toward a Dual Process Conception and a Model of Selective Optimization with Compensation, in *Life-Span Development and Behavior* (Vol. 6), P. B. Baltes and O. G. Brim (eds.), Academic Press, New York, pp. 33-76, 1984.
35. K. W. Schaie, The Hazards of Cognitive Aging, *Gerontologist, 29*, pp. 484-493, 1989.
36. T. A. Salthouse, Effects of Age and Skill in Typing, *Journal of Experimental Psychology: General, 113*, pp. 345-371, 1984.
37. K. W. Schaie and S. L. Willis, Can Intellectual Decline in the Elderly Be Reversed? *Developmental Psychology, 22*, pp. 223-232, 1986.
38. C. Hertzog, K. W. Schaie, and K. Gribbin, Cardiovascular Disease and Changes in Intellectual Functioning from Middle to Old Age, *Journal of Gerontology, 33*, pp. 872-888, 1978.
39. K. Gribbin, K. W. Schaie, and I. A. Parham, Complexity of Life Style and Maintenance of Cognitive Abilities, *Journal of Social Issues, 36*, pp. 47-64, 1980.
40. P. B. Baltes and S. L. Willis, Plasticity and Enhancement of Intellectual Functioning in Old Age: Penn State's Adult Development and Enrichment Project (ADEPT), in *Aging and Cognitive Processes*, F. I. M. Craik and S. E. Trehub (eds.), Plenum, New York, pp. 353-389, 1982.
41. P. B. Baltes, Theoretical Propositions of Life-span Developmental Psychology: On the Dynamics Between Growth and Decline, *Developmental Psychology 23*, pp. 611-626, 1987.
42. P. B. Baltes, F. Dittmann-Kohli, and R. Kliegel, Reserve Capacity of the Elderly in Ageing-Sensitive Tests of Fluid Intelligence: Replication and Extension, *Psychology and Aging, 1*, pp. 172-177, 1986.
43. P. B. Baltes and R. Kliegl, Further Testing of Limits of Cognitive Plasticity: Negative Age Differences in a Mnemonic Skill Are Robust, *Developmental Psychology 28*, pp. 121-125, 1992.
44. G. H. Bower, Analysis of a Mneumonic Device, *American Scientist, 58*, pp. 496-510, 1970.
45. M. Marsiske, F. R. Lang, P. B. Baltes, and M. M. Baltes, Selective Optimization with Compensation: Life-Span Perspectives on Successful Human Development, in *Psychological Compensation: Managing Losses and Promoting Gains*, R. Dixon and L. Bäckman (eds.), pp. 35-79, Erlbaum, Hillsdale, New Jersey, 1995.
46. F. R. Lang and L. L. Carstensen, Close Emotional Relationships in Late Life: Further Support for Proactive Aging in the Social Domain, *Psychology and Aging, 9*, pp. 315-324, 1994.
47. L. L. Carstensen, Age-Related Changes in Social Activity, in *Handbook of Clinical Gerontology*, L. L. Carstensen and B. A. Edelstein (eds.), Pergamon Press, New York, pp. 227-237, 1987.
48. N. J. Osgood, Theory and Research in Social Gerontology, in *The Science and Practice of Gerontology. A Multidisciplinary Guide*, N. J. Osgood and A. H. Sontz (eds.), pp. 55-87, Greenwood Press, New York, 1989.
49. E. Cumming and W. E. Henry, *Growing Old: The Process of Disengagement*, Basic Books, New York, 1961.
50. M. M. Baltes and L. L. Carstensen, The Process of Successful Aging, *Ageing and Society, 16*, pp. 397-422, 1996.

51. L. L. Carstensen, Motivation for Social Contact Across the Life Span: A Theory of Socioemotional Selectivity, in *Nebraska Symposium on Motivation: Developmental Perspectives on Motivation* (Vol. 40), J. Jacobs (ed.), University of Nebraska Press, Lincoln, pp. 209-254, 1993.

52. L. L. Carstensen and F. R. Lang, Social Relationships in Context and as Context: Comments on Social Support and the Maintenance of Competence in Old Age, in *Societal Mechanisms for Maintaining Competence in Old Age*, S. Willis and K. W. Schaie (eds.), Springer, New York, pp. 207-222, 1997.

53. J. Heckhausen and F. R. Lang, Social Construction in Old Age: Normative Conceptions and Interpersonal Processes, paper prepared for *Applied Social Psychology*, G. Semin and K. Fiedler (eds.), Sage, London, 1996.

54. F. R. Lang, Die Gestaltung informeller Hilfebeziehungen im hohen Alter—Die Rolle von Elternschaft und Kinderlosigkeit [Social Support Management in Late Life—The Role of Parenthood and Childlessness], *Max-Planck-Institut ffr Bildungsforschung, Studien und Berichte, Band 59*, Berlin, 1994.

55. F. R. Lang and C. Tesch-Römer, Erfolgreiches Altern und soziale Beziehungen: Selektion und Kompensation im sozialen Kontaktverhalten [Successful Aging and Social Relationships: Selection and Compensation in Social Contact Behavior], *Zeitschrift ffr Gerontologie, 26*, pp. 321-329, 1993.

56. L. L. Carstensen, Socioemotional Selectivity Theory: Social Activity in Life-Span Context, *Annual Review of Gerontology and Geriatrics, 11*, pp. 195-217, 1991.

57. L. L. Carstensen, Social and Emotional Patterns in Adulthood: Support for Socioemotional Selectivity Theory, *Psychology and Aging, 7*, pp. 331-338, 1992.

58. P. B. Baltes, K. U. Mayer, H. Helmchen, and E. Steinhagen-Thiessen, The Berlin Aging Study (BASE): Overview and Design, *Ageing and Society, 13*, pp. 483-515, 1993.

59. R. L. Kahn and T. C. Antonucci, Convoys over the Life Course. Attachment, Roles and Social Support, in *Life-Span Development and Behavior*, P. B. Baltes and O. G. Brim (eds.), Academic Press, New York, pp. 254-283, 1980.

60. L. J. Beckman, Effects of Social Interaction and Children's Relative Inputs on Older Women's Psychological Well-Being, *Journal of Personality and Social Psychology, 4*, pp. 1075-1086, 1981.

61. M. Ishii-Kuntz, Social Interaction and Psychological Well-Being: Comparison Across Stages of Adulthood, *International Journal of Aging and Human Development, 30*:1, pp. 15-36, 1990.

62. D. J. Lee and K. S. Markides, Activity and Mortality among Aged Persons over an Eight-Year Period, *Journal of Gerontology: Social Sciences, 45*, pp. 39-42, 1990.

63. M. F. Lowenthal and C. Haven, Interaction and Adaptation: Intimacy as a Critical Variable, in *Middle Age and Aging*, B. L. Neugarten (ed.), University of Chicago Press, Chicago, pp. 390-400, 1968.

64. K. S. Rook, The Negative Side of Social Interaction: Impact on Psychological Well-Being, *Journal of Personality and Social Psychology, 46*, pp. 1097-1108, 1984.

65. L. F. Berkman and S. L. Syme, Social Networks, Host Resistance and Mortality: A Nine-Year Follow-Up Study of Alameda County Residents, *American Journal of Epidemiology, 109*, pp. 186-204, 1979.

66. D. Blazer, Social Support and Mortality in an Elderly Community Population, *American Journal of Epidemiology, 115*, pp. 684-694, 1982.

67. M. Hammer, Core and Extended Social Networks in Relation to Health and Illness, *Social Science and Medicine, 17*, pp. 405-411, 1983.

68. K. Orth-Gomer and J. V. Johnson, Social Network Interaction and Mortality. A Six Year Follow-Up Study of a Random Sample of the Swedish Population, *Journal of Chronic Diseases, 40,* pp. 949-957, 1987.
69. U. Steinbach, Social Networks, Institutionalization, and Mortality among Elderly People in the United States, *Journal of Gerontology: Social Sciences, 47,* pp. 183-190, 1992.
70. H. Sugisawa, J. Liang, and X. Liu, Social Networks, Social Support, and Mortality among Older People in Japan, *Journal of Gerontology: Social Sciences, 49,* pp. S3-S13, 1994.
71. K. S. Rook, Strains in Older Adults' Friendship, in *Older Adult Friendships,* R. G. Adams and R. Blieszner (eds.), Sage, Newbury Park, California, pp. 166-194, 1989.
72. N. Bolger and S. Kelleher, Daily Life in Relationships, in *Social Context and Relationships,* S. Duck (ed.), Sage, Newbury Park, California, pp. 100-108, 1993.
73. T. C. Antonucci, Social Support: Theoretical Advances, Recent Findings and Pressing Issues, in *Social Support: Theory, Research and Application,* I. G. Sarason and B. R. Sarason (eds.), Nijhoff, Dordrecht, The Netherlands, pp. 21-37, 1985.
74. S. Duck, *Human Relationships,* Sage, London, 1986.
75. F. R. Lang, D. L. Featherman, and J. R. Nesselroade, *Managing Short-Term Variability in Personal Relationships: Evidence from the MacArthur Successful Aging Studies,* unpublished manuscript, Free University, Berlin, 1995.
76. D. L. Morgan, Combining the Strengths of Social Networks, Social Support, and Personal Relationships, in *Personal Relationships and Social Support,* S. Duck and R. C. Silver (eds.), pp. 190-215, Sage, Newbury Park, California, 1990.
77. S. E. Crohan and T. C. Antonucci, Friends as a Source of Social Support in Old Age, in *Older Adult Friendships,* R. G. Adams and R. Blieszner (eds.), Sage, Newbury Park, California, pp. 129-146, 1989.
78. D. Field and M. Minkler, Continuity and Change in Social Support Between Young-old and Old-old or Very-old Age, *Journal of Gerontology: Psychological Sciences, 43,* pp. 100-106, 1988.
79. J. P. Scott, Sibling Interaction in Later Life, in *Family Relationships in Later Life,* T. H. Brubaker (ed.), Sage, Beverly Hills, California, pp. S86-99, 1990.
80. G. Caplan, The Family as a Support System, in *Family Stress, Coping, and Social Support,* H. I. McCubbin, A. E. Cauble, and J. E. Patterson (eds.), Thomas, Springfield, Illinois, pp. 200-220, 1982.
81. C. E. Depner and B. Ingersoll-Dayton, Supportive Relationships in Later Life, *Psychology and Aging, 3,* pp. 348-357, 1988.
82. N. L. Chappell, Informal Support Networks among the Elderly, *Research on Aging, 5,* pp. 77-99, 1983.
83. R. Larson, R. Mannell, and J. Zuzanek, Daily Well-Being of Older Adults with Friends and Family, *Psychology and Aging, 1,* pp. 117-126, 1986.
84. P. M. Keith, K. Hill, W. J. Goudy, and E. A. Powers, Confidants and Well-Being: A Note on Male Friendship in Old Age, *The Gerontologist, 24,* pp. 318-320, 1984.
85. L. A. Strain and N. L. Chappell, Confidants. Do They Make a Difference in Quality of Life? *Research on Aging, 4,* pp. 479-502, 1982.
86. W. K. Rawlins, Friendship Matters, in *Communication, Dialectics, and the Life Course,* Aldine de Gruyter, New York, 1992.
87. C. J. Johnson, Fairweather Friends and Rainy Day Kin: An Anthropological Analysis of Old Age Friendship in the United States, *Urban Anthropology, 12,* pp. 103-123, 1983.
88. G. R. Peters and M. A. Kaiser, The Role of Friends and Neighbors in Providing Social Support, in *Social Support Networks and the Care of the Elderly,* W. J. Sauer and R. T. Coward (eds.), pp. 123-158, Springer, New York, 1985.

89. M. M. Baltes and S. B. Silverberg, The Dynamics Between Dependency and Autonomy: Illustrations Across the Life-Span, in *Life-Span Development and Behavior* (Vol. 12), D. L. Featherman, R.M. Lerner, and M. Perlmutter (eds.), Erlbaum, Hillsdale, New Jersey, pp. 41-90, 1994.

90. M. M. Baltes, E.-M. Neumann, and S. Zank, Maintenance and Rehabilitation of Independence in Old Age: An Intervention Program for Staff, *Psychology and Aging, 9,* pp. 179-188,1994.

91. M. M. Baltes, Dependencies in Old Age: Gains and Losses, Current Directions, *Psychological Science, 4,* pp. 14-19, 1995.

92. F. R. Lang, M. M. Marsiske, P. B. Baltes, and M. M. Baltes, *Selective Optimization with Compensation: Different Facets of Control?* paper presented at the 13th biennial meeting of the International Society for the Study of Behavioral Development, Amsterdam, The Netherlands, June 28-July 2, 1994.

93. A. Bandura, Self-Efficacy Mechanism in Human Agency, *American Psychologist, 37,* pp. 122-147, 1982.

94. R. L. Kahn, Aging and Social Support, in *Aging from Birth to Death,* M. W. Riley (ed.), American Association for the Advancement of Science, Boulder, Colorado, pp. 77-91, 1979.

95. T. C. Antonucci, Social Supports and Social Relationships, in *Handbook of Aging and the Social Sciences* (3rd Edition), R. H. Binstock and L. K. George (eds.), Academic Press, San Diego, pp. 205- 226, 1990.

96. D. L. Morgan, T. L. Schuster, and E. W. Butler, Role Reversals in the Exchange of Social Support, *Journal of Gerontology: Social Sciences, 46,* pp. 278-287, 1991.

CHAPTER
3

A Social Psychology of the Life Cycle: Interdisciplinary Social Policies, Perceptions, and Prospects

Jeffrey Michael Clair, William C. Yoels,
and David A. Karp

Gerontology has become an increasingly popular area of study, with courses and research agendas proliferating in the social and behavioral sciences, humanities, professions, and schools of public health, nursing, and medicine. Most texts now available focus on the *aged* rather than *aging as a life-long social process*. In so doing, they concentrate on a specific group of persons at one point in time, rather than on general social processes affecting us continually throughout our lives. In addition, most current studies deal with the objective correlates of aging—with matters such as health, poverty, unemployment, housing, social security status, and retirement.

But even such objective issues have their *subjective foundation*. In this chapter, we want to focus on the subjective implications of current policy issues that impact us all. Our intention is to connect such issues as intergenerational conflict, multiracial integration, child care, and long-term care with the *subjective, personal responses* persons make when dealing with these issues and their own aging [1]. We do this realizing that any focus on the *meanings* of aging throughout the life cycle also must remain sensitive to the dynamic interplay between face-to-face relations and the world "behind our backs," the macro domain of history, demography, and social structure. To comprehend the aging process, we need to examine how persons occupying different locations in social space interpret and respond to repeated social messages about the meanings of age and their place within the life course. For this reason, we attend to such matters as the role of historical factors in defining aging, the significance of the general values of the larger society, the structure of family life, the importance of work careers, and the role of gender and race in the aging process.

We generate our discussion from a social psychological framework, but pose questions that are broad and sufficiently live enough to reflect a commitment to interdisciplinary thinking. The fruits of such a commitment will only be seen if we draw from the research of multiple disciplines, for example, the anthropologists, demographers, historians, and psychologists to supplement the underlying symbolic interactionist view presented here.

While we highlight the most significant age-related policy issues in need of interdisciplinary attention, the description of such issues alone is not our sole purpose. We strive to make a *theoretical statement* as well. Our aim is to infuse a *point of view*, an organized framework for thinking about these life-cycle policy issues. Our emphasis throughout is on persons' continual efforts to give meaning and significance to their lives.

We experience many seasons during our life cycle in search of purpose and meaning. Our experiences and aspirations branch out rather than form singular truths. Although we are varied and change significantly over a lifetime, the universal metaphors of stages and journeys help us situate aging within the life cycle. The metaphorical stages convey a sense of fixed periods, or perhaps significant milestones throughout life. The motif of journey, highlights dynamically patterned movement—the drama being the traveler's search [2].

We are living in times when ideas about the life cycle are undergoing fundamental transformations. We have become uncertain about what it means to grow old. The process of aging has increasingly come to be viewed as a troublesome, problematic aspect of identity. We can even dare to ask the question of whether aging has any intrinsic purpose?

The meaning of aging has been linked historically to the way cultures symbolize life as a whole. Any understanding of the aging process requires knowledge of the cultural definitions given to that process. Meanings given to chronological age categories are not constant but vary by socio-historical context and audience. From an interactionist perspective, different groups respond to age in terms of quite different inventories of symbols and thereby create among their members quite different aging selves. Meanings attached to age will vary with persons' social attributes such as gender, race, ethnicity, occupation, social class, and marital status. In a larger sense, our conceptions of aging and personal experience of the life cycle will be shaped by our place in history, by the historical epoch in which we live. Although we acknowledge the existence of age norms, we remind you that the aging experience also is a *subjective* one and must be viewed from the perspective of persons moving through that experience. In this sense, our culture lives in every community, within each of us, having a unique historical value which tells our story.

One common dimension throughout the life cycle is that all people desire meaningful social relationships, satisfying work, and a sense of self-efficacy in their daily lives. The historical period in which one lives is crucial here, however, as issues facing our aging society today are qualitatively different from those we faced, for example, during *The Great Depression* [3]. Social scientists have described a traumatized cohort of Depression children in the 1930s; a scared cohort of 1940s, World War II teenagers who gained maturity through war-time experience; a relatively affluent but anxious postwar cohort in the late 1950s; a post-Vietnam cohort with new ideas in the late 1960s and early 1970s. The 1980s produced a cohort confronted with shrinking horizons in terms of occupational opportunities [4]. The 90s have left many with cloudy expectations about a retirement with stability, dignity, and honor. So, despite all the similarities across times and places, each cohort faces unique challenges, resulting from its "collective memory" of the distinctive social and political events of its youth [5]. We use the term cohort instead of the frequently used generic and historical term "generation." Bengtson, Cutler, Mangen, and Marshall have pointed out that the term generation is no longer useful when referring to groups of different ages in the broader society [6]. The term *cohort* refers to those individuals who have been born at roughly the same point in time and who, together, experience specific social events at a common point in their individual life course. The use of the term *generation* primarily reflects ranked-descent ordering of individuals within families. *Cohorts* are to societies what *generations* are to families. Societal cohorts can be seen as expressions of the mentalities of the people that populate that era. Sharing the same "age location" in history, each cohort's "collective consciousness" shapes its members in varied ways—whether they agree with it or spend a lifetime in opposition [7].

We stand at the convergence of a new century and millennium. Rarely have so many lived through so much social change (see Cutler, this volume). It is perhaps the first time in history that significant numbers of first, second, third, and fourth generation members are alive *at the same time* (see Bengston et al. this volume). Policies of the 1980 and 90s, such as the "Contract with America," echoed a number of conservative-based, traditional themes such as the "preservation" of the family and respect for "law and order." The end of this century has seen our society develop new rationalizations for a retreat from the 1960s "Great Society" ideals of equal opportunity and compassion for the less fortunate. These rationalizations are experienced individually in face-to-face situations, and collectively through their institutionalization in governmental policies. Many experience the fact that differences seem to matter more than what we have in common. The new millennium may be the place where we learn to respect one another's differences and embrace and value policies that unite us or we may witness increasingly narrowed horizons for most groups within our society.

Our multigenerational society has to deal with the historical legacy of past problems and the immediacy of policy issues. The overall theme of the White House millennium programs is "Honor the past; imagine the future." We are now confronting the core values and sensibilities in American culture while facing the many "isms" (i.e., ageism, racism, sexism) at the root of present tensions. It is not hard to see our movement into the twenty-first century as the possible beginning of a crisis era, in terms of its potential for unprecedented social struggles.

Any time a country struggles to sustain economic growth and social psychological well-being, the class system becomes more rigid. Competition increases, especially among the young who must compete for a diminishing supply of resources. Those from poverty backgrounds find themselves falling further and further behind. Women, many burdened with child rearing, and members of traditional minority groups simply have fewer of the advantages, the "social boosters" so to speak, that make the quest for old age fun and challenging; and at the end of life, the economic security of our elderly, both present and future, depends importantly on good will and a sense of obligation from those engaged in productive labor, as well as on the efficacy of that labor [4]. So, while ideally some might view the elderly, because of their wisdom and experiential knowledge, as prized resources, others see them as competitors for resources—just another cohort in need of public welfare entitlements. At the same time, we can view our youth as the future leaders of our country with unique creativity and energy, or as other self-interest groupings. This is particularly important when you consider that we are becoming more and more diverse. It appears during our own individual walks that we are more likely to find others dwelling on differences, which has become easier than building shared values.

If different cohorts do not honor and respect each others' contributions and sacrifices, conflicts will intensify. Through a process of reciprocal obligations generations support one another. Thus, you help your parents and children, then after your parents' deaths, your children help you while raising their own children; after your death your grandchildren then raise their own children while helping their parents (your children) and so on. Since the above proposition assumes a degree of social stability and minimal intergenerational conflict, a major concern is that particular cohorts may break this ongoing chain of reciprocal obligations [8]. This is especially crucial in that those in the middle will pay disproportionately more for general living needs than their predecessors [9]. All one need do is talk to some sixteen to thirty-year-olds and ask them what they expect from our current retirement system. The majority response is staggering. Most do not expect to receive any benefits and would like to see government find a way to let them keep their current and promised future contributions.

THE SOURCES OF POTENTIAL CONFLICT

The goals of all generations are usually couched in sweeping language encompassing difficult but laudable objectives. We are all interested in a good education, adequate income, the best possible physical and mental health, suitable housing, and opportunity without regard to race, gender, and age. We would like to think that we all have a chance to get ahead with hard work, and we can live in safe communities, with strong families, and schools, and health services. And, at the end, we wish to retire in good health, honor, and dignity, with efficient social services available when needed. Since everyone wants such comfort in their lives, it is easy to imagine conflict over what persons define as their fair share of the "resource pie." Potential generational and racially based conflicts quickly come to mind when we look at changing demographics and policy issues in the near future.

To be sure, we are an *aging society*. The population of the United States will never again—not even when the "baby boomers" pass through the scene—be nearly as "youthful" as it is today. Once the age composition peaks in the next twenty years, the "aging of America" will be more or less permanent. This is an enduring reality to which our economic, political, and social institutions must adapt. Most significant today is the growing political power of the elderly in tandem with the presence of increasingly younger multiracial cohorts who can expect to live longer [10].

We also are at the tail end of times in which the descendants of Anglo-Europeans dominate culturally and demographically. Within the first part of the twenty-first century, about half, or perhaps even the majority of our population, will consist of African Americans, Hispanics, Asians, and Native Americans. This demographic fact raises two realities: not only will we witness more minority elderly, a life experience often characterized as multiple jeopardy, but young minority populations will become more essential parts of the work force. This labor force will carry the responsibility and burden of maintaining productivity and economic prosperity. Such minorities often face restricted educational and employment opportunities. In an economy that truly honors opportunity, all Americans must be able to reap rewards. Expressions of feeling a sense of outrage about the reality of "The American Dream" for those outside the mainstream is lyrically and visually portrayed through the here to stay hip hop culture. Other forms of impassioned challenges are lurking everywhere as long as we do not attend to policies that ensure opportunity and fairness for all. We are hopeful for policy development that builds greater understanding across relationship and communication lines—to find resolutions to honest differences, and to enact solutions to identified problems.

Another historically unique sociodemographic fact concerns those born between 1946 and 64— those called "baby boomers." Based on mere numbers, this cohort has the potential political clout to establish public agendas as it moves through the life cycle [10]. Besides influencing popular culture, politically this cohort can make politicians accountable. Whether this trend setting cohort develops a collective identity that can be mobilized into concerted political action is an intriguing question in need of empirical data.

The "baby boomers" will have to acknowledge many problems which affect all cohorts as they move through the life cycle: parents' problems in obtaining access to child care and quality education for their children; the universal need for health care; and ameliorating current racial tensions. They also may witness a labor force increasingly embittered about supporting an expanding retired elderly population. Those born between 1910 and 26 are approaching their 80s and 90s and will need social and health services. Another group, those born in the 30s, will begin to obtain their share of public benefits and services just when the stability and fiscal soundness of many entitlement programs become increasingly problematic. Those demanding new programs for children, universal health care for all, reinvestments in the industrial infrastructure, and minority job-training programs, will all simultaneously compete for funding. This also is the time when the baby boomers may start exerting their political muscle [10].

We want to pose some critical questions about the meanings of policy and politics for all generations as we move into the twenty-first century. In so doing, we will highlight challenges demanding immediate action. We will focus on the issues of: accepting an intergenerational society; integrating a multiracial population base; providing health and longterm care; and child care and women in the workforce [1]. We conclude with the challenge of incorporating the politics of the life cycle into a national policy agenda in need of interdisciplinary scientific support.

We are currently presented with an opportunity for reassessing policy developments while creating appropriate political strategies cutting across demographic and social class lines. With meaningful opportunities and honest communication, is it possible we can unite such a diverse people in freedom and mutual respect? The politics of the life cycle center on changes in public values and attitudes about aging, race, and gender. In this regard, 1988 marked the passing of a cohort of leaders who have shaped social policies since *The New Deal*. Such leadership changes signify a move from a politics of the life cycle rooted in the experiences of the Depression, World War II, and the Cold War, to one of a baby-boom cohort which will age in the next century. This cohort, and its newly emerging leaders, will confront a different set of intergenerationally-based problems as they assume leadership on life-cycle social policies. They will need to decide what we value and intend to preserve of our past for the new millennium. And they are faced with developing solutions to the competing demands of social differentiation and integration. What will their creative solutions to these seemingly polar social and psychological processes look like. Each era is stamped by its own characteristic way of resolving this twin problem of how to divide and integrate. The dynamic of these processes are the trust for social change. It also is here that we will find the possibilities of generating work careers that offer opportunity, a society rooted in responsibility, and a people that live as a community. This is the place where we move toward general well-being.

ACCEPTING AN INTERGENERATIONAL SOCIETY

We begin with the basic fact that the average age of Americans is rising. A decline in birth rates and a rise in longevity have produced unprecedented demographic swings. The proportion of the population over sixty-four years of age has risen continuously while the proportion under twenty has steadily decreased. Future projections through the year 2060 show a continuous rise in the elderly population with young-to-old ratios about equal. The share of the elderly population will continue to rise slowly until about 2010 and then will rapidly increase over the following three decades as the baby boomers retire.

Vern Bengtson et al. (this volume) pose the challenge of assessing just how individual family units, communities, and larger social institutions can maintain continuity over time, while facing the persistent changes in population composition resulting from the life cycle of individual members—birth, aging, generational succession. Changes in our population's age structure have important implications for service demands and our ability to finance social entitlement programs. The aging of our population also implies a decline in the proportion of both the young and working age populations, as the absolute size of these groups shrink. Such population trends suggest that the elderly will consume a growing proportion of our nation's total output if their living standards remain similar to those of the rest of the population. Many already think that America is spending too much on its elderly and too little on its young. This is a crucial issue facing U.S. society. Unless something changes, this gap will only widen, with potentially devastating economic and social consequences.

Throughout the life cycle, persons also suffer from more open and visible social problems: the drug-related violence in the inner-cities, homelessness, the inadequate provision of health and long-term care coverage, struggling schools, and an explosive racial climate. Without large scale, long-term social programs, these problems will continue to worsen.

Currently we spend more than $11,000 on every American over sixty-five and only about $4,000 on each youngster under eighteen. Thirty years ago these proportions were roughly reversed [11, 12]. Will our children become a "treasured resource, nurtured all the more for their scarcity and importance to the nation's future?" [13, p. 161). Many are concerned that as younger generations mature they will not have the necessary skills to keep the economy productive. This is especially worrisome since today's children will one day feed and nurse an unparalleled army of elders— the seventy-six million baby boomers born between 1946 and 1964. This cohort begins reaching retirement age in just over ten years. What is often called a dependency ratio, dividing the nonworking elderly by the total workforce, also portends trouble considering predictions about fewer younger workers to support future baby-boom elders on pensions. Data, in fact, suggest that by the year 2025 there will be 4.3 retirees for every ten employed workers, compared to 2.7 retirees in 1990, an increase of almost 60 percent in the number of retirees per worker during the next thirty-five years or so [14]!

Social Security funds will be especially affected by this shrinking supply of workers needed to support baby-boom pensioners. Social Security pensions are funds generated primarily through a tax on paid labor, an employer-employee payroll tax. FICA (Federal Insurance Contributions Act) is the 7.65 percent payroll tax, on the first $68,400, of income you see automatically deducted from your check each month, thereafter it continues at 2.45 percent.

Each month, the revenues collected through the payroll tax are forwarded from the IRS to the SS Administration, where they are appropriated, under a formula set by Congress, to each of the system's three major trust funds. About 70 percent of the revenue is entered into what the government calls the Old Age Survivors Disability Insurance (OASDI) trust fund to cover the month-to-month cost of providing pensions for today's elderly. Another 20 percent of those revenues go to the Hospital Insurance (HI) trust to finance current hospital care benefits for the elderly under the Medicare program. The remaining 10 percent of your payroll tax goes to Disability Insurance (DI) paying benefits to the physically challenged.

Current projections show the Hospital Insurance trust, or main Medicare trust fund, slipping into deficit with reserves being challenged. Medicare benefits accounted for over 40 percent of total welfare spending in 1990, an increase of over 10 percent from ten years earlier [15]. The disability fund could be exhausted by 2026 and the pension trust fund is projected to run in the red by 2020 and toward bankruptcy by 2054, a phenomenon which will affect today's children [16]. President Clinton's 1998 State of the Union address with plans to use 100 percent of any deficit surplus to shore up this system is already being met with mixed reviews, and surely will result in drawn out political party battles.

How likely is it that Social Security (SS) will go "belly-up," so to speak? As Gelfand has noted, it is important to emphasize that "best guess" government forecasts arguing for the soundness of the Social Security system assume that: 1) any reserves built up in one trust won't be used in another; 2) wages will rise above inflation by at least 25 percent before the end of the century, double by 2032, and triple by 2059; 3) there will be no more recessions and the economy will grow by two to three percent annually; 4) unemployment will not exceed 6 percent after 1993; 5) fertility will rise by 10 percent by the year 2010; and 6) life expectancy at age sixty-five will increase by no more than three years and four months for men and four years and four months for women by the year 2060 [16]. These are all very questionable assumptions even with recent economic events showing some strength.

Responding to a projected financing crisis in the SS system, Congress has addressed the issue of increasing the workforce by attempting to add more workers to the tax base, while encouraging people to retire later, thereby paying into the system longer. As of 1983, all new federal workers are required to pay Social Security taxes. Secondly, in 1983 Congress enacted a delay beginning in the year 2000 in the normal age for SS eligibility. Eligibility at sixty-five for an unreduced SS benefit will be delayed two months for those born in 1938, four months for those born in 1939, and so on, with normal retirement age set at sixty-six for those born between 1943 and 1954. Another round of retirement reductions is scheduled in the law to begin 2016, affecting those born in 1955 or later and pushing normal retirement age up to sixty-seven by 2022.

Finally, legislative developments also have liberalized the mandatory retirement test, with the permissible age for forced retirement moved from sixty-five to seventy, as a result of the 1979 Age Discrimination in Employment Act. This has had little impact on retirement age. In fact, during the past three decades, the average age of retirement underwent significant decline [17]. It is not clear whether the SS changes will result in wide change in retirement patterns, given the fact that many retirements already precede SS eligibility, with *most of them due to health limitations.*

There are basically two arguments for raising the age of eligibility for Social Security benefits. The first argues that in the 1930s when SS was enacted, life expectancy for men at age twenty was only an additional 45.1 years, so the average male worker would only live to about sixty-five (life expectancy for women was only 1 year longer). Thus, one had to live longer than average to collect any benefits. Social Security was not a universal pension, and in a sense could even be described as an insurance against not dying young. By 1990, life expectancy at age twenty for all men and women was an additional fifty-seven years which would lead to twelve years of retirement benefits past the age of sixty-five. Secondly, it also has been argued that since jobs have become less strenuous, later retirement is now more appropriate.

In considering such policies, however, opponents of deferred retirement counter with qualitatively different arguments. They note that many early retirements are taken because of ill health and fatigue. Moreover, it is important for us to realize that public benefits provide for the *majority.* Many private plans provide for full retirement at fifty-five but such benefits currently serve only a minority. As we have seen in the early 1990s, such plans also are susceptible to financial crises which provide corporations with a rationale for reducing the pension and health benefits paid to former employees. Ninety percent of the current retired population rely on SS for at least 50 percent of their income. More importantly, over 25 percent of the retired population get 90 percent of their income from SS. So, for sizable chunks of the population, SS income is their *main or only* source of economic support [16].

Those against extending the retirement eligibility age also point out that most lower paid workers, such as minority group members and women, rely entirely on public pension policy. By contrast, skilled technical and professional workers can look forward to early retirements knowing that they are financially secure and not dependent on SS benefits. Thus, pushing back the retirement age will be detrimental to the economically disadvantaged who have no choice but to remain in the work force. Opponents and advocates of current retirement policy can both agree that change and a shoring up of pension plans is necessary. Ironically, even though we currently spend more on our elderly population than on our youth, the disturbing fact is that the elderly need more—especially widows, single females, members of racial minority groups, and the "oldest-old," those over eighty.

Kingson cogently poses the issue before us:

> . . . in the absence of commonly-agreed upon standards of social justice empha-
> sizing egalitarian concerns or the importance of distributing resources in relation
> to social need, consistent standards of adequacy for income, health services,
> housing and other needed services for all simply do not exist . . . Those concerned
> with advancing policies based on egalitarian or needs-based concepts of social
> justice ought to seek ways to transform interest-group politics and establish
> adequate income, health, housing, and educational guarantees *for all* (italics
> added) [18, p. 769].

We are facing opportunities for the government, the private sector, and taxpayers to understand that it is in our nation's best interest to launch a massive reinvestment in the human infrastructure (education, health care, jobs) while combating all forms of institutional discrimination (ageism, racism, sexism) hindering such objectives. Unresolved issues could foster intense conflict along generational, gender, and racial lines. We must creatively synthesize the "liberal" agenda of creating opportunities with the "conservative" argument about personal responsibility. In a larger sense, there is a need to heighten the public's *sociological imagination* [19] by helping it understand how personal *troubles* relate to the way resources and opportunities are *socially distributed in the larger society*. This imagination helps us realize that social problems result from historically structured, socioeconomic inequality rather than individual and family-based deficiencies. It is here, where sociologists, economists, political scientists, historians, psychologists, and public health officials can play a crucial role toward informing policy makers with real life data.

INTEGRATING A MULTIRACIAL POPULATION BASE

In discussing the integration of a multiracial population base, we are calling attention to minority groups *and* to social class. It is important to realize that when we refer to minority groups, we are, in fact, not just talking about numbers, which is why the label "minority" is often misleading. Women, for instance, are not numerical minorities, but neither are they full members of the dominant culture. The term "dominant culture" involves the issue of power—those who historically or traditionally have had the most persistent impact on culture, on what we think and say. In America, dominant culture significantly reflects the precepts and artifacts of Anglo-culture, and thus is not necessarily a reference to numbers but to power.

We also want to discuss some numbers, however. Future projections show minorities comprising at least 50 percent of our population by the middle of the next century. Along with issues of class, the sheer growing number of minority group members has great significance for members of *all* age categories. We can safely predict that this growing minority population will provide the basic foundation for our work force in the next century.

In terms of minority communities, there are noticeable class-based trends within the African-American community which run in opposite directions. On one hand, there has been significant improvement in the socioeconomic status of a sizable number of middle class Black Americans, whom Gilliam and Whitby [20] refer to as the "new ethclass" [21]. By contrast, there still exists a disturbingly large African-American "underclass." The existence of such a sizable underclass raises serious *life cycle policy* questions. Can we expect children from backgrounds of poor nutrition and health care, inadequate education, and deteriorating neighborhoods to develop into strong, effective adults capable of participating in governing our nation? In the face of institutionalized discrimination, will our country be able to produce enough skilled workers to sustain continued economic growth and prosperity? Will there be sufficient opportunities for our unemployed teenagers to stay out of gangs and find meaningful employment? Will our middle-aged minority population be given the chance to serve as "old heads," as sources of knowledge and expertise, to their families and communities [22]?

At the same time as the number of retirees will be rapidly growing relative to the number of employed workers, the work force will be increasingly reliant on the work of those from the most disadvantaged backgrounds. Will our need to enhance the economic security of our growing elderly population lead us to expand avenues for minority success in the work force? Moreover, African Americans and Hispanics, for example, tend not to live as long as whites, thereby gaining less benefits from Social Security retirement arrangements. Will they be more likely, then, to prefer public expenditures targeted on programs for children rather than aimed at the elderly [23]? Unfortunately, the political communication between racial groups has traditionally been uneasy and tension-laden. Questions such as the above, however, must be addressed.

It can be argued that political attitudes are the product of distinct political subcultures [24]. Martin Luther King, Jr., for example, believed that African Americans and whites have fundamentally different definitions of the term "equality":

> Negroes have proceeded from the premise that equality means what it says, and they have taken white Americans at their word when they talked of it as an objective. But most whites in America in 1967, including many persons of

goodwill, proceed from a premise that equality is a loose expression for *improvement*. White America is not even *psychologically organized* to close the gap— essentially it seeks only to make it less painful and less obvious but in most respects to retain it. Most abrasions between Negroes and white liberals arise from this fact. (emphasis added) [25, p. 8].

In *Black and White Styles in Conflict*, Thomas Kochman argues that the black mode of public debate is "animated, interpersonal, and confrontational," while the white mode is relatively "dispassionate, impersonal, and nonchallenging" [26]. Influenced by the notion of scientific detachment, whites believe reason and emotion work against each other. African Americans on the other hand see their emotion and anger as part of their grievances to be negotiated, not something to be set aside prior to debate [27].

Currently many minority group members feel that they have been assigned a permanent place as people of lower status. Edith Folb has pointed out that the "white, male, heterosexual, able-bodied, youthful person" sets the standards and is the human yardstick by which people are measured and treated [28]. She suggests there is a cultural prescription to keep minority peoples in their place, sustained by the *subterranean self*:

the culture-bound collection of prejudices, stereotypes, values, and beliefs that each of us embraces and employs to justify our world view and the place of people in that world . . . our subterranean selves . . . provide fuel to fire the normative in our lives—what roles people ought and ought not to perform, what and why certain individuals are ill- or well-equipped to carry out certain roles, and our righteously stated rationalizations for keeping people in their places as we see them [28, p. 127].

The 1992 Rodney King incident in Los Angeles, and the initial verdict of not guilty for the four police officers captured on video pummeling Mr. King, spawned racial violence not witnessed since the Civil Rights Movement of the 60s. Those looting were the children of blacks who rioted in Watts in 1968, as well as some recent immigrants from Latin America for whom the Southern California dream has turned into a nightmare. Conflicts across ethnic group lines, such as between African-American community residents and Korean store owners, manifest the despair of those at the bottom rungs of the social ladder who increasingly compete against each other for scarce resources. Such actions illustrate the racial tension underlying our social fabric. Arthur Schlesinger, Jr. suggests that ethnic and racial conflict is the "explosive issue of our times," with racism being a "great national tragedy" [29]. In this regard, he sadly echoes the words of Gunnar Myrdal [30], uttered almost fifty years ago, about race relations as the most significant issue in American life.

People of color remain convinced that they live in a world of historically generated ceilings, restrictions, and obstacles. Societal policies have proven incredibly resistant to demands for change. There are many signs that poverty and hopelessness pervade the diverse ranks of minority groups [22]. Consider the African-American experience. Males account for only 5 percent of all corporate officers,

3 percent of Ph.D. candidates, and despite some recent political gains still hold less than 3 percent of all elective offices in the United States [31]. In contrast, African Americans make up over 40 percent of death row inmates and nearly half of state and federal inmates [32].

No matter how one "crunches" recent numbers from the United States Census Bureau, the Bureau of Labor Statistics, and the National Center for Health Statistics, they demonstrate sizable gaps between minority and white America. Despite growth in the African-American middle class, for example, a larger percentage of urban African-American people live in poverty today than at the time of the Los Angeles Watts riots in 1968. The unemployment rate among non-whites is twice that for white people and has been at least twice that of whites for as long as the U.S. Bureau of Labor Statistics has been tracking such demographics. The median household income for whites is almost double compared to African-American median income.

African Americans trail whites in earnings even when education is equal. While overall homeownership is close to two-thirds, 69.2 percent are occupied by whites, while only about 43.6 percent of African Americans and 41.4 percent of Hispanics can make such claims [33]. Additionally, we have known for some time that health indicators show infant mortality rates among Blacks to be more than double that for whites along with considerably lower life expectancies. Most importantly, over 40 percent of Black youths under eighteen and about 39 percent of Hispanics under eighteen live in poverty, compared to about 15 percent of similarly-aged white youths [34, Table 737]. Minority youths also are quite likely to be living in female-headed (i.e., male absent) families, and, as Fitzpatrick and Yoels' study of high school dropouts indicates, this family arrangement is a powerful predictor of dropout rates [35]. Such families typically lack the economic resources for upward mobility.

On top of all the struggles of surviving and raising children in this world, ethnic parents have the additional problems of battling oppression while preparing their children to feel good about themselves and proud of their ethnic identity. They must work as advocates for their children and families while at the same time attempting to survive economically.

While we have painted a picture of considerable bleakness, there is room for optimism about our ability creatively to confront some of these issues (also see Stanford and Stanford, this volume). In *Within Our Reach: Breaking the Cycle of Disadvantage,* Lisbeth Schorr documents a wide range of successful programs targeting problems in minority communities [36]. In terms of "bottom line," dollars and cents criteria, many of these efforts have been quite cost effective. In a program providing outside support for families called Homebuilders, the social policy interventions resulted in "savings [that] were calculated to amount to three to three and a half times the expenditures" [36, p. 271]. The Yale Child Study Center's day care family support program in New Haven led to a savings in welfare costs alone which came to more than $60,000 at the time of a ten-year follow-up study [36, p. 272]. The Perry Preschool program in Ypsilanti, Michigan estimated that it saved several times its beginning annual cost of $5,000 per child because of a variety of associated consequences—lower crime rates and reduced costs of public assistance [36, p. 272].

Finally, and perhaps most importantly in terms of intergenerational relations, she reports on how Dr. James Comer, a child psychiatrist at the Yale Child Study Center, achieved remarkable success in turning around schools in New Haven's inner city that ranked among the lowest of the city's public schools in academic achievement, attendance records, and behavior problems. Between 1968 and 1983 the two inner city schools in which his demonstration project unfolded—one of which was actually in the Brookside Public Housing Project—moved from thirty-second and thirty-third in reading and math achievement out of thirty-three New Haven elementary schools, to third and fifth in composite fourth grade scores [36, p .231]! The involvement of parents in this project provided an important source of educational continuity for the children as they moved back and forth from home to school. As Schorr notes in this regard, such a program not only benefitted the children but the *parents* as well. In fact, as a result of this program "it turned out that some parents, their own confidence bolstered by their school activity, went back to school themselves and some took jobs they previously thought they couldn't handle" [36, pp. 233-234]. We can see clearly here how programs aimed at one age group can have important beneficial "spin-off" effects on others.

When one compares the fact that the costs associated with building one prison cell amount to $75,000, or $7.5 million per 100 inmates, and that the yearly costs for incarceration run about $20,000 per year per inmate [37], it certainly seems sensible to consider the kinds of successful program interventions described by Schorr.

HEALTH AND LONG-TERM CARE

The health care crisis facing Americans today is staggering. Lacking money and insurance, thousands of Americans die every year of curable diseases and injuries. As the following data from the U.S. Buerau of Census [15] indicate, an estimated forty-one million Americans, primarily the young and working poor, lack any medical insurance. Between 1960 and present, the percentage of the nation's gross national product consumed by health care has more than doubled from 5 to 14 percent. About one-third of all health care spending is consumed by the 12 percent of the population over sixty-five years of age. As the elderly population increases, so too will the demand on health care.

The most rapidly growing age group is the population aged eighty and over. The "oldest-old" will disproportionately require more sustained medical care. We can expect that our population will continue to die at older ages, since close to 71 percent of all deaths now occur in people ages sixty-five and over, with 30 to 35 percent occurring in those age eighty and older [38]. While only 2 to 3 percent of the elderly in their early sixties and seventies require nursing home care, over 23 percent of all those above eighty-five eventually require such care [16, 39]. Additionally, individuals over sixty-five account for about 33 percent of all hospital stays and about 42 percent of the days of care provided by hospitals [40, 41]. There is no way for society to avoid these burdens. Even if the proportion of institutionalized elderly remains stable, the absolute number of those institutionalized and the estimated demand for services will continue to grow.

Younger and middle-aged people increasingly realize that aging is not simply about being old but, rather, about growing older and living longer. The rise of long-term care as a policy priority signifies the newfound awareness by younger groups that policy decisions concerning the elderly can have a direct impact on *their own* lifestyle choices, economic status, social relationships, and general well-being.

In addition to private health insurance, currently there are two protective devices for the aged to meet their medical costs—*Medicare* and *Medicaid*. The Medicare program is an integral part of the SS pension system. Medicare covers persons age sixty-five and over. There are currently close to thirty million medicare recipients with expenditures reaching fifty billion. To control hospital costs, a new system of prospective payment for hospital care was developed. The Prospective Payment System uses standardized payments for particular conditions. The results of this system have been controversial. The average length of stay in hospitals has been reduced from 7.3 days in 1980 to 5.7 now [41]. Critics have argued, however, that the elderly are being discharged prematurely despite assurances from the Medicare Quality Protection Act requiring hospitals to prepare alternative discharge plans for patients who might be adversely affected by discharge.

The Medicare program is divided into two parts: *Part A—hospital insurance* and *Part B—medical insurance*. All persons sixty-five or older receive part A benefits without any additional costs. Part B benefits are available only to those who join and pay a certain amount each month [42]. Most Americans are unaware of the limited coverage provided by Medicare Part A. After paying for the first day of care, each individual is essentially entitled to sixty days of hospitalization. If additional days beyond the first sixty are necessary the consequences can be staggering. Let us consider a few examples. For thirty additional days of coverage, an individual can expect to pay as much as $5,000 out of pocket if they have not secured "additional" private insurance, which can easily run to several hundred dollars a month in insurance policy premiums. If an additional, let's say, ninety days are needed, individual or family costs could be as high as $25,000. A fair estimate is that the cost of full-time institutionalized long-term care can cost as much as $38,000 per year [43, p. 985]. How much of this will come from personal savings depends on whether or not persons were able to invest in "private" retirement plans. For those without private coverage, an eventual depletion of lifetime savings is the only way they can secure long-term care.

None of the above hospital charges include the services of such specialists as anesthesiologists, pathologists, and radiologists. They are billed separately from the hospital charges and are considered a Part B, Supplemental Insurance, expense. Many elderly cannot afford the Part B Costs, which are about $30 a month with an annual deductible of about $100. After the first $100, insurance will cover 80 percent of medical services. Expenses for drugs and dental services are not included, which can lead to serious health consequences. Many elderly who cannot pay for prescribed medications will not take them. Those who cannot afford dental services often suffer from malnutrition, thereby producing additional chronic health problems. Outpatient psychiatric services are reimbursed at 50 percent, with no more than $1,100 annually reimbursed. This too can be problematic, especially when considering the rising prevalence of Alzheimer's disease and the often inordinate difficulty in diagnosing such a disease [44].

Medicaid varies from state to state, with states deciding whom to include and exclude. Medicaid is the major source of public funds for longterm care. Currently, about 70 percent of federal medicaid funds are used to pay for nursing home care, 17 percent for hospital care, and 12 percent for in-home care. Half of all nursing home residents are below the poverty level and are *totally* covered by Medicaid.

In total, private insurance pays for about 27 percent of all medical costs in the nation, while the government pays, mainly through Medicare and Medicaid, about 42 percent. Individual direct payments cover about 27 percent, and a very small percentage is covered through philanthropy. As one can easily calculate, if you were to become chronically ill there is a very frayed safety net, indeed, to "catch" you in later life. Many people must eventually deplete all of their personal resources to deal with such illnesses. While many of our medical advancements are contributing to extended life, they also are posing monumental quality of life issues.

We have no demonstrably effective forms of intervention for most of the diseases that degeneratively cause suffering and dependent disability among our elderly. These chronic illnesses can be "skillfully overseen, may occasionally abate or be arrested, and are sometimes cured; but by and large, these are illnesses that are incrementally progressive" [45, p. 15]. As a result, Alzheimer's disease, along with other chronic illnesses, will continually increase the demand for long-term care services. Where such funding will come from remains to be seen.

We currently lack useful measures for predicting and determining the health care needs of our aging society [46]. We would argue here that *identifying predictors of healthy aging* seems like a reasonable alternative to greater medical intervention. This is an important policy issue since a change in focus, from intervention to prevention, will require a commitment to reordering our health care priorities [47]. Devoting more funds to medical intervention strategies perpetuates an ideology that medical intervention can incrementally eliminate one disease after another. Even if we develop some miraculous cure for cancer, this still does not mean that you have a better chance of living forever. Rather, you now have a better chance of dying from *some other disease,* such as a circulatory disease, for example.

A recent survey of adolescents revealed that they expected to live beyond 100 years and to be able to buy organs right off the shelf. We need to be cautious about encouraging persons' expectations about controlling specific disease, lifestyle, and socio-environmental factors since freedom from all diseases is incompatible with the process of living. Future cohorts who remain committed to increasing medical intervention spending and the medicalization of the life cycle will likely resist any reordering of social health priorities. Inevitably, however, the growing number of elderly in need of sustained care will be at the center of future domestic policy priorities.

The concepts of healthy or "successful" aging, "high levels of physical functioning," "continued physical ability" generated by our Public Health scholars [48-50] require identifying socio-environmental and physiologic correlates of biological aging amenable to prevention strategies as an alternative to more medical intervention. Work in this direction has identified behavioral and lifestyle risk factors that correlate with the absence of chronic disease, such as never smoking, a low body mass index, exercise, nutrition and dietary practices, consumption of minimal amounts of alcohol, and avoidance of drugs. Relevant social structural factors concern education, income, occupational stress, social support, and isolation. Increasingly, future health-care policy decisions must focus on how social stressors affect health. A critical discourse enlightens us on how medicine may move beyond its focus on biomedical goals and values, to a recognition that illness may result from the unmet needs and social stresses of everyday life [51, also see Baker, Clair, Yoels, and Allman, this volume].

Great expectations accompany the funding of research into the multi-system degenerative diseases, but it would be a mistake to base social-health policy on an assumption that the coming years will provide major biomedical breakthroughs for such problems as Alzheimer's, arthritis, circulatory diseases, or various forms of central nervous system degeneration prevalent among elderly long-term care patients. Although the burdens originating in the above illnesses and diseases show some room for improvement, we can expect a vast number of aging persons to still require long-term care services. In essence, changes in our society's age composition insure high levels of future dependent disability, with the social services and medical sector responses struggling to catch up while families are forced to fill in the ever-widening gaps [47].

The aging of our society will continue challenging the ability of the public and private sectors to provide support solutions for long-term care problems [52, 53]. Past solutions include: the Social Security Act in 1935; passage of the Older Americans Act and development of Medicare and Medicaid in 1965; the establishment of Social/Health Maintenance Organizations in the 1970s; the imposition of a prospective payment system, Diagnostic-Related Groups, in 1983; and most recently, the passage of and then repeal of the Medicare Catastrophic Coverage Act (CHI) of 1988 (see Torres-Gil, this volume). These past and current policy solutions will still leave a large and increasing number of Americans excluded from adequate access and coverage. Even when sustained care is provided by informal caregivers, the economic burden on society is still felt through the decrements in informal caregivers' economic, physical, and psychological well-being.

We know that long-term care is inadequately provided by publicly supported nursing homes [54]. To compound matters, recent evidence informs us that while hospital stays have been reduced through the prospective payment system, the demand for nursing home care is *increasing*. Shortcomings in our current modes of dealing with dependent disability require us to pursue alternatives to institutionalized care. Such alternatives include board and care, adult foster care, life care, and domiciliary care. Efforts to find alternatives illustrate the interrelations between living arrangements and long-term care services, since the aging process reduces persons' ability to meet activities of daily living. In fact, about 85 percent of all nursing home residents have some form of dependency in activities of daily living. Estimates are that the number of elderly needing help with ADLs and/or IADLs may grow from 7.3 million now, to ten to fourteen million by 2020 and fourteen to twenty-four million by 2060 [55].

Even though there is only limited evidence to support the cost-effectiveness of alternative home care and community-based service programs, these efforts are in their infancy and the development of an adequate supply of residentially-based and community-based services is still desirable, especially since this is what *many aged and their families prefer* [56]. A linkage of residentially and community-based services with public services and programs will meet more needs and enable us to address the transition of elders through different stages of dependency. Unfortunately, our awareness of the relationship between housing and long-term care occurs too late, "when the functional independence of an individual has been threatened and families can no longer cope" [57, p. 341].

Evidence about family caregiver alternatives are more critical than ever because of their implications for policy. Findings from forty years of gerontological research suggest that families will continue to provide substantial care for their aged, even in the absence of formal incentives to assume these responsibilities (also see Cutler this volume, and Baker, Clair, Yoels, and Allman, this volume). Since care giving often has very negative effects on families, and women in particular, it must be assisted and strengthened through a variety of formal programs and economic supports such as respite care and state tax incentives. As Olesen notes, the amount of *hidden care* provided by women is enormous:

> The Older Women's League (OWL) estimates that the value of women's unpaid work in American society is $515 billion annually, more than twice that of men. OWL's figures do not specify how much time spent in the case of the sick contributes to that figure, but it is reasonable to surmise that it must be substantial [58, p. 5].

Women can expect to spend as much time caring for an aging parent as raising children—eighteen years for the former, compared with seventeen years for the latter; women comprise about 75 percent of the unpaid caregivers to the elderly [59, p. 39]; 80 percent of family caregivers to the elderly provide care seven days a week, and it has been estimated that caregivers to the elderly provide over twenty-seven million days of unpaid care every week; and finally, about one-third of the caregivers are themselves sixty-five or older [60]. It has long been pointed out that family members care for their dependents because alternative options are not available, rather than because they value this role [61]. We must question our long-standing belief that the family is individually responsible for its dependents. This should become part of a national debate on political agendas for the future.

Supplementing the numerous "hidden" family caregivers will contribute to their overall well-being while keeping elderly relatives in more familiar and caring environments [58]. Many families take on caregiving activities, through a sense of duty, filial responsibility, or love, and if their well-being can be improved by the availability of supportive physical and social services then this is an agenda issue for practice and policy consideration. Certain sub-groups within the population should be targeted when designing caregiver support services: 1) those with health declines, 2) those with lower socioeconomic status, 3) those with troubled family relationships, and 4) caregivers who are themselves older [47]. These factors as well as other social and demographic trends noted earlier, such as lower mortality and fertility, increases in life expectancy, higher divorce rates, and gender role changes, diminish informal caregivers' ability to provide services.

Torres-Gil has pointed out many times that the provision of health and long-term care as a "domestic policy rallying point," because family caregivers are realizing the importance of having health care support services. For many people, families and friends orchestrate a continuum of care. However, as the population requiring continuing care grows, the health care system will come under multiple and increasing pressures to cooperate with and assist the informal caregivers we have become so dependent on.

CHILD CARE AND WOMEN IN THE WORK PLACE

Millions of American women—over twenty-three million at last count—face a common dilemma each day as they seek care for their children while they work [62]. There are ten million female headed families [12]. Currently, two-thirds of preschool children and three-fourths of school age children, have mothers in the work force [42]. Yet, America stands alone with South Africa as the only industrialized nation without formal policies for enhancing family well-being [63]. In most West European countries, as well as Canada and Israel, the government helps pay for child care, requires private employers to provide generous paid leaves for childbirth, and encourages flexible work schedules. French families, for example, receive a monthly allowance to help them rear each child and children enter free public schools at age two and a half. In Sweden, *both* men and women are allowed one year of leave at 90 percent of their earnings after they have a child. They also can take up to sixty paid days leave per year to care for a sick child [63].

Unlike these countries with national family policies, the United States has a disorganized hodgepodge of public and private responses. In many communities, mothers turn to neighbors, and others are forced to leave their children in unlicensed and unregulated care each day. According to the Children's Defense Fund (1996), only about 5 percent of our nation's employers with 100 or more employees report offering on-site child care. Three out of five American women work for companies without any maternity leave [64]. Many are docked a day's pay for each one taken to care for a sick child.

Why, we might ask, does the United States, the richest nation on earth, lack a clear national policy on children and families? In our current economy, most parents work harder than ever. They face a constant struggle to balance their obligations to be good workers—and their even more important obligations to be good parents. Child care is the next frontier we must face to enable people to succeed at home and at work. Current policy reflects the weight of American historical traditions and the deeply entrenched ideology of *individualism* [65]. Large numbers of Americans are wary of government intervention and believe in a more traditional role for mothers. The child care impasse also is related to an American ideology that views child rearing, like other spheres of family life, as a *private* affair best handled by families themselves. Parents, so far, have been noticeably absent from the debate, even though cries for more help and resources seem to be intensifying.

The role of labor unions also is critical here since in most Western European nations they have been a potent political force for programs aimed at women, children, and families. Through organized labor parties, of various sorts, workers have managed to wield considerable power in Western Europe. In the United States, the percentage of workers in unions has dropped from 24 percent in 1977 [66] to 16 percent now [67]. This is rather startling when compared to that for other advanced industrial countries such as the following: Scandinavian countries (80% +), in Europe as a whole about 50 percent, and Canada, Switzerland, and Japan (33%) [68]. More importantly, data indicate that when a host of other worker and occupational characteristics are statistically controlled for, results show that "*all workers* gain a wage and benefit premium from unionization, with women and minorities benefiting the most" (italics added) [66, p. 105].

There is an old African phrase, now popularized by Hillary Clinton, "It takes a village to raise a child." In many cultures, children are seen as *everyone's* concern and child rearing is viewed as a service to the community. Americans, however, seem to view children as the sole responsibility of their parents [69], a stark contrast to the European concept of children as a resource for the society as a whole, and thus worthy of investment [70].

The European tradition has its roots partly in the devastation of World War II. After the war, governments were eager to increase fertility rates to rebuild their nations and to improve the situation of children. To accomplish this, many countries established family allowances to help defray the cost of raising a child, and offered families other support to balance the conflicts between work and family responsibilities. In France, for example, families receive an allowance to help pay for better housing and four-week vacations in summer, as well as an annual vacation bonus, free preschools, and medical care. Children are valued as the nation's future, and preschool is seen as a way to enrich every childs' world [70].

France spends more than $7 billion annually on publicly sponsored child care and education, which include child care services for infants and toddlers, as well as before- and after-school [71]. In addition, France's Maternal and Infant Protection Service offers prenatal care and preventive health services to children. Richardson and Marks point out that if the United States were to spend equivalent public funds on child care and preschool programs, we would have to *triple* our present public expenditures [71]. How will those without children and those who have already raised their kids, feel about spending their tax money on *other people's* kids? Unfortunately, in many communities these two groups are in fact voting down school financing and taxation referendums.

Demands for job-protected leaves to care for a newborn or sick relative, for better health and safety standards for children cared for outside of the home, and for tax policies that help middle-class parents with child-rearing costs could become claims competing with others for national resources. Will Americans be able to reach a consensus that caring for our children, all of our children, should be as "American as apple pie"? Our world has changed, families have changed, and our social policies must address such changes. We are at a point similar to the one education faced toward the end of the last century when most children were taught at home and our nation, after having debated the need for mass public education, decided to institute just such a system.

Interestingly, current child care policies have important consequences which affect us at the social psychological level. For instance, many parents believe that if they cannot cope with their child rearing responsibilities, something must be "wrong" with them. Families, therefore, are willing to piece together a constantly changing patchwork of child care arrangements rather than demand that the government step in and provide a coherent, national plan. This attitude is bolstered by the ideology of individualism, that if you just try hard enough, you can overcome adversity.

The absence of powerful organizations representing children and families is critical here since legislation is often brought about by those having access to important organizational resources, especially those of a corporate kind [72]. There is an urgent need to convince corporation executives, overwhelmingly male, that child care is an issue affecting everyone, including the national interest [64, 73].

Conflict over womens' "proper" role in society is another theme affecting child care policy issues. The United States has one of the highest proportions of women in the paid labor force of any industrialized country, but we also seem to have a built in ambivalence toward women working and being away from their children during the day. Debates over mothers' "real" role have an added political consequence in that they divide women, thereby diluting women's political power. Stay at home mothers often feel that employed mothers have a certain disdain for them. Employed moms often feel guilty that they are not at home with their children. Clearly, both women who work in the paid labor force and those who do the hidden and necessary unpaid work at home could benefit from government policies giving them more buying power and more help rearing their children. Seminal longitudinal child development research implicitly adds to this debate, suggesting that if at all possible, it is best for a child's development for a parent to be at home for the first twenty-four months of the child's life.

Our social programs have traditionally been geared toward the poor who need aid. Day care comes to be seen, then, as the last resort of the truly needy—a badge of shame, so to speak, for those who are helpless in caring for themselves. Without universal coverage, such an approach pits the middle class against the poor. Many middle class people resent paying taxes to care for someone else's children when they, too, could use some help. The potential power of families, linked by their mutual interest in children, thus evaporates; instead there is anger directed at the poor.

Increased interest in child care also derives from concerns that some mothers are kept out of the labor force because of child care problems [74]. Poor single mothers in pursuit of greater self-sufficiency for their families may be especially vulnerable [42]. However, bill after bill has been blocked to improve child care, billions of dollars in federal aid for children have been slashed, and state licensing standards for day care centers are continually relaxed. This remains a policy issue begging for support.

With declining numbers of workers available to support non-working elderly, policymakers will be forced to come up with solutions. A growing body of research shows what most working parents already know—productivity suffers, absenteeism grows, and many workers will be forced to quit jobs when they lack resources for adequate child care. In this sense, a lack of support for families, working women, and children will result in fewer workers to support the old [62].

Parents in our society remain liable for the cost of raising children, with mothers paying the highest cost in terms of interrupted careers and forgone wages. Yet, as Longman points out, such sacrifice results in the eventual economic reward divided among all members of one's generation in the form of "across-the-board" old age subsidies [75]. This creates the classic "free-rider" problem, wherein the support of persons in old age does not depend on their having made any personal sacrifice to raise up the next generation; instead they rely *on others* to make the effort. Longman concludes that the "obvious incentive is to remain childless and let other people's children pay for one's old age" [75, p. 139]. Social justice suggests that parents should be compensated for the sacrifices they make in raising children and for their contributions to their cohort's well-being in retirement. One way or another we will have to pay for this country's falling birthrates. A significant challenge is to make it easier for "working women also to be mothers."

Child care is not an ancillary matter in the grand policy scheme. It is central to questions of productivity, establishing a living wage, creating fair labor standards, and the investment value of consistent nurturing. These are mainstream political issues and, as has become evident in our discussion of the many policy challenges facing our nation, providing child care support adds one more competing demand on our nation.

CONCLUSION

The reality of aging is ultimately a social construction given "objective" character through human thought and action. Thus, it is subject to change as human beings both transform their social conditions and in turn are transformed by them. Problems within the life cycle lie in everyone's future. Solutions to these problems, however, will take shape in the collective meanings and practices people create as they conduct their everyday lives.

Life-cycle experiences, while currently a personal and private affair, nevertheless have public policy implications. What is privately felt and experienced can only be changed when brought into the public arena. We are suggesting that issues of age, gender, and race must move beyond just being personally felt and must instead be transformed into something more objective, real, and immediate on the national level. But this means more than the awareness of individuals about the plight of the living and dying, this awareness also must be coupled with concrete actions and political organizations committed to change as interdisciplinary researchers inform policy makers searching for answers.

We cannot afford to address our social problems through narrowly defined stop-gap, partial solutions [76]. We cannot continue to allow the solutions to be developed individually, case by case. Experiences throughout the life cycle need to be seen in the context of larger social meanings. The growing elderly population, increasing minority populations, and the "baby-boom" cohort will help define the many issues discussed here as they move through the life cycle.

By nurturing a sense of mutual interdependence among cohorts, we can avoid intensified intergenenrational competition for resources. It is exciting to realize that different groups, such as children, young adults, the middle aged, the elderly, women, African Americans, etc., all have something to contribute to society. Moreover, they need each other and have reciprocal responsibilities. Together they can develop a united and viable national community. Such a notion leads us to consider policies enabling each group to make their unique contribution.

We need more of the kinds of programs recently described by Lisbeth Schorr [36] and Melissa Ludtke [77, p. 84] where, in Pittsburgh, an organization called Generations Together has connected the elderly with children home alone ("latchkey" kids) through telephone hook-ups. Visionary companies such as Stride Rite Corporation in Cambridge, Massachusetts have organized day care facilities for *both* the elderly and the young. They've designed those facilities with space available for members of those different generations to meet one another.

Our purpose in this chapter has been to convey a sense of urgency about the potential effects of aging on our society. We have elaborated on some issues which will confront us in the not too distant future—issues affecting children, the elderly, women, minorities, families, as well as the labor force, the health care system, the political system, and many other facets of our national life. Dealt with now, these issues can become the basis for a new national policy agenda; if ignored, they will cause severe social tensions in the immediate years ahead and possibly even shatter that sense of community needed to sustain a nation. From a symbolic interactionist perspective, we have stressed that nothing is preordained. The future aging of our society, thus, holds within it the promise of a better society for all, or a far worse one.

We have conveyed the idea that our experience of the aging process depends upon where we stand in society. Persons living out their lives as members of different social classes, races, and ethnic and occupational groups perceive their life cycles in subjectively distinctive ways. One of our messages has been, it follows, that we too much oversimplify the aging process if we think of it only in chronological terms. It is worth restating that age carries no intrinsic meaning. Human beings in communication with one another attach meanings to age. Our feelings about growing up, older, and old are formed by the values of the society at large and by the particular groups we belong to. Interdisciplinary research giving special attention to the importance of our several "places" in the world: our gender, our place in the family life cycle, our rung on the occupational career ladder, and, more broadly still, our place in history, needs to be encouraged and supported. We need to better understand how significantly these social locations shape the way we conceive of the world.

Certainly we feel that the above policy issues represent significant research issues in the burgeoning gerontological prism. We would like to make a *theoretical statement* as well. We believe that we need to highlight the subjective, personal dimensions of the aging process—dimensions needing more attention by those researching the life cycle. In this respect, we view ours as a work of revision. We are not claiming available aging theories to be incorrect. Our task is a more modest one of amendment and specification of existing theoretical explanation. The theoretical perspective informing our inquiry—*symbolic interaction*—requires responses to the question: How do persons give meaning to, adapt to, and make intelligible their passage through the life course? This global question, in turn, supposes a number of additional assumptions concerning the way to understand aging.

Human beings are not simply objects in nature, not simply passive receptacles for biological processes associated with the passage of time. Rather, human beings shape the aging process by thinking about it, interpreting it, defining it, categorizing it, labeling it, and attaching values to it. Too, these mental activities have critical consequences for our actual behaviors. We have presented a simple truth that chronological age is a symbol and consequently subject to continuous human definition and redefinition. Our future inquiries need to be centered on the interplay of social structure, biological change, human beings' definitions of situations, and their actual beliefs and behaviors. In this way, we may be able to generate interdisciplinary research agendas that help contribute to individual's ability to avoid *dis-ease*, maintain high cognitive and physical function, and to remain actively engaged with life [78]. These interconnections define the substance of a *social psychology of the life cycle*. The above challenges represent the stuff for the development of interdisciplinary research and policy foundations.

REFERENCES

1. (We borrow from material) in J. Clair, D. Karp, and W. Yoels, *Experiencing the Life Cycle: A Social Psychology of Aging,* Thomas, Illinois, 1993.
2. T. Coe and M. Winkler (eds.), *The Oxford Book of Aging: Reflections on the Journey of Life,* Oxford University Press, New York, 1994.
3. G. Elder, *Children of the Great Depression,* University of Chicago Press, Chicago, 1974.
4. T. Williams and W. Kornblum, *Growing Up Poor,* D. C. Heath, Lexington, Massachusetts, 1985.
5. H. Schuman and J. Scott, Generations and Collective Memory, *American Sociological Review, 54,* pp. 359-381, 1989.
6. V. Bengtson, N. Cutler, D. Mangen, and V. Marshall, Generations, Cohorts, and Relations between Age Groups, in *Handbook of Aging and the Social Sciences,* Van Nostrand-Reinhold, New York, 1985.
7. W. Strauss and N. Howe, *Generations: The History of America's Future, 1584 to 2069,* William Morrow, New York, 1991.
8. E. Wynne, Will the Young Support the Old, in *Our Aging Society: Paradox and Promise,* A. Pifer and L. Bronte (eds.), Norton, New York, 1986.
9. K. Kressley, Intergenerational Equity and Interdependence: A Public Policy Issue for the 1990s, *Journal of Health and Human Resources Administration, 16,* pp. 359-376, 1991.
10. F. Torres-Gil, Aging for the Twenty-First Century: Process, Politics, and Policy, *Generations,* pp. 5-9, Spring 1988.
11. A. Benjamin, P. Newacheck, and H. Wolfe, Intergenerational Equity and Public Spending, *Pediatrics, 88,* pp. 75-83, 1991.
12. United States Bureau of Census: Statistical Abstract of the United States, Government Printing Office, Washington, D.C., 1997.

13. H. Richman and M. Stagner, Children: Treasured Resource or Forgotten Minority? in *Our Aging Society: Paradox and Promise,* A. Pifer and L. Bronte (eds.), Norton, New York, 1986.
14. (For a less pessimistic view of this issue) see K. Easterlin, C. MacDonald, and D. Macunovich, Retirement Prospects of the Baby Boom Generation: A Different Perspective, *The Gerontologist, 30,* pp. 776-783, 1990.
15. United States Bureau of Census, Health Insurance Coverage, table 171, Government Printing Office, Washington, D.C., 1996.
16. D. Gelfand, *The Aging Network: Programs and Services,* Springer, New York, 1993.
17. J. Quinn and R. Burkhauser, Work and Retirement, in *Handbook of Aging and the Social Sciences,* R. Binstock and L. George (eds.), Academic Press, New York, 1990.
18. E. Kingson, Generational Equity: An Unexpected Opportunity to Broaden the Politics of Aging, *The Gerontologist, 28,* pp. 765-772, 1988.
19. C. W. Mills, *The Sociological Imagination,* Oxford University Press, New York, 1959.
20. F. Gilliam, Jr. and K. Whitby, Race, Class, and Attitudes Toward Social Welfare Spending: An Ethclass Interpretation, *Social Science Quarterly, 70,* pp. 88-100, 1989.
21. (Also see) N. George, *Buppies, B-Boys, Baps, and Bohos: Notes on Post-Soul Culture,* HarperCollins, New York, 1993.
22. E. Anderson, *Street Wise,* University of Chicago Press, Chicago, 1990.
23. M. Minkler and A. Robertson, Generational Equity and Public Health Policy: A Critique of 'Age/Race War' Thinking, *Journal of Public Health Policy, 12,* pp. 324-344, 1991.
24. C. P. Henry, *Culture and African American Politics,* Indiana University Press, Bloomington, Indiana, 1990.
25. M. L. King, Jr., *Where Do We Go From Here: Chaos or Community,* Harper and Row, New York, 1967.
26. T. Kochman, *Black and White Styles in Conflict,* University of Chicago Press, Chicago, 1981.
27. W. Donohue, Ethnicity and Mediation, in *Communication, Culture, and Organizational Processes,* W. Gudykinst et al. (eds.), Sage Publications, California, 1985.
28. E. Folb, Whot's Got the Room at the Top? Issues of Dominance and Nondominance in Intracultural Communication, in *Intercultural Communication: A Reader,* L. Samovar and R. Porter (eds.), Wadsworth, Belmont, California, 1988.
29. A. M. Schlesinger, Jr., *The Disuniting of America: Reflections on a Multicultural Society,* Norton, New York, 1992.
30. G. Myrdal, *An American Dilemma: The Negro Problem and Modern Democracy,* Harper and Row, New York, 1944.
31. *Glass Ceiling Commission,* Government Printing Office, Washington, D.C., 1995.
32. Bureau of Justice: Jodi Brown et al., *U.S. Department of Justice Statistical Bulletin on the Correlational Population in the United States: 1996 Annual,* U.S. Government Printing Office, Washington, D.C., 1996.
33. Bureau of Census, *HUD American Housing Survey on US Homeownership,* Government Printing Office, Washington, D.C., 1996.
34. Bureau of Census, *Trends in Well-Being of American Children and Youth,* Government Printing Office, Washington, D.C., 1996.
35. K. Fitzpatrick and W. Yoels, Policy, School Structure, and Sociodemographic Effects of Statewide High School Dropout Rates, *Sociology of Education, 65,* pp. 76-93, 1992.
36. L. Schorr, *Within Our Reach: Breaking the Cycle of Disadvantage,* Anchor Books, New York, 1989.

37. K. N. Wright, *The Great American Crime Myth,* Greenwood Press, Westport, Connecticut, 1985.
38. NCHS, *Advanced Report of Final Mortality Statistics,* Department of Health and Human Services, Government Printing Office, Washington, D.C., 1996.
39. Bureau of Census: F. Hobbs and B. Damon, *Sixty-Five Plus in the US,* Government Printing Office, Washington, D.C., 1996.
40. NCHS, *Data on Health Resources Utilization, Vital and Health Statistics, Series 13,* Government Printing Office, Washington, D.C., 1996.
41. NCHS: E. Graves and B. Gillum, *National Hospital Discharge Survey,* Government Printing Office, Washington, D.C., 1996.
42. House Ways and Means Committee, *Green Book Overview of Entitlement Programs,* Government Printing Office, Washington, D.C., 1996.
43. American Hospital Association, *Annual Hospital Statistics,* Government Printing Office, Washington, D.C., 1996.
44. W. Haley, J. Clair, and K. Saulsberry, Family Caregiver Satisfaction with Medical Care of their Demented Relatives, *The Gerontologist, 32,* pp. 219-226, 1992.
45. R. Fox, *The Sociology of Medicine: A Participant Observer's View,* Prentice-Hall, Englewood Cliffs, New Jersey, 1989.
46. E. Brody, The Informal Support System and Health of the Future Aged, in *Aging 2000: Our Health Care Destiny, Vol. 2, Psychosocial and Policy Issues,* C. Gaitz, G. Niederehe, and N. Wilson (eds.), Springer-Verlag, New York, 1985.
47. J. Clair, Old Age Health Problems and Long Term Care Policy, in *The Legacy of Longevity: Health, Illness, and Long Term Care in Later Life,* S. Stahl (ed.), Sage, Newbury Park, California, 1990.
48. J. Brody, Toward Quantifying the Health of the Elderly, *American Journal of Public Health, 79*:6, pp. 685-686, 1989.
49. J. Guralnik and G. Kaplan, Predictors of Healthy Aging: Prospective Evidence from the Alameda County Study, *American Journal of Public Health, 79*:6, pp. 703-709, 1989.
50. T. Harris, M. Kovar, R. Suzman, J. Klein, and J. Feldman, Longitudinal Study of Physical Ability in the Oldest-Old, *American Journal of Public Health, 79*:6, pp. 698-702, 1989.
51. R. Allman, W. Yoels, and J. Clair, Reconciling the Agendas of Doctors and Patients, in *Sociomedical Perspectives on Patient Care,* J. Clair and R. Allman (eds.), University Press of Kentucky, Lexington, Kentucky, 1993.
52. A. Achenbaum, *Shades of Gray: Old Age, American Values, and Federal Policies Since 1920,* Little, Brown and Co., Boston, 1983.
53. P. Starr, *The Social Transformation of American Medicine: The Rise of a Sovereign Profession and the Making of a Vast Industry,* Basic Books, New York, 1982.
54. NCHS: E. Hing, E. Sekscenski, and G. Strahan, *The National Nursing Home Survey: 1985 Summary for the U.S. Vital and Health Statistics, Series 13,* U.S. Government Printing Office, Washington, D.C., 1989.
55. NCHS, *Data on Nursing Homes, Vital and Health Statistics,* Government Printing Office, Washington, D.C., 1994.
56. G. Maddox and T. Glass, Health Care of the Chronically Ill, in *Handbook of Medical Sociology,* H. Freeman and S. Levine (eds.), Prentice-Hall, Englewood Cliffs, New Jersey, 1989.
57. C. Estes, *The Aging Enterprise,* Jossey-Bass, San Francisco, 1979.
58. V. L. Olesen, Caregiving, Ethical and Informal: Emerging Challenges in the Sociology of Health and Illness, *Journal of Health and Social Behavior, 30,* pp. 1-10, 1989.
59. J. Waldrop, Who Are the Caregivers? *American Demographics, 11,* p. 39, 1989.

60. P. Lamey, *The Geriatrics Triangle,* The Association of Gerontology in Higher Education, Washington, D.C., 1991.
61. E. Borgatta and R. Montgomery, *Critical Issues in Aging Policy: Linking Research and Values,* Sage, Beverly Hills, 1987.
62. Children's Defense Fund, *The State of America's Children,* CDF, Washington, D.C., 1996.
63. S. Kammerman, Child Care Policies and Programs: An International Overview, *Journal of Social Issues, 47,* pp. 179-196, 1991.
64. F. Schwartz, *Breaking New Ground: Women and Work, The New Facts of Life,* Warner Books, New York, 1992.
65. R. Bellah, *The Good Society,* Knopf, New York, 1991.
66. L. Mishel and D. Frankel, *The State of Working in America,* M. E. Sharpe, Armonk, New York, 1991.
67. J. Macionis, *Sociology,* Prentice-Hall, Englewood Cliffs, New Jersey, 1998.
68. B. Western, Post War Unionization in Eighteen Advanced Capitalist Countries, *American Sociological Review, 58,* pp. 266-282, 1993.
69. A. Kahn and S. Kammerman, *Child Care: Facing the Hard Choices,* Auburn Press, Westport, Connecticut, 1988.
70. S. Kammerman and A. Kahn, *Innovations in European Parenting Policies,* Greenwood Press, Westport, Connecticut, 1991.
71. G. Richardson and E. Marks, *A Welcome for Every Child: Practical Ideas for the United States,* French American Foundation, New York, 1990.
72. D. Karp, G. Stone, and W. Yoels, *Being Urban: A Sociology of City Life,* Praeger, New York, 1991.
73. R. Kanter, *When Giants Learn to Dance,* Simon and Schuster, New York, 1989.
74. Kids Count Data Book, *State Profiles of Child Well-Being,* Annie E. Casey Foundation, Baltimore, Maryland, 1997.
75. P. Longman, *Born to Pay: The New Politics of Aging in America,* Houghton Mifflin, Boston, 1987.
76. R. Atchley, Renewing Gerontology's Commitment to Interdisciplinary Discourse in the Face of Growth and Postmodernism, *Contemporary Gerontology, 3,* pp. 79-80, 1996.
77. M. Ludtke, Getting Young and Old Together, *Time,* p. 84, April 1990.
78. J. Rowe and R. Kahn, *Successful Aging,* Pantheon, New York, 1998.

CHAPTER
4

Clinical and Health Services Delivery Research

Richard M. Allman, Patricia S. Baker,
and Richard S. Maisiak

Medical research of aging ranges from the biological, molecular level to clinical research. The focus of clinical and health care delivery research is the patient. In contrast, basic biomedical research focuses on the cellular or tissue level of organisms. Clinical and health services delivery research addresses the interaction of normal aging and disease in individual humans with the preventive, therapeutic, and palliative interventions of medicine as well as the process through which these procedures are obtained. Clinical research includes the broad categories of the investigation of the pathophysiology of aging, the identification of at-risk and special populations, the classification and diagnosis of specific conditions and diseases, and the evaluation of preventive and therapeutic interventions. Health services delivery research investigates the process and consequences of distributing healthcare to patients, including cost, access, and healthcare settings and delivery systems. The efficacy of healthcare services are evaluated in terms of universality, effectiveness, quality improvement, and quality of life. Thus, variables of interest for clinical and health services research may include biological, psychological, social, and the spiritual aspects of the patient.

The purpose of this chapter is to provide the reader with an understanding of the importance of clinical and health services delivery research among older adults. Examples of some of the reseach progress made in the last decade, as well as within the broad categories of clinical and health services delivery research are discussed. Throughout the chapter, the importance of an interdisciplinary approach to clinical and healthcare delivery research is highlighted.

THE AGING POPULATION AND CLINICAL RESEARCH

Projections of increasing numbers of older adults and the increasing proportion of old and very old adults within the U.S. population pushed aging to the forefront of scientific inquiry in the early 1990s. The proportion of persons aged sixty-five and older has risen from 4.1 percent (3.1 million) at the beginning of the century to a projected 13 percent (34.7 million) at the end of the century. Moreover, there will be more persons over the age of eighty-five at century's end than there were sixty-five and older in 1900. A rapid increase in this population is expected to occur as the "baby-boom" generation reaches age sixty-five, between 2010 and 2030; by 2030 it is expected that 20 percent of the population will be over the age of sixty-five (69.4 million). Aging research must also incorporate demographic projections that predict an increasing minority elderly population as well as the already established difference in life expectancy for men and women.

In response to this demographic imperative, in November 1990 the U.S. Congress authorized the Task Force on Aging Research [1] to look at the progress that had already been made in aging research and to give recommendations for future topics. Their report, published in 1995, expands the biomedical focus set by the Institute of Medicine's 1991 [2] research agenda on aging, and identifies research priorities related to social, economic, psychological, biological, and medical domains.

Among the conclusions reached was the assessment that "real potential exists for major scientific advances in the near future." All research recommendations incorporate an additional focus on the predominance of women and the changing ethnic and racial composition of the aging population. In using a multidisciplinary approach, many topics were considered under multiple domains. Additionally, the criteria of social value, scientific merit, the cost-benefits of research, and governmental benefits were used to establish guidelines for future research. Issues discussed at length in this chapter have been identified by the Task Force on Aging [1] as being among those "most important," having immediate priority. Broad categories of clinical or patient-oriented research include: 1) investigation of the pathophysiology of aging; 2) the identification of at-risk and special populations; 3) the classification and diagnosis of specific conditions and diseases; and 4) the evaluation of preventive and therapeutic interventions.

The Pathophysiology of Aging

The variation in individual aging patterns and the response of the patient to treatments and drugs is difficult to evaluate since no single measurement is currently available to assess the rate of aging. One goal of the search for biomarkers of aging is to identify specific indicators of the aging process beyond chronological aging that would facilitate patient assessment and the evaluation of interventions [3]. Basic biomedical research has provided evidence that longevity is governed by the action of multiple genes; the genetics of longevity explores family specific traits that are associated with an age related onset of clinical symptoms. Longevity Assurance Genes (LAGs) [1] have been identified as specific genes that promote longevity and extend health span. Future clinical research will need to study whether or not these and other candidate genes lead to prolongation of life and improved function among older adults.

One area in which particular advances have been made in the last decade is in the understanding of the pathophysiology of wounds and wound healing. Age related differences in all phases of wound healing are well documented; the elderly have an impaired healing process. Although the rate of wound healing is only slightly reduced in patients not suffering from concomitant diseases, diseases that affect wound healing are more prevalent in the elderly and the effect may be greater than for younger patients [4, 5]. The improved understanding of wound healing has led to promising new developments and clinical research related to the role of growth factors in the healing process [6, 7].

The elderly are the largest consumers of pharmaceuticals, purchasing 30 percent of all prescription drugs and 40 percent of over-the-counter medications [8]. Not only are the elderly more likely to take multiple medications increasing the risk of drug interactions, unwanted effects, and adverse reactions, but there are age related changes in drug metabolism [9]. Thus, the need for increased knowledge about age-related changes in the absorption, metabolism, elimination, and cellular effect of drugs has been increasingly conducted. While general rules are difficult to formulate about the effects of aging on specific drugs, pharmacokinetics describe processes that determine the rate that drugs appear (bioavailabilty) and are cleared from the body, and the distribution of the drugs in bodily tissues [10]. Noted pharmacokinetic changes include an increase in the volume of distribution, as in diazepam; and a reduction in drug clearance, as in digoxin [9]. The study of pharmacodynamics provides a means of approximation of the drug dose to the intensity of response at a particular site in the body [10]. Changes in pharmacodynamics and pharmacokinetics may result in a prolonged drug half-life, increased potential for drug toxicity, and a greater likelihood for adverse drug reactions [11]. While knowledge of the changes in drug metabolism is critical to the physician in prescribing drugs, it also is beneficial in the development of new drugs [12]. The increasing variability in persons as they age and the lack of female subjects, old-old, and target populations are significant areas of current research [10].

Another area of pathophysiology that is currently receiving increased attention is recovery from strokes. Stroke is the third leading cause of death among older adults in the United States and a major cause of disability, such as paralysis or loss of speech. The changing population profile, preventive measures, and increased changes of survival have resulted in a decreased incidence but increased prevalence of persons recovering from stroke [13]. The prognosis for both mortality and functional recovery varies greatly, and is dependent on the patient's age, other medical conditions, the type and extent of the stroke, and associated neurological deficits [14]. While clinical factors are known to be the major predictive variables in determining outcome from stroke, research is inconclusive since most of the patients studied are those selected for rehabilitation programs. The Copenhagen Stroke Study found that age should not be the primary selection criterion for rehabilitation [15]. Innovative approaches for stroke rehabilitation have been developed and need further evaluation [16].

Identification of At-Risk and Special Populations

Older people are clinically different from younger people. This is based not only on chronological age, but different rates of aging among individuals and different rates of aging for biologic processes and organ systems within individuals. One consequence is increasing diversity among individuals as they age; biologic systems minimally affected by the aging process may have physiologic changes due to environmental and lifestyle factors [17]. This diversity mandates the research directed to special populations, particularly women, racial and ethnic minorities, persons with lower socioeconomic status, rural residents, disabled persons, and the oldest-old. As Jackson notes, the need for increased research on women deserves special attention since traditional aging research assumed that findings from male populations apply equally to women [18]. Sex differences in longevity predict an older and larger population of women in the near future, and women are more likely to report functional disability. This interaction of increased morbidity and longevity means that older women, especially those over seventy-five, are at a relatively higher risk than men for health problems, and these differences may be correlated with socioeconomic, racial, and ethnic groupings.

Specific areas affecting older women targeted by the Task Force on Aging [1] include frailty, bone loss and osteoporosis, falls, hypothyroidism, and urinary incontinence. The ongoing Women's Health and Aging Study [19] and the Women's Health Initiative [20] were designed to help address some of these questions, as well as defining ways to prevent cardiovascular disease, cancer, and osteoporosis in older women.

Research on hormone replacement therapy (HRT) for postmenopausal women to alleviate effects of hormone deficiency such as vasomotor symptoms, dyspareunia, and the progressive development of osteoporosis continues to receive increased emphasis in the 1990s. In 1996 there were over 700 studies listed under estrogen replacement therapy in MEDLINE [21] (from more than 500 in 1995). Besides the basic effects noted above, HRT has been studied in relation to body mass, the risk of dementia, and even intellectual decline [22-24]. Despite advances, there still is a gender gap both in research and clinical care [25]. Recently, it has been noted that Alzheimer's disease should be considered a women's health issue, not only because women are more likely to have the disease than men (since the incidence increases with age and the population over the age of 85 is 72% female), but women bear a disproportionate share of the informal caregiving burden associated with persons suffering from Alzheimer's disease [26].

Although differences in the health of African Americans and whites have long been recognized, the interaction of race and aging on health status has not been well defined. Examination of the association of aging and race is necessary to see whether racial and ethnic differences continue during the aging process, and, if they do, whether they become of greater or lesser significance [27]. Currently, life expectancy of African Americans is lower than that of whites. Reed summarizes the difference between African Americans and whites: African Americans between the ages of sixty-four and eighty-four are more likely to die than whites [28]. Also at these ages,

African-American elderly are at greater risk of dying from cardiovascular disease, accidents, diabetes, and homicide. Both male and female African Americans are more likely to suffer from chronic diseases, including hypertension, diseases of the circulatory system, diabetes, and arthritis. In addition, the number of restricted-activity days and the number of bed-disability days tend to be greater for elderly African Americans than for elderly whites. Differences in racial and ethnic subgroups continue to be a priority to identify both the differing risk factors of specific diseases and conditions and to evaluate treatments. In addition to basic research, epidemiological analysis can sensitize physicians in the identification and treatment of patients [29].

The Classification and Diagnosis of Specific Conditions and Diseases and the Evaluation of Preventive and Therapeutic Interventions

These interrelated foci of clinical research represent the interaction of individual patients with the health care system. The identification of existing diseases and/or conditions and assessing individual risk factors allows application of appropriate and effective interventions which then must be evaluated. We highlight examples of current research.

Alzheimer's Disease

Aging is the most prominent risk factor in Alzheimer's disease [1], and many research efforts are directed to discovering the linkages between the aging process and this particular form of dementia. One such discovery is the association of Apo E with AD, first discovered by epidemiologic findings. A review by Cotton summarizes the association of the Apo E4 allele with the greatest risk of developing late-onset Alzheimer's, especially in patients with mild memory problems [30]. The genetic profile defines populations at varying risks by age such that persons with two copies of the E4 allele have onset before the age of seventy, for those with no copies of the allele the average age of onset is over eighty-five. For example, a seventy-eight-year-old with two E4 alleles has a 98 percent chance of having the disease, with one E4 allele a 68 percent chance, and with no E4 alleles a 25 percent chance. Although there may be prognostic value in knowing a patient's Apo E status, at the present time the evidence is preliminary. Evidence does suggest that the allele does not cause Alzheimer's pathology but speeds up the development. A recent study established the association of Apo E4 to AD in the African-American population [31]. Other research has shown that this allele is not associated with either Parkinson's disease nor the dementia associated with Parkinson's [32]. Moreover, a protective effect seems to be associated with the presence of the Apo E2 [33]. Current and future research will focus on identifying the role of Apo E for the purpose of advising families and patients as well as exploring the possiblity of treatments to alleviate the presence of the allele [30].

Designation of the 1990s as the "Decade of the Brain" has accelerated the development of pharmacologic agents [34]. In particular, tacrine and donepezil, oral antidementia agents, were approved by the Food and Drug Administration in the mid 1990s. Both of these agents have been shown to have beneficial effects in cognition and memory when used in the treatment of AD [35, 36]. While beneficial, the effectiveness of both of these agents is somewhat limited by their side-effect profiles. Moreover, many patients with AD do not show benefits with these therapies [37]. The development of new therapeutic agents for Alzheimer's and related dementias will remain a priority.

Prostate Cancer

Controversy continues over the use of prostate-specific antigen (PSA) levels to screen for prostate cancer. PSA is based on a kallikrein-like serine proteinase produced by epithelial cells of both benign and malignant prostate tissue. Partin and Oesterling [38] note that PSA is the first prostate specific serum marker of clinical usefulness and effective in detecting early prostate cancer and monitoring response to therapy. No study has established that early detection decreases the prostate cancer specific mortality rate. It is suggested that long-term research is necessary to establish whether PSA testing should be done routinely, at what intervals, and if it should be accompanied by ultrasound or biopsy [39]. Ongoing clinical trials should address these issues over the next several years.

Thrombolytic Therapy for Coronary Artery Disease

Acute myocardial infraction is the most common threat to health in the United States and in other Western industrialized societies [40], and the mortality of infarction increases steeply with increasing age [41]. Yet age as an independent risk factor is not established among the more commonly acknowledged risk factors, such as hyperlipidemia, hypertension, obesity, smoking, and lack of exercise [42]. Age has been a factor in the determination of recommended therapy regimens, and the efficacy of thrombolytic treatment for older adults continues to be a focus of research [41, 43, 44]. One side of the argument is that thrombolysis may be under-used for elderly patients because of the greater risk of stroke resulting from cerebral hemorrhage in spite of the absolute increase in benefit from such treatment [45, 46]. Of the three commonly used thrombolytic agents, current research focuses on the early application of tissue plasminogen activator (TPA) [47, 48]. The Global Utilization of Streptokinase and Tissue Plasminogen Activator for Occluded Coronary Arteries (GUSTO) trial followed 41,021 patients. Among the conclusions were that for all subgroups, including elderly patients, there was improved outcome with accelerated treatment and that the risk/benefit ratio clearly supported this therapy for all patients [48]. Smith suggests that overall clinical results will be improved by minimizing the time from diagnosis to therapy and, although cautioning that contraindications should be a consideration, infers that age alone should not determine nonapplication of accelerated treatment and suggests that an aggressive approach to treating elderly patients is warranted in view of their higher mortality rate [49]. Although mortality continues to decline, there is some question if advances in treatment with thrombolytic agents have benefitted women [40].

Cataract Surgery

In 1990, the method of cataract surgery techniques became much simpler from the patient's perspective with the adoption of phacoemulsification as the preferred method. In this procedure, ultrasonic vibrations are used to the diseased lens is reduced to a liquid which can be drained from a much smaller incision in the eye. Surgery can be an ambulatory procedure using local or topical anesthesia in which the patient's eye is dilated and evaluated one hour preceding the surgery. Surgery generally takes an hour, and after post-operative observation lasting another hour the patient can be escorted home. Very little pain is associated with uncomplicated surgery and some aspects of vision improve immediately. Enhanced safety, more rapid rehabilitation, and reduced postoperative astigmatism are associated with this technique. Visual stability is achieved within four weeks compared to eight weeks for the older method of extracapsular surgery. This surgery is very successful and functional outcome measures are positive based on improvement in activities of daily living and the patient's perceived satisfaction with the procedure. With these techniques it is generally better to have surgery performed before the cataract becomes too advanced [50, 51].

HEALTH SERVICES DELIVERY

Research in health services delivery relates to all aspects of providing and distributing health services. In general, such research has been empirical rather than theoretical, with a goal of providing documentation for application to policy [1]. For the elderly population, health care can be conceptualized as a continuum ranging from the acute care focusing on cure to continuous care or treatment for chronic, comorbid conditions in a variety of long-term care settings. The Task Force on Aging identified a research need to develop and evaluate models of geriatric care to coordinate prevention, primary care, rehabilitation, mental health, and long-term care services that would build on existing programs [1]. They note that it is often erroneously assumed that the need for services among older persons is always from a state of health and independence to steady and permanent decline and dependency. Using simulation techniques, Zedlewski and McBride showed that future demand for long-term services may surpass expectations, and, although future elderly may have a better economic status, most elderly Americans will probably not be able to afford insurance [52]. The rising numbers of elderly of increasingly older ages with differing healthcare needs combined with uncertain direction in terms of cost, access, and quality of care have been impacted by the changing structure of health care delivery systems.

Specific interest in the health of elderly persons and problems of aging is historic, although the establishment of geriatrics as a distinct medical specialty is fairly recent [53]. Healthcare provision to the elderly was specifically labeled "geriatrics" in 1909 by Ignatz Nascher [54]. The focus of geriatrics is broad, encompassing biological, psychological, pathological, and socio-environmental factors. Aging is not a disease, and geriatricians are trained to "distinguish disease states from the normal physiological changes associated with aging" [54, p. 11]. The clinical perspective of geriatric medicine focuses not only on the establishing underlying disease diagnoses but helping the elderly person cope with illness. Medicine's contribution to elderly persons' well-being encompasses chronic illness in which medical goals may be redefined as improving patient function and satisfaction without providing cure [17].

Long-term care is typically differentiated by the site of delivery and characteristics of the caregiver (paid/formal vs. unpaid/informal). Persons who have limitations in activities of daily living are considered to need long-term care. Current estimates are that approximately 5 percent of the elderly population are in nursing homes and that another 10 percent are equally disabled but living in the community [55]. There are difficulties in projecting accurate long-term healthcare needs for the increasing older population because of the apparent declining rate of age-related disability, but it is likely that the absolute number of persons with needs will continue to rise for the next three decades [56].

The Task Force on Aging notes the need to assess and evaluate home-based long-term care in terms of decreased cost compared to nursing home placement, especially in light of the preference of most disabled older persons to remain in their own homes [1]. In addition, they note the scarcity of information about minority and poor older persons in spite of research that indicates that minority and lower socioeconomic status are associated with a greater likelihood of chronic illness and disability.

Healthcare Costs

Regardless of the type or location of healthcare delivery, central issues in the United States concern the cost, equity, and distribution of services in relation to need [57]. Healthcare costs, the actual costs of providing services related to the delivery of health care, include the costs of procedures, therapies, and medications, and are differentiated from healthcare expenditures, which reflect the amounts spent for total health care. Healthcare costs in the United States comprised 14 percent of the gross national product in 1992, up from 9 percent in 1980 [58]. Contributing factors to these escalating costs are consumer demand, rising costs of health providers, hospitals, medical equipment, nursing home care and medications, longer life expectancy, increased costs of malpractice insurance, and improved technology [59]. Not surprisingly, cost analyses show that increased disability is associated with increased costs. For most elders the cost of a complete substitution of informal care for formal services, including living expenses, was less than nursing home care [60]. Keeping elderly persons independent and community dwelling as long as possible is identified as one of the goals of healthcare providers, both for cost and quality of life issues.

In the United States, health care has traditionally been fragmented with little integration of its components [61]. One feature of the fragmented nature of healthcare delivery for the elderly is the development of separate systems providing and paying for acute and long-term care. Rising cost is but one consequence of the lack of coordination as patients change from one treatment type and location to another. Elder care often involves an interface between systems, and only recently has systematic study of health services delivery for the elderly focused on the movement of elderly persons between and within both systems. One report noted that in 1987, 8.5 percent (816,000 persons) of all Medicare hospital admissions for persons aged sixty-five and older were transfers from nursing homes [62]. Another 347,000 persons were originally community dwelling elderly who had hospital stays and were transferred to nursing homes, suggesting that the movement between nursing homes and hospitalization should be examined to contain hospital costs. One of the problems that occurs is identified as the loss of some independent physical function when elderly persons are in the hospital for an acute illness [63]. Between 25 percent and 60 percent of elderly patients experience this loss, with outcomes of increased hospital stay, nursing-home placement, and even death.

The current trend to reorganize healthcare delivery is largely driven by economic concerns. As a result, smaller healthcare organizations are merging and boundaries that previously separated components of the industry are disappearing [61]. Managed care plans, designed to provide incentives to reduce unnecessary healthcare costs, have evolved and grown to be a dominant pattern of healthcare delivery in the 1990s [64]. The impact of such plans on care of elderly patients has yet to be fully evaluated. Recent work has suggested those elderly with chronic illness and the poor may have worse functional outcomes in managed care settings [65].

There is a general belief that too great a share of Medicare resources are expended in the last year of life, with the implication that expensive technology is futilely utilized by terminally ill persons [66]. In an analysis of twelve years of data on persons 65+, expenses in the last year of life rose in proportion to all expenses. Of these expenses, about half are spent in the last sixty days of life, and about 40 percent in the last thirty days, reflecting the likelihood that elderly will die in hospitals [67]. The authors note, however, by age, Medicare payments generally decreased as age of death increased, perhaps suggesting that medical care is not being mistargeted, especially since survival is not known a priori.

Provision of Health Care

Organized on the basis of payment, there are three basic types of healthcare systems in the United States: traditional fee-for-service; managed care; and public health [59]. Types of care include acute, long-term, mental health, chronic, and preventive care. Elderly persons have access to medical care through private health insurance, Medicare, Medicaid, and the Department of Veterans Affairs. The introduction of Medicare and Medicaid in 1965, providing health services for older and poor Americans, was followed by a rise in healthcare costs. At the same time, lack of access for the poor and maldistribution of physicians were also seen as problems [68].

By the late 1970s an era of cost containment began [69] and during the 1980s issues of inaccessibility were almost totally ignored [68]. One result of the focus on cost containment has been a shift in the organizational structure of healthcare delivery to include a growing managed care component. Managed care programs are a form of health insurance designed to reduce "unnecessary health care costs through a variety of mechanisms, including: economic incentives for physicians and patients to select less costly forms of care; programs for reviewing the medical necessity of specific services; increased beneficiary cost sharing; controls on inpatient admissions and lengths of stay; the establishment of cost-sharing incentives for outpatient surgery; selective contracting with healthcare providers; and the intensive manage-ment of high-cost heath care cases" [21]. The "managing" of managed care is based on administrative oversight and includes budgeting and bargaining as a method of controlling costs [68]. Managed care plans, although more effective in controlling costs than traditional health insurance, vary in the return to enrollees for premium dollars invested [68]. By 1993, most private physicians had become involved with a form of managed care, typically working with at least four different managed care plans [68]. Although managed care plans have curbed the inflation of employer paid health benefits, some of the costs to employees are increased personal expendi-tures, less choice of providers, and an increasing proportion of premiums spent on administrative management tasks [68]. Advantages of managed care for older persons may include an emphasis on prevention, more flexibility in care delivery, fewer restrictions, and better coverage than the traditional Medicare supplement [70], although at the current time, potential benefits of managed care have not been achieved [71].

Innovative Care Plans

Currently the Medicare program is seeking ways to expand managed care options for older adults [72]. Many Medicare reform proposals seem to encourage older persons to select managed care plans offered by private insurance companies, suggesting that both the quality and extent of medical coverage will be enhanced [73].

One program with reported success is On Lok, established in the 1980s and targeted to the Chinese community of San Francisco [71]. The approach was to allow persons eligible for nursing home placement to remain in the community, utilizing integrated service delivery through adult day health centers with case management by interdisciplinary teams [74]. Replication of the success of the On Lok program at nine additional sites (Program of All-inclusive Care for the Elderly or PACE), however, has been limited by slow enrollment and/or systematic exclusion criteria [74], suggesting that site-specific variables may need to be considered.

Structural modeling of nursing home usage reveals that there are strong effects of family helpers and living arrangements associated with long nursing home stays, and that after controlling for the effects of physical and cognitive functioning, adequate community help reduces the risk of permanent nursing home residence but not that of short-term stays [75, 76]. The problem of loss of function increases as older adults become frail, especially in a fragmented healthcare delivery system [76]. Day hospitalization or treatment is one of the methods that is currently under study.

The Collaborative Assessment and Rehabilitation for Elders (CARE) program is a nurse-managed out-patient program designed to improve function of frail elderly [76]. This program attempts to provide comprehensive care and serves as a bridge between acute, home-based care and institutional long-term care, yet still be reimbursable by Medicare and other third-party payers. This program provides an intensive, individualized program of nursing, rehabilitation, mental health, social, and medical services in one setting for several days a week over a limited time period. Primary care is also available at the same location, if needed. Preliminary data supported the feasibility of such a program in terms of health improvement and economics. Hui et al. compared outcomes of elderly stroke victims treated in a geriatric day hospital versus conventional medical management and found that care in the day facility hastened functional recovery, reduced out-patient visits and did not differ in cost [77].

Nursing homes have typically provided a single service, long-term institutionalized care, isolated from other sectors of healthcare provision [78]. With shorter hospital stays, nursing homes now have sicker patients more in need of physician services. Innovative approaches based on changing the role of nursing homes to provide continuum of care for frail elderly patients have been developed [80]. Burton suggests that nursing homes would be "ideal sites as centers of operation for comprehensive geriatrics health care, and are well suited to respond to the public cry for innovation and leadership in community based long term care" [78, p. 795]. One example of such a program is the Johns Hopkins Geriatrics Center in which physician office practices are located in the nursing home along with adult day-care centers as a way of achieving cost effective and quality care. With the addition of a physician house call component to serve community dwelling residents, a continuum of care between home, day care, nursing home, and hospitals is provided. This network of care allows the movement of patients to the optimal placement location.

Methodologic Issues

The ability to measure and report health outcomes has become a critical focus in evaluating the delivery of health care. Not only are survival or occurrence or non-occurrence of a specific event (clinical measures), episodes of care, and days of restricted activity (economic measures) important, but patient-oriented measures such as satisfaction, symptom improvement, quality of life, and functional status (humanistic concerns) also must be considered. These factors become even more necessary in consideration of elderly patients with chronic conditions, wherein cure is not an expected outcome. Although not specifically targeting the elderly, Epstein and Sherwood note that outcomes research incorporates epidemiology, health services research, health economics, and psychometrics, with the goal of improving outcomes and controlling costs [79]. Measurement issues include the assessment of functional status, the need to differentiate disease from age-associated changes, the assessment of comorbities, and severity of illness.

Studies comparing plans generally focus on utilization and outcomes. In one of the few studies of access and outcomes of elderly patients enrolled in managed care,

Clement et al. noted that there was decreased utilization of services for persons with chest pain or joint pain if they were enrolled in HMOs, measured by specialist care, follow-up recommendations, and monitoring of progress [80]. HMO patients were also less likely to report symptomatic improvement of joint pain. The Medical Outcomes Study followed elderly and poor, chronically ill patients for a four-year period [81]. Overall, for elderly patients (65+) declines in physical health were more common when they were enrolled in HMOs. A study of rheumatoid arthritis patients, however, showed no differences in either utilization or outcomes between HMO and traditional patients over an eleven-year period [82].

Inclusion of Elderly in Research Studies

Other methodological issues in health services delivery research include the recruitment and retention of older people, especially those with disability. Much of the data on which health care is based comes from studies in which exclusion criteria eliminate older persons with comorbidities. Practice-based research would include these patients and provide knowledge based on typical adults presenting in primary care settings [1]. Many of these patients suffer from comorbidity, the presence of co-existing diseases that may affect the ability of affected individuals to function. These multiple problems can exacerbate the effects of a single other problem. For instance, treatment of depression can enhance rehabilitation after an illness episode, lead to better compliance, and reduce the need for expensive diagnostic and therapeutic services [1]. There is no standardized instrument for assessing comorbidity in the clinical setting, although most studies look at various associated conditions and diseases [83] and the Charlson comorbidity index [84] has been used as a prognostic indicator for length of hospital stay, cost factors, and outcome or survival.

With the changing population demographics, there are increasing numbers of racial and ethnic minority elderly. Currently these groups are designated as African American, Hispanic American, Native American, and Asian American, but these divisions can mask the diversity within groups. Although it is generally accepted that minority elderly populations have a higher need for health and social services, utilization research is limited and the differences within subgroups may be significant [85]. Research indicates that minorities do not obtain health services as often as whites [85]. Rubenstein and Kramer remind us that differing health promotion behaviors and health outcomes are an outcome of macro sociocultural, environmental, and biological factors and result in different patterns of aging among population subgroups [86]. They note that the interpretations of differences in healthcare service utilization are complex, related to access, disease prevalence, patient preferences, and/or regional preferences. Further obstacles in studying minority populations result from the difficulty in identification of ethnic elderly, small samples, aggregation of persons into single subgroups, and cohort variability [86].

Specific research notes methods of recruitment and retention that are successful in recruiting minority persons. A sub-study of research designed to study risk factors in African-American post-menopausal women focused on factors influencing the women's decisions to participate in the clinical trial [87]. They found that working with community churches to recruit participants was the most successful, yielding a 10:1 ratio of screened applicants to those eligible and willing to participate in the clinical trial. Other recommendations included making transportation available or not requiring travel by taking the research to the residences, involving healthcare providers that are members of the subgroup being studied, having adequate funding to reach eligible subjects and collect quality data, recruiting from an organizational, affiliated source, targeting mass media approaches directly to the subgroup, and responding to special needs of the participants. This study was successful in recruitment considering the 27:1 ratio reported by others. A study to increase minority participation in Alzheimer's Disease Diagnostic Centers noted the importance of establishing priorities to recruit minorities, having specific funding for such efforts and hiring bilingual and bicultural staff to assist in recruitment [88]. Although costly and time intensive, recruitment and retention of subjects will continue to be a research priority.

Studies to Improve Quality of Care

The measurement of quality of life and outcomes presents a challenge to researchers. A six-part series in the *New England Journal of Medicine* delineates the need to define, measure, and finally improve quality of care [89-94]. Outcomes research attempts to assess the quality and effectiveness of health care as measured by the attainment of a specified end result or outcome. Typical measures include improvement in health, decline in symptoms, lowered morbidity or mortality. The Task Force suggests that quality be conceptualized in a multidimensional way, considering the structure, process and outcomes of health care, and evaluating quality both from the perspective of the provider and recipient of care [1]. They note that the application of such methods to the evaluation of long-term care would lead to a "less litigious and more rational, compassionate, and efficient" approach in policy and planning. One reason for the current focus on quality of care and outcomes is the inherent conflict in interest manifest in managed care delivery systems in which economic incentives depend on providing minimal care for an increased number of patients [95].

Three approaches to improving quality of care include management plans, assessment of patient satisfaction, and determining benchmarks of achievable performance [96-98]. Critical pathways as a technique to improve delivery of service within hospitals were adapted from industry [96]. Application to health care generally focuses on the goals of selecting a "best" practice style, defining standards for hospital stay, use of tests and treatments, finding ways to coordinate or decrease time spent in the various stages of treatment, giving a common ground to all hospital staff, decreasing documentation burdens, improving patient satisfaction through education [96]. Pearson et al. note that critical pathways are multidisciplinary, designed along timed sequences of care, enumerate intermediate and end patient outcomes, and, perhaps most importantly, are applied after a decision has been made for patient treatment [96]. Early evaluation of the technique notes that hospital stays and costs have been significantly reduced as well as significant improvements made in other clinical outcomes (lower readmissions, lower rates of wound infection, higher compliance). However, this method has been criticized as constraining physicians in their treatment of patients.

Another focus on quality of care issues is patient satisfaction. In some health plans, physician renumeration is based, in part, on patient evaluations, which it is assumed reflect the quality of care received [97]. In a study of office-based preventive care for the elderly, Weingarten et al. found that patient satisfaction, although related to physician competence and quality of care, was an inadequate measure [97]. Patients were generally satisfied with their physicians (95% thought their doctors were friendly, 92% thought they were competent) and were more likely to be satisfied when specific preventive procedures were offered. However, the authors concluded that patient expectations prior to the encounter may confound patient assessment of care. The difficulty in utilizing patient satisfaction as an outcome measure in this study is typical of other research [99].

As a method of evaluating hospital performance, benchmarking strives to identify a practical goal that is both desirable and attainable [98]. The concept has been adapted from continuous quality improvement research in which benchmarking is defined not as an established guideline but a process through which achievable performance can be continually assessed. Kiefe et al. use data of what is being done in healthcare procedures in acute myocardial infarction care to demonstrate the applicability of the procedure [98]. Establishing healthcare standards by the "best" (care procedures utilized) gives underachieving hospitals a goal to emulate. This is a practical and pragmatic approach to improving quality of care.

The increase in life expectancy brings with it a concern for the quality of life in these added years. Understanding the components of quality will be critical to designing healthcare programs and interventions resulting in maximum health status in a cost effective way [1]. Lacking a consistent and comprehensive definition of health for the elderly population, it is difficult to evaluate the success of healthcare provision. Klinkman et al. suggest that health for the elderly be defined by the absence of disease, the maintenance of optimal function, and the presence of an adequate support system, with a primary goal of disease prevention and the compression of morbidity [100]. Clinical and health services delivery research is directed toward meeting these goals.

REFERENCES

1. Task Force on Aging Research, *The Threshold of Discovery: Future Directions for Research on Aging* (DHHS Administrative Document), U.S. Government Printing Office, Washington, D.C., 1995.
2. Institute of Medicine, Committee on a National Agenda for Prevention of Disabilities, *Disability in America: Toward a National Agenda for Prevention,* National Academy Press, Washington D.C., 1991.
3. R. A. Miller, The Biology of Aging and Longevity, in *Principles of Geriatric Medicine and Gerontology,* W.R. Hazzard, E. L. Bierman, J. P. Blass, W. H. Ettinger, Jr. and J. B. Halter (eds.), McGraw-Hill, Inc., New York, pp. 3-18, 1994.

4. P. C. Van de Kerkhof, B. Van Bergen, K. Spruijt, and J. P. Kuiper, Age-Related Changes in Wound Healing, *Clinical & Experimental Dermatology, 19,* pp. 369-374, 1994.
5. A. D. Gerstein, T. J. Phillips, G. S. Rogers, and B. A. Gilchrest, Wound Healing and Aging, *Dermatologic Clinics, 11,* pp. 749-757, 1993.
6. T. A. Mustoe, N. R. Cutler, R. M. Allman, P. S. Goode, T. F. Deuel, J. A. Prause, M. Bear, C. M. Serdar, and G. F. Pierce, A Phase II Study to Evaluate Platelet-derived Growth Factor-BB in the Treatment of Stage 3 and 4 Pressure Ulcers, *Archives of Surgery, 129,* pp. 213-219, 1994.
7. V. Falaga, Growth Factors and Chronic Wounds: The Need to Understand the Micro-environment, *Journal of Dermatology, 19,* pp. 667-672, 1992.
8. I. L. Salom and K. Davis, Prescribing for Older Patients: How to Avoid Toxic Drug Reactions, *Geriatrics, 50,* pp. 37-40, 43, 1995.
9. P. A. Rochon and J. H. Gurwitz, Drug Therapy, *Lancet, 346,* pp. 32-36, 1995.
10. J. B. Schwartz, Clinical Pharmacology, in *Principles of Geriatric Medicine and Gerontology,* W. R. Hazzard, E. L. Bierman, J. P. Blass, W. H. Ettinger, Jr., and J. B. Halter (eds.), McGraw-Hill, Inc., New York, pp. 259-276, 1994.
11. D. S. Chutka, J. M. Evans, K. C. Fleming, and K. G. Mikkelson, Symposium on Geriatrics—Part I: Drug Prescribing for Elderly Patients, *Mayo Clinic Proceedings, 70,* pp. 685-693, 1995.
12. L. Z. Benet and K. Zech, Pharmacokinetics—A Relevant Factor for the Choice of a Drug? *Alimentary Pharmacology & Therapeutics, 8,* pp. 25-32, 1994.
13. P. W. Duncan, Stroke Disability, *Physical Therapy, 74*:5, pp. 399-407, 1994.
14. L. M. Cooney, Jr. and T. F. Williams, Rehabilitation of Specific Conditions, in *Principles of Geriatric Medicine and Gerontology,* W. R. Hazzard, E. L. Bierman, J. P. Blass, W. H. Ettinger, Jr., and J. B. Halter (eds.), McGraw-Hill, Inc., New York, pp. 349-355, 1994.
15. H. Nakayama, H. S. Jorgensen, H. O. Raaschou, and T. S. Olsen, The Incidence of Age on Stroke Outcome, *Stroke, 25*:4, pp. 808-813, 1994.
16. E. Taub, J. E. Crago, L. D. Burgio, T. E. Groomes, E. W. Cook III, S. C. DeLuca, and N. E. Miller, An Opperant Approach to Rehabilitation Medicine: Overcoming Learned Nonuse by Shaping, *Journal of the Experimental Analysis of Behavior, 61*:2, pp. 281-293, 1994.
17. M. E. Williams, Clinical Management of the Elderly Patient, in *Principles of Geriatric Medicine and Gerontology,* W. R. Hazzard, E. L. Bierman, J. P. Blass, W. H. Ettinger, Jr., and J. B. Halter (eds.), McGraw-Hill, Inc., New York, pp. 195-201, 1994.
18. J. S. Jackson, Special Populations, in *The Threshold of Discovery: Future Directions for Research on Aging* (DHHS Administrative Document), U.S. Government Printing Office, Washington, D.C., pp. 253-257, 1995.
19. National Institute on Aging, *The Women's Health and Aging Study: Health and Social Characteristics of Older Women with Disability* (NIH Pub. No. 95-4009), J. M. Lguralnik, L. P. Fried, E. M. Simonsick, J. D. Kasper, and M. E. Lafferty (eds.), Bethesda, Maryland, 1995.
20. Anonymous, Design of the Women's Health Initiative Clinical Trial and Observational Study. The Women's Health Initiative Study Group, *Controlled Clinical Trials, 19*:1, pp. 61-109, 1998.
21. National Institute of Health, National Library of Medicine, Medlars OnLine (MEDLINE) Bibliographic Data Base, 1998.
22. B. E. Reubinoff, J. Wurtman, N. Rojansky, D. Adler, P. Stein, J. G. Schenker, and A. Brzezinski, Effects of Hormone Replacement Therapy on Weight, Body

Composition, Fat Distribtion and Food Intake in Early Postmenopausal Women: A Prospective Study, *Fertility and Sterility, 64,* pp. 963-968, 1995.

23. K. F. Mottel and J. S. Meyer, Lack of Postmenopausal Estrogen Replacement Therapy and the Risk of Dementia, *Journal of Neuropsychiatry and Clinical Neuroscience, 7,* pp. 334-337, 1995.

24. D. Kimura, Estrogen Replacement Therapy May Protect Against Intellectual Decline in Postmenopausal Women, *Hormones and Behavior, 29,* pp. 312-321, 1995.

25. R. N. Butler, Taking the Pulse of Older Women's Health. Despite Advances, Gender Gap Still Exists in Medical Education, Research and Clinical Care, *Geriatrics, 50,* pp. 6-8, 1995.

26. J. J. McCann, L. E. Herbert, D. A. Bennett, V. V. Skul, and D. A. Evans, Why Alzheimer's Disease Is a Women's Health Issue, *Journal of the American Medical Womens Association, 52*:3, pp. 132-137, 1997.

27. K. Blakemore and M. Boneham, *Age, Race and Ethnicity,* Open University Press, Bristol, Pennsylvania, 1994.

28. W. L. Reed, Health Care Needs and Services, in *Black Aged: Understanding Diversity and Service Needs,* Z. Harel, E. A. McKinney, and M. Williams (eds.), Sage Publications, Newbury Park, California, pp. 183-204, 1990.

29. R. Lavizzo-Maurey and E. R. Mackenzie, Cultural Competence: Essential Measurements of Quality for Managed Care Organizations, *Annals of Internal Medicine, 124,* pp. 919-921, 1996.

30. P. Cotton, Alzheimer's/Apo E Link Grows Stronger, *Journal of the American Medical Association, 272*:19, p. 1483, 1994.

31. H. C. Hendrie, K. S. Hall, S. Hui, F. W. Unverzagt, C.E. Yu, D. K. Lahiri, A. Sahota, M. Farlow, B. Musick, C. A. Class et al., Apolipoprotein E. Genotypes and Alzheimer's Disease in a Community Study of Elderly African Americans, *Annals of Neurology, 37*:1, pp. 118-120, 1995.

32. W. C. Koller, S. L. Glatt, J. P. Hubble, A. Paolo, A. I. Troster, M. S. Handler, R. T. Horvat, C. Martin, K. Schmidt, A. Karst et al., Apolipoprotein E Genotypes in Parkinson's Disease With and Without Dementia, *Annals of Neurology, 37*:2, pp. 242-245, 1995.

33. E. H. Corder, A. M. Saunders, N. J. Risch, W. J. Strittmatter, D. E. Schmechel, P. C. Gaskell, Jr., J. B. Rimmler, P. A. Locke, P. M. Conneally, K. E. Schmader, G. W. Small, A. D. Roses, J. L. Haines, and M. A. Pericak-Vance, Protective Effect of Apolipoprotein E Type 2 Allele for Late Onset Alzheimer Disease, *Nature Genetics, 7,* pp. 180-184, 1994.

34. C. H. Gunderson, The Impact of New Pharmaceutical Agents on the Cost of Neurologic Care, *Neurology, 45*:3 Pt 1, pp. 569-572, 1995.

35. L. Parnetti, Clinical Pharmacokinetics of Drugs for Alzheimer's Disease, *Clinical Pharmacokinetics, 29*:2, pp. 110-129, 1995.

36. C. A. Kelly, R. J. Harvey, and H. Cayton, Drug Treatments for Alzheimer's Disease, *British Medical Journal, 314*:7082, pp. 693-694, 1997.

37. A. Kurz, R. Marquand, and D. Mosch, Tacrine: Progress in Treatment of Alzheimer's Disease [German]. *Zeitschrift fur Gerontologie und Geriatrie, 28*:3, pp. 163-168, 1995.

38. A. W. Partin and J. E. Oesterling, The Clinical Usefulness of Prostate Specific Antigen: Update 1994, *Journal of Urology, 152*:5 Pt 1, pp. 1358-1368, 1994.

39. W. J. Catalona, D. S. Smith, T. L. Ratliff, and J. W. Basler, Detection of Organ-Confined Prostate Cancer is Increased Through Prostate-Specific Antigen-Based Screening, *Journal of the American Medical Association, 270,* pp. 948-954, 1994.

40. K. M. Hussein, L. Gould, B. Sosler, T. Bharathan, and C. V. Reddy, Clinical Science Review: Current Aspects of Thrombolytic Therapy in Women with Acute Myocardial Infarction, *Angiology, 47*:1, pp. 23-33, 1996.

41. P. Sleight, Is There an Age Limit for Thrombolytic Therapy? *American Journal of Cardiology, 72*:19, pp. 30G-33G, 1993.

42. J. Owen, Thrombotic and Hemorrhagic Disorders in the Elderly, in *Principles of Geriatric Medicine and Gerontology,* W. R. Hazzard, E. L. Bierman, J. P. Blass, W. H. Ettinger, Jr., and J. B. Halter (eds.), McGraw-Hill, Inc., New York, pp. 775-789, 1994.

43. J. H. Gurwitz, J. M. Gore, R. J. Goldberg, M. Rubison, N. Chandra, and W. J. Rogers, Recent Age-Related Trends in the Use of Thrombolytic Therapy in Patients Who Have Had Acute Myocardial Infarction, *Annals of Internal Medicine, 124*:3, pp. 283-291, 1996.

44. D. D. Tresch and D. Berkompas, Management of Acute Myocardial Infarction in the Elderly, *Cleveland Clinic Journal of Medicine, 62*:3, pp. 156-162, 1995.

45. B. Morgan and C. L. Emerman, Effect of Age on Myocardial Infarction and Thrombolysis, *American Journal of Emergency Medicine, 13*:2, pp. 196-198, 1995.

46. P. Sleight, Thrombolysis: State of the Art, *European Heart Journal, 14*(Suppl G), pp. 41-47, 1993.

47. R. E. Fowles, Myocardial Infarction in the 1990's, Complications, Prognosis, and Changing Patterns of Management, *Postgraduate Medicine, 97*:6, pp. 155-157, 161-162, 165-168, 1995.

48. D. R. Holmes, R. M. Califf, and E. J. Topol, Lessons We Have Learned from the GUSTO Trial. Global Utilization of Streptokinase and Tissue Plasminogen Activator for Occluded Arteries, *Journal of the American College of Cardiology, 25*:7(Suppl.), pp. 10S-17S, 1995.

49. S. M. Smith, Current Management of Acute Myocardial Infarction, *Disease-A-Month, 41*:6, pp. 363-433, 1995.

50. Agency for Health Care Policy and Research, *Clinical Practice Guideline, No. 4: Cataract in Adults: Management of Functional Impairment* (AHCPR Publication No. 93-0543), U.S. Department of Health and Human Services, Rockville, Maryland, 1993.

51. S. A. Obstbaum, An 82-Year-Old Woman With Cataracts, *Journal of the American Medical Association, 275*:21, pp. 1675-1680, 1996.

52. S. R. Zedlewski and T. D. McBride, The Changing Profile of the Elderly: Effects on Future Long-Term Care Needs and Financing, *Milbank Quarterly, 70*:2, pp. 247-275, 1992.

53. S. A. Gaylord and M. E. Williams, A Brief History of the Development of Geriatric Medicine, *Journal of the American Geriatrics Society, 42*:3, pp. 335-340, 1994.

54. Alliance for Aging Research, *Meeting the Medical Needs of the Senior Boom,* The National Shortage of Geriatricians (Report), Washington D.C., 1992.

55. C. S. Kart, *The Realities of Aging: An Introduction to Gerontology,* Needham Heights, Massachusetts, 1997.

56. A. Ford, Long-Term Care: A New Model, in *Quality Care in Geriatric Settings,* P. R. Katz, R. L. Kane, M. D. Mezey (eds.), Springer, New York, 1995.

57. W. C. Cockerham, *Medical Sociology,* Englewood Cliffs, New Jersey, 1998.

58. U. E. Reinhardt, Reforming the Health Care System: The Universal Dilemma, in *The Social Medicine Reader,* G. E. Henderson, N. M. P. King, R. P. Strauss, S. E. Estroff, and L. R. Churchill (eds.), Duke University Press, Durham, North Carolina, 1997.

59. American Association of Retired Persons (AARP), *Health Care Delivery and Insurance*, Washington, D.C., 1996.
60. B. S. Harrow, S. L. Tennstedt, and J. B. McKinlay, How Costly Is It to Care for Disabled Elders in a Community Setting? *Gerontologist, 35*:6, pp. 3-13, 1995.
61. J. M. Harris, Disease Management: New Wine in New Bottles? *Annals of Internal Medicine, 124*:9, pp. 838-842, 1996.
62. M. P. Freiman and C. M. Murtaugh, Interactions between Hospital and Nursing Home Use, *Public Health Reports, 110*:5, pp. 546-554, 1995.
63. R. M. Palmer, Acute Hospital Care of the Elderly: Minimizing the Risk of Functional Decline, *Cleveland Clinic Journal of Medicine, 62*:2, pp. 117-128, 1995.
64. R. H. Miller and H. S. Luft, Managed Care Plans: Characteristics, Growth, and Premium Performance, *Annual Review of Public Health, 15*, pp. 437-459, 1994.
65. J. E. Ware, M. S. Bayless, W. H. Rogers, M. Kosinski, and A. R. Tarlov, Differences in 4-Year Health Outcomes for Elderly and Poor, Chronically Ill Patients Treated in HMO and Fee-for-Service Systems. Results from the Medical Outcomes Study, *Journal of the American Medical Association, 276*, pp. 1039-1047, 1996.
66. J. D. Lubitz and G. F. Riley, Trends in Medicare Payments in the Last Year of Life, *New England Journal of Medicine, 328*, pp. 1092-1096, 1993.
67. A. McMillan, R. M. Mentnech, J. Lubitz, A. M. McBean, and D. Russell, Trends and Patterns in Place of Death for Medicare Enrollees, *Health Care Finance Review, 12*:1, pp. 1-7, 1990.
68. D. L. Madison, Paying for Health Care in America, in *The Social Medicine Reader*, G. E. Henderson, N. M. P. King, R. P. Strauss, S. E. Estroff, and L. R. Churchill (eds.), Duke University Press, Durham, North Carolina, 1997.
69. L. DeBrock, Efficient Allocation of Health Care to the Elderly, in *Set No Limits*, R. Barry and G. Bradley (eds.), University of Illinois Press, Chicago, Illinois, 1991.
70. R. N. Butler, F. T. Sherman, E. Rhinehart, S. Klein, and J. C. Rother, Managed Care: What to Expect as Medicare-HMO Enrollment Grows. 1, *Geriatrics, 51*:10, pp. 35-42, 1996.
71. R. L. Kane, The Role of Geriatric Assessment in Different Countries, in *Geriatric Assessment Technology: The State of the Art*, L. A. Rubenstein, D. Wieland, and R. Bernabei (eds.), Kurtis, Milan, Italy, 1995.
72. J. Garriss, J. Aistrop, B. Slavic, K. Wagner, J. Calvaruso, R. Reiner, J. Dille, and R. Schrock, The Market Made Them Do It. Participants in the Medicare Choices Project Say They're Nudging Out the Insurance Middleman—and Insuring Their Own Survival, *Hospitals and Health Networks, 712*:13, pp. 32-34, 36, 1997.
73. J. B. Oberlander, Managed Care and Medicare Reform, *Journal of Health Politics, Policy and Law, 22*:2, pp. 595-631, 1997.
74. L. G. Branch, R. F. Coulam, and A. Zimmerman, The PACE Evaluation: Initial Findings, *The Gerontologist, 35*:3, pp. 349-359, 1995.
75. D. G. Blazer, L. R. Landerman, G. Fillenbaum, and R. Horner, Health Services Access and Use among Older Adults in North Carolina: Urban Vs. Rural Residents, *American Journal of Public Health, 85*:10, pp. 1384-1390, 1995.
76. L. K. Evans, J. Yurkow, and E. L. Siegler, The CARE Program: A Nurse-Managed Collaborative Outpatient Program to Improve Function of Frail Older People. Collaborative Assessment and Rehabilitation for Elders, *Journal of the American Geriatrics Society, 43*:10, pp. 1155-1160, 1995.
77. E. Hui, C. M. Lum, J. Woo, K. H. Or, and R. L. Kay, Outcomes of Elderly Stroke Patients. Day Hospital Versus Conventional Medical Management, *Stroke, 26*, pp. 1616-1619, 1995.

78. J. R. Burton, The Evolution of Nursing Homes into Comprehensive Geriatrics Centers: A Perspective, *Journal of the American Geriatrics Society, 42*:7, pp. 794-796, 1994.
79. R. S. Epstein and L. M. Sherwood, From Outcomes Research to Disease Management: A Guide for the Perplexed, *Annals of Internal Medicine, 124*:9, pp. 832-837, 1996.
80. D. G. Clement, S. M. Retchin, R. S. Brown, and M. H. Stegall, Access and Outcomes of Elderly Patients Enrolled in Managed Care, *Journal of the American Medical Association, 271*:19, pp. 1487-1492, 1994.
81. J. E. Ware, M. S. Bayliss, W. H. Rogers, M. Kosinski, and A. R. Tarlov, Differenes in 4-Year Health Outcomes for Elderly and Poor, Chronically Ill Patients Treated in HMO and Fee-for-Service Systems: Results From the Medical Outcomes Study, *Journal of the American Medical Association, 276*:13, pp. 1039-1047, 1996.
82. E. H. Yelin, L. A. Criswell, and P. G. Feigenbaum, Health Care Utilization and Outcomes Among Persons With Rheumatoid Arthritis in Fee-for-Service and Prepaid Group Practice Settings, *Journal of the American Medical Association, 276*:13, pp. 1048-1053, 1996.
83. A. A. Jaeger, M. A. Hlatky, S. M. Paul, and S. R. Gorner, Functional Capacity after Cardiac Surgery in Elderly Patients, *Journal of the American College of Cardiology, 24*:1, pp. 104-108, 1994.
84. M. Charlson, T. P. Szatrowski, J. Peterson, and J. Gold, Validation of a Combined Comorbidity Index, *Journal of Clinical Epidemiology, 47*:11, pp. 1245-1251, 1994.
85. J. Damron-Rodriquez, S. Wallace, and R. Kington, Service Utilization and Minority Elderly: Appropriateness, Accessibility and Acceptability, in *Cultural Diversity and Geriatric Care: Challenges to the Health Professions,* D. Wieland, D. Benton, B. J. Kramer, and G. D. Dawson (eds.), Haworth Press, Inc., Binghamton, New York, pp. 23-43, 1994.
86. L. Z. Rubenstein and B. J. Kramer, Health Populations in Old Age: Cross-Population Comparisons, in *Cultural Diversity and Geriatric Care: Challenges to the Health Professions,* D. Wieland, D. Benton, B. J. Kramer, and G. D. Dawson (eds.), Haworth Press, Inc., Binghamton, New York, pp. 23-43, 1994.
87. L. E. Moody, S. J. Gregory, T. Bocanegra, and F. Vasey, Search and Research, Factors Influencing Post-Menopausal African-American Women's Participation in a Clinical Trial, *Journal of the American Academy of Nurse Practitioners, 7,* pp. 483-488, 1995.
88. V. R. Hart, D. Gallagher-Thompson, H. D. Davies, M. DiMinno, and P. J. Lessin, Strategies for Increasing Participation of Ethnic Minorities in Alzheimer's Disease Diagnostic Centers: A Multifaceted Approach in California, *The Gerontologist 36*:2, pp. 259-262, 1966.
89. D. Blumenthal, Quality of Health Care, Part 1: Quality of Care—What Is It? *New England Journal of Medicine, 335*:12, pp. 891-894, 1996.
90. R. H. Brook, E. A. McGlynn, and P. D. Cleary, Quality of Health Care, Part 2: Measuring Quality of Care, *New England Journal of Medicine, 335*:13, pp. 966-970, 1996.
91. M. R. Chassin, Quality of Health Care, Part 3: Improving the Quality of Care, *New England Journal of Medicine, 335*:14, pp. 1060-1063, 1996.
92. D. Blumenthal, Quality of Health Care, Part 4: The Origins of the Quality-of-Care Debate, *New England Journal of Medicine, 335*:15, pp. 1146-1149, 1996.
93. D. M. Berwick, Quality of Health Care, Part 5: Payment by Capitation and the Quality of Care, *New England Journal of Medicine, 335*:16, pp. 1227-1231, 1996.
94. D. Blumenthal, A. M. Epstein, Qualtiy of Health Care, Part 6: The Role of Physicians in the Future of Quality Management, *New England Journal of Medicine, 335*:17, pp. 1328-1331, 1996.

95. M. Angell and J. P. Kassirer, Editiorials and Conflicts of Interest, *New England Journal of Medicine, 335*:14, pp. 1064-1065, 1996.

96. S. D. Pearson, D. Goulart-Fisher, and T. H. Lee, Critical Pathways as a Strategy for Improving Care: Problems and Potential, *Annals of Internal Medicine, 123*:12, pp. 941-948, 1995.

97. S. R. Weingarten, E. Stone, A. Green, M. Pelter, S. Nessim, H. Huang, and R. Kristopaitis, A Study of Patient Satisfaction and Adherence to Preventive Care Practice Guidelines, *American Journal of Medicine, 99,* pp. 590-596, 1995.

98. C. Kiefe, T. W. Woolley, J. J. Allison, J. B. Box, and A. S. Craig, Determining Benchmarks: A Data-Driven Search for the Best Achievable Performance, *Clinical Performance and Quality Health Care, 2*:4, pp. 190-194, 1994.

99. R. M. Allman, W. C. Yoels, and J. M. Clair, Reconciling the Agendas of Physicians and Patients, in *Sociomedical Perspectives on Patient Care,* J. M. Clair and R. M. Allman (eds.), Lexington, Kentucky, pp. 29-46, 1993.

100. M. S. Klinkman, P. Zazove, D. R. Mehr, and M. T. Ruffin, 4th, A Criterion-Based Review of Preventive Health Care in the Elderly. Part 1. Theoretical Framework and Development of Criteria, *Journal of Family Practice, 34*:2, pp. 205-209, 213-218, 221-224, 1992.

SECTION II

Key Substantive Issues

CHAPTER 5

Diversity as a Catalyst for Change

E. Percil Stanford and Gwendolyn E. Stanford

Diversity, aging, and social change are seemingly at once dissimilar, but yet have numerous common elements. They are concepts that aid in explaining the status of highly visible social conditions. Diversity as a more recent social concept has not been easy to sort out. Therefore, diversity has emerged as a way of not only assisting in explaining similarities and differences among population groups, but has begun to be accepted as a way of justifying social, political, and economic actions.

The 1970s represented the first decade in which there was an earnest attempt to carefully consider the impact of emerging diversity among the elderly. Bass, Kutza, and Torres-Gil pointed out that the rapid transition to an aging society finds us continuing to view the elderly as a nameless and faceless mass of persons whose age bracket—sixty-five years and older—gives each the same needs and wants [1]. It is too often taken for granted that older people are more alike than unlike with regard to their experiences, needs, and aspirations. We continue to seek labels and descriptions that are easily and quickly communicated. Bass et al. make it clear that the "rocking-chair" image of older people has been a dominant stereo-type and it has been fully resisted by groups who represent older people, such as the Gray Panthers [1].

As a nation, the United States has a more diverse aged population than any other country in the world. The historical make-up of society dictates the hetero-geneity of the current aging and aged population. People differ by race, ethnicity, social economic status, religious preferences, political backgrounds, sexual per-suasion, outlook on family configuration, regional preferences, and general life-styles. While the traditional discussion of embracing a "melting pot" society has continued, the reality is that society has steadily moved in the direction of being heterogeneous.

DIVERSITY IN THE FOREFRONT

Gerontologists and others in the academic arena concerned with gerontology and geriatrics have an opportunity to influence social change at a level never before recognized. Scholars in age-related disciplines have the tools to shape theory and methodology and fuel the debate around the impact of age and the older person in today's social world. Gerontologists and other colleagues are well positioned to effectively describe the many dimensions of aging, and highlight the significance of understanding those dimensions in varied disciplines. While doing so, it is inevitable that the paradoxes inherent in theoretical issues versus practical concerns, individual needs versus group demands, or whether or not gerontology is a discipline or theme for disciplinary investigation, must be rightfully confronted. Stanford and Schmidtke maintain that there is a remarkable inter-connectedness between gerontology and the diversity agenda in higher education [2]. The analogy of a prism, one in which light enters into a spectrum and bursts forth, helps explain the inter-connectedness.

If considering diversity as a prism, the essence of the analogy is that the main focus of attention is on the prism, not just on the light or the spectrum. The prism works because of the light and its unique shape. It follows that we too need our identities, our group affiliations, our habits, and special ways of surviving. Our lives, like a prism, do not exist merely in a homogeneous world. The nature of the color spectrum is that there is no connectedness between colors, meaning there is no identifiable demarcating line that defines the end of one color and the beginning of another. Cultural and ethnic groups have many general traits that are shared, but there are often not enough specific well-defined characteristics to clearly separate individuals from each other.

It is essential to realize that one of the colors in the spectrum of diversity is gerontology. Its boundaries blend and merge with the agenda and concerns of race, ethnicity, religion, gender, sexual preference, and impairments. These colors share a paradoxical and asymmetrical nature. At the policy level, we are dealing with the economies of a minority population which has considerable wealth, comfort, and a significant degree of poverty [2].

> On a social level, there are prejudices and discriminations that lead to "pathological" views and attitudes toward older people, as well as self-fulfilling prophetic behaviors. Yet, we cannot ignore the realities of growing older. At the academic/institutional level, gerontologists face "marginalized" attitudes of acceptance in administrative, curricular, funding, and staffing decisions, even though "aging" is the wave of the future. We travel a comparable road with those fellow travelers sharing our color spectrum, and all too often we disregard what we can learn from our companions. We tenaciously cling to a narrow agenda and fail to focus on the breadth and depth of the prism that is available [2, p. 1].

For curriculum purposes, cultural diversity in gerontology can be examined microscopically within the boundaries of institutions of higher education. It is within these boundaries that cultural diversity can be managed to derive the best possible benefits for all concerned. Institutions of higher education are responsible for insuring that their actions are effective beyond the confines of the institution. They have a major role in shaping the social and political values of students, the surrounding community, and beyond. Within the institution, many roles and responsibilities collide. The prism effect is abundantly at work. Faculty are charged with providing guidance and setting the tone for students to ensure appropriate input from an intellectual and social perspective. Considerable variances are introduced, because faculty come from multiple backgrounds and their definitions of reality correspond to their level and quality of experiences. The degree to which faculty communicate their life experiences and philosophy depends on the intensity of the interaction with those in their environment. Faculty become role models by their mere presence in the institution. Unlike few other individuals, they have the power to direct and guide the thinking and actions of students who ultimately affect the prism of the future.

Administrators represent a key link to the success of diversity as a part of social change in the institution. Administrators, as individuals, represent a wide range of ideas, visions, and cultural experiences. Leadership is key as change evolves in the institution. Their commitment to fostering change, based on the needs of the surrounding population and their understanding of those needs, is most critical. Therefore, administrators, as an intricate part of the institutional culture, must have the vision to realize the magnitude of their influence. Influence at the policy and decision making level can do more to lay the foundation for institutional change than any other single act. The "culture" of the institution is shaped and guided by administrative policies and directives.

> The prism analogy could be helpful if faculty and administrators recognize that programming needs to focus upon process, interdependence, and consensus. We need to overcome our pre-occupation with specialization and keep it in its proper perspective. It is necessary to foster research, scholarship, and knowledge. It becomes worthwhile and important when research, scholarship, and knowledge become part of the light sent through a prism and when they become a process that calls for synthetic thinking and inter-dependent curricular opportunities. Not only should we expect students to think interdependently, faculty should foster activities and programming that help us see the narrowness of our social ordering process [2, p. 2].

DIVERSITY AND BEYOND

The rapidly burgeoning aging population, which consists of a higher percentage of ethnically and culturally different older people more than ever before, is cause for concern, but not alarm. With the prospect of approximately sixty-five million persons—22 percent of the U.S. population—being sixty-five and older by the year 2030, there is an urgent need to plan for the acceptance, recognition, and utilization of the skills and talents of diverse groups [3, p. 6]. It is clear that the aging population in the United States will continue to become more diverse by race, gender, income, ethnicity, immigration, and language. The younger population will mature and soon represent the aged population in large numbers, and therefore accentuate the diversity that now exists in the older population. The emerging diversity causes questions to be raised relative to how we can respond to the myriad social, cultural, and economic needs; understand and incorporate the effects of race, language, ethnicity, and other variables on the aging process; and simultaneously make public benefit programs responsive. As curricula are forged, faculty and administrators will be forced to distinguish between the common needs of all persons. It is at this point that the prism effect must be taken into consideration.

There are compelling reasons to go beyond the common definition of diversity. The concept can be used not only to explain variances, differences, and dissimilarities, but also to highlight strengths within groups. More emphasis must be placed on the importance of within-group strengths and variances. As the traditional melting pot philosophy fades, diversity must be incorporated into the philosophy of acculturation. The goal of acculturation has been to enable individuals to function successfully in society by eliminating barriers, such as racism and nativism (favoring native born citizens against immigrants), and promoting economic and social opportunities. There are very few critical areas in society that will escape the effects of diversity in efforts to come to terms with assimilation and acculturation as related to aging. Emerging generations will become more aware of and show evidence that diversity must be a leading force in determining the essence of lifestyles of older people as anchors in society. Diversity should be viewed as an enabling concept rather than an end unto itself.

As philosophies, ideas, and pedagogic preferences continue to emerge, diversity looms even larger. It is of utmost importance that administrators, faculty, and others in institutions of higher education abstain from the age old practice of equating diversity and minority with Americans of African descent. Too often, the first response to hearing the terms is that the reference is to Americans of African descent. Having highlighted the notion that diversity is multifaceted throughout the discussion thus far, it is also appropriate to indicate that some of the guiding principles which help define the roots of diversity have been centered around older Americans of African descent. Historical experiences shaping their unique experiences have a tendency to reflect a variety of issues that confront other individuals from minority/ethnic backgrounds.

Several changes and opportunities for ethnic elders can be attributed to the civil rights activities of the 1960s and 1970s. In the 1980s older minorities took more responsibility for political and social economic change that would noticeably affect their lives. The current cohort of ethnic elders has had a tremendous sense of responsibility, but simultaneously has been forced to exhibit a sense of helplessness. Such helplessness is gradually being removed and replaced by an emerging sense of political potency and a feeling of enfranchisement. The ethnic older adult of the 1960s and 1970s, and to an extent the 1980s, carries what may be referred to as "vestiges of the slave culture" that set the stage for the status of older Americans of diverse cultural backgrounds in our society during the nineteenth and twentieth centuries [4, p. 34].

As scholars fully appreciate the breathe and depth of the concept of "diversity," negative connotations will ease. It is time in our social, political, and economic history to identify other constructive means of explaining how individuals and groups throughout society can coalesce. There is no need to equate diversity with ineffectiveness, negative actions, or anything that does not connote a positive force. Older individuals labeled as minority have suffered with the negativism accompanying the label. Minority, as a designation, renders individuals as less than equal to someone or something regardless of their educational, economic, or political standing. As we develop curricula and put forth ideas for change, it is appropriate to gauge the status and standing of individuals and groups in society by their contributions.

Older persons of diverse cultural backgrounds have experiences stemming from lives that have been culturally circumscribed in ways that are somewhat similar. The primary issue is that scholars in academia should take the experiences of diverse groups of older individuals and examine them for positive ways of bringing about change in society. Lessons learned can be extremely catalytic in providing examples of how to move ahead.

Diversity would not be considered a major catalyst for change if it were not for the major revolution taking place in the aging population. As the population matures, medicine and technology have made it possible for more individuals from different backgrounds and environments to live healthier longer. Bass et al. indicated that there is perhaps no other change that is as visible and omnipresent as the demographic revolution [1, pp. 157-158]. They are certain that the forces of this revolution will fundamentally change how we live our lives and will create new meanings about "old age."

The baby-boom generation is targeted to represent the most effective demographic change ever and will, most likely, produce our largest group of older persons beginning around the year 2010. This change will cause shifts in dependency ratios and, in the fifteen years between 2010 and 2025, the number of persons in the work force will decline by nearly twelve million. At the same time the older population will grow from approximately forty-two million to sixty-two million. It is an inescapable fact that we must make better use of the impending older diverse population which will include large numbers of individuals from diverse cultural backgrounds and women.

Those opting for and promoting change must be certain that data are accurate and represent the population under consideration. As change is forced and evolves, scarce resources dictate that planners, legislators, and others possess the most current and accurate information. It is not enough to make decisions based on raw data, there must be an ability to interpret data based on the background and circumstances of the population. If major changes in policy or general laws were to have serious negative effects on certain population groups, it would be important to have information which would make it possible to target programs in certain directions [5, pp. 46-47].

Bass makes it clear that we will have a more ethnically and racially diverse older population in the very near future [1, p. 6]. When the population is examined, based on the 1990 census, 28.3 million elderly are white, 2.6 million are black, 603 thousand are other races, and 1.1 million are of Hispanic origin. When looking ahead to 2050, the projection shows that nearly ten million would be black, five million would be persons of races other than white or black, and eight million would be Hispanic. Currently, races other than white constitute about one in ten of the elderly and by 2050 that proportion is likely to increase to two in ten. It is expected that by 2030 when the baby-boom generation is sixty-five to eighty-five years old, nearly 18 percent of Black Americans and 13 percent of Hispanics will be sixty-five or older.

David Hayes-Bautista feels that because of the rapid change, ethnic and inter-generation conflict may be a reality in the near future [6, pp. 37-38]. His outlook is greater cause for social scientists to review the parameters within which diversity forces change in society. The census of 1970 showed that Anglos were 79 percent of California's total population and by 1990 they were only approximately 54 percent of the States total population. The Anglo population continues to shrink while the Latino segment continues to burgeon. Hayes-Bautista indicates that in 1970 Latinos were roughly 10.9 percent of the population in the state of California, by 1990 the figure had grown to 25.7 percent, and by the year 2000 it will be around 35 percent [6]. The Anglo population is older than the Latino population which is more fertile and is increasing because of immigration. From a demographic perspective, change is inevitable because Latinos will not only be a younger population, but will be the working age population and will therefore inevitably develop economic practices that will have a domino effect on how change takes place.

DIVERSITY UNBRIDLED

As diversity in its many contexts is examined as a social and cultural force, architects of change must be careful to cultivate all aspects of diversity. One of the most important is the cultural fiber that extends beyond the visual entities that cause actions and re-actions. Cultural and ethnic backgrounds not withstanding, old age brings with it physical changes. There are, for example, undeniable changes in appearance, such as gray hair and wrinkled skin. It is acknowledged that in the absence of severe disease, these changes seldom prohibit the ability to pursue activities or to fulfill normal social obligations [7].

As social scientists ponder the impact of aged-related changes on society, there has been little attention given to the impact of diversity within the perimeters of this discussion. Changes which may have been easy to explain within cultures and ethnic groups are now more difficult to explain as varying degrees of accul-turation and assimilation occur. The "sloughing-off-effect" that occurs over time is not easy to account for. There is not only a "sloughing-off-effect," there is also a "bundling- effect" that occurs as individuals age. The "bundling-effect" suggests that as individuals age there is a tendency to try to extricate those customs, traditions, and values encountered in a society that does not easily meld with their traditional belief patterns. However, there are aspects of society that they encounter which are attractive and are difficult to dismiss. Bundling provides a security blanket for those who are not prepared to consciously assume a greater degree of acculturation.

Stoller and Gibson discuss cultural images and ways in which older people respond to them [7, p. 47]. They emphasize images of old age as reflected in cultures and how they vary along gender, race, and class hierarchies. They also raise to a conscious level how these images for older persons are used to help maintain positive self-concepts in face of negative images. These authors propose that the contemporary culture in the United States reflects mixed images of older individuals. They are simultaneously viewed on the positive side as wise, understanding, generous, happy, knowledgeable, and patriotic; and on the negative side, seen as forgetful, lonely, dependent, demanding, complaining, senile, selfish, and inflexible.

Given the statistics available, it is unlikely that patterns now in motion will be reversed. There is little doubt that many planned and unforeseen adjustments will emerge as the configuration of the population changes [8].

> As the older population increases and becomes more diverse, it becomes a driving force for changes required to meet the challenge of providing the quality of life we have come to expect. Aggregate skills and energy will need to be mobilized. Diversity as a social force will require us to consider how different needs can be met without disrupting those entities that represent the common good.

> Older Americans are no longer bound by locale as they once were. The diversity they have brought to many communities has caused community leaders to re-think the way they plan programs and services. They can no longer plan as if the aged were homogeneous. Diversity as a social force will help change the way bureaucracies perceive their roles and responsibilities and the way they operationalize their activities [8, p. 1].

Societal change cannot take place without the ongoing involvement of working units in varied social environments. The family and other units that provide support and cohesion in social environments, usually defined as communities, are significant elements for diversity to survive and be a force in change. The way the family is defined and viewed has, in large part, come about because of diverse elements in society. More persons define themselves as family units in a variety of situations and circumstances than ever before. Units defined are not necessarily traditional nuclear family units. The pressures to marry young and have children has changed considerably, to the extent that many are marrying later and having children later. Age differences within families and among couples has increased.

As laws have become more open and liberal to permit greater formal interaction, the diverse makeup of the family has changed immensely. It is safe to postulate that had formal sanctions, in the form of laws, not been in place, the diverse nature of family structures would be further advanced. As families become more culturally and ethnically integrated through marriage and other formal and informal alliances, diversity will evolve more naturally. Cohorts of older persons from different backgrounds will interact in ways they have not thought possible. At the same time, cohorts of younger generations will begin to interact at a much earlier stage of their lives and will consider their interactions "normal." The net results of inter- and intra-generational involvement at the family level has unlimited potential for bringing about change.

Language is another area that must be considered. The issue is quite often what language should be more dominant in the household. That often leads to protracted discussions around what language is more beneficial for individuals at different age levels. Past history shows that there are many situations in which families have made conscious decisions to prohibit younger persons in the family from speaking a traditional language, because they want the younger people to be more assimilated and acculturated. At the same time, there are situations in which conscious efforts are made to retain languages in order to have a vehicle for maintaining connectedness with ones traditional culture. Types of foods, eating patterns, and habits are also at the top of the list when considering those things that help bring about immediate change at the family level and therefore at the larger societal level. It is not just the food that is important, it is the degree to which food serves as a focal point to draw people together.

As communities change, it is imperative that bureaucracies which serve the needs of the population change as well. A major impediment is that bureaucracies comprise leadership which is not always sympathetic to, nor do they understand the needs of, some of the emerging populous. The first order of business for many agencies and institutions, as they begin to modify their approach to surrounding communities, is to examine their missions. Many organizations hold tenaciously to irrelevant missions. An organization that was effective and served a major community need in the 1950s will not necessarily be relevant today. To bring about change, it is necessary to involve those whom will be affected by impending changes. Therefore, the planning process will of necessity draw in individuals who most nearly represent the cultural and ethnic makeup of the community.

Work published by the National Association of Social Workers outlines major actions that can be taken to improve agency response to diversity in the community. They are as follows:

> Examine how well staff represent the diversity of those in their client pool; insure that staff in outreach, case management, and information and referral are representative of the community; insure that minority contractors are given an opportunity to be providers of services; use culturally appropriate sites, materials, and individuals in outreach efforts; constantly review the demographics of the community to determine whether all aspects of the population are being served; recruit and use ethnically diverse volunteers for aging and inter-generational programs; and incorporate older community members as volunteers, advisors, and paid workers [9].

THEORY AND RESEARCH

Gerontologists continue to be criticized for the lack of comprehensive theory and adequate research designs to test proposed theories. Social scientists in general, and gerontologists in particular, have continued to debate whether or not theoretical developments in social gerontology are advanced enough to declare a relevant and coherent body of theory. The discussion becomes more intense when questions are raised about the presence of theory to appropriately explain ethnicity, culture, and aging. It is only in the 1990s that any protracted discussion has evolved relative to diversity and aging and its conceptual impact on understanding aging populations.

Burton, Dilworth-Anderson, and Bengtson indicate that it is important to move beyond traditional discipline-bound research methods, data resources, and theories when studying diversity and aging [10]. Three ways of developing theoretical perspectives relevant to diverse aging populations are offered: 1) the use of grounded theory; 2) the use of resources in the humanities (art, music, dance, literature, and folklore) as a basis for understanding and interpreting important themes in the lives of ethnic-minority elderly; and 3) incorporating a life-course perspective (temporal context and interdependence among generations) in the study of ethnic-minority aged. Markides et al. confirm that many new fields of inquiry typically do not have theoretical integration [5, pp. 24-25]. Gerontology has been no exception. The concept of diversity in gerontology must be understood in the context of other theoretical and conceptual outlooks. Before that can be achieved, it must be accepted that social and behavioral studies in gerontology have not been carried out to the extent that research on clinical and biological aspects have been studied and embraced. Social gerontologists continue to focus on predicting adaptation or adjustment in old age, while considering measures of well-being, such as moral, life satisfaction, and mental health. Very little has evolved during the past half century to adequately explain the impact of an aging population, as an aggregate, on society. Diversity as a catalyst for change is an appropriate vehicle to further examine the direct and indirect impact of diverse populations on society.

Diversity among populations and age groups, in its truest form, serves as a mechanism for examining the many facets and variations among groups. The added dimension of culture provides a patterned way of thinking, perceiving, believing, acting, communicating, and evaluating [11]. More than national origin, this is an expanded view of culture as a reflection of a shared outlook of a group. Any group with sufficient cohesion may be associated with its own unique culture. Accordingly, one can refer to various types of cultures formed along lines of racial, ethnic, professional, organizational, and even age-group identification. Individuals perform multiple social roles as members of multiple cultures [12].

Using the premise that diversity is a major catalyst for change, the earlier expressed ideas of Waiet et al. [12], diverse aged individuals may have a more potent impact on how society is shaped and values established. Other's interaction with the older population may no longer be based on former expectations of individuals outside the age group(s). Interaction patterns may be more formally arranged, based on what the older population expects. The shift may be slow and subtle, but may come about because of cultural expectations and gradual deference paid to older individuals. Several scholars have advanced theoretical ideas to explain social and behavioral actions as individuals age. Had the basic research and/or ideologies which spawned the original theoretical notions been attentive to the need for the inclusion of diversity from a cultural, gender, and environmental perspective, it would have been possible to have made diversity an intricate part of the theoretical discussion.

RESEARCH AS AN ANCHOR

The prominence of research in explaining the many facets of diversity, aging, and social change has not reached its potential. To carefully explain the genesis of behavior and, therefore, expectations of older people of diverse, cultural, and ethnic backgrounds within the context of the present society, extensive research is needed. The type of research relied upon may not be the most effective or efficient research to fully understand and document the role of diversity as exemplified and represented within diverse aged populations.

Social scientists can no longer reasonably take the position that research methods used for larger less complex populations are as effective for smaller and often more complex groups. It has taken several decades for many "purists" in the social science research community to acknowledge that their approaches to data gathering and, therefore, evaluation as related to diverse ethnic populations may of necessity vary from their normal mode(s) of operating. For example, it is not uncommon for a researcher to be in the position of having to examine all available subjects represented by a population group in order to establish a reasonable sample from which to discuss the findings in an appropriate manner.

During the past two decades, minor signs of movement beyond traditional discipline oriented research methods and procedures have been vaguely visible. The involvement of those who understand the need to delve into the intra-operational facet of groups from a political, economic, social, and behavioral standpoint have helped make the case for analyzing small groups of diverse individuals using a combination of qualitative and quantitative methods. When appropriately applied, these approaches have not diluted the quality nor significance of findings. In fact, the reliability of the findings are enhanced, because of the depth of understanding afforded by the approaches used. Burton et al. suggested that the primary method for generating knowledge and information about minority older persons has been cross-sectional survey research [10]. They further acknowledge that this research has been a bountiful source for descriptive information, but has not provided the conceptual foundation needed to develop culturally relevant theories of diversity and aging. Most survey research including ethnic/diverse older persons examines relationships between constructs derived from studies of white middle-class aged populations; however, the major exception is the National Survey of Black Americans [12].

The grounded theory approach, in combination with survey research, has made it possible to generate culturally relevant concepts. Grounded theory provides a pathway for theoretical concepts and constructs to emerge from the data. The grounded theory approach has been used in qualitative research to systematically identify and highlight relationships among variables. The significance is that the constructs and relationships among variables are thought to be relevant to the diverse group, because they emerge from the agendas and meanings which are assigned by the respondents to the phenomena under consideration [10, p. 69].

Scholars from diverse cultural and ethnic backgrounds have been persistent in their argument that research on diverse groups of older persons enriches conceptualizations of aging phenomena generally [13, p. 242]. Jackson also highlights that the literature emphasizes simple racial comparisons that have affected the investigation of importance within group differences and a clearer understanding of the significance of racial status for well-being [13]. He suggests that there are three important influences on aging processes that have received attention in work on minority elderly. They are social system forces, cultural factors, and life-span issues.

Research on diverse cultural elder groups has begun to highlight the claim that many of the theories and methodological approaches to gathering data are not fully relevant to some minority groups. Jackson argues that there is evidence disputing the proposed universality of the disengagement process and its normative basis [13, p. 244]. Research on older blacks provides an example for demonstrating the variability of aging processes and the presence of a different set of cultural values. Specifically, it is suggested that older African Americans, as a group, hold more positive attitudes toward their own aging and regard the elderly with respect. Research has a vital role in determining the direction of change for diverse populations and also affecting the degree to which diverse populations bring about change. Much of the potency evolves from the impact of research on social and economic policy. When data are convincing enough, change may emerge as a result of political and social interest through policy, revision, and manipulation. As research in the area of ethnicity, age, and diversity evolves, there is likely to be more attention given to the volumes of data addressing conditions and situations of diverse populations and the effect of those populations on society.

CONSUMER PERSUASION

Demographics and research clearly show the direction in which many key operational elements in society must move to facilitate the lifestyles of a major segment of the population. Population aging is destined to be reckoned with on all fronts, regardless of the lag created by many in responsible social, political, and economic positions. The greater aggregation of older persons in society will drive the direction in which many organizations and institutions move. Further, the "power" exhibited by older persons from many backgrounds will be manifest in ways previously unimagined. One area in which older persons will influence change is as consumers. Not only will older persons, in general, have a major influence on the marketplace, those from diverse backgrounds will have a telling influence on the types of products in demand in their various communities. Although assimilation and acculturation will account for a high degree of sameness in some areas, the diverse life patterns and expectations within groups will also retain a reasonable profile that will distinguish groups.

As major contributors to the work force, and as a more significant force as consumers, older people will help dictate the configuration of the work force and available goods and services. Vaidyanathan [14, p. 555] pointed out that having a high proportion of older persons in the work force can result in obsolescence of skills at a time when rapid technological change is taking place, unless opportunities are made for older workers to upgrade their skills. Many diverse ethnic middle-age older workers do not have highly honed skills which may become obsolete. They may need training in the use of basic technology prior to being introduced to more sophisticated methods in the work place.

As all older consumers become more central to the force of change as diverse individuals, there must be more attention given to their various roles in the community. One emerging role is that of caregiver, both as formal support persons and informal. It is necessary to impress upon trainers and educators to be more aware of the skills needed to meet the physical and psycho-social needs of older diverse clients. Both the client and the potential caregiver must be focused upon as the consumer. As consumers, they will of necessity need information, material goods, technical support, and skills that commensurate with their expectations, as well as their immediate and unique needs. Selker insists that consumer and family education are important elements as attention for care shifts to the community [15].

Older citizens of diverse backgrounds, as consumers, make their presence known in ways that go far beyond their influence on materials and services. As diverse elders become more entrenched and effective in manipulating political system(s), they will become an important link in the chain of events that make diversity a powerful catalyst for change. Their numbers and political acumen will challenge traditional wisdom. Most communities have not had to seriously consider the influence of diverse elders as consumers of community politics. As they become more aware of the effect of their involvement and participation they will demand more access to the political arena as social minded consumers.

Torres-Gil [16, p. 53] was clear in his assessment regarding access to the political arena by older diverse individuals. He pointed out that access is broad in scope in that it takes into consideration the legal, physical, social, and environmental barriers to participation in areas such as education, health, income, and choice of residence. Older consumers are inadvertently bringing about change as they participate in the political process; however, the major concern is that their basic physical and social needs are met. Torres-Gil further indicates that without sufficient food, good health, and an adequate income to buy basics, the older individual will not be able to be concerned with politics. If an individual must concentrate the majority of his or her energies on survival, they cannot be effective consumers of politics.

Estes' [17, pp. 20-21] words resonate vigorously as she cogently outlines how political and economic conditions help determine how social problems, including those of the aged, are defined and dealt with. She relates that when the economy is expanding, optimism is plentiful and resources for dealing with problems are likely to increase, while in times of sparse resources, inadequate programs are likely to be produced and their failure predictable. This scenario has brought about cynical thinking and therefore the rationale for dismissing efforts to induce social change and limit resources that assist disadvantaged older persons. As consumers of programs developed through the Older Americans Act and other human service policies, diverse elders, those with disabilities, women, and ethnic elders have every reason to lack confidence in hollow promises. The notion that as consumers with insufficient economic resources, many diverse elders find themselves living in undesirable environments unable to meet their basic health and traditional needs is further sanctioned by Williams [18, pp. 146-147].

Most ordinary older citizens do not value their composite strengths as power brokers in the political, economic, or social milieu. Estes' insights related to power and participation have been extremely helpful [17, pp. 199-200]. She suggests that legislative enactment's and government policies determine the degree of formal and discretionary power given to those who plan and operationalize policies. This practice regarding who has power in areas of policy may serve to reduce the need for participation by some groups, while dramatically increasing the need for involvement by others. It becomes evident that the provision of participatory roles for diverse elders does not automatically mean there is power. To be effective as a part of the change process, diverse elders must understand the differences between the various aspects of participatory power. Alford and Freidland make distinctions between categories of participatory power which are: 1) participation without power—symbolic power; 2) participation with power—access to officials and regulatory bodies; and 3) power without participation—systemic or structural power [19].

POLICIES RULE

Social policies which impact the lifestyles of older people and others from diverse backgrounds will continue to have a profound impact on the degree to which the elderly are full partners in the development of the society of the twenty-first century and beyond. The elderly, as a major link in the diversity chain, will demand a level of attention that will place them in a position of respectability and power that has not been in evidence to date. Well established policies and the politics of establishing policies will of necessity change given the nature and backgrounds of those involved. A torrid change in policies affecting the ambiance of our social situation would come about due to the surge in the older population and the percentage consisting of individuals from diverse, cultural, and ethnic backgrounds.

Policies that reflect the care of older persons as a diverse group span several political and historical periods in our society. Kutzik highlights the colonial period where public assistance was provided by politically organized communities [20]. Care and treatment was provided to members of the community who needed it and this sympathetic and generous treatment was largely due to the fact that it was an ethnic social institution in which both those receiving and those providing assistance, from overseers of the poor to Almshouse staff, were nearly always of the same English (Protestant) background [20].

Markides et al. emphasize that it took the Great Depression of the 1930s, followed by the enactment of the Social Security Act of 1935, to make drastic changes in the ethnic character of aid for the poor and older persons [5]. As grand as the Social Security Act is, the assumptions behind the original program have not worked to the advantage of many culturally diverse individuals. The initial concept was built on the notion of social insurance. This meant that payments into the social security program by the individual were to be premiums for a benefit that was to be received upon retirement. The benefit upon retirement was looked upon as an insurance against a major reduction in income as a consequence of retirement. As history has shown, large numbers of older persons from diverse cultural backgrounds have not had the luxury of having employment situations which would make them eligible for social security. The 1960s represented a major ground swell for policies which would influence change from a diversity and cultural perspective. The Older Americans Act, Medicare, Medicaid, the Economic Opportunity Act, and the Community Mental Health Center Act were among the major laws passed during the 60s. None was as important in affecting the lifestyles of older people as the Older Americans Act of 1965. The Older Americans Act brought about the first real national policy effort to develop programs exclusively for older people [4, 17].

In its initial form, the Older Americans Act was rather mute and blind to nearly all aspects of diversity. It is fair to say that those involved in the initial development of the law were striving to address the needs of older people from a generic perspective. In doing so, the generic perspective was not inclusive of those who may have been outside the mainstream. Therefore, the implementation of the law had severe shortcomings as it pertained to those from various ethnic and cultural backgrounds. It was not until the early to mid-1970s, when amendments were included to specify targeting services to minority elders, that they began to reap some of the positive benefits of the act.

To insure that diverse older persons are a part of the force for change, there must be opportunities for input into policy and legislation. Elders from diverse cultural backgrounds must be involved in activities that exemplify their uniqueness and diverse life patterns [4, p. 46]. Torres-Gil [16, p. 28] indicates that political participation has translated into the development of senior citizen political movements and age-based organizations. He further asserts that a variety of movements and organizations have been developed to advocate for older persons and they have had a dramatic impact on the formulation and implementation of public policy.

Connolly says, "The classical theory of pluralism . . . portrays the system as a balance of power among overlapping economic, religious, ethnic, and geographical groupings . . ." [21, pp. 3, 13]. Estes correctly frames the discussion surrounding pluralism when she points out that policy issues and alternatives cannot be appropriately examined without fully considering the political process that created and sustains the basic law [17]. She asserts that pluralism in the political process and the role and influence it provides for special interests and ambiguous legislative mandates are causes for the breakdown in the Older Americans Act as a full-service act for all diverse population groups. A salient point is that policies derived from bargaining among interest groups cannot be assumed to be the product of open and fair competition, nor can it be assumed to represent the larger public good [17, p. 72].

Policy as a central element in the matrix of diversity as a catalyst for change will be sharpened by the input of advocates from diverse cultural backgrounds. As the aged population continues to diversify, future policies will reflect their input, perhaps as special interest groups within the aged population. With greater influence and power at the community level through advisory groups and task forces, diverse groups of older persons will have a stronger voice in shaping legislation.

CONCLUSIONS

Older persons, as a significant element in the matrix for diversity, emerge as a major determinant in the aggregate force of diversity as a catalyst for change. The diverse nature of the elder population further magnifies the significance of roles older people play in shaping the future diverse society. Education, training, and research are major areas of consideration as diversity and the older person are viewed as major cohorts in the chain of events that bring about change from a diverse perspective. In addition to the aforementioned areas, the impact of diverse elders as consumers and emerging participants in the political process must be understood in order to take full advantage of their power as catalysts for change.

To better understand the status of diverse elders, as relevant entities in the diversity matrix as catalysts for change, religion, caregiving roles, and social support must be taken into consideration. Social support and caregiving are core elements in the matrices of social change for diverse aging populations. Antonucci expresses social supports as "interpersonal transactions involving key elements such as aide, affect, or affirmation" [22]. Lockery cautions, "the informal support network of the racial and ethnic minority (family, friends, and neighbors, particularly the family) has been the fulcrum of their social integration. Later in life this same support system becomes the primary source of caregiving for the older racial and ethnic minority adult" [23, p. 59]. Educators, researchers, legislators, and service providers must learn to appreciate the substantial diversity in caregiving and social support systems across cultural and ethnic groups. Within this context, there should be a greater appreciation for the degree to which inter-generational variations sway the type of care.

Coke and Twaite confirm the notion that religion is important in the lives of many diverse older individuals [24]. Religion and spirituality will be significant factors in determining the ease of acceptance of change on the part of many diverse elders. In particular, religion may temper the level of leadership provided by diverse elders to bring about change in certain practices that may negatively reflect on their religious beliefs. Nevertheless, religion continues to be on the leading edge of the factors that influence the lives of diverse older persons. For many, it is the primary element that symbolizes strength and forbearance. Religion is also said to be a predictor of life satisfaction among both the general population and older individuals. It is important that religion continues to be a focal point for providing strength to diverse elders as they participate voluntarily or involuntarily in the sometimes turbulent vestiges of social change.

As the population of diverse elders becomes more educated and aware of their power base, they will exhibit greater influence over political decisions and directions. As diverse elders begin to become more aware of the need for them to be involved politically, they will be powerful forces in shaping the political agenda at the community level. This will represent a major change for politics. For some diverse cultural groups of elders, their ability to communicate more effectively in English will be a factor in their political power base. As previous barriers that prevented full participation are removed, diverse elders will not only pursue the opportunity to be involved in the change process, but will of necessity be at the center of the process, primarily because of their numbers.

The dreams, hopes, and expectations of diverse elders are no different than anyone of any age in the main stream of society. The difference is that many diverse elders understand that their potential for having a major positive impact on change as diverse individuals is minimized. Their histories speak clearly to the barriers and deficits that have been a part of their life course. It is through older persons from diverse cultural backgrounds that we may most clearly see diversity as a catalyst and opportunity for quality change in society. Older diverse individuals have the best perspective for the future because of their experiences, insight, and hindsight.

If diversity is to be seriously considered as a major catalyst for change with older diverse individuals at the center, a commitment must be made at all levels of society. It is important to honor the dignity, wisdom, and courage of diverse older persons who have provided the foundation for our existence. Without their myriad experiences and a high level of tolerance for injustices, younger and middle-aged diverse individuals would not be able to effectively become a part of the catalyst for change as diverse individuals. Again, it is through the respect for "diverse life patterns," that positive change will evolve. Without mutual respect for diverse life patterns and experiences, there will be very little on which to build. Diversity as a catalyst for change is well rooted and will continue to blossom as a major force in our society.

REFERENCES

1. S. Bass, E. Kutza, and F. Torres-Gil, Challenges Facing Planners and Policy Makers in the 1990s, in *Diversity in Aging,* Professional Books on Aging, Scott, Foresman and Company, Illinois, 1990.
2. P. Stanford and C. Schmidtke, Diversity: A Prism of Strength, *AGHExchange, 17*:4, pp. 1-2, 1994.
3. P. Stanford and F. Torres-Gil, Diversity and Beyond: A Commentary, *Generations, XV*:4, pp. 5-6, 1991.
4. E. P. Stanford, Diverse Black Aged, in *Black Aged Understanding Diversity and Service Needs,* Z. Harel, E. McKinney, and M. Williams (eds.), Sage, Newbury Park, California, 1990.
5. S. Markides, K. Mindel, and C. Mindel, Aging and Ethnicity, *Sage Library of Social Research* (Vol. 163), Sage, Newbury Park, California, 1987.
6. D. E. Hayes-Bautista, Young Latinos, Older Anglos, and Public Policy: Lessons from California, *Generations, XV*:4, pp. 37-38, 1991.
7. E. P. Stoller and R. C. Gibson, *Worlds of Difference—In Equality and the Aging Experience,* Pine Forge Press, Thousand Oaks, California, 1994.
8. E. P. Stanford, Diversity as a Social Force in an Aging Society, *Diversity and Long-Term Care News, 1*:2, pre-summer 1994.
9. National Association of Social Workers, *Social Work with Older People: Understanding Diversity,* Washington, D.C., 1993.
10. L. M. Burton, P. Dilworth-Anderson, and V. L. Bengtson, Theoretical Challenges for the Twenty-First Century—Creating Culturally Relevant Ways of Thinking About Diversity and Aging, *Generations, XV*:4, pp. 67-72, 1991.

11. W. H. Goodenough, *Description and Comparison of Cultural Anthropology,* Aldine, Chicago, 1970.
12. M. S. Waiet, J. O. Harker, and L. I. Messerman, Interdisciplinary Team Training and Diversity Problems, Concepts and Strategies, *Gerontology and Geriatrics Education, 15*:1, p. 73, 1994.
13. J. S. Jackson (ed.), *The Black American Elderly, Research on Physical and Psycho Social Health,* Springer, New York, 1988.
14. K. E. Vaidyanathan, Some Key Indicators on the Economic Aspects on Aging, in *Population Aging: International Perspectives,* T. M. Shuman, E. P. Stanford, A. S. Harbert, M. G. Schmidt, and J. L. Roberts (eds.), San Diego State University, San Diego, California, pp. 554-563, 1993.
15. L. G. Selker (Guest ed.), The Implications of an Aging Society for Health Care Needs, *Journal of Allied Health, 16*:4, p. 321, 1987.
16. F. M. Torres-Gil, *Politics of Aging Among Elder Hispanics,* University Press of America, Inc., Washington, D.C., 1982.
17. C. L. Estes, *The Aging Experience,* Jossey-Bass, San Francisco, 1979.
18. M. Williams, African American Elderly Experiences with Title II—Programs Assumptions and Economic Well-Being, in *Black Aged—Understanding Diversity and Service Needs,* Z. Harel, E. A. McKinney, and M. Williams (eds.), Sage, Newbury Park, California, pp. 146-147, 1990.
19. R. Alford and R. Friedland, Political Participation and Public Policy, *Annual Review of Sociology, 1,* pp. 429-479, 1975.
20. A. J. Kutzik, American Social Provision for the Aged: An Historical Perspective, in *Ethnicity and Aging: Theory Research and Policy,* D. E. Gelfand and A. J. Kutzik (eds.), Springer, New York, 1979.
21. W. E. Connolly, *The Bias of Pluralism,* Atherton, New York, 1969.
22. T. C. Antonucci, Personal Characteristics, Social Support and Social Behavior, in *Handbook of Aging and the Social Sciences* (2nd Edition), E. Shanas and R. H. Binstock (eds.), Van Nostrand, New York, p. 96, 1985.
23. S. L. Lockery, Family and Social Supports: Caregiving among Racial and Ethnic Minority Elders, *Generations, XV*:4, 1991.
24. M. M. Coke and J. A. Twaite, *The Black Elderly—Satisfaction and Quality of Later Life,* The Haworth Press, Binghamton, New York, pp. 41-44, 1995.

CHAPTER 6

Intergenerational Relationships and Aging: Families, Cohorts, and Social Change

*Vern Bengtson, Timothy Biblarz, Edward Clarke,
Roseann Giarrusso, Robert Roberts,
Judith Richlin-Klonsky, and Merril Silverstein*

Intergenerational relationships are often tense. Relations between age groups, and between younger and older generations within the family, have been the source of both the most serious conflict and the most profound solidarity recorded throughout human history. In Western literature we have, for example, the Biblical accounts of Job and his ungrateful sons; the revolt Jeremiah had to deal with between rebellious youth and the leaders of their parents' generation; and, of course, the problems King David had with his son Absalom, probably the source of several woeful Psalms and certainly the cause of a bloody revolution in David's newly unified kingdom. Added to this is the saga of the unfortunate Oedipus, killing his father and marrying his mother unawares, and (according to the playwright Sophocles) forever cursed as the result; and the mistaken confidence of King Lear in his daughters, leading another playwright (Shakespeare) to cry: "O, the infamy of youth!"

In America, recently the drama of intergenerational relationships—and their subtheme, the negotiation of conflict and solidarity between age groups—may appear more muted than some of yesterday's confrontations, for example those of thirty years ago. During the 1960s, American society appeared to be pulling apart on the basis of cleavages between age groups. Youth during this tumultuous decade were questioning their elders' authority and legitimacy on several ideological battlefields. The results included the civil rights movement, the student movement, the Vietnam anti-war movement, the counter-culture movement, and perhaps the feminist movement [1]. Each and all of these irrevocably changed America's outlook and sociopolitical institutions during the last three decades.

But today, especially as we look toward the new century, the drama in intergenerational relationships is unfolding under new and quite unprecedented circumstances in human society [2]. The circumstances arise out of the worldwide trend of population aging during the last half-century which has resulted in a striking change in the age composition of both societies and families over recent time. The drama involves the interplay between solidarity and conflict as age cohorts and families attempt to adapt to the realities of population aging and the changing relationships of generations in the future.

In this chapter we address three issues in the continuing drama of intergenerational relationships, focusing on families, aging, and social change. Of course the only sensible basis for predicting the future lies in reviewing research concerning past and present conditions and extrapolating them to possible tomorrows. Thus we will draw from recent data concerning: 1) the "American family decline" debate; 2) solidarity and conflict within multigenerational families; and 3) solidarity and conflict between age cohorts. Based on this discussion a model for future research on multigenerational family relationships over time is developed, leading to a speculative forecasting of intergenerational relationships in the early twenty-first century. We conclude that a scenario of less, rather than more, conflict between generations and cohorts is likely in the future.

THE "AMERICAN FAMILY DECLINE" DEBATE

That the family is no longer the important institution it once was in American society has become the orthodox view of many pundits and politicians. That many elderly Americans are isolated from, or abandoned by, the families they have created is a frequent corollary to this view. It was almost three decades ago that Shanas [3] called this a "hydra-headed myth": social scientists with their empirical data lop one head of the stereotype off, only to see a newer myth, also about elders ignored by their families, quickly growing in its place. But today this perception still seems to persist—not only in the mass media, but among scholars outside gerontology as well.

Is the Family Declining?

Popenoe [4, 5] argues that "the family has been stripped down to its bare essentials—just two adults and two main functions: childbearing and the provision of affection and companionship to its members" [5, p. 540]. The result is that Americans today are less willing than ever before to invest time, money, and energy in family life, and are turning more to other groups and activities in this age of the "me-generation": "Adults for their own good purposes, most recently self-fulfillment, have stripped the family down to its nucleus. But any further reduction—either in functions or in number of members—will likely have adverse consequences for children, and thus for generations to come" [5, p. 540].

Among family sociologists, Popenoe's views have touched off spirited debate, and critics of Popenoe's view [6-8] counter with several arguments: 1) His view of "family" rests on an outmoded and conservative structural-functionalist interpretation of what families are, or should be; this minimizes, and in fact scapegoats, non-nuclear families: those with single parents, those without children, or those "unconventional" in other ways. 2) His attribution of change in family structure and function to "a decline in family values" is misplaced or myopic; the growth of other institutions, rather than a lessening in family values, is the principal cause for nuclear family change. 3) But most importantly, in our opinion, is the fact that Popenoe confuses families with households: his definition of family is a "relatively small domestic group of kin (or people in a kin-like relationship) consisting of at least one adult and one dependent child" [5, p. 545], which ignores the substantial evidence of cross-generational kinship support structures that exist between adult children and grandchildren and their parents and grandparents.

Are Elders in Particular Victims of Declining Family Functions?

As applied to the elderly, the "family decline" debate involves several issues: 1) the fragility (or strength) of intergenerational bonds between elders and their descendants; 2) the disengagement (or engagement) of family in care giving for dependent elders; 3) the marginality (or centrality) of kinship roles for family elders; and 4) the rejection (or acceptance) of norms and values of intergenerational cohesiveness. It should be noted that each of these reflect empirical questions, and a good deal of research during the past decade has been carried out to assess these issues.

First, existing research evidence indicates that *intergenerational bonds are perceived as remarkably strong* by most family members in contemporary American society; that this is true for both emotional and instrumental connections involving family elders; and that there are positive consequences for both older and younger generations of such linkages (see research reviews in [9-16]). Several important studies support this conclusion. Rossi and Rossi have documented the extensiveness of intergenerational solidarity (in terms of affect, interaction, and help exchange between generations) in their Boston-area study—providing a model for the complexities of "bonding" activities involving older and younger generational kin [17]. Bengtson and Harootyan report data from a nationally representative survey that indicate extensive linkages across generations involving older family members [18]. Elder, Rudkin, and Conger demonstrate the strength of intergenerational ties even during recent economic duress, among Iowa families who lost the "family farm" during the economic downturn of the 1980s [19]. Soldo and Hill [20] document the extensive nature of intergenerational transfers in the recently completed Health and Retirement Survey, as do Eggebeen and Hogan [21] in the National Survey of Families and Households. Silverstein and Bengtson examine the long-term consequences of parent-child solidarity over time in the Longitudinal Study of Generations, and find that close ties enhance not only the psychological well-being but also the survival of aging parents [22, 23]. Roberts and Bengtson found that close relationships with parents is related to self-esteem and psychological well-being of young adults, an effect that lasts into middle age [24, 25].

Second, the voluminous body of research concerning long-term care given to frail elders in American society suggests one principal conclusion: *families are the primary, preferred, and most effective source of support*. Family members provide 60 to 80 percent of long-term care for dependent elderly members, and formal or institutional mechanisms become activated only after family caregiving resources are expended. This is documented in extensive research reviews by Abel [26], Brody [27], Dwyer [28], Gatz, Bengtson, and Blum [29], Maddox and Lawton [30], and Matthews [31] (also see Clair et al., this volume).

Third, it is becoming clear that large numbers of grandparents (and great-grandparents) are playing *central kinship roles.* Many are "surrogate parents," primary care givers to their grandchildren (or great-grandchildren) following the divorce or incapacity (through disease, drugs, AIDS, or incarceration) of the middle generation. Chalfie has demonstrated that an increasing proportion of grandparents are assuming full-time responsibility for their grandchildren: the number of youngsters in households headed by grandparents has increased by over 50 percent since 1970, to more than three million, and in 33 percent of these families neither parent of the grandchild resides in the household [32]. Troll [33] suggests that grandparents are often the "family watchdog," keeping a low profile until a crisis threatens the younger generations; Johnson [34] documents increased involvement with grandchildren following divorce; Burton [35] describes the activities of both grandparents and great-grandparents raising children of drug-addicted parents. Doka and Mertz [36] and Wentowski [37] discuss great-grandparenthood as an increasingly common social role which was virtually unknown only a few decades ago. These kinship functions of elders have been ignored in the "American family decline" arguments to date.

Fourth, *norms and values supporting intergenerational connections* appear to have high salience for most Americans today—contrary to conventional wisdom about the detachment of "Generation X" from such linkages [38]. Recent data from national and cross-national surveys [18, 39] provide evidence for strong normative support of cross-generational linkages, reflecting equally strong values about the desirability of such connections.

THE FAMILY LEVEL: SOLIDARITY AND CONFLICT WITHIN MULTIGENERATIONAL FAMILIES

By now we have many reviews of studies concerning multigenerational families, and these uniformly conclude that the evidence points to considerably greater inter-generational *solidarity* than is commonly assumed in contemporary debates [40-43]. However, none of these reviews have indicated very much about interpersonal *conflicts* within aging families. Nor have proponents of the "American family decline" position ever argued that intergenerational conflict has played a role in the downfall of the extended family. This is a surprising omission given the widespread trend of population aging during the last half-century. With family members living longer and having many more years of shared lives and shared relationships with kin, there exists today a greater potential for "long-term lousy relationships" [2] between parents and children, grandparents and grandchildren, than in previous eras of family history. However, results from our long-term study demonstrate that intergenera-tional family relationships evidence *both* solidarity *and* conflict over time, supporting the proposition that American families are considerably more resilient and functional than their contemporary critics suggest.

The Longitudinal Study of Generations

Since the data and examples cited throughout this section come from the Longitudinal Study of Generations (LSOG), we begin with a description of the methods and procedures of this research. The study began in 1971 with data from 2,044 individuals—grandparents, their middle-aged children, and their young-adult grandchildren aged sixteen to twenty-six—who were surveyed concerning their perceptions of intergenerational relationships as well as their values, opinions, and well-being [44]. The population from which the study sample was obtained represented 840,000 employee members and their dependents enrolled in the first large HMO established in California in the 1950s. Most were beneficiaries of labor union health benefits packages negotiated in the rapidly-expanding postwar manufacturing boom in Southern California, resulting in a sample which is of working-class background, with stable employment history since WW II, and 90 percent white (a figure consistent with the distribution of labor-union families in southern California at that time, although certainly less ethnically diverse than the region is today).

The 1971 cross-generational survey has become a longitudinal investigation of family relationships, aging, and social change since three-year survey assessments were begun in 1985.

Table 1 provides the numbers of participants in each survey of the Longitudinal Study of Generations. As can be seen, there is sample attrition over time, due mostly to the deaths of grandparent (G1) generation family members. We have added a fourth generation, the great-grandchildren of the original grandparents, beginning in 1991, as eligible G4s turned age sixteen.

(Our sample was drawn from a prepaid medical group program which started with Kaiser steel mill workers in Los Angeles and Fontana during the 1950s.) However, an important minority of families represented in the sample are from Hispanic-, African-, Asian-, and Native-American ethnic backgrounds.

Is There a "Generation Gap" in Perceptions About the Intergenerational Relationship?

In pilot testing twenty-five years ago for the first LSOG survey, we were struck by what appeared to be a "generational bias" in perceptions. Why were parents and children far apart in their views of their common relationship? Descriptions of relationships *downward* in the generational chain—toward children—were consistently more positive than reports of relationships *upward*—toward parents.

We proposed what we called the "developmental stake hypothesis" to explain these findings [45]. Our data indicated that middle-aged parents consistently reported higher levels of closeness, interaction, and consensus in the parent-child relationship, relative to the perceptions of their adolescent and young adult children, who reported

Table 1. Cross-Sectional and Longitudinal Samples

| | Cross-Sectional | | | | | | | | | | Longitudinal Sample 1971-1994 | |
| | Time-1 1971 | | Time-2 1985 | | Time-3 1988 | | Time-4 1991 | | Time-5 1994 | | | |
	N	$\bar{X}$ Age	N	$\bar{X}$ Age	N	$\bar{X}$ Age	N	$\bar{X}$ Age	N	$\bar{X}$ Age	N	$\bar{X}$ Age
G1:												
Male	266	68	91	79	64	81	44	83	27	86	34	84
Female	250	66	130	77	111	79	93	83	75	86	76	83
G2:												
Male	322	46	243	59	240	61	204	65	213	68	147	65
Female	379	42	313	56	327	59	291	62	311	64	220	62
G3:												
Male	385	20	226	33	313	36	297	40	280	43	122	40
Female	442	19	328	33	427	35	401	39	386	41	221	39
G4:												
Male	—	—	—	—	—	—	82	20	111	22	—	—
Female	—	—	—	—	—	—	117	20	179	22	—	—
Total N:	2044		1331		1482		1529		1582		820	

lower levels. We suggested that such systematic contrasts emerge because each of the generations—some thirty years apart in individual life-course transitions—have different developmental concerns, and in consequence a different "stake" or invest-ment in their mutual relationship. We reasoned that the developmental stake of the older generation centers on continuity and transmission, while the quite different developmental stake of the younger generation focuses on autonomy and innovation. The contrast between these developmental stakes provides an important mechanism for differences observed between parents and young adult children in perceptions of their common solidarity.

Twenty years later, we have revisited what we now call the *intergenerational stake hypothesis* with longitudinal data [46]. Our goal was to examine whether the phenomenon of generational bias persists over time, with the aging of parents and their now middle-aged children. These data are summarized in Figure 1.

Perhaps the most striking thing to note is that the affectual solidarity average scores—based on a five-item index with high internal reliability—are high, and considerably over the expected midpoint of the scale: response distributions are skewed in the positive direction. Second, the mean scores are remarkably consistent over the four measurement points. There are no significant differences between 1971, 1988, 1989, and 1991 for any of the parent-child dyads, and correlations over time range between .5 and .8. Third, there is indeed empirical support for the intergenera-tional stake hypothesis: parents consistently report higher affect than their children,

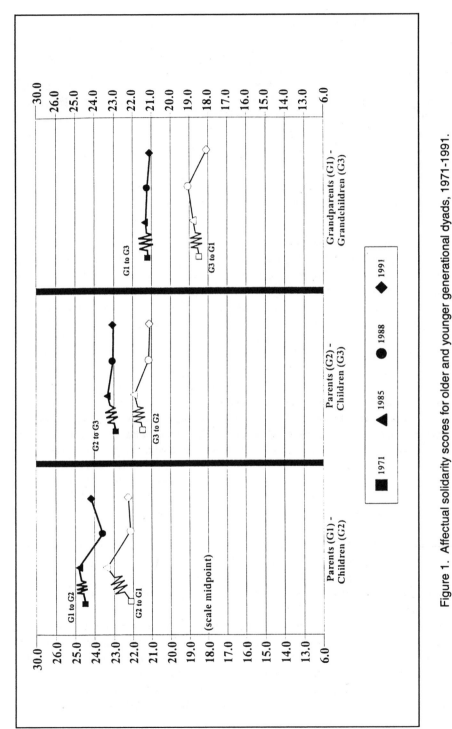

Figure 1. Affectual solidarity scores for older and younger generational dyads, 1971-1991.

and the magnitude of such difference does not change much from one time of measurement to another. This is even more evident for grandparent-grandchild dyads, with the grandparents' perceptions of affectual solidarity considerably higher than grandchildren's at each point of time.

Thus, there appear to be systematic differences in older and younger generation's perceptions of their joint relationship across the life course: the older generation's perception of affection is consistently higher than the younger generation's. That this occurs for all three generations at all four times of measurement suggests that the perceptual gap may be universal and not evidence of historic decline in family solidarity.

Transmission of the "American Dream" Across Three Generations

Another way of examining historic decline (or continuity) in family solidarity is to assess the extent to which values, status, and behaviors are transmitted or perpetuated from one generation to the next. A lack of intergenerational transmission over time would not only indicate the family's failure to reproduce or modify the social structure through the socialization of children, but also sets the stage for potential conflict by creating a "generation gap" in values and orientations [44]. Thus, a second dimension of the debate over "American family decline" [5] concerns how social changes in the recent twentieth century have affected family transmission of socioeconomic and cultural resources.

To explore this question, we examined within-family socioeconomic attainment and the intergenerational transmission of socioeconomic levels over time [47]. We compared the level of inheritance of occupational stratum experienced by three successive generations of offspring in the LSOG: grandparents (G1s), who inherit great grandparents' (G0s) socioeconomic positions; parents (G2s), who inherit G1s socioeconomic positions; and adult children (G3s), who inherit G2s' socioeconomic positions (the analysis of a fourth generation, the G4s, is currently under way).

In this analysis we focused on the implications of four twentieth-century social changes—expanding universalism, a shift in childrearing values from obedience to autonomy, the growth of alternative family structures, and changing gender role attitudes—for intergenerational social mobility. We predicted that 1) each successive generation would have higher occupational attainments than the one before; and 2) the effect of parents' statuses on children's occupational outcomes would decline with each successive generation.

We found that each successive generation of offspring in the LSOG sample had higher occupational attainment than the one before, but that the rate of upward mobility slowed across generations. That is, the association between parents' socioeconomic stratum and children's socioeconomic stratum weakened across generations (independent of structural shifts in the distributions of occupations). G3s were less likely than G2s (who, in turn, were less likely than G1s) to stay in or remain near the same socioeconomic stratum they were born into.

Using the LSOG to track intergenerational transmission of occupations, we found these normative patterns: In the early 1900s, many white families and individuals immigrated to Southern California. The men worked primarily in farming, manufacturing, and other manual occupations. Their children (who represent the first generation sampled in the LSOG—the G1s) moved out of farming, and became concentrated in blue collar, manufacturing occupations. In turn, their children—the next generation (G2s)—crossed the line from manual to nonmanual work. They moved out of production and into the white collar work world as clerks, managers, technicians, administrators, and professionals. Many of their children—the third generation (G3s)—in turn became concentrated in the higher echelons of the white collar work world, as professionals and managers. At the family level, the processes described mean that adult children in the LSOG have tended to occupy positions in the social structure that are different (and typically "higher") than the positions occupied by their parents, and that are very different than the positions occupied by their grandparents.

These patterns suggest a decline in family transmission of social position to offspring over three and four generations, perhaps reflecting a more meritocratic opportunity structure and greater availability of education in the United States over the twentieth century. Increasing individualization would appear to support the decline of the family's role as an economic engine in society. In the language of Bengtson's original paper, the "generation gap" in social class may be widening [44]. This increase in intergenerational fluidity of social class inheritance may, of course, come at the expense of family integration. However, at the same time families may have played an important role in socializing children to adopt values that legitimate and encourage occupational mobility from their social class of origin.

The Paradoxes of Multigenerational Families Over Time

These group-level statistics, reflecting the large-scale survey research program, present a disembodied picture of the families who comprise the LSOG. For that reason we want to describe one of our multigenerational families, the "Potters" [48], and use the changes they have experienced over the past quarter-century to highlight what we consider to be an enduring theme of multigenerational family life over several decades: "drifting apart" and "pulling together" in response to individual development, family events, and social structural change.

The Potters' multigenerational family structure when the LSOG began in 1971 is depicted in Figure 2. The grandfather is G1 Robert Potter Sr., then age sixty-nine, a house painter who had divorced his first wife Leah, the mother of this three children, two decades earlier. Baseline survey data came from him and from his three G2 children: Robert Jr. (then age 45), Roberta (age 43), and Maria (age 38). In addition, seven grandchildren (G3s) provided responses to the 1971 survey—including David, Maria's twenty-year-old son, who filled out his survey from prison. Thus, this one multigenerational family provided a complex array of survey data concerning intergenerational structures and relationships. Moreover, they appeared to be a family with considerable intergenerational conflict; their scores on our measures of

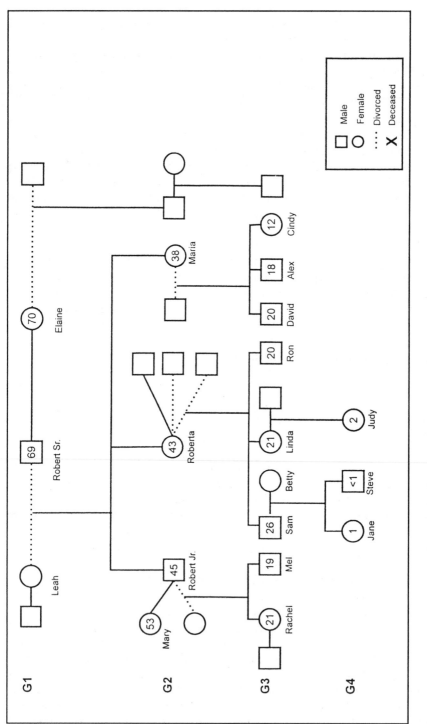

Figure 2. The "Potter" multigenerational family at the beginning of the study in 1971.

intergenerational solidarity appear to be much lower than most in our 1971 survey. For example, Robert Potter Sr. indicated he had no contact with Maria, his youngest daughter, for some time; there appeared to be feelings of estrangement up and down the generational ladder. In short, at the time of our baseline (1971) survey, this family appeared to be "drifting apart" across generational boundaries [48].

In 1991, twenty years later in our longitudinal study, the Potter family structure is even more complex, as can be seen in Figure 3. In the G1 generation, Robert Sr. is still alive at the age of eighty-nine, having outlived his first wife, Leah, and his second wife, Elaine. In the G2 generation, Robert Jr. has died, as has Roberta's second husband. In the G3 generation there have been marriages, divorces, remarriages, and one death (David's, at the age of 38, a few years after his release from prison). A G4 generation of adults has emerged. And there are two G5s, great-great grandchildren in Robert Sr.'s lineage; Roberta, age sixty-two, is now a great-grandparent.

Moreover, as we examine both survey and interview data from the Potter family members in the interval since 1971, another theme emerges: "pulling together" over time, especially in response to health crises of older and younger generation members [48].

What can be summarized about such family intergenerational relationships over time, given the complex changes in their intergenerational structures over two decades? We conclude the following:

The Potter family demonstrates that levels of interpersonal closeness—of solidarity—are neither consistent across the many relationships which constitute a family or constant over the years they share together. Even within this single family, we see the diverse possibilities for types of family relationships. From person to person, from subsystem to subsystem, the place and meaning of "family" varies among the Potters. At any given point, some members' lives are closely woven together, as they actively share care-giving alliances or family traditions. Others hang on by a thread, connected to the family by their relationship with just one other member . . . [And] family relations are not static: members who are estranged at one point may well reestablish relations later on, while close ties may ultimately be severed. Furthermore, the evolution of family life is not linear. Over time the Potters become closer and more distant, and back again, within and between generations [48 p. 277].

The Potters, as a case study of one multigenerational family over time, illustrate an important paradox about the American family: *long-term family relationships evidence both solidarity and conflict,* the balance between which changes across the life course in conjunction with individual development, health crises, changes in marital status, and family life events, all within the context of broader societal changes. The pattern of solidarity or conflict in the family over time is not linear, it is dynamic. The Potter family "comes together" around some issues and at some times (such as caregiving for their elderly family member) but "drifts apart" at other times and in relationship to other issues (such as the divorce of several family members). Notwithstanding the antagonisms and apathies among the Potters, something members recognize as "family" seems to have been maintained across more than two

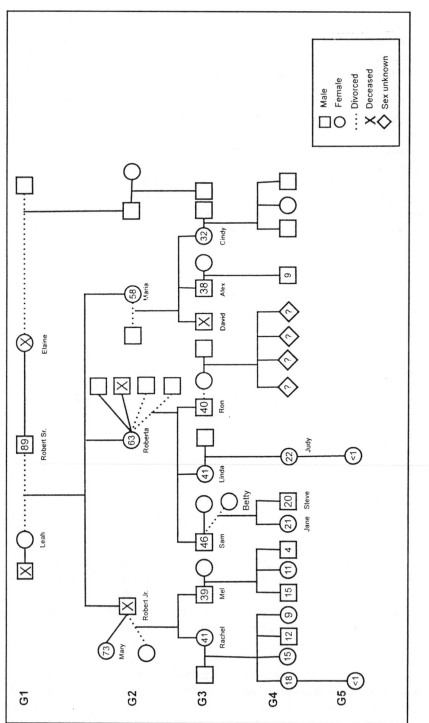

Figure 3. The "Potter" family twenty years later in 1991.

decades through a variety of elastic bonds. Intergenerational families are not static or abstract; rather they are dynamic entities with a constantly changing metabolism. This dynamism perhaps reflects the adaptability of the American family to changing developmental, familial, and social structural circumstances, rather than its decline.

The Dimensions of Intergenerational Conflict

Thus, it is inaccurate to stereotype relationships between parents and their adult children as purely cohesive—as having little or no conflict. Such a view is not supported by our description of the "Potter family" nor by a small, but growing number of studies of intergenerational conflict in later life. These studies document conflict as a common feature of essentially stable adult parent-child relations, especially when parent and child co-reside [49]. Moreover, several important correlates of intergenerational conflict in adulthood have been identified, including: psychological distress of parent and child [50], negative health outcomes [51], and caregiver depression [52] and anger [53, 54].

Research on intergenerational family conflict has been limited, however, by two issues: 1) the reluctance of respondents to report conflict (social undesirability); and 2) the lack of adequate conceptualizations and measurement [55, 56]. In response to the second issue, Clarke et al. (in press) developed a typology of adult intergenerational conflict based on LSOG data [56]. The typology was derived from open-ended responses to the question we have asked of our survey families since 1971: "What do you and your child (or parent) disagree about most these days?" Results indicated that the six most often-mentioned themes or areas of disagreement were (in order of frequency): 1) relational styles within family roles, 2) lifestyle, 3) childrearing, 4) ideology, 5) work habits and orientations, and 6) household labor. These are more fully described in Table 2.

The issues of focal concern to parents and children reflect both sociohistorical and developmental factors. For example, when the LSOG began in 1971, the G3 children (average age was 19) most frequently identified intergenerational conflicts were about ideology (43%) and differences in lifestyle (28%). At that time their G2 parents also noted conflict in these areas, but rated lifestyle differences (35%) as slightly more salient than ideology (28%). By 1991, as both G2s and G3s had grown older over two decades, we noted both similarities and differences in the areas of conflict reported by these parents and children. Among the G3 children (now averaging 39 years old), lifestyle (36%) was the most frequently noted area of conflict, followed by relational style and ideology (both 26%). Their parents (now in their 60s and 70s) also cited concern over family relational style (18%), and they were also as likely to note conflict over lifestyle (18%) and ideology (17%).

Past research has tended to portray families either as places of peace, refuge, and harmony, *or* as places of abuse, anger, and violence. These are extremes and fail to characterize accurately the vast majority of American families today. There appears to be an interplay between dimensions of solidarity and conflict as family members

Table 2. Typology of Intergenerational Conflict
Themes in Later Life

Theme	Description
Family Relational Style	Conflict over relationship expectations and behaviors. • Critical Issues: communication styles, situational responses, interpersonal power, etc.
Lifestyle	Conflict over lifestyle and personal habits. • Critical Issues: appearance, sexuality, substance use or abuse, living arrangements, etc.
Child rearing	Conflict over methods or philosophy of parenting. • Critical Issues: permissiveness vs. control, support and involvement, rules, etc.
Ideology	Conflict over attitudes, ideas, and beliefs. • Critical Issues: religion, ethics, morality, politics, etc.
Work	Conflict over work habits and orientations. • Critical Issues: degree of dedication to work and school performance, etc.
Household Labor	Conflict over distribution of and commitment to household labor. • Critical Issues: housework, yardwork, maintenance, etc.

age, and each are negotiated with the passage of time. Families are typically the source of our greatest pleasure and our greatest pain throughout life. *Both* aspects of intimate relationships—concern, caring, and support on the one hand; or differences, tensions, and anger, on the other—are inevitably part and parcel of the interactions between family members over time, as they grow up and grow old [41]. There can be high solidarity *and* high conflict (what might be termed "enmeshed" or "intense" families) between kin members, just as there can be high solidarity and low conflict (the "placids")—or low solidarity and low conflict ("disengaged"), and finally low solidarity and high tensions ("conflicted").

However, family relationships cannot be understood in isolation: they must be examined in the context of wider demographic, economic, and political trends. Relationships between generations in the family are profoundly affected by demographic changes such as population aging and by macrosocial trends involving tensions or reciprocities between age cohorts. In what ways does the balance between solidarity and conflict for age cohorts have repercussions for multigenerational family relations?

THE COHORT LEVEL: SOLIDARITY AND CONFLICT
BETWEEN AGE COHORTS

The Demographics of Population Aging

Population aging is a worldwide issue. An historical review of America's population aging since 1900 helps to illustrate the rapid changes that have been occurring in industrialized nations during the last century. Figure 4 portrays the age distribution of our country from 1900 to 2030 (projection). At the beginning of the twentieth century, the median age of Americans was twenty-three years; average life expectancy was forty-seven years. In 1900, there were 3.1 million older persons in the United States. One out of every twenty-five Americans was age sixty-five and over, representing 4.1 percent of the total population [57].

The "Baby Boom" which began at the end of World War II resulted in seventy-five million births during the period between 1946-1964. In Figure 4 the effects of the baby boom can be seen as a bulge in the age-population distribution that has been described as the "hour glass" curve or the "pig-in-a-python" phenomenon moving through historical time. These Baby Boomers, who in 2000 will be between thirty-six to fifty-four years old, will contribute to a large expansion of the American elderly population after the year 2011, when the first of them will reach retirement age. By the year 2030 the last of the "Baby Boom" cohorts will have become age sixty-five and older, and they will constitute 18 percent of the U.S. population. Then, after 2030, the rate of increase in the older population will fall sharply as the smaller "Baby Bust" birth cohorts begin to turn age sixty-five. Consequently, dependency ratios—the number in the working age population needed to support each retiree—are expected to increase only through the first quarter of the next century, and then they will begin to stabilize. Inter-cohort tensions over support and care for the elderly may follow a parallel trajectory to that of ratios, with intergenerational conflict increasing and then subsiding by mid-century.

Over 31.1 million people age 65+ were counted in the 1990 U.S. Census, which was ten times more elderly than were alive in 1900. As of 1990, the median age in the United States was thirty-four years, while the average life expectancy of Americans was about seventy-nine years for women and seventy-two years for men [57]. For those who have already reached sixty-five, women can expect to live on average another twenty years; men, another fifteen years [58].

Almost one in eight Americans were aged 65+ as of 1990, representing almost 13 percent of the total population. Between 1990 to 2020, the U.S. older population is projected to increase to some fifty-four million people. By 2020 one in six Americans will be elderly, representing 17 percent of the total population [57]. These projections assume that present mortality rates will persist. However, if people continue to live longer and healthier lives, the projected number of elderly will increase even more [59, 60].

In 1990 the oldest-old, those eighty-five and over, constituted about three million persons and 1.2 percent of the total U.S. population. These "oldest-old" represent the fastest growing age segment of the American population. By 2020 it is projected

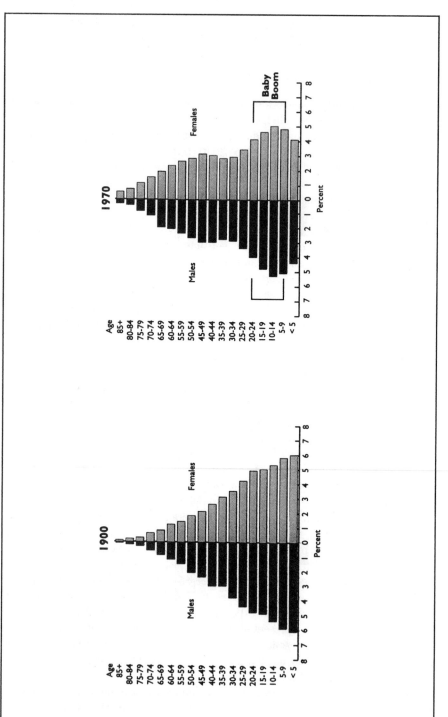

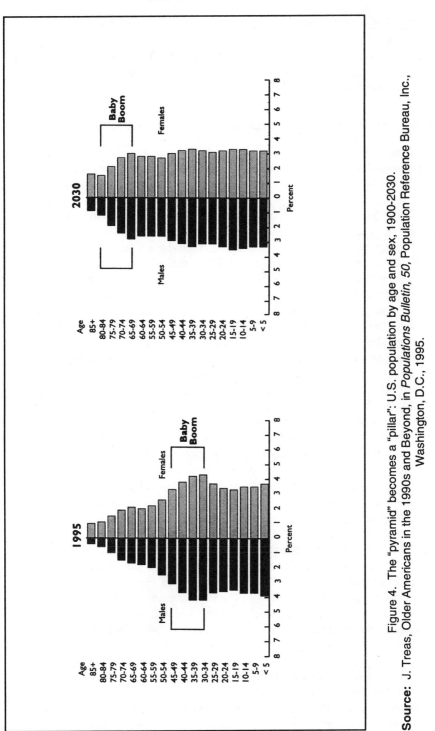

Figure 4. The "pyramid" becomes a "pillar": U.S. population by age and sex, 1900-2030.

Source: J. Treas, Older Americans in the 1990s and Beyond, in *Populations Bulletin, 50,* Population Reference Bureau, Inc., Washington, D.C., 1995.

that the "oldest-old" will increase to about 6.5 million and by 2050, they will have more than doubled, to 17.7 million [61]. The total U.S. elderly population will have grown to about eighty million, which is more than twice the size of the present U.S. elderly population. One of every five, or 20 percent, of all Americans will be elderly in 2050.

The Elderly as "Scapegoats" of Current Economic Problems

These demographic trends have frightened some people, suggesting that our present economic and policy arrangements cannot sustain our increasingly aging population. And this leads to the specter of conflict between generations and age groups.

A headline in the *Los Angeles Times* asked, "Is it fair to tax 20-somethings to pay Social Security and Medicare for their great-grandparents?" [62]. This type of pointed and one-sided commentary has become standard fare in the United States press during the past decade [63]. Similar headlines have warned that the elderly are greedy geezers who are not "footing the bill" for their own costs to society [64], and that "generational economics" [65] are leading to a "financial tug of war" between generations [66]. The cover story for *Worth* magazine said, "They fed you. They clothed you. They love you madly. ARE YOUR PARENTS ROBBING YOU BLIND?" [67]. A recent Sunday news magazine cover story continued the theme: "Golden oldies: The WWII generation got it all. What's left for the rest of us?" [68].

These media images of intergenerational equity conflicts are dramatic, and their use can be a powerful political tool that helps shape sentiment and form public opinion [69]. And, at times, the media can be the source of biased information. Pitting the old against the young ignores the diversity within each group as well as the heterogeneity of their needs. The media crusade aimed at identifying inequities has contributed to the myth that equity between age groups means that funds should be diverted from the elderly to the young, thereby solving all of our nation's economic problems. This over-simplifies the true economic issues, and does so at the expense of achieving real reform in programs that benefit all age groups. Rather than assessing the successful outcomes of old age programs for the elderly, their families, and different age groups—*all old age assistance programs are deemed too costly.*

Are elderly persons in the United States in an advantaged economic position, relative to younger generations? An examination of census data reveals that the rhetoric in the mass media does not match the reality [13]. Poverty, as well as affluence are found among the older population. In Figure 5 we divide elderly Americans into four income groups: 1) The Poor—those with annual incomes below the government poverty line, which in 1989 was $7,495; 2) The Near Poor—individuals with an annual income of no more than 150 percent above the poverty line or $11,250; 3) The Middle Income Group—those with incomes above 150 percent, but less than five times the government poverty line, $37,475; and 4) The Comfortable Group—those with incomes of $37,475 and above—more than 500 percent of the government poverty line.

Figure 5 shows the distribution of elderly men and women across the four income groups. Eight percent of U.S. men aged 65+ and 16 percent of elderly

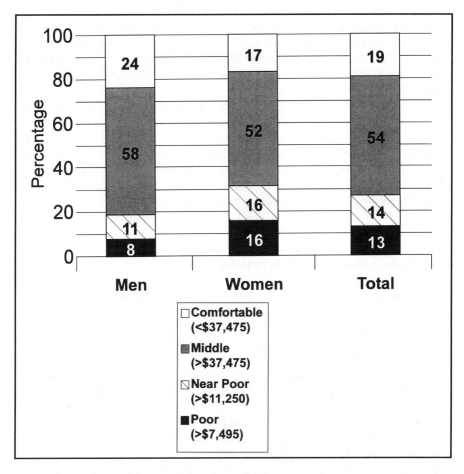

Figure 5. The distribution of "greedy geezers" in the American population: income categories by sex, 1989. **Source:** U.S. Bureau of the Census. 1990 Public Use Microsample Data 5 percent file.

American women are living below the poverty line. The near-poor category comprises 11 percent of men and 16 percent of women. The near-poor are a setback away from slipping into poverty. Nearly 25 percent of elderly men are in the comfortable income category, and only 17 percent of women aged 65+ have comfortable incomes.

Why are there so many poor or near-poor elderly in America? One reason is that Social Security is insufficient to meet the financial needs of the elderly without other, substantial income sources. The intention of Social Security was to be a supplemental retirement benefit, coupled with savings and private pensions. This trebled support was known as the "three-legged stool" of support. When considering men in the aggregate, the three-legged stool does indeed characterize the financial position of men aged sixty-five and over. However, for elderly women Social Security remains the primary source of retirement income. This can be partially attributed to women's weak ties to the U.S. labor market. More than 50 percent of U.S. women aged 75+ are poor, compared to around 45 percent of men aged 75+. The young-old (age 65 to 74) occupy the comfortable income category. This is explained as an outcome of the young-old entering old age with higher levels of educational attainment and economic resources.

So, there are relatively few "greedy geezers" in American society today. Still, how many people—apart from politicians and op-ed writers—feel that the old are getting an unfair advantage in distribution of public money like Social Security and Medicare? How widespread is the perception of generational conflict? The empirical evidence discussed below suggests that actual public sentiment differs from the tone portrayed in media accounts [18]: that is, there is little evidence based on national probability surveys of a "war" escalating between "the generations."

Are Younger Cohorts in Conflict with Older Cohorts Over Policy Issues Across Age Groups?

In 1990, the American Association of Retired Persons fielded a nationwide survey of 1,500 adults, ages eighteen to ninety, to examine perceptions of inter-age inequities and potential conflicts [18]. It was designed to explore various aspects of contemporary "linkages" between age groups and to discern areas in which inter-generational and intercohort stresses or conflicts may exist. The study focused on assistance, emotional, and financial links between adult generations and on the prevailing attitudes, values, and opinions that are related to these behaviors among different birth cohorts.

Data from these respondents were used to assess the degree of perceived con-flicts and tensions between age groups as representatives of different birth cohorts in American society. These tensions and conflicts are usually framed as economic issues surrounding the general principle of "intergenerational equity." Equity was defined in the survey as the perceived well-being of different age groups and the equitable distribution of government benefits among them.

First we examined to what extent age groups differ in their perceptions of the elderly as a group deserving of privileges, and age-based entitlements. Figure 6 shows the percent of each age group that agree and strongly agree with four state-ments. The first reflects the perceived value of older people, that is, whether they contribute to their communities. There is a clear age-cleavage showing that the youngest adults, those age eighteen to twenty-four, are the least likely to agree with this statement. Among age-groups over the age of twenty-five, there were few differences in levels of agreement.

The second statement concerns whether cuts in programs for the elderly are perceived as hurting the public-at-large. Young adults age eighteen to twenty-four are the least likely to agree that "programs for the elderly are linked to the general social welfare." While there are only minor differences among age-groups over twenty-four years old, those sixty-five and older are most likely to *strongly* agree with this statement. These findings demonstrate that the oldest and the youngest adults differ in how they view the interdependence of the aged with other generations.

Third, we asked about perceptions of the fairness of senior citizen discounts. Interestingly, older adults are the *least* likely to endorse such discounts. While overall in this sample there is broad support for senior discounts, the elderly express opinions that appear to be inconsistent with their self-interest. The fourth statement deals with attitudes toward social security as an earned right of the elderly. Here there is nearly perfect concordance among age-groups. However, shades of age-group disagreements are found in that the youngest group of adults are less likely than the elderly to *strongly* support social security as an earned right.

In summary, the results reveal broad support for programs that serve the needs of the aged, with about 80 percent favoring existing policies. However, the relatively weak support expressed by the youngest adults in the sample may be cause for concern. Whether their opinions are the product of their chronological distance from old age, or the product of fears for their generation's future in a period of growing economic uncertainty, cannot be known from these data. Nevertheless, this age-group represents a generational splinter from the otherwise great support for age-based entitlements.

Another issue in the "generational equity" debate concerns whether the elderly benefit from programs in amounts disproportionate to their need. This issue is quite apart from attitudes about the legitimacy of programs and policies designed to help elderly. Do age groups differ in the perception that current levels of spending on the elderly represent a financial burden to society and that the elderly should give more back?

Attitudes toward four statements concerning the perceived injustice in current aging policy is shown Figure 7. A third or less of all respondents feel that programs for older people are too costly. Curiously, both the oldest and youngest adults are most likely to endorse this attitude, while those thirty-five to forty-four are the least likely. When asked whether they think social security benefits should not be taxed, fewer than a third of respondents agreed, but comparing across age groups the youngest adults were most opposed to taxation and the middle-aged the least opposed. These age patterns are duplicated in opinions about whether older people receive more than their fair share of government resources. While fewer than 25 percent of the whole sample agreed with this statement, the elderly are most likely to endorse this position, followed by young-adults. Finally, when respondents were asked to consider whether the elderly are the financially best off age-group, nearly half of those sixty-five years of age and one-third of those eighteen to twenty-five agreed with this statement.

The results from this survey portray great public support for programs and policies serving the needs of the elderly, and weak opposition toward cutting existing levels of benefits. Contrary to views that older people are "greedy geezers," most of the evidence points to altruism on the part of the elderly, who may believe that their benefits unfairly come at the expense of other age-groups. Perhaps the strongest evidence for inter-cohort solidarity is found among the middle-aged adults who exhibit the strongest support for public spending on the elderly. Many of these

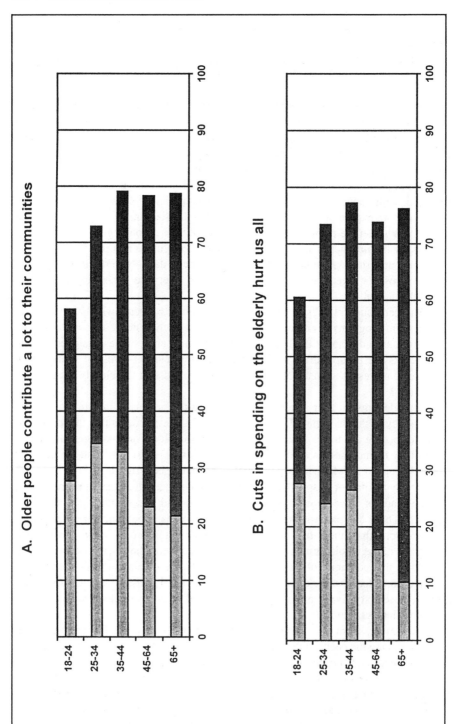

A. Older people contribute a lot to their communities

B. Cuts in spending on the elderly hurt us all

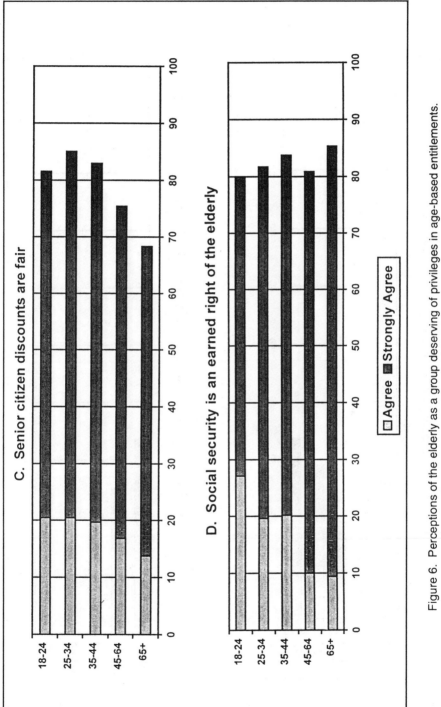

Figure 6. Perceptions of the elderly as a group deserving of privileges in age-based entitlements.

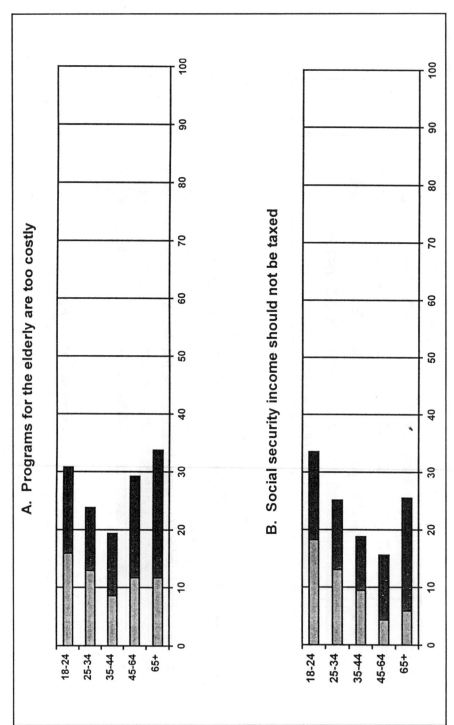

A. Programs for the elderly are too costly

B. Social security income should not be taxed

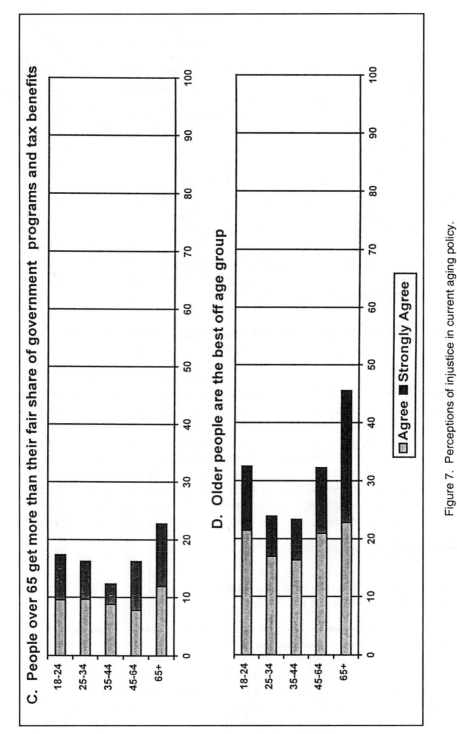

Figure 7. Perceptions of injustice in current aging policy.

middle-aged adults may be caring for older parents, and thus support a strong government commitment to the aged to complement their private contributions.

However, an ominous note for the future may be found in the relatively greater hostility toward entitlement programs for the elderly and age-based public spending among those eighteen to twenty-four years of age. From current data it is unclear whether their negative attitudes are the product of cohort-specific factors (and thus an immutable characteristic of Generation "X" cohort members) or the product of their chronological distance from old age (and thus likely to change with the aging of Generation "X"ers).

In sum, while the AARP survey suggests that as of 1990 there is strong cross-age support of public programs for the elderly, increased tensions may be signaled by the aging and subsequent retirement of the baby-boom generation. If younger adults continue to worry about the prospect of paying more taxes to support a larger and more prosperous generation ahead of it, then the contract between generations, at least at the aggregate or population level, may erode to the point of becoming untenable. However, several factors will likely mitigate such conflict, such as improvements in the nation's economic well-being and continued high levels of personal commitment to older family members.

FORECASTING INTERGENERATIONAL RELATIONSHIPS IN THE EARLY TWENTY-FIRST CENTURY

What, then, are the prospects for generational and age group relations in the future? Is there likely to be more, or less, generational and age group conflict in industrialized societies? Are future age groups likely to support each other? Will there be solidarity and will there be reciprocities?

It is difficult to predict the future, and sociologists have seldom been highly regarded as prophets. Moreover, events that occur in economic and sociopolitical areas—effects exogenous to the process of aging and succession—will determine much of the fate of generational age group conflicts and solidarities in the future. Be that as it may, we can explore some reasons why conflict will be more likely in the next few decades, at least in some Western industrialized societies, and reasons why it will be less likely. Again, micro- and macro-level processes should be differentiated.

The Prospects for Increased Age Group or Generational Conflict in the Future

First, let us list some reasons why there might be an increase in age group or generational conflict between now and 2030 [2]:

1. *Increases in the dependency ratio.* The decline in fertility translates into fewer workers left to support aging retirees. Indeed, it has been estimated by Soldo that, while the ratio of "dependent" aged to working-age population was 18 to 100 in 1980, by 2000 it will be 26 to 100, and by 2030 it may be 32 to 100 [70]. Thus, there will be fewer and fewer workers per dependent—along with increased medical care

expenditures for older people. Unless there are marked increases in productivity, or a real "Cold War peace dividend" that will spread across the industrial world in the next decade, it will be increasingly difficult to continue as is without setting limits on medical care for the elderly or on pensions [71, 72]. This might this have an impact on families (shifting burden to families).

2. *Increased perceptions of "generational inequity."* This is a particularly likely scenario in the United States. If inflation continues to rise (especially in housing costs), the elderly are more and more likely to be perceived as "greedy geezers" in their mortgage-free houses. It will be increasingly argued that public support for the aged comes from funds that could be allocated to other segments of society, such as youth, and to affordable housing for young families. This is the "generational equity" scenario, as discussed above; Callahan goes along with this by calling for "voluntary restraints" on pension and health care expenditures by tomorrow's aged [72].

3. *Increased "ageism."* There will probably be a continuation of negative stereotyping that sees the elderly as rigid, terribly old-fashioned, unable to cope, irrelevant, and worthless. As more of the elderly population of the future live past eighty-five, and as more live with mental impairments like Alzheimer's disease and strokes, it could be that aging itself will be more negatively viewed. But characteristics of future cohorts of elderly will be efficient—*more highly educated,* which might close the "generational cohort gap" between high and low tech cohorts. Moreover, if technological advances become even more a part of personal life, those who cannot or will not learn the new techniques involving man-machine interfaces (such as computerized home banking) may be left behind. On the other side of the coin, there may be even greater emphasis on the virtues of youth. With fertility low and children proportionately less common, youth will be valued even more highly and attention will be turned to the young at the expense of the old.

Prospects for Less Age Group Conflicts in the Future

Other reasons suggest that there may be less intergenerational conflict in the twenty-first century, and that solidarity between generations at both the micro- and macro-social levels may be high.

1. *The cultural lag (or structural lag) hypothesis.* We may be in a situation of temporary normlessness now with regard to the longevity revolution; our social structures and norms may not have caught up to changes in the population age structure [73]. This argument would suggest that in another several decades social structures and cultural values will have evolved to reflect our changing age composition, with the result that we will have created more and more effective mechanisms to deal with large numbers of aged people, such as new work roles for elderly, loosening of rigid family-career-leisure sequencing, and new forms of elder-care combining adult and child daycare.

2. *Norms of solidarity and support.* Many studies have described significant intergenerational solidarity at the family level, with relations between generations solid and rewarding and with a great deal of mutual support taking place [17]. This solidarity reflects norms of 1) *filial piety,* 2) *reciprocity,* 3) *altruism,* and

4) *self-interest* (individuals' expectations for their own future). Cannot similar arguments be advanced at the macrosocial level? Are there not social or cultural values of elder caring, reciprocity, and self-interest—all of which may dampen possible "generational inequity" conflicts between age groups? It can be argued that the welfare state is not likely to go back on the moral principles that have been in effect for so many decades.

3. *Norms of reciprocity.* While we have only begun to research them [74], life course and intergenerational norms of reciprocity are very high. That is, people believe in a cyclical process of being helped and helping throughout life; they believe this is "normal" and so do not resent it (much of the time). The "burdens" of caretaking for a child are taken for granted. So too are many of the burdens of elder caring.

4. *New roles for the aged.* As suggested earlier, we may also see the development of collective change in the definition of what older people can and should contribute to society. For example, they may be seen as the resource for noneconomic capital—knowledge about relationships and history. They may be increasingly viewed as repositories of wisdom.

Thus, while the basis for intergenerational conflict does exist [75], there are several reasons to predict future solidarity rather than conflict across age groups and generations. There may be an emergence of new roles for older persons as day-care volunteers or teachers in economically-strapped school districts. There may be more seniors working part-time jobs in lieu of full retirement. Some seniors may reciprocate to future age groups by working to preserve the environment. There may also be greater "elder altruism" in support of proposals to cut the deficit, with wealthy elders paying a greater share of the tax burden than their less well-off peers. Elders may increase their power of self-determination and choose to have living wills and other advance directives which stipulate the circumstances under which they no longer want life-sustaining treatment or expensive and heroic medical measures to save their lives.

Further, more years of shared lives across generations may increase solidarity within families, bringing with it a valued "kin-keeping" role for elders who create new norms of old age. Last, there will undoubtedly be greater potential for both instrumental and socio-emotional support from elders to younger generations within families in the future, such as the support grandparents can provide to grandchildren and adult children during destabilizing periods of divorce or poverty. This issue is the wildcard for the future—blended families, step-relations. Now we see an "ideological lag"—we still view the intact nuclear family as the ideal.

In other nations, it is likely the same basic concern leading to conflict or solidarity will arise [38]. What is a fair distribution of public and private resources, obligations, and expectations? However, the context in which these issues are addressed in other nations may be different from the United States, and the mix of other social influences (especially the high unemployment rates of middle-aged and older persons) and political history will undoubtedly impact public perceptions of fairness. In Canada, for example, conflict between generations has not yet materialized in the media [13], and in Britain the issue of intergenerational equity has been less publicized by the press than it has been in the United States [76]. Some explanations offered for the greater salience of the issue in America but not in Canada or Britain are that 1) the United States lacks comprehensive welfare policies that regulate relations between age groups; 2) the United States has historically preferred individual, market-oriented solutions over government interventions to solve social problems; and 3) greater inequality, in general, in the United States leads to populist movements (e.g., Pat Buchanan), which seeks to scapegoat the most vulnerable, *and* those perceived to have the most wealth. This indicates the inextricable lineage between macro-policy and micro-family interactions. Private family transfers take place in the context of societal structures (e.g., conflict might go up with policies that increase old age poverty because exchange relation within family may become imbalances).

We suggest that gerontologists and policy makers utilize three important lessons from the U.S. experience as they address these issues [38]. First, the expectations and obligations across family generations must be distinguished from those that exist between age groups; the micro-level must not be confused with the macro-level in terms of intergenerational supports. Second, the objective of "justice across genera-tions" can mean either equity or equality across generations and age groups. Which of these two goals dominates will determine the path of debate, reform, and possible conflict. Third, political and media rhetoric do not always match empirical evidence; less rhetoric and more facts are needed.

CONCLUSION

The purpose of this chapter has been to examine trends in families, aging, and social change, looking toward intergenerational relationships in the future. While it has been suggested that the American family is declining in importance and function, we see evidence of strong kinship ties between adult generations despite the presence of intergenerational conflict. Data we have been collecting from over 300 multi-generational families for more than two decades as part of the Longitudinal Study of Generations suggest that extended-generational families' constantly changing metabolism—as a result of the interplay between solidarity and conflict over time—is an indication of its resiliency. Results from the LSOG run contrary to the argument that there is a decline in American family structures and functions. This appears to be true even when intergenerational family relationships are considered within a macro-social context, looking at solidarity and conflict between age cohorts. We suggest a model for future research on multigenerational families that incorporates society-level, family-level, and individual-level mechanisms. Our conclusion is that, as we look toward the future, the "social optimists" are more likely than the "social pessimists" to be correct concerning intergenerational relationships in the twenty-first century.

ACKNOWLEDGMENTS

Authors' names are listed alphabetically; this has been a collaborative research effort in every sense. Research was supported by grant #R37 AG07977 from the

National Institute on Aging. We want to acknowledge with gratitude the many contributions of Linda Hall, Christopher Hilgeman, and David Sharp to the technical development of this and many other papers from the Longitudinal Study of Generations over the past years.

REFERENCES

1. V. L. Bengtson, The Problem of Generations: Age Group Contrasts, Continuities, and Social Change, in *The Course of Later life,* V. L. Bengtson and K. Warner Schaie (eds.), Springer, New York, pp. 25-54, 1989.
2. V. L. Bengtson, Is the "Contract Across Generations" Changing? Effects of Population Aging on Obligations and Expectations Across Age Groups, in *The Changing Contract Across Generations,* V. L. Bengtson and W. A. Achenbaum, Aldine de Gruyter, New York, pp. 3-24, 1993.
3. E. Shanas, Social Myth as Hypothesis: The Case of the Family Relations of Old People, *The Gerontologist, 19,* pp. 3-9, 1979.
4. D. Popenoe, *Disturbing the Nest: Family Change and Decline in Modern Societies,* Aldine de Gruyter, New York, 1988.
5. D. Popenoe, American Family Decline, 1960-1990: A Review and Appraisal, *Journal of Marriage and the Family, 55,* pp. 527-555, 1993.
6. P. Cowan, The Sky is Falling, but Popenoe's Analysis Won't Help Us Do Anything About It, *Journal of Marriage and the Family, 55,* pp. 548-553, 1993.
7. A. Skolnick, *Embattled Paradise: The American Family in an Age of Uncertainty,* Basic Books, New York, 1991.
8. J. Stacey, Good Riddance to "the Family": A Response to David Popenoe, *Journal of Marriage and the Family, 55,* pp. 545-547, 1993.
9. V. L. Bengtson, C. J. Rosenthal, and L. M. Burton, Paradoxes of Families and Aging, in *Handbook of Aging and the Social Sciences* (4th Edition), R. H. Binstock and L. K. George (eds.), Academic Press, San Diego, pp. 253-282, 1995.
10. V. L. Bengtson and M. Silverstein, Families, Aging, and Social Change: Seven Agendas for 21st Century Researchers, in *Kinship, Aging, and Social Change, Vol. 13, Annual Review of Gerontology and Geriatrics,* G. Maddox and M. P. Lawton (eds.), Springer, New York, pp. 15-38, 1993.
11. R. Blieszner and V. H. Bedford (eds.), *Handbook of Aging and the Family,* Greenwood, Westport, Connecticut, 1995.
12. F. Goldscheider, The Aging of the Gender Revolution, *Research on Aging, 12,* pp. 531-545, 1990.
13. V. W. Marshall, S. Matthews, and C. J. Rosenthal, Elusiveness of Family Life: A Challenge for the Sociology of Aging, in *Annual Review of Gerontology and Geriatrics, Vol. 13, Kinship, Aging, and Social Change,* G. Maddox and M. P. Lawton (eds.), Springer, New York, pp. 39-72, 1993.
14. G. O. Hagestad, Parent-Child Relations in Later Life: Trends and Gaps in Past Research, in *Parenting Across the Life Span,* J. B. Lancaster, J. Altmann, A. S. Rossi, and L. R. Sherrod (eds.), Aldine de Gruyter, New York, pp. 405-434, 1987.
15. C. D. Ryf and M. M. Seltzer, Family Relations and Individual Development in Adulthood and Aging, in *Handbook of Aging and the Family,* R. Blieszner and V. H. Bedford (eds.), Greenwood, Westport, Connecticut, pp. 95-113, 1995.

16. J. Treas and L. Lawton, Early and Middle Adulthood, in *Handbook of Marriage and the Family* (2nd Edition), M. B. Sussman and S. K. Steinmetz (eds.), Plenum Press, New York, in press.

17. A. S. Rossi and P. H. Rossi, *Of Human Bonding: Parent-Child Relationships Across the Life Course,* Aldine de Gruyter, New York, 1990.

18. V. L. Bengtson and R. Harootyan (eds.), *Hidden Connections: Intergenerational Linkages in American Society,* Springer, New York, 1994.

19. G. H. Elder, Jr., L. Rudkin, and R. Conger, Intergenerational Continuity and Change in Rural America, in *Intergenerational Issues in Aging: Effects of Societal Change,* V. L. Bengtson, K. W. Schaie, and L. M. Burton (eds.), Springer, New York, pp. 30-60, 1994.

20. B. Soldo and M. C. Hill, *Intergenerational Transfers and Family Structure in the Health and Retirement Survey,* Health and Retirement Working Paper #94-1004, University of Michigan Institute for Social Research, Ann Arbor, Michigan, 1994.

21. D. Eggebeen and D. Hogan, Giving Between the Generations in American Families, *Human Nature, 1,* pp. 211-232, 1990.

22. M. Silverstein and V. L. Bengtson, Do Close Parent-Child Relations Reduce the Mortality Risk of Older Parents? A Test of the Direct and Buffering Effects of Intergenerational Affection, *The Journal of Health and Social Behavior, 32,* pp. 382-395, 1991.

23. M. Silverstein and V. L. Bengtson, Does Intergenerational Social Support Influence the Psychological Well-Being of Older Parents? The Contingencies of Declining Health and Widowhood, *Social Science and Medicine, 38,* pp. 943-957, 1994.

24. R. E. L. Roberts and V. L. Bengtson, Relationships with Parents, Self-Esteem, and Psychological Well-Being in Young Adulthood: A Further Examination of Identity Theory, *Social Psychology Quarterly, 56,* pp. 263-277, 1993.

25. R. E. L. Roberts and V. L. Bengtson, Affective Ties to Parents in Young Adulthood and Self-Esteem Over 20 Years, *Social Psychology Quarterly, 59,* pp. 96-106, 1996.

26. E. K. Abel, Family Care of the Frail Elderly, in *Circles of Care: Work and Identity in Women's Lives,* E. K. Abel and M. K. Nelson (eds.), State University of New York Press, Albany, New York, pp. 65-91, 1990.

27. E. Brody, Parent Care as a Normative Family Stress, *The Gerontologist, 25,* pp. 19-29, 1985.

28. J. W. Dwyer, The Effects of Illness on the Family, in *Handbook of Aging and the Family,* R. Blieszner and V. H. Bedford (eds.), Greenwood, Westport, Connecticut, pp. 401-421, 1995.

29. M. Gatz, V. L. Bengtson, and M. Blum, Caregiving Families, in *Handbook of the Psychology of Aging* (3rd Edition), J. E. Birren and K. W. Schaie (eds.), Academic Press, New York, pp. 404-426, 1990.

30. G. Maddox and M. P. Lawton (eds.), *Kinship, Aging, and Social Change, Vol. 13, Annual Review of Gerontology and Geriatrics,* Springer, New York, 1993.

31. S. H. Matthews, The Burdens of Parent Care: A Critical Evaluation of Recent Findings, *Journal of Aging Studies, 2:2,* pp. 157-165, 1988.

32. D. Chalfie, *Going it Alone: A Closer Look at Grandparents Parenting Grandchildren,* AARP Women's Initiative, Washington, D.C., 1994.

33. L. Troll, The Contingencies of Grandparenting, in *Grandparenthood,* V. L. Bengtson and J. F. Robertson (eds.), Sage, Beverly Hills, California, pp. 135-150, 1985.

34. C. L. Johnson, Marital Instability and the Changing Kinship Networks of Grandparents, *The Gerontologist, 27,* pp. 330-335, 1987.

35. L. M. Burton, Black Grandparents Rearing Children of Drug-Addicted Parents: Stressors, Outcomes, and Social Service Needs, *The Gerontologist, 32:6,* pp. 744-751, 1992.

36. K. J. Doka and M. E. Mertz, The Meaning and Significance of Great-Grandparenthood, *The Gerontologist, 28,* pp. 192-197, 1988.
37. G. J. Wentowski, Older Women's Perceptions of Great-Grandmotherhood: A Research Note, *The Gerontologist, 25,* pp. 593-596, 1985.
38. V. L. Bengtson and T. M. Parrott, Intergenerational Conflicts about Social Equity, Expectations and Obligations: Lessons from the United States, *Southern African Journal of Gerontology, 3:*2, pp. 6-14, 1994.
39. D. P. Hogan and J. I. Farkas, The Demography of Changing Intergenerational Relationships, in *Adult Intergenerational Relations: Effects of Societal Change,* V. L. Bengtson and K. W. Schaie (eds.), Springer, New York, pp. 1-18, 1995.
40. V. L. Bengtson, N. E. Cutler, D. J. Mangen, and V. W. Marshall, Generations, Cohorts, and Relations between Age Groups, in *Handbook of Aging and the Social Sciences,* Vol. 2, R. Binstock and E. Shanas (eds.), Van Nostrand Reinhold, New York, pp. 304-338, 1985.
41. V. L. Bengtson, C. J. Rosenthal, and L. M. Burton, Families and Aging: Diversity and Heterogeneity, in *Handbook of Aging and the Social Sciences* (3rd Edition), R. Binstock and L. George (eds.), Academic Press, New York, pp. 263-287, 1990.
42. M. B. Sussman, The Family Life of Old People, in *Handbook of Aging and the Social Sciences,* R. H. Binstock and E. Shanas (eds.), Van Nostrand Reinhold, New York, pp. 218-243, 1976.
43. M. B. Sussman, Aging and the Family, in *Handbook of Aging and the Social Sciences* (2nd Edition), R. H. Binstock and E. Shanas (eds.), Van Nostrand Reinhold, New York, pp. 294-326, 1985.
44. V. L. Bengtson, Generation and Family Effects in Value Socialization, *American Sociological Review, 40,* pp. 358-371, 1975.
45. V. L. Bengtson and J. A. Kuypers, Generational Differences and the "Developmental Stake," *Aging and Human Development, 2,* pp. 249-260, 1971.
46. R. Giarrusso, M. Stallings, and V. L. Bengtson, The "Intergenerational Stake" Hypothesis Revisited: Parent-Child Differences in Perceptions of Relationships 20 Years Later, in *Intergenerational Issues in Aging: Effects of Societal Change,* V. L. Bengtson, K. W. Schaie, and L. M. Burton (eds.), Springer, New York, pp. 227-263, 1995.
47. T. J. Biblarz, V. L. Bengtson, and A. Bucur, Social Mobility Across Three Generations, *Journal of Marriage and the Family, 58,* pp. 188-200, 1996.
48. J. Richlin-Klonsky and V. L. Bengtson, Pulling Together, Drifting Apart: A Longitudinal Case Study of a Four-Generation Family, *Journal of Aging Studies, 10,* pp. 255-279, 1996.
49. J. J. Suitor and K. Pillemer, Explaining Conflict When Adult Children and Their Elderly Parents Live Together, *Journal of Marriage and the Family, 50,* pp. 1037-1047, 1988.
50. D. Umberson, Relationships between Adult Children and Their Parents: Psychological Consequences for Both Generations, *Journal of Marriage and the Family, 54,* pp. 664-674, 1992.
51. T. L. Campbell, Family's Impact on Health: A Critical Review, *Family Systems Medicine, 4,* pp. 131-200, 1986.
52. S. Zarit, N. Orr, and J. M. Zarit, *The Hidden Victims of Alzheimer's Disease: Families under Stress,* New York University Press, New York, 1985.
53. S. J. Semple, Conflict in Alzheimer's Caregiving Families: Its Dimensions and Consequences, *The Gerontologist, 32,* pp. 648-655, 1992.
54. N. Sheehan and P. Nuttall, Conflict, Emotion, and Personal Strain among Family Caregivers, *Family Relations, 37,* pp. 92-98, 1988.

55. E. Clarke, *Effects of Conflict on Adult Children's Relationship to Parents: A Multi-Dimensional Approach to Parent-Child Conflict,* doctoral dissertation, Department of Sociology, University of Southern California, 1996.
56. E. J. Clarke, M. Preston, J. Raksin, and V. L. Bengtson, Types of Conflicts and Tensions between Older Parents and Adult Children, *The Gerontologist,* in press.
57. J. Treas, Older Americans in the 1990s and Beyond, *Population Bulletin, 50*:2, May 1995.
58. R. Atchley, *Social Forces and Later Life* (7th Edition), Wadsworth, Belmont, California, 1994.
59. E. M. Crimmins, Changes in Life Expectantcy and Disability-Free Life Expectancy in the United States, *Population and Development Review, 15,* pp. 235-267, 1989.
60. J. F. Fries, Compression on Morbidity 1993: Life Span, Disability, and Health Costs, *Facts and Research in Gerontology,* pp. 183-190, 1993.
61. U.S. Bureau of the Census, *We the American Elderly,* September 1993.
62. J. P. Pinkerton, Economy Bites the Edge off Generation X, *Los Angeles Times,* B7, February 24, 1994.
63. V. W. Marshall, F. L. Cook, and J. G. Marshall, Conflict over Intergenerational Equity: Rhetoric and Reality in a Comparative Context, in *The Changing Contract Across Generations,* V. L. Bengtson and W. A. Achenbaum (eds.), Aldine de Gruyter, New York, pp. 119-140, 1993.
64. R. A. Rosenblatt, Footing the Bill for Our Future, *Los Angeles Times, A1,* pp. 8-9, October 28, 1992.
65. R. J. Samuelson, Generational Economics: The Gap is Real, *The Washington Post National Weekly Edition, 28,* p. 28, April 18-24, 1994.
66. P. Galloway, Financial Tug of War, *Chicago Tribune,* pp. 1, 4, August 10, 1992.
67. J. Weisberg, Are Your Parents Robbing You Blind? The Coming War between the Old and the Young, *Worth,* pp. 68-75, June/July 1992.
68. M. D'Antonio, The New Generation Gap: Golden Oldies, *Los Angeles Times Magazine,* pp. 16-20, 46-49, March 14, 1997.
69. M. Edelman, *Constructing the Political Spectacle,* University of Chicago Press, Chicago, Illinois, 1988.
70. B. Soldo, America's Elderly in the 1980s, *Population Bulletin, 35*:4, 1981.
71. V. L. Bengtson and D. Dannefer, Families, Work and Aging: Implications of Disordered Cohort Flow for the 21st Century, in *Health in Aging: Sociological Issues and Policy Directions,* R. A. Ward and S. S. Tobin (eds.), Springer, New York, pp. 256-289, 1987.
72. D. Callahan, *Setting Limits,* Simon and Schuster, New York, 1987.
73. M. W. Riley and J. W. Riley, Connections: Kin and Cohort, in *The Changing Contract Across Generations,* Aldine de Gruyter, New York, pp. 169-190, 1993.
74. A. S. Rossi, Intergenerational Relations: Gender, Norms, and Behavior, in *The Changing Contract Across Generations,* V. L. Bengtson and W. A. Achenbaum (eds.), Aldine de Gruyter, New York, pp. 191-211, 1993.
75. V. L. Bengtson and W. A. Achenbaum (eds.), *The Changing Contract Across Generations,* Aldine de Gruyter, New York, 1993.
76. A. Walker, Intergenerational Relations and Welfare Restructuring: The Social Construction of an Intergenerational Problem, in *The Changing Contract Across Generations,* V. L. Bengtson and W. A. Achenbaum (eds.), Aldine de Gruyter, New York, pp. 141-165, 1993.

CHAPTER
7

Interdisciplinary Health Care in the Twenty-First Century: Fantasy or Fundamental?

Theresa J. K. Drinka

BACKGROUND

The road to perfect health care is paved with the carcasses of interdisciplinary teams that fought the good fight and died in a quest for some healthcare ideal that was always beyond their reach. Interdisciplinary healthcare teams embody the type of health care that makes so much sense for those patients who are dubbed by some as "chronic high-end users of the system" or have so many interacting problems that they threaten to unbalance the delicate system that has come to be known as managed care. Yet, the practice of interdisciplinary health care appears so difficult to effect that many have abandoned it in favor of other "new" models of care that frequently turn out to be some form of team care. In reality, different forms of team delivered health care have been around for all of this century. Since they don't seem to be disappearing, perhaps it would be wise to try to understand teams in the context of our healthcare system.

In the past 100 years, numerous factors have coalesced to create the matrix of confusion that represents the United States' healthcare enterprise. The sovereignty of the medical profession, the lure of medical technology, the changing nature of health care and healthcare consumers, diverse views of disease, fear of making and admitting mistakes, and denial of conflict all relate to interdisciplinary practice. The responses of physicians, other health professionals, and patients to these issues have added to the healthcare maze.

As the twenty-first century approaches, the topic of healthcare delivery remains highly visible. Escalating health care costs and an expanding geriatric population, with increasing needs for both chronic and acute care, are givens. These realities, coupled with a decreasing base of economic support from income-producing segments of the population dictate that continued changes in healthcare delivery are inevitable. In medicine as in other fields that must adapt to change, survival and growth often depend on adopting complexity by integrating diverse perspectives. The integration of differing approaches to healthcare provision would require professionals to problem solve and practice in an interdependent and collaborative manner. An interdisciplinary healthcare team is a vehicle that provides structure and method for collaborative interprofessional practice, potentially improving the efficiency and effectiveness of health care to select populations.

Developing an interdisciplinary approach to care appears common sense in a healthcare delivery system that frequently ignores the psychosocial concerns of the patient. In fact, interdisciplinary healthcare teams have maintained a presence in health care since the 1940s. Evolvement of this mode of healthcare delivery has been both stifled and promoted by numerous factors ranging from education to politics and economics, and the healthcare industry has never fully endorsed the concept of interdisciplinary practice. Because half-hearted attempts, by healthcare providers and policy makers, to establish interdisciplinary teams have appeared costly and inefficient they have moved to establish other models like quality improvement, virtual teams, and custom care planning. Healthcare providers have also tried training medical providers in topics such as customer service, handling difficult patient situations, communication, and risk management. As these methods prove to be insufficient to create quality geriatric care in integrated managed care systems, perhaps policy makers will re-consider interdisciplinary teams. Hopefully this time they will do it right. Moving to an interdisciplinary approach to health care will require transformations in policies, structures, and process by those in the forefront of revamping our healthcare system.

THE HEALTHCARE SYSTEM AS A SETTING FOR INTERDISCIPLINARY PRACTICE

Rise of Medicine as a Sovereign Profession

The French revolution in medicine in the early 1800s released two possibilities for medical care. One became modern clinical medicine, focused on science and technology; the other, social medicine, focused on the human factor. Their relative priority was a political response defining social and economic conflict over the emergence of new hierarchies of power and authority, new markets, and new conditions of belief and experience. The germ theory guided the developing science of medicine. The medical profession focused on scientific technology and rose to power in the late nineteenth and early twentieth centuries. In the United States, science has dominated the art of medicine and from the early 1900s through the 1980s the acute care teaching hospital became the primary symbol of medical care.

Additionally, in the early 1900s physicians banded together and created a more unified front within their profession. Consequently, they distanced themselves from their patients through internal cohesiveness and strong collective organization. This contributed to the rise in the medical profession and its structuring of a bureaucratic regime to support itself [1].

Technology vs. Human Issues

Technology grew out of the science of medicine and has directed our efforts at health care for almost a century. Technology has also reified the hierarchies of power in medicine as it is practiced in the United States. The best medical technology is displayed in the teaching hospitals that are used to train our physicians. Technology is supported by the political and economic systems that the medical profession has structured to support itself. Technology is alluring because it can produce dramatic results. Because of this allure, health professionals and patients look to technology for solutions to problems. However, when patient problems require human intervention, patients and physicians are frequently disappointed with the results of their medical care. The glorification of technology with its rapidly changing and esoteric nature and the value placed on active technological intervention has limited the potential for rational control over the healthcare system [2].

Changing Nature of Health Care and Health Care Consumers

During the last half of the twentieth century, the nature of healthcare consumers in the United States has been rapidly changing [3]. Diseases like Acquired Immune Deficiency Syndrome and Alzheimer's and conditions like the frailty of old age are altering the healthcare system's view of disease from ailments that can be treated and cured with technology, to ailments that also need long-term care and management. In the 1990s the number of people who receive Social Security Disability is at an all time high. People are living longer and previously fatal conditions are treated and managed as long term chronic and complex problems that are more human than technology intensive. Treatment of these conditions requires more than science and technology.

Demands for Care

Despite the increased need for non-technological intervention in chronic care, the healthcare system is fueled and encouraged by healthcare consumers who allow and demand healthcare resources to be spent on acute or end stage problems that might have been prevented. If technology is available and offers a potential solution to their problem, consumers may cry out for its application. In the late 1990s pharmaceutical companies began advertising prescription drugs in the popular media in hopes of encouraging patients to ask their physicians for the most recent drug therapy.

Health professionals may contribute to consumer's demands by inadequately presenting options or by not realizing their own fears about death, disability, or the wrath of the health maintenance organization. As such, different health professionals may give "shopwise" consumers confusing messages about the costs and benefits of treatments.

Dissatisfaction with Health Care

Concurrent with demands for "high tech" care, consumers exhibit a dissatisfaction with the shortcomings of the healthcare system. There is a growing feeling in health care that the basic human needs of many patients are being ignored, that the personal emphasis is gone from health care; that machines alone can't make people better; and that the culture of the patient must be understood in determining what is "best" for that particular patient [4]. The consumption of organic foods, nutritional supplements, and alternative medicine is increasing as people seek alternatives and/or additions to their traditional medical care [5, 6].

Increase in Litigation

In the United States, the doctor-patient relationship can also be confrontational as the media delivers hopeful messages about experimental treatments and lawyers, specializing in medical injuries, hawk their wares. Throughout the decade of the 1980s, medical professionals experienced an upswing in the frequency of lawsuits [7]. In one review of malpractice claims against physicians, over 70 percent were related to breakdowns in doctor-patient communications [8]. As managed care has emerged in the 1990s, there has been a dramatic increase in lawsuits related to outpatient care [9].

The litigation trend is not directed solely at physicians as other professionals are also being included in malpractice suits. Also, while acute care providers still receive the market share of lawsuits, long-term care providers are experiencing an increase in lawsuits directed at patterns of mistreatment abuse and neglect [10].

Diverse Views of Health and Disease

Health and disease have long been considered opposite entities. The science of medicine has viewed health as the absence of disease while the World Health Organization defines health as a state of complete physical, mental, and social well-being [11]. The difference in perspectives may be based in two divergent views of disease, *normatist* and *nonnormatist*. The *normatist* view defines disease in the context of the values of a given individual or group [12]. The *nonnormatist* perspective views disease as a value free concept [13] and leads those trained in the medical model to determine disease according to certain well-defined parameters.

The controversy over diverse views of health and disease raises questions of which professions are best suited to promote health and contend with disease. The chosen view will determine which professions gain relative status and power. Exploration of these diverse views could also encourage an integration among the approaches of the different health professions. While the *nonnormatist* view of disease has been the predominant view of medical care since the early 1900s, more recently, policy makers have seen health and disease as complementary, albeit parallel concepts [14]. As managed care has grown and vies for "customers," the notion of patient satisfaction has become increasingly important. Believing that they can satisfy an ever increasing load of patients, physicians have dutifully responded by attending training on topics related to meeting patient needs [15].

Fear of Making and Admitting Mistakes

Health professionals as a group have a highly developed sense of responsibility, a strong sense of professional autonomy, difficulty admitting that they make mistakes, and an inability and/or unwillingness to constructively address interprofessional conflict. All of these attributes combine to make it difficult for professionals from multiple disciplines to openly collaborate and to use the conflict created by error for constructive and creative change. All disciplines, especially physicians, are socialized to strive for error free practice. They view mistakes as unacceptable and error as a failure of character. It is also difficult for a physician to view error without considering negligence. It may be that health professionals are afraid to share what they know across disciplines for fear that they will lose their autonomy. However, it is just as likely that the practiced autonomy of each profession is a way of guarding against exposing their errors to other disciplines.

Denial of Conflict

The complexity inherent in geriatrics and in interdisciplinary teams can lead to chaos or conflict and conflict is very uncomfortable. Denial of complexity as denial of conflict is an additional quality that allows professionals to practice under the secure and sanctioned blanket of what they were taught to do, i.e., autonomous discipline-specific practice. Denying the existence of conflict establishes a team culture that prevents collaboration from occurring and negates the usefulness of the interdisciplinary team. What is left is the tedious work of trying to keep the team together without the diversity of opinions that produce creative solutions to complex problems.

THE EMERGENCE OF INTERDISCIPLINARY HEALTH CARE

History

In the early part of the twentieth century, it was commonplace for physicians to make house calls and the doctor's wife might assume the role of office nurse, thus creating an informal team. Interdisciplinary healthcare began formally in this country in the 1940s with the interdisciplinary home health care team that was created at Montefiore Hospital in New York City. Interdisciplinary health care was popularized in the early 1970s through the establishment of neighborhood health centers. It was evident that health providers from different professions needed to understand each others' viewpoints and strengths and learn to work together.

Training for Interdisciplinary Health Care

In the 1970s, large interdisciplinary training grants were funded by the U.S. Public Health Service Bureau of Health Professions and the Veterans Affairs (VA) Office of Health Manpower. In the 1980s, the VA funded twelve Interdisciplinary Team Training Programs to provide both basic and continuing education in interdisciplinary team practice for health professionals. In the late 1980s and early 1990s, the U.S. Public Health Service funded Area Health Education Centers to establish rural interdisciplinary health training projects. In the mid 1990s, the John A. Hartford Foundation established eight model Geriatric Interdisciplinary Team Training Programs.

One problem with some of these training programs was that, while they called themselves interdisciplinary, the teams that provided the training often operated in a more multidisciplinary model of practice. Also, if the program or grant developed a team, they may not have been given the resources to maintain that team or to increase its efficiency over a sufficient period of time.

State of Interdisciplinary Geriatric Practice

Despite the training attempts, the engagement of physicians with interdisciplinary practice has grown in some spheres and not in others. The field of geriatrics is a good example of how interdisciplinary health care has and has not evolved. Teams within the following settings may have varying functionality depending on variables like team training for new staff, ongoing team development, and focus on an integrated assessment and treatment process. Even in the most well developed teams, treatment plans may be static documents that reflect input from and not ongoing interaction between health workers from multiple disciplines.

Geriatric Evaluation and Management Units in clinic and hospital settings have developed over the past fifteen years. Traditionally, physicians are an integral part of the problem solving that occurs on these units.

For the most part, nursing home care is still nurse directed care. Physicians function more as consultants as they write orders and make cursory rounds. Despite the fact that the Joint Commission on Accreditation of Health Care Organizations (JCAHO) requires interdisciplinary treatment plans in nursing homes, the physician is not necessarily in on the treatment planning process, nor does the physician necessarily read the ongoing interdisciplinary progress notes.

In general, house calls in home care programs are made by professional nurses, rehabilitation therapists and social workers, or paraprofessional nursing assistants and chore workers. Most home care professionals practice rather autonomously within the context of a loosely knit team. However, the physician is rarely an integral part of the team.

Adult day health care (ADHC) is another model of geriatric care that has been tried in some communities. In general, ADHCs have integrated medical and psychosocial approaches to care and their teams of practitioners may include physicians. However, ADHC teams commonly neglect the team process and maintenance issues that could increase their efficiency.

Outpatient clinics are beginning to establish team care for geriatric patients with complex problems. Since Medicare does not reimburse for physical exams but does reimburse for technical interventions based on those exams, geriatric team care has grown around geriatric specialty clinics like memory disorders, incontinence, or falls. The general geriatric clinic is likely to be a loss leader that attracts older patients to a larger system of care. The ideal core of health professions is considered to be a nurse, physician, and social worker. However, the actual mix of the geriatric clinic team may be more dependent on the type of reimbursement available.

THE PROFESSIONS' READINESS FOR INTERDISCIPLINARY PRACTICE

Training of Health Professionals

The training of physicians and non physician healthcare professionals is often incongruous with the problems they see in practice. Until recently, physician training ignored the changing nature of health care. Emphasis was placed on training with the most acutely ill patients in tertiary and quaternary care hospitals [16]. Health professions' students have been trained to view "high tech" care as exciting, even though, most of the time, patients required a small "low tech" practice. The human and psycho-social side of physician training has not been emphasized [17]. In addition, each profession has been trained separate from other professions to view problems according to the unique framework of their particular profession.

Since the mid-1990s, most of the U.S. medical schools have increased their emphasis on training for primary care practice and more medical students are announcing their intention to become primary care practitioners. Medical schools are initiating courses on ethics, behavior, communication, coping with death, etc., hoping to sensitize physicians to the psycho-social side of patient care. Despite adding these courses, medical students are acutely aware that this is "soft science" and that it is the "hard science" on which they will be tested.

Physicians are still being trained to view themselves as a one person team. They are not being trained to understand or appreciate the knowledge, skills, and values of other disciplines. They are not being trained to know when they might need a team; how or when to hand off problems to other disciplines; or when to problem solve with other disciplines. When, in practice, physicians face a situation where they cannot do everything or do not have time to address a need, they will hand off referrals expecting that their communication is understood by other disciplines. They become frustrated when the patient's needs are not met, thus increasing their distrust of professionals from other disciplines.

Medicine as a Business

The current managed care market rewards systems for generating high numbers of "covered lives." Ideally, most are relatively healthy people who do not require complex approaches to care. Physicians are assigned to see patients in ten to twenty minute blocks of time. One study found that general practitioners spent an average of 11.2 minutes with older patients and that physicians take less time with older patients than younger patients [18]. For the growing numbers of older patients with complex issues, who have difficulty expressing themselves, who don't know how to report a vague symptom, or who don't recognize a symptom, the allotted time is seldom adequate. In such a short amount of time it would be difficult to ascertain the potential environmental, psychological, and social contributors to interacting problems; explain the costs and benefits of treatment options; or to educate the patient about treatment. In their brief encounters with patients, physicians have little time to learn about people's lives.

An issue of a popular magazine [19] featured an article that gave tips on how to talk to your doctor. The article outlined over fourteen questions to ask your doctor ranging from "What should a medicine do for me?" to asking "why?" as a response to a doctor's advice. With approximately fifteen minutes allowed for a typical office visit, the patient who followed this advice might likely be seen as a "crock" or someone to be avoided by the physician. Patients make comments like, "When I write down my questions the doctor seems upset"; or, "When I ask questions the doctor changes the subject." A distraught caregiver recently commented to me, "It is hard working with health professionals when you have six minutes to get your point across." In the current system there is no time to adequately address patients' concerns. Partly it is a problem of economics. Physicians must generate enough money to pay their salary and satisfy the administrators of the clinical operation.

Policy makers, physicians, malpractice attorneys, and healthcare administrators share responsibility for building a high technology healthcare empire that is now facing the long-term needs of an aging population. Physician training is expensive and physicians must often work many years to pay off student loans. During this time they feel entitled to be rewarded for their hard work. Although the current healthcare system still rewards physicians and health systems for generating patient volume and using technology, the system is attempting to change to meet the demands of decreasing Medicare payments and a policy shift toward primary care and low technology. Physicians are feeling pressed by a perceived loss of power and autonomy [20] and are often caught in a double bind between the threat of reprimands or rejections from the system that pays them and the fear of lawsuits from disgruntled patients. Primary care physicians are led to believe that if they work harder they can meet the needs for low tech care without the additional services that are needed to manage complex illnesses in older patients over the long term.

Rise and Fall of Other Health Professions

Physicians, given their external demands to generate high revenues both to cover their salaries and to support the bureaucracy, have had difficulty meeting healthcare needs of individuals with permanent or chronic ailments and disabilities. Medicine's inadequate response to the social aspects of illness and disease partly spawned the rapid growth of other non-physician healthcare disciplines in the middle to last half of the twentieth century. Non-physician healthcare disciplines have carried out established healthcare treatment plans and performed ongoing assessment and trouble shooting of health problems. As integrated care systems formed, some disciplines like social work, occupational therapy, and clinical pharmacy have been squeezed. Clinical departments have been closed or merged. As certain disciplines were eliminated, nursing was expected to fill the void and is emerging as another discipline that is expected to do everything.

Isolation of Other Health Professions

Rather than integrating new health professions into the medical establishment, the expansion of health professions was accomplished in a separatist way and the result led to patient care that is often segmented and off target [21]. As healthcare regulations increasingly promote reimbursement for some non-physician interventions, physicians have been losing their grip on the management of medical care. Unfortunately, the result has not necessarily been more comprehensive or improved coordination of health care.

While non-physician professionals could perform many tasks relegated to physicians [22], other disciplines like social work or occupational therapy or dietetics are rarely an integral part of a medical practice. Netting and Williams found that even when social workers were case-managers for physicians they were seldom integrated into the practice setting [23]. The potential roles of these disciplines may be unclear to other providers or not valued by them. This may be due to the inability of professionals from these disciplines to clearly describe what it is they could do. It may also be due to a continuing lack of appreciation for the role that psychosocial issues play in health care.

Nurse practitioners or physician assistants have been added to some medical practices to relieve physicians of the burden of routine assessment and care. However, these disciplines often hold the same medical focus as the physicians they replace. And increasingly, they are being encouraged by administrators and their own professions to think (like physicians) that "they can do it all." This is also threatening to the autonomy and power status of physician providers.

Registered nurses and licensed practical nurses are often represented as part of medical clinics. However, their use is often more for technical procedures and clinic coordination than it is for gathering information and collaborative problem solving. Most other disciplines are only consulted for non-routine issues and are not a part of integrated problem solving. Thus, it has become clear that having many professional disciplines available does not equate with interdisciplinary practice.

THE HEALTH CARE SYSTEM'S READINESS FOR INTERDISCIPLINARY COLLABORATION

Controlling the Demand for Health Professionals

The numbers and mix of professions that are promoted by policies for education of health professionals and policies for healthcare system reimbursement will greatly influence interdisciplinary collaboration and the potential to deliver comprehensive health care. By using paramedical workers, keeping surgeons working full time, and monitoring physician performance, HMOs began to operate successfully in the 1980s with significantly lower ratios of doctors to patients than did the United States as a whole. Additional attempts to regulate demand for health professions in the 1990s have included managed competition, integrated delivery networks, downsizing and merging departments, and the emergence of healthcare technicians.

Rationing certain health services could affect demand for both medical and nonmedical health professions. The demand for some non-physician disciplines like physical therapy or dietetics might rise if fee-for-service prevails, or it might drop if prepaid plans succeed. As capitation increasingly takes hold in integrated systems of care, demand for other non-physician disciplines could rise when the need for efficient teams to care for certain segments of the population becomes evident.

Fear and Conflict among Health Professions

There is fear among health professionals that the changing healthcare system and potentially rationing certain types of care will continue to create schisms between the various professional health disciplines and between different segments of the medical profession. As our healthcare systems change they must address the impact the changes will have for encouraging or discouraging collaboration among diverse health professions. Those considerations involve reimbursement mechanisms, integrated training programs, expectations for joint problem solving, and altering the message that physicians must be the center of the system.

Inequities Driven by Market Competition

Market competition driven by supply, demand, reimbursement patterns, and political lobbying has encouraged salary inequity between different health professions and technical specialists. A physical therapist with a bachelors degree may earn $20-$30,000 more than an occupational therapist with a bachelors degree. Nurses with masters degrees may earn $20-$30,000 more than medical social workers with master degrees. In some cases a physical therapist with a four-year degree will earn more than a nurse with a four-year degree. A recently advertised position, in the upper midwest, for a doctorally prepared educator with experience in clinical geriatrics attracted three physical therapists (2 had masters degrees and 1 had a Ph.D.). All were earning $20,000 more than the top salary for the advertised position. That was $35,000 more than the masters prepared social workers were making at the facility and $15,000 more than the master and Ph.D. prepared nurses were making. Physical therapists are a scarce commodity because the profession has maintained entrance limits over a long period of time. These and similar factors will play a part in how much collaboration professionals from different disciplines achieve. Thus, supply and demand and reimbursement mechanisms must be factored into any plan to make true interdisciplinary practice a viable commodity.

PROFESSIONAL RESPONSIBILITIES FOR CHANGE

Acculturation of Health Professionals

In general, health professionals from different disciplines are educated and trained in separate and very strong cultural entities. The values and theories of health care are not the same across these cultural enclaves. Physicians and pharmacists are trained in the nonnormatist philosophy. Social workers and nurses are trained more in a normatist mode. Even problem-solving strategies differ between health professions. For example, professionals like social workers and psychologists are trained to problem solve by ruling in information. Other professionals like physicians are trained to rule out information [24].

Although the disciplines of medicine, nursing, and social work all take a global view of patient function, the word *function* has different primary meanings for different disciplines. Psychiatrists and psychologists use the term function to refer to mental health function while an internist refers to physiological function. A nurse might refer to the function of input, output, and mobility. A social worker might view function in terms of the structures for social support. A physical therapist might view function as it relates to basic activities of daily living, and an occupational therapist usually refers to the more cognitive instrumental activities of daily living. The interface between biological, psychological, social, environmental, and spiritual perspectives requires a mutual understanding of several languages and a willingness to establish mechanisms for interactive communication. Health professionals must be exposed to these diverse languages and values in order to learn, retain, and use their meanings.

Bringing diverse healthcare disciplines together can be likened to a struggle between different cultures that are continually changing. This is illustrated in "The Doctor-Nurse Game" [25] and the subsequent "Doctor-Nurse Game Revisited" [26]. In the original game the nurses behaved in a subservient manner and the doctors and nurses both knew the rules. In the revised game the nurses had changed the rules and the doctors were still playing the old game. The struggle for a collaborative environment between health professions is also constantly changing. Thus, it will require more than one training experience to assure professionals from different disciplines work together. It is unlikely that different health professions will, by their own choice, band together to provide integrated health care.

Different Views of Interdisciplinary Practice

As they have different views of disease and health care, health professionals have different views of interdisciplinary practice. A physicians view of interdisciplinary practice is likely that of several medical subspecialties talking to one another [27]. Another discipline might view interdisciplinary teamwork as professionals from several disciplines performing independent assessments and presenting data on the same patient. Most health professionals have not been trained to know what other disciplines do. Few healthcare curricula in the United States require students to learn about what other health professions might contribute to managing the care of a patient with complex problems. It is quite certain that professionals from most disciplines have felt frustrated by trying to do their job when other professionals don't understand or don't value what it is they do.

Prior experiences of health professionals on teams may have been negative. Common perceptions may be those of lack of power, uncertain roles, and time wasted in senseless meetings and discussions. If interdisciplinary practice is to become a reality, these perceptions must be recognized and the need for training in diverse languages and perspectives, reimbursement for meetings, negotiated leadership, and interpersonal processing of conflicts must be addressed.

RECOGNIZING LIMITATIONS AND POSSIBILITIES

Physicians Cannot Do Everything

A call for more primary care physicians has been raised [28], and more primary care physicians are being trained as a response to that call. However, even with more family practitioners and general internists the healthcare needs of an aging society with an increasing population of frail old patients probably could not be met in a way that would address both the needs of the patients and the requirements of the physicians for *adequate* compensation. To expect that primary care practitioners alone can manage most of the problems of the very frail or complex patient is placing an unreasonable burden on both the practitioner and the patient.

Targeting Complex Cases

For a patient with complex problems, a typical office visit might proceed as follows. The physician prescribes a number of medications for the patient who has unstable cardiac disease, hypertension, osteoarthritis, depression, and seizure disorder. The physician and/or clinic nurse give instructions on taking the medications. The patient picks up the medicine at one pharmacy and the pharmacist might give instructions on those medications and potential interactions between them. The patient may have ordered other medications through the mail or from another pharmacy that is not linked into the computer system of the first pharmacy. Some of those medications may have potentially harmful interacting effects. Perhaps the patient is involved with a community outreach social worker who discovers that he is not taking some of his medications because they interfere with his ability to leave his home at certain times of the day so he can visit the neighborhood restaurant to eat certain high fat foods that he refuses to give up. Additionally, the patient forgets to take his medicine before bed as it is too difficult for him to make another trip down the stairs to get it. The social worker might call a pharmacist to discuss all of the medications and to consult on a better way to fit the medication regimen into the patient's schedule. The social worker might feel that consultations by an occupational therapist and a dietitian were necessary and call the nurse who might decide the patient needed to be seen again in the clinic.

Increasing Efficiency of Targeting Complex Cases

Delivery of the necessary information and assessment of the outcome might be accomplished in a more efficient and cost effective way. Healthcare practitioners who worked together on an ongoing basis could assess and analyze the patient's situation and plan interventions up front. By structuring an integrated assessment process, they could also minimize duplication of efforts. The solution requires several healthcare professions to work together to establish an integrated assessment protocol, a working treatment plan, and integrated progress notes that relate to the plan. If a professional from a discipline like nursing or social work could obtain the patient's perception of the problems and their preferred approaches to them before the patient saw the physician and could communicate the information to the physician, the exam could be more thorough and accurate. The physician's acceptance of input from other disciplines is predicated on the team's understanding of the entire assessment process, deleting redundancies how all parts interrelate, and trusting others to perform parts of the assessment. If a dietitian and perhaps an occupational therapist had been involved in the assessment and plan, the problems might have been prevented. The team would need to take time to work out when or if other disciplines needed to be brought (permanently or transitionally) into the team.

The cost of interventions can be estimated. It is more difficult to estimate the costs of not intervening in time to avert inevitable problems. It is also difficult to estimate the cost of a team that does not function well together. However, costs for each of these situations must be factored into equations for efficiency of care.

A VIEW FOR THE FUTURE

So, what is a team? The terms *unidisciplinary, bi-disciplinary, multidisciplinary, interdisciplinary, transdisciplinary,* and *pandisciplinary* have all been applied to teams. These terms relate to the variety of disciplines, amount of collaboration, and interdependence for problem solving that team members assume. An internist working with a surgeon would be considered as a unidisciplinary team because they are both physicians. These team types are confusing and the terms are used interchangeably and without context [29]. In reality it might be easier to refer to *ad hoc group, formal work group,* and *interactive teams.* Autonomous practice plays a role in each type of team. Without working knowledge of what other disciplines can do and a knowledge of how an interactive team operates, a professional is incapable of appropriately choosing autonomous practice.

Continuum of Professional Practice

There is a continuum of professional practice—from individual problem solving to interdisciplinary collaborative problem solving (Figure 1). One assumption is that health professionals practice autonomously most of the time. In reality, a good part of the time health professionals recognize the need to interact with others in the healthcare community. Thus, they are continually choosing where on the continuum

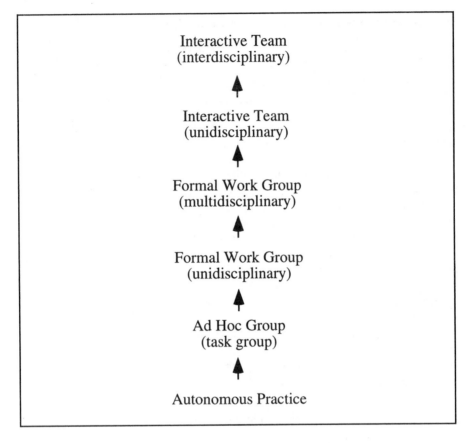

Figure 1. Continuum of healthcare practice.

they want to practice. The choice is not only dependent on their philosophy of practice and their training but is also situation specific. If a given situation calls for the skills of a particular profession and the representative from that profession feels comfortable applying those skills, they will likely work independently. If a situation is seen as demanding of skills a professional doesn't have and they feel uncomfortable, they might consult another professional, either from the same or another discipline. The discipline that is chosen will depend on availability, access, and a knowledge of what that discipline has to offer. It might also involve some degree of individual trust; meaning that the professional requesting help might need to know something about the person they are contacting, i.e., how they process information, that they are accurate, knowledgeable, and reliable.

A second assumption related to the continuum of practice is that preparation for autonomous practice also prepares a professional for the other types of practice on the continuum. One only needs to look at the history of health care to realize the fallacy in this assumption.

An additional belief related to the continuum of practice is that learning about each of the modes of team practice must be sequential, i.e., that professionals cannot learn to practice with other disciplines until they are secure in the autonomous practice of their own discipline. Although this assumption has great allure, it is open to debate. Because the practice of health care is seldom a solo venture, it is important for health professions students to learn the type of interaction necessary for different levels of patient problems. There is every reason to believe that this skill can and should be learned in conjunction with every level of their professional training.

Continuum of Health Team Operation

If healthcare practice is thought of not as a continuum but as a system, it becomes obvious that healthcare professionals need to learn how to efficiently operate within the system of interdisciplinary practice which encompasses all of the six approaches to care (Figure 2). In addition to autonomous practice there are at least five types of teams, from the *ad hoc group* or *task group* which meets to work on a specific issue and then disbands; the *formal work group* that is ongoing and consists of professionals from one discipline; the formal work group of many disciplines; the *one-discipline interactive team* that works on its developmental processes, and the *interactive team* that is interdisciplinary. The need for ongoing interdependence and collaboration are triggers to which part of the system or team type is used for an interaction. As individual practitioners and teams learn about the six approaches to care and the most appropriate approach for a given problem, they gain depth and breadth in their ability to problem solve. Both the team's members and the team become able to address increasingly complex issues.

There are advantages and disadvantages to each of the team types [30]. The *ad hoc group* might be the appropriate mechanism to rapidly address a unique problem that had implications for the larger organization. However, because solutions often lack breadth and depth, it would not be an effective mechanism for addressing complex ongoing practice issues. The multidisciplinary formal work group might be a good format for discussing routine health care that needs to involve input from many disciplines. Because solutions from this type of team often lack depth, it is not a format for addressing complex issues that tend to be ongoing. Learning to function efficiently as a potential member of the six types of care is not necessarily progressive. Also, if a team member knew how to function in an ad hoc task group they would not necessarily know how to function in the other four types of teams. Whereas, if a person learned how to function in an interdisciplinary team, they should also know how (not necessarily when) to function in each of the other four types of teams. Healthcare professionals cannot choose the most appropriate type of practice if they are not familiar with and comfortable with their options.

Healthcare teams provide structure that enables health professionals to work efficiently on different types of problems. The ideal is to structure a team system that allows professionals to belong to an interdisciplinary team and at the same time work in other types of teams or groups as needs dictate (Figure 2). Using this model, a physician who belonged to an interdisciplinary healthcare team in a geriatric clinic

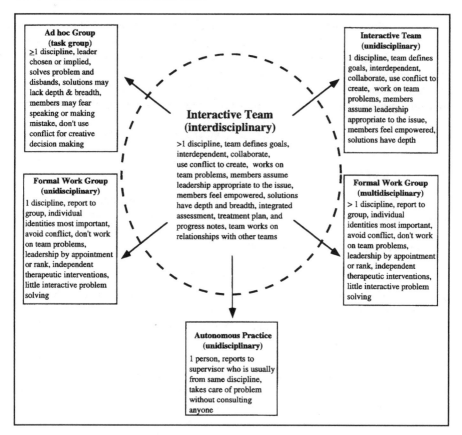

Figure 2. Interdisciplinary teamwork system.
Source: © 1997, Theresa Drinka, River's Edge Consulting[SM].

setting might meet briefly with a nurse and an occupational therapist (ad hoc group) to discuss a hospitalized patient's needs for mobility while hospitalized. That same physician might sit in once a week on a multidisciplinary planning conference (formal work group) in a nursing home. The physician might meet monthly with a group of clinic staff physicians (unidisciplinary formal work group) to discuss policies relative to medical care. The physician might meet regularly with the other physicians who are on the interdisciplinary clinic team to discuss their ongoing relationship with each other and with the other health professionals on the team (unidisciplinary interactive team). The interdisciplinary clinic team will meet regularly to discuss patient care plans and will periodically meet to discuss the team's function.

An interdisciplinary health care team has certain requirements to ensure its survival, efficiency, and effectiveness. As a team clarifies and re-clarifies its practice objectives, those objectives must meet the needs of the patients the team is attempting to serve. The team clarifies and engages in an ongoing symbiotic relationship with the broader organization. Both must establish a structure and rules for process that will support a culture of collaborative problem solving, communication, and conflict management. Both must recognize the need for initial team training and continued team development.

Interdisciplinary Clinical Practice Linked to Education and Research

It is useful to view clinical practice, education, and research as integrated entities. Promoting collaborative relationships among different professions makes sense within a teaching/research context. Demanding integration of health professions would help lend critical perspectives to the most difficult and complex issues in health care, like how to provide comprehensive care with limited resources and when to limit or stop medical care. Linking research with clinical practice would help to evaluate practice protocols, to raise and research clinical questions, and to remain on the cutting edge of clinical care. Linking education with clinical practice would promote a questioning environment, teach ways to model interdisciplinary teamwork, and to mentor other team members. Both education and research are essential ingredients to challenge assumptions about clinical practice.

A well-developed interdisciplinary team learns from past experiences of its members and has the potential to be the foundation for many other team models of clinical care, teaching, and research in geriatrics and complex care situations; models that measure change/complexity/and chaos. It will take more than didactic training and problem based learning modules to assure that the complex health care needs of geriatric patients are met by the most efficient and effective team method possible. We will need well-developed clinical teams which can function as teachers and role models to students and health professionals. Such teams can function as a central focus for other less resource intensive teams. There is evidence for the value of a well-developed healthcare team that has members who engage in critical reflection. Once we recognize the value of developed interdisciplinary health care teams, we must learn how to use them effectively in primary and continuing education processes. It is crucial for the team's members to model the processes for confronting conflict and negotiating roles. It takes time, effort and resources to create a team culture that fosters critical questioning. Ideally the vehicle should exhibit high performance and durability even as it engages in frequent internal controversies. Paradoxically, this focus on critical questioning fosters an open and supportive work environment which in turn can lead to reduction of fear and prevention of errors [31].

Patients are not exempt from the need for education. Patients cannot continue to expect that their physicians alone can meet all of their healthcare needs. They too must be taught what to expect from a team, how to work with a team, and how to tell when a team is not functioning as it should. The rise in the number of patients shopping for healthcare alternatives is an opportunity for health professionals to teach that a well-functioning interdisciplinary healthcare team can provide more comprehensive care and that the patient's views and values will be represented in the treatment plan.

The questions when should teams function, how should they function, how should team members be trained to function, and what is the support for teams to function must be answered in a systematic way. Since professional disciplines are sensitive to using scientific methodology in their pursuit of truth, it is surprising that the study of healthcare teams has largely escaped scientific methodology. In medical and research circles science gets funded and funneling capital into the study of healthcare teams will provide evidence for what kinds of teams are the most effective for different needs in complex care settings. Additional studies should help indicate the most appropriate ways to train health professionals to function in the continuum of interprofessional care. Studies of these questions need not be solely through the process of quantitative scientific inquiry. They can be through ongoing processes of inquiry such as quality improvement, organizational feedback at all levels, and action science. However, for all of these methods, target outcomes must encompass real changes in patient care and/or in team function.

CONCLUSION

A recognition of the need for integrated interprofessional practice is the first step to improving the efficiency and effectiveness of caring for patients with complex problems. With such recognition by health care reimbursement and review systems, all of the other issues could eventually be resolved. Without such recognition, there is little hope for survival of interdisciplinary practice.

Healthcare teams have been around since at least the early twentieth century. The interdisciplinary teamwork system is the epitome of team delivered care and when it is understood and executed as it is meant to be has a high likelihood of providing health care that is comprehensive and responsive to the changing needs of both the patient and the healthcare system. However, this type of team is complex and like many complex entities is misunderstood. When things go wrong and efficiencies are not achieved we blame what we do not fully understand—the interdisciplinary team. Rather than looking at the team's context in terms of history and systems (delivery, training, and funding) we blame the team and do away with that which is so complex and ill understood. However, because health care involves human systems it requires human communication. The best way to assure effective and efficient communication is with a structure and process that is matched with what needs to be communicated (its complexity and frequency). Thus, as we destroy teams, we keep creating them in new forms, except we do not match them to the complexity and frequency of what needs to be communicated.

Helping interdisciplinary healthcare teams meet the challenge of collaborative practice in the twenty-first century will require systematic intervention. A basic understanding of different types of teams and why they work in some situations and not in others is another essential step. Initial team training, use of reliable and valid assessments of team function, training for interdisciplinary team development, and structures and processes for team maintenance will all be necessary mechanisms to keep interdisciplinary healthcare practice at optimal levels.

We remain skeptical of interdisciplinary teams in health care. They have been said to be too cumbersome, too costly, too time consuming, too resource intensive; and yet, they just won't go away. The question is not whether interdisciplinary healthcare practice is possible in the twenty-first century; the question is, "can we afford not to develop the technology of interdisciplinary practice?" What will be the results of many disciplines not working together or of one discipline trying to do it all?

REFERENCES

1. P. Starr, *The Transformation of American Medicine*, Basic Books, NewYork, 1982.
2. D. B. Smith and A. D. Kaluzny, *The White Labyrinth: Understanding the Organization of Health Care*, McCutchan Publishing, Berkeley, California, 1975.
3. A. R. Tarlov, The Coming Influence of a Social Sciences Perspective on Medical Education, *Academic Medicine, 67*, pp. 724-731, 1992.
4. Corporation for Public Broadcasting, *Medicine at the Crossroads*, PBS Series for Television, 1993.
5. E. Ernst and T. J. Kaptchuk, Homeopathy Revisited, *Archives of Internal Medicine, 156*, pp. 2162-2164, 1996.
6. J. Kluger, Mr. Natural, *TIME Magazine, 149*:19, pp. 68-76, 1997.
7. E. C. Annandale, The Malpractice Crisis and the Doctor-Patient Relationship, *Sociology of Health Care and Illness, 11*, pp. 1-23, 1989.
8. H. B. Beckman, K. M. Markakis, A. L. Suchman, and R. M. Frankel, The Doctor-Patient Relationship and Malpractice: Lessons from Plaintiff Depositions, *Archives of Internal Medicine, 154*, pp. 1365-1370, 1994.
9. S. A. Cole, Reducing Malpractice Risk Through More Effective Communication, *American Journal of Managed Care, 3*:4, pp. 649-653, 1997.
10. J. Bowe, Imminent Danger: Surge in Lawsuits Jeopardizes Providers, *Contemporary Long Term Care*, pp. 31-32, July 1993.
11. World Health Organization, *World Health Organization Constitution in Basic Documents*, World Health Organization, Geneva, 1948.
12. A. Caplan, H. T. Englehardt, Jr., and J. McCartney (eds.), *Concepts of Health and Disease*, Addison-Wesley, Reading, Massachusetts, 1981.
13. J. Scadding, Health and Disease: What Can Medicine Do for Philosophy? *Journal of Medical Ethics, 14*, pp. 118-124, 1988.
14. A. Caplan, Can Philosophy Cure What Ails the Medical Model? in *The Second 50 Years: Promoting Health and Preventing Disability*, R. L. Berg and J. S. Cassells (eds.), National Academy Press, Washington, D.C., pp. 291-310, 1990.
15. P. Reich, Physician Education in the Management of Managed Care, *Medical Interface, 10*, pp. 3, 17, 1997.
16. M. Catley-Carlson, Global Considerations Affecting the Health Agenda of the 1990s, *Academic Medicine, 67*, pp. 419-428, 1992.
17. M. R. Greenlick, Educating Physicians for Population-Based Clinical Practice, *Journal of the American Medical Association, 267*, pp. 1645-1648, 1992.
18. S. E. Radecki, R. L. Kane, D. H. Solomon, R. C. Mendenhall, and J. C. Beck, Do Physicians Spend Less Time with Older Patients? *Journal of the American Geriatrics Society, 36*, pp. 713-718, 1988.
19. E. Ubell, Talk Back to Your Doctor, *Parade Magazine*, pp. 8-11, April 4, 1993.

20. E. Ginzberg and M. Ostow, Managed Care—A Look Back and a Look Ahead, *New England Journal of Medicine, 336,* pp. 1018-1020, 1997.
21. J. R. Evans, The Health of the Public Approach to Medical Education, *Academic Medicine, 67,* pp. 719-723, 1992.
22. J. R. Knickman, M. Lipkin, Jr., S. A. Finkler, W. G. Thompson, and J. Kiel, The Potential for Using Non-Physicians to Compensate for the Reduced Availability of Residents, *Academic Medicine, 67,* pp. 429-438, 1992.
23. F. E. Netting and F. G. Williams, Case Manager-Physician Collaboration: Implications for Professional Identity, Roles, and Relationships, *Health and Social Work, 21:3,* pp. 216-224, 1996.
24. S. H. Qualls and R. Czirr, Geriatric Health Teams: Classifying Models of Professional and Team Functioning, *The Gerontologist, 28,* pp. 372-376, 1988.
25. L. I. Stein, The Doctor-Nurse Game, *Archives of General Psychiatry, 16,* pp. 699-703, 1967.
26. L. I. Stein, T. Howell, and D. Watts, The Doctor-Nurse Game Revisited, *New England Journal of Medicine, 322,* pp. 546-549, 1990.
27. S. E. Skochelak and T. C. Jackson, An Interdisciplinary Clerkship Model for Teaching Primary Care, *Academic Medicine, 67,* pp. 639-641, 1992.
28. R. G. Petersdorf, The Doctor Is In, *Academic Medicine, 68,* pp. 113-117, 1993.
29. T. J. K. Drinka and R. O. Ray, Health Care Team Does Not Equal Health Care Team, in *Proceedings of the Fourteenth Annual Conference on Interdisciplinary Health Care Teams,* J. Schneider (ed.), University of Indiana, Indianapolis, Chicago, Illinois, pp. 1-12, 1992.
30. T. J. K. Drinka, Applying Learning from Self-Directed Work Teams in Business to Curriculum Development for Interdisciplinary Geriatric Teams, *Educational Gerontology, 22,* pp. 433-450, 1996.
31. L. L. Leape, Error in Medicine, *Journal of the American Medical Association, 272,* pp. 1851-1857, 1994.

CHAPTER
8

Organizing Chronic Care: The Value of Organization Theory to Gerontology

William E. Aaronson, Connie J. Evashwick, and Richard M. Shewchuk

The field of aging research has flourished in recent decades. At the same time, a rich body of organizational theory and empirical research has arisen which focuses on long term and acute care services in an organizational context [1]. Organization theory is valuable in helping us to understand the evolution of the healthcare system. It helps us to understand the influence of environment on organizational structure and strategy, how structures evolve to gain greater control over the environment, and the forces that inhibit organizational change. However, much of the organizational context is devoid of connection to the clients served by the organization. Clients have often been considered as control variables in empirical models. Thus, there has not been a clear and consistent link in the empirical literature between organizational research and other social sciences research.

Organizational theory, itself having an interdisciplinary foundation, is insufficient to model or understand the behavior of health services organizations. Knowledge of the health and medical sciences, social sciences, and the applied social science disciplines are essential to the study of health services organizations. Thus, interdisciplinary research, that includes organizational theory and medical and social sciences, is essential to the pursuit of knowledge in the area of chronic care services organization, financing, and delivery. That is, it is essential that chronic care research be based on a theoretical understanding of the technical basis of service delivery and of the behavior of organizations that deliver the services.

This effort bridges the gap in that we envision a continuum of care as an organizational solution to chronic care needs. Organizations form when it is not possible for individuals to adequately complete important or desired tasks alone. This effort assesses organizational evolution of a chronic care system using chronic care need as an evaluation criterion. That is, we examine the changing roles of health services organizations as they relate to environmental contingencies. Historically, hospitals, nursing homes, and physician practices operated as if they were closed systems. That is, they valued predictability, order and efficiency over openness, adaptability, and innovation [1]. A fee-for-service payment system protected health services organizational boundaries and allowed them to act as independent agents in service provision. However, capitated payment systems will result in erasure of the organizational boundaries and creation of newer, more adaptable systems. Organizational theory allows us to hypothesize about the nature of systems evolution.

As a point of caution, the approach we are taking does not assume that the "chronic care system" is distinct and separate from the healthcare system. Rather, the chronic care system is a subsystem within the general healthcare system. However, what makes the chronic care system unique is that it has a boundary spanning components that link the healthcare delivery system to the social service delivery system, the family and community informal support networks, and the welfare system. These system linkages are complex. We are not ignoring the significance of the informal support systems as important environmental contingencies. In light of the complexity of interactions within the system as a whole, we will focus on those subsystems that include formal care providers and purchasers of care within the healthcare delivery system. In this way, we will be able to describe a continuum of care within an organizational theoretic framework.

CHRONIC CARE: DEFINING THE PARAMETERS OF A CONTINUUM OF CARE

Understanding chronic care requires that researchers examine the medical and social conditions related to the chronic illnesses and disabilities. Medical science provides a basic understanding of the pathophysiologies that are the basis of chronic illness. In addition, medical research can provide answers about the probabilities of change in the disease process, known as the trajectory of illness. Trajectory of illness is influenced by social and environmental factors. For example, the progress of coronary heart disease is influenced by smoking behavior, exercise, and stress, among other factors. Thus, behavioral research is essential in understanding the trajectory of illness. Finally, epidemiologists can describe the disease profile (distribution and risk) for a population. Studying chronic illness requires an interdisciplinary effort.

Gerontological and health services research has helped us to understand the causes and effects of chronic illness on the population. Improved living standards (economic, sanitary, food preparation, distribution, etc.) and medical technology have resulted in a general aging of the population. The aging of the population has resulted in the increased prevalence of chronic conditions such as heart and pulmonary disease, cerebrovascular disease, and arthritis [2]. Chronic disease is a progressive process. It requires both medical care and personal supportive care over the trajectory of illness as the acute exacerbation of the conditions increase and the disease process reduces functional capacity [3]. The problem of chronic illness has been associated principally with an aging society, due to the sheer numbers of older persons in society. The aging of North American society has been well documented. However, the problems of chronic illness are not confined to the elderly. The numbers of chronically ill children have increased dramatically as a result of medical interventions that reduced risk of premature death in at-risk children. Also, with advances in medical treatment, persons with the human immunodeficiency virus are likely to live longer. With an extension of the natural history of HIV over many years, this disease for all intents and purposes should be classified as a chronic disease. Better trauma care has also resulted in increased survival rates from motor vehicle accidents, falls, and gunshots—but with a high likelihood of chronic medical conditions requiring long-term medical, psychological, and social supportive services. Thus, improved living conditions and better medical care have resulted in increasing rates of survival with higher prevalence rates of morbid conditions.

Thus, it is nearly impossible to discuss chronic illness without referring to services that are required by persons with chronic illness. Services are provided in an organizational context. Thus, research focusing on chronic illness must of necessity consider the organizational context(s) within which care is organized and delivered.

Chronic disease affects persons of all ages and presents the single most important challenge to the healthcare system—i.e., organizing and financing services given a resource base that is growing at a slower rate than healthcare resource use. This is reflected in the well-documented increases in healthcare spending as proportion of gross national product. As chronic disease prevalence increases it will become more important to design care systems that are both effective and efficient.

The present system of care tends to dichotomize need between acute medical care and long-term custodial care [4]. The use of the former has been considered to be an insurable event; while the latter is considered a personal responsibility and, therefore, a welfare issue for those unable to fulfill that responsibility [5]. The need for a continuum of institutional and home based services that includes intermediate levels between acute and custodial care has been well documented [3, 4, 6, 7]. Early reform efforts were directed toward motivating the development of less expensive non-institutional services. For example, the Omnibus Reconciliation Act (OBRA) of 1981, Medicaid waiver programs, and the federal Community Long-Term Care Demonstration Project resulted in the legitimization of additional services as important components of a care continuum. Additionally, the Tax Equity and Fiscal Responsibility Act of 1982 provided incentives to include Medicare beneficiaries in managed care plans, which Congress believed would exert greater control over costly inpatient expenditures. There were also several federal demonstration projects which allowed for experimentation with various payment arrangements, organizational structure, and use of health professionals. On balance, the federal effort did not result in the creation of integrated delivery systems, but has smoothed the way for market reform of the healthcare delivery system [8].

The market for chronic care services has changed considerably in recent years, resulting in a substantial increase in non-institutionally based long-term care and innovative approaches to the design and delivery of institutionally based services. The chronic care system is far from integrated. However, the need to more efficiently and effectively deliver services is creating an environment that is right for the development of an integrated continuum of care for persons with chronic illnesses and disabilities across the age spectrum. This chapter examines the trends and organizational changes that will lead to better organized systems of care. In particular, we will examine the changing roles of institutional providers and their likely contributions to integrated delivery systems (IDSs).

GETTING IT RIGHT THROUGH INTEGRATED DELIVERY SYSTEMS

Ideally, all persons should have continuous access to a seamless continuum of care. This system would include primary, secondary, and tertiary prevention services, rationally organized and coordinated, so that consumers will optimize use of it and experience optimal health states. Evashwick defined a continuum of care as:

> a client-oriented system of care comprising both services and integrating mechanisms that guides and tracks an enrolled client population over time through a comprehensive array of health, mental health and social services spanning all levels of intensity of care, with common financial incentives among providers, payers, and participants [7, p. 6].

The definition makes reference to both services and to integrating mechanisms. What is not referenced are the organizational structures that provide the services, and how those services are linked across organizational boundaries. The services of the continuum include medical, psychological, and social services, and range from short-term, acute medical care to long-term personal, supportive services. These services tend to be delivered in discrete units by provider organizations, including physician practices, hospitals, home health agencies, nursing homes, adult day care, hospice, and specialized housing units. What makes the continuum complete is when the services are coordinated and integrated in such a way that the consumer is able to access needed services through a central source, services are non-duplicative and the client receives complementary, coordinated services that assure the best outcome.

The integrating mechanisms are the means by which the continuum of care is completed. These mechanisms include interorganizational planning, care management, integrated information systems, and capitated payment systems [7]. Essentially, the integrating mechanisms include the managerial strategies to coordinate services delivered by different provider organizations. The evolution of the integrated delivery system (IDS) is a means to achieve a continuum of care for all consumers, not just those with long-term need for care management. However, we are far from the ideal system. Current efforts to develop IDSs are limited to the formation of provider networks, including physician practices, hospitals, and occasionally long-term care organizations as well. Ultimately, the IDS will need to be flexible and change in response to environmental pressures, including changing health and social ills, technology, and the national/global economy. More diversified organizations will form, the focus of which is the integration of clinical services.

These newer organizational forms are likely to be dynamic and more resemble the "virtual corporation" [9] than the traditional static, bureaucratic organizational form health services executives are used to. The virtual health care company is likely to have management teams that represent a network of collaborating providers and support companies linked by capitation contracts and economic joint ventures [10].

In the interim, the chronic care system will continue to evolve in response to changing payment and market incentives. In particular, there are two changes that will most directly effect motivation and ability for health services providers to enter into arrangements that set the conditions necessary for a continuum of care. The first is the growth in information technology, the cost of information technology, and growth in organizational information management capability. The challenge is in developing a system that provides instant access to information by clinical decision makers and facilitates communications among management and clinical care teams [10]. Second, change from fee-for-service to case-based to partial risk to full risk capitation payment will gradually increase the motivation of providers to form integrated delivery systems as they become more responsible for health of enrolled populations [8]. The growth in information technology is necessary in order to estimate and manage risk. However, this chapter is concerned primarily with understanding the conceptual foundations of service integration, not the technology required to support it.

The trend toward capitated payment systems has resulted from the desire at each level of payment to shift risk onto the level below, and ultimately onto providers. The federal government shifts risk to HMOs through Medicare risk contracts; to states through block grants. The HMO passes risk to providers through capitated partial risk contracts. HMOs and providers pass risk onto the consumer through service and access limits and diminution of quality. This trend is based on the ethical principle of subsidiarity which states simply that decisions should be made at the lowest level possible and that individuals should not receive assistance when they are capable of acting as a self-governing agent. Regardless of the potential for ethical analysis, the conclusion is that shifting risk from government and private insurers onto providers allows for a strong incentive to create systems that reduce financial risk related to use of services. This is a profound change in incentives to providers as they scramble to serve enrolled populations optimally and limit service use by individuals.

The nature of this change is important to understand. First, the move toward capitated, rather than fee-for-service, payment reduces the entitlement mentality of federal health insurance programs. The federal budget becomes more predictable as financial risk is shifted onto states and private insurers. States in turn follow the same strategy with the same result. Second, this forces communities, payers, and providers to develop managerial solutions to the health needs of constituent populations or communities (depending on who is served).

This chapter will examine some of these changes and the likely impact on the roles and relationships of institutional providers in the 1990s. The creation of integrated delivery systems that provide a seamless continuum of care is an ideal that the authors believe we should continue to strive for. However, it may be difficult to predict the actual behavior of providers. The wild card in this process is the role of financial risk reduction—an important moving force behind system evolution. Long-term incentives of capitated systems may present a new risk to consumers—related to quality [11]. We will not address this issue directly. The future roles of system providers may be influenced by incentives to reduce quality and limit access in order to maintain system profitability.

MEDICARE AND MEDICAID PAYMENT CHANGES

Medicare is the primary source of health insurance for Social Security beneficiaries and the permanently disabled. Medicaid is the primary third-party payer for long-term nursing home care. Regardless of how draconian the cuts in the Medicare and Medicaid budgets, the programs will continue to be an essential ingredient in financing the continuum of care for the chronically ill. It is likely that Congress will find ways to move more Medicare beneficiaries into managed care plans without appearing to eliminate essential freedom of choice. The number of states with mandated Medicaid managed care or limited mandates are growing rapidly.

The market has spoken as well. Voluntary HMO enrollment by Medicare beneficiaries has increased dramatically in recent years. Between 1986 and 1992 enrollment in HMOs tripled from 440 thousand to 1.4 million [12]. Unpublished HCFA Region III (Pennsylvania, Maryland, West Virginia) indicates that from January to November, 1995, enrollment in Medicare risk plans increased in Region III from 64 k to 161 k, a 250 percent increase. At a minimum, Congress will include cost and benefit incentives in the Medicare program that will make managed care plans very attractive to the typical Medicare beneficiaries.

Medicare risk contracts are a means to transfer financial risk of beneficiary service use from the federal government onto the risk contractor, usually an HMO, or managed care plan [8]. The HMO enters into a contract with the HCFA whereby HCFA pays the HMO a capitated payment per enrollee per month. The HMO is then required to provide Medicare covered services, with the HMO at-risk for Medicare service costs that exceed the amount paid per capita by Medicare. HMOs in turn may choose to share the risk with providers by negotiating favorable pricing structures or capitated rates with providers for a defined list of services to be made available to enrollees. This is referred to as a partial risk contract. This arrangement puts the provider organization at risk for use of services, but is limited to the service-use risk agreed to in the contract.

The Medicare and Medicaid programs form the backbone of the payment system for persons with complex chronic illnesses and disabilities. The influence that these two payers have on shaping the system of chronic care is considerable. The future role of chronic care service providers will largely depend on the methods of payment, what organized entities are selected as risk contractors, and the methods by which they organize and compensate providers for services rendered.

SERVICE MANAGEMENT, FINANCIAL RISK,
AND UNCERTAINTY REDUCTION

In order to understand the incentives of capitated risk contracts, it may be useful to consider the sources of risk and methods to manage risk in an enrolled population. The contract defines the services that the contractor agrees to provide to a group of enrolled persons in exchange for per member per month payment from the purchaser. In this type of an arrangement, in contrast to fee-for-service, the contractor assumes the risk of service use. Service use generates financial risk for the contractor. Financial risk is the risk related to availability and use of services by the enrolled population. Assuming that revenue generated per member is fixed, expenses are a function of fixed investments (capital and human resources), and variable costs related to service use. The availability of services is a function of the investment made by communities, governments, provider organizations and payers in the technology, and people necessary to provide the services. These costs tend to be fixed or sunk costs. This investment is manifested in the number of hospital beds, nursing home beds, physicians, nurses, etc. per capita among a defined population. Use of services will be influenced by available services and by the health or medical need of individuals within the population and the total population.

While investment in resources is a sunk cost to the system, use of services is a function of the extent to which services are used and the combination of those services, resulting in the variable cost component. The use of services, in theory, should be driven by the health needs of consumers and communities. If this were the case, then in making decisions about service use by individuals, the identification of the least cost (discretionary use of services—variable costs) service combination that will not violate a quality constraint is the solution. The search for such a solution begins a priori. The solution is based on an understanding of probabilities. These probabilities are used to predict the likely trajectory of disease given the application of various resources/services. Potential outcomes are ranked according to value to the consumer or provider. The decision maker then must select the combination of services that will optimize outcome. Keep in mind that outcomes include positive and negative results of services/procedures, and the resultant cost to the individual and the system. If the theory is sound, then a mathematical solution is possible. If so, then the decision maker only needs to identify the current condition (inputs). Given that outcome values are relatively static, the solution can be derived. Sounds simple—a problem that can be solved by linear programming. Thus, the search for critical paths and the development of physician practice guidelines can be understood as an effort to reduce financial risk through the identification of a least cost solution defined by the condition of the patient, given a quality constraint. That is, given the medical and social condition of the patient, there exists a combination of medical services that will provide the best outcome at the lowest cost. Again, developing this methodology requires a strong interdisciplinary theoretical base.

There are several problems with this conclusion, however. Each problem is related to some faulty assumptions contributed by exclusion of or faulty interpretation of disciplinary research. First, chronic and degenerative disease processes have illness trajectories that carry considerable uncertainty (uncertainty in medical decision making). Second, the trajectories of illness are influenced strongly by social, psychological, and economic factors related to personal support and care (behavioral research). Third, services are fungible—witness current attempts to define subacute care and to identify whom should provide it. Fourth, even full risk contracts will have service gaps and holes. Small contributory errors by each discipline can result in conclusions for which errors are magnified (organizational research).

The fungibility (substitutability) of services provided by hospitals, physicians, nursing home, home health providers, clinics, among others, presents a dilemma to anyone seeking to predict the future role for service providers. Now, enter the role of managed care.

THE ROLE OF MANAGED CARE IN THE CONTINUUM

In theory, managed care is the process by which services are managed for an enrolled population in such a manner so as to provide a seamless and cost-appropriate system of care. Since managed care is a process, it can be identified as a role and a function of providers, payers, or dynamic consortia of providers. Ultimately, the managed care organization will become what has been described as the virtual corporation [9], which forms around specific population needs. The virtual corporations will be dynamic and shift as population health needs shift, and as payment methods change. In the interim, it is important to identify the roles of institutional providers in affecting the changes that will lead to virtual managed care organizations.

SERVICES OF THE CONTINUUM

In understanding the future roles of provider organizations, it is important to understand that we are really addressing the issue of who stakes claim to the provision of which services. Evashwick has developed a system of service classification which is useful in understanding future institutional roles [7, 13]. She defined over sixty distinct services. These services were grouped into seven categories: extended care, acute inpatient care, ambulatory care, home care, outreach, wellness, and housing. These categories represent the basic types of health and health-related assistance that a person would need over time, through periods of both wellness and illness of a chronic care patient.

Some services are clearly health or health-related and are likely to be included as part of a health benefits package. However, some are not directly health-related and may not be included in a benefits package. Non-mandated services, nonetheless, may reduce total cost of service to an enrolled population. Capitated risk contracts allow the provider more discretion in determining which services to include. For example, a hospital that has an outreach program in place may be able to reduce lengths of acute, inpatient stays more effectively than a hospital without such a program. Thus, the optimal mix of services may include health and non-health services. This is a different mindset than is typical of most providers who were enculturated into a fee-for-service system. In a fee-for-service system, if a payer will only pay for services from list X, and not Y, than providers would only provide services from list X. However, when the provider bears the financial risk for service use, and the optimal mix includes services from each list, than the provider will provide the service mix that meets financial and quality objectives. But the provider may not be organizationally capable of providing services from list Y, so the incentive is set for development of networks and integrated delivery systems.

CLINICAL INTEGRATION AND SERVICE MANAGEMENT: STRUCTURAL PROTOTYPES

The crux of the problem inherent in creating a continuum of care is understanding that the continuum by definition is based on the vertical integration of patient care [14]. It is the integration of clinical services that creates a continuum of care, not the integration of administrative structures. Gillies et al. define integration as

> the extent to which functions and activities are appropriately coordinated across operating units—that is, any organization within the system that is involved in the provision of health care services such as acute care and specialty hospitals, home health agencies, nursing facilities and medical group practices—to maximize value of services delivered to the patient [15, p. 468].

Thus, integrated delivery systems are those that have "the capacity to plan, deliver, monitor, and adjust the care of an individual over time" [14, p. 492].

According to Hurley, a continuum of care can be implemented by provider-sponsored integrated care systems or by purchaser-driven provider networks, such as managed care organizations (MCOs) [16]. That is, integrated delivery structures can be fostered by community-based health services providers entering into service networks; or they can be fostered by service purchasers who enroll providers into integrated networks.

PURCHASER-DRIVEN INTEGRATED SYSTEMS

Purchaser-driven systems are those systems in which the purchaser organizes the delivery system for an enrolled population. The enrolled population is likely to be spread over several communities [17]. The mode of service delivery is through purchaser owned subsidiaries and/or through service contracts with local health services providers. The purchaser (hereafter called the managed care organization—MCO) coordinates and integrates services into a rationalized continuum. Provider contracts are likely to be consummated on an at-risk basis, with the purchaser and provider sharing the financial risk of service use by the enrolled population.

Purchaser-driven systems of care tend to focus on efficiency and costs in delivering services to a defined population, primarily due to the ease with which costs can be modeled. While quality is an important consideration, quality management focuses on the development of critical paths and clinical outcomes. (A critical path is an optimal sequencing and timing of interventions by physicians, nurses, and other staff for a particular diagnosis [18].) Clinically defined pathways or medical practice guidelines can be easily monitored given modern information technology, thus simplifying the task of managing services for the enrolled population.

Current managed care systems directed by MCOs make primary care physicians formally responsible for case management and provide them incentives to manage the use of services efficiently and in accord with practice guidelines. The physician serves as the first gatekeeper in managing the use of services. MCOs have an incentive to reduce financial risk through oversight of the gatekeeper function. This incentive creates an ethical dilemma for the MCO and for the primary care physician. It places the physician in a position to balance the demands of the MCO and personal economic health against the legitimate professional and consumer expectations of quality and accountability [11, 19]. While most physicians are not directly motivated by financial incentives to prescribe the least cost alternative treatment, MCOs indirectly increase leverage on physicians by refusing to pay for a higher cost alternative. The emerging focus on subacute care [20] provides an illustrative example. Patients requiring intravenous antibiotic therapy and close medical supervision (i.e., subacute care) may be treated either in an acute care hospital, or in a lower cost skilled nursing facility (SNF). The role of the MCO as backup gatekeeper enters, protecting the MCO from the uncertainties of opportunistic physician behavior. Primary care physicians may be given no choice in treatment site if the MCO refuses to pay for a hospital admission. Thus, MCOs have the incentive and ability to restructure use of services by the way in which payment for services is determined, and by carefully monitoring or micromanaging the use of the services.

PROBLEMS WITH PURCHASER DRIVEN NETWORKS

Capitated systems of payment provide strong incentives to select the least cost service option. Thus, MCOs will monitor service use and take corrective action if providers are not following the guidelines established by the MCO. This process is called micromanaging services. Micromanagement of services by case managers external to the community is an inadequate strategy to assure access and expenditure control, especially for persons with complex chronic illness and social network deficits. Medical decisions are fraught with uncertainty [21]. While uncertainty is inherent in medical practice, the identification of need becomes less clear as the condition moves from emergent to long-term, chronic. Service need is affected by measurable medical conditions (pathophysiology) and intangible social support needs. Coordination of services for older and chronically ill clients becomes integral in assuring that service needs are identified and met equitably [3].

However, case managers working for managed care organizations (MCOs) make service choice decisions based on critical path analysis, clinical protocols, and least-cost options. As medical conditions become more complex, as they do for persons with multiple, chronic illnesses, critical pathways become more obtuse, clinical decisions less clear, and outcomes more uncertain [22]. Case managers who are external to the care system have less ability to manage care. As a result, outcome uncertainty and financial risk to the MCO increase.

While critical path analysis is an important tool, community-based case management systems are more likely to identify personal, cultural, or community factors that influence care outcomes. As a result, locally sponsored care management efforts have a greater likelihood of applying clinical practice guidelines flexibly and effectively. In the future, much of the clinical management activity will occur in close proximity to patients—at the bedside, in physician group offices, satellite clinics, and other care settings [10]. Case management will occur through communication linkages among management and clinical teams, including e-mail, fax, phone, and other venues not yet imagined.

Locally organized care management strategies which focus on use of nurse specialists or interdisciplinary clinical teams to coordinate care are more likely to be perceived as augmenting, rather than controlling, the primary medical care practice [14]. Practice guidelines will emerge through consensus, not by edict [10]. Thus, local control of service access is likely to be more cost effective than external control due to the greater ability to compensate for uncertainty in medical decisions, the greater likelihood of attaining physician participation in the continuum, and clinical service integration. These factors are critical to the successful development of IDSs. Local versus external control will also influence the roles and functions of providers within the system.

PROVIDER-SPONSORED INTEGRATED SYSTEMS

The provider-sponsored, fully integrated system is less developed, but may be a more appropriate vehicle for developing a community-based care continuum fully responsive to constituent preferences. As an example of a provider-sponsored system, Shortell et al. describe what they call organized delivery systems (ODS). An ODS is ". . . a network of organizations that provides or arranges to provide a coordinated continuum of services to a defined population and is willing to be held clinically and fiscally accountable for the outcomes and the health status of the population served" [23, p. 447]. The American Hospital Association defines community care networks (CCNs) as:

. . . any system of health care delivery that has made great progress toward community care network vision, especially by planning and operating itself through the pursuit of improving community health. It delivers or enables the delivery of a comprehensive array of health and health-related services from preventive to acute to chronic services, in a well-coordinated, high quality, cost effective manner. It operates within the constraints of a budget fixed by capitated payments or a global budget" [24, p. 3].

While community hospitals may belong to horizontally integrated hospital systems or alliances, the extent of hospital affiliation with community care providers will determine the breadth of delivery [25] offered within a geographically concentrated sphere of health care interest, known as a community. The hallmark of provider-sponsored, community-focused care systems is that the population of a culturally and geographically bound community is the denominator in the health status measures used for purposes of accountability [17].

The CCN consists of a network of service organizations, as well as access to tertiary care systems. The CCN is pictured in this figure as comprehensive. However, the reality is that payers and consumers are likely to drive the compositions of special need networks (virtual networks) given the special service needs and payment sources necessary to support such systems of care.

We will now focus on the roles that critical providers in the system play at present and how these roles are likely to change.

THE HOSPITAL'S ROLE IN SYSTEM DEVELOPMENT

The traditional role of the hospital as an inpatient facility providing short-term acute care primarily is diminishing rapidly. Read and O'Brien [26] identified a new imperative for hospitals to become the focus of integrated, comprehensive, and coordinated care systems. The hospital's link into the range of community-based health and social services historically has been through the post-hospital care planning process and physicians on the hospital's medical staff. The critical nature of these links became more apparent as a result of the Medicare Prospective Payment System (PPS). Perceived limitations placed on hospital length of stay has caused many hospitals to explore diversification[1] into related services within the continuum [27, 28]. Forward integration and diversification (e.g., acquisition of nursing homes or home health agencies) became desirable in order to control hospital length of stay by providing easier access to post-discharge placement options.

Backward integration (e.g., acquisition of medical practice organizations or managed care plans) has become important as a result of the growing power and system control exercised by MCOs [29, 30]. Despite the obvious need for diversification and integration, hospital response has been mixed, as has been the resulting performance [31]. That is, hospitals have developed, acquired, or joint ventured to sponsor nursing homes and home health providers; the ventures generally have not resulted in more effective clinical service integration across a continuum of services.

Integration of clinical services across the health and non-health services organizational boundaries is critical to the cost-effective delivery of services to a geographically defined region or community [14]. Thus, hospitals must participate fully in the vertical integration of clinical services in order to meet the health needs of the hospital's constituent community. Conrad states further that administrative and

---

[1] For greater discussion of conceptual basis for diversification and vertical integration, see Clement [32].

organizational-managerial integration is a necessary complement to the clinical integration of patient care.

EVALUATION OF HOSPITAL-BASED SYSTEMS

Although the need is evident, the state of research on effective continuum of care models is underdeveloped. Early results from the Health Systems Integration Study (HSIS), funded by nine participating hospital systems, were reported recently [15, 23]. Relatively little is known about organized healthcare delivery systems that embrace all levels of care, including primary, secondary, tertiary, and rehabilitative care services [23]. There is considerable evidence that some hospitals have developed sophisticated methods of care coordination and case management [33, 34]. Social models of case management have become more sophisticated as a result of federal long-term care demonstration projects, such as the Community Long-Term Care Project and the Medicaid 2176 waiver program [28]. However, applications of lessons learned from these projects to hospital-based coordinated care have not worked well, partly because program planners have not adequately factored important organizational contingencies, such as hospital-physician relations, into the program designs.

Two funded research projects, the Robert Wood Johnson Foundation Hospital Initiative Program in Long-Term Care and the Flinn Foundation Hospital-Based Coordinated Care Program, focused on the hospital's role in coordinating care for persons with long-term care needs [33, 35]. These projects encountered short run successes, but many were not sustained beyond the grant periods. The failure of grant-funded demonstration projects to produce sustained coordinated care systems may be a function of the approaches taken. First, the projects did little to encourage or facilitate hospital structural change or managerial paradigm shifts. For example, the projects encouraged expansion of hospital efforts in care management, but did not require integration with other service organizations, such as medical practice organizations or community long-term care programs. Second, the projects failed to incorporate physicians into program planning and implementation. Thus, without physician support, efforts to coordinate care were doomed to failure.

The critical role of physicians in affecting system integration is further supported in the HSIS study [15]. The study found that the level of physician integration influences both the level of clinical and functional integration. Thus, the success of care coordination efforts is linked to physician participation and integration into the delivery system. Newly emerging structures must be based on partnerships between physicians and hospitals, since new delivery models could result in financial ruin for hospitals if the major source of revenue and cost generation (the physician) is not co-opted into the process of structural redesign [30].

This approach to hospital-led IDSs ignores a fundamental problem with current approaches to the IDS organization for persons with complex chronic care needs. That is, the approach emphasizes medical components and services, and ignores or marginalizes services (community based or nursing facility based) that may be more cost effective. Further, a hospital-centered model may perpetuate what Shortell calls the hospital paradigm. The hospital paradigm conflicts the value base of a continuum of care, as we have described it, in two respects. First, hospitals have an inordinate power base, which is enhanced through further integration with physician services. In terms of contract negotiation, hospitals have been guilty of opportunistic accounting practices [36] that may jeopardize the financial stability of non-hospital partners. Second, hospital culture and acute care practice differ markedly from nursing homes and community care providers. Hospitals were never designed to improve function, but to deliver short-term curative services. Hospitals that will be in the best position to take advantage of newer constituent preferences will be those who have developed parallel structures to support a community care orientation, thus avoiding the limitations of organizational inertia. These structures can accommodate problems related to perceived inequities in the system and would allow for accommodation of cultures.

THE FUTURE ROLE OF HOSPITALS

The traditional functions performed by acute care hospitals have diminished in importance as the health needs of the population have shifted from short-term, acute to long-term, chronic, and as payment methods have emphasized shorter hospital stays and alternative care sites. Shortell et al. believe that acute care is no longer the core business of health care, having been displaced by the growing emphasis on primary care and wellness, to which we add prevention and long-term chronic care [23]. They identify the organized delivery system as one that will provide a comprehensive and coordinated system of care. However, the source(s) of community health system leadership is not clear. Major participants in the system, as defined by Shortell and others, include hospitals, physicians and payers, and the communities they serve; minor participants (at present) include a host of health, long-term care and social service providers. Transformational leadership for health system development must come from among these participants.

The hospital, as the dominant provider of services in existing community care systems [37], is a logical choice to serve as the fulcrum, or pivot point, of a seamless system. Kenkel suggests that hospital systems are positioning themselves to provide medical services to large groups of consumers on a fixed budget, based on capitated payment [30]. While community care networks do not necessarily depend on hospital-based leadership for system formation to occur, hospitals are the only participants that are sufficiently capitalized to provide the support for community care network development and at the same time ward off "takeover" of community care systems by external forces. Hospital system executives' failure to recognize the potential for system leadership and act accordingly will result in hospitals becoming more subject to micromanagement of services by increasingly powerful managed care organizations [29, 36]. The requirements of a chronic care system that provides a continuum of care may provide hospitals with the leverage to establish locally organized IDSs.

ROLE OF THE NURSING FACILITY

Nursing homes have traditionally been considered to occupy space at the edge of the health services delivery system. The current implementation of IDSs is manifested as a hospital, a medical group, and a managed care company joining together in a three-way partnership to reach as many enrollees as possible. Long-term care, and nursing homes in particular, have been viewed as outside of the normal health services continuum, with the exception of services that are provided on an interim basis. The reason is that nursing homes provide a range of services, which include housing, nutrition support, and personal care—none of which are directly defined as health care. For persons with intractable chronic conditions and limited social network support, the nursing home provides a relatively closed system of care. Nursing homes also provide short-term, rehabilitation and special services. For individuals who enter the nursing home for short-term interventions, it is part of the open system continuum of care.

Evashwick and Langdon identify nursing home as a broad category of health facility that encompasses a wide spectrum of organizational units from twenty-bed units in community hospitals to 1200 bed government operated institutions [38]. There is considerable variability among nursing facilities in terms of the types of services provided and the clients served. Under the broad umbrella are included freestanding facilities, units within hospitals, and integral components of multilevel retirement centers. Clients can be of any age, but the predominant group can be characterized as older (median age—81), female (75%), and of European descent (90%). Nursing home residents are characterized by multiple chronic conditions, functional deficits, incontinence, mental confusion, and limited social network support. Nursing home residents can also be short-stay (rehabilitation, hospice, or respite) or long-stay (custodial).

The role played by nursing homes in integrated delivery will depend largely on their ability to identify unique factors that build synergies within integrated systems. Nursing homes that are weak imitations of hospitals, or that poorly execute residential care are unlikely to survive. Nursing facilities that are seen as contributing to the cost effective, long-term management of populations characterized by high rates of complex, chronic illness within capitated systems are most likely to survive [39]. An issue of *Generations: Journal of the American Society on Aging* (Vol. XIX, No. 4, Winter 1995-6) was dedicated to an assessment of evolving roles of nursing homes.

Integrated delivery systems offer potential for nursing facilities to assume a significant role in the healthcare delivery system [40]. Nursing homes play a pivotal role between the acute care hospital and the chronic care system. However, nursing homes have been sheltered from much of the environmental change that has caused hospitals to form IDSs. With the exception of growing pressure for quality reform and the community long-term care demonstrations, nursing homes experienced few substantial threats. Utilization has remained high, while hospital use has declined. The future will not be as promising for nursing facilities that have not adjusted their strategies to take advantage of opportunities to enhance position. By the early 1990s, nursing home occupancy had begun to decline [41]. This is probably due to tighter utilization review, managed care, and competition from non-institutional providers [38]. Aggressive actions are required to identify the strengths that nursing homes bring to IDSs and to use these strengths as an opportunity for assuming a role in the chronic care system.

PERSONAL AND CUSTODIAL CARE

Nursing facilities have traditionally been a major source of non-family support for persons requiring custodial care. The nursing home has historically filled a gap between the curative system of hospital and physician, and the social care system, the family, and community [42]. This role is likely to continue. While that is true, the medicalization of nursing homes that resulted from Medicare and Medicaid regulations, increasing patient acuity, and more recently, the Nursing Home Reform title of the Omnibus Budget Reconciliation Act of 1987, have resulted in rapidly escalating costs. Nursing home care is still paid for largely out-of-pocket (48%—[43]), suggesting that consumer price sensitivity may induce competition for less expensive products within the multi-product firm we call a nursing home. There have been a plethora of alternative residential settings developed in recent years that provide assisted living and personal care. Home care technology and support systems have also improved. It is not the intent of this chapter to explore all possible iterations of the intermediary (between family and institutional care—[42]) market. However, nursing homes are threatened by competition for the low end of the medical care continuum. At the same time, case mix payment systems for nursing homes make that resident unprofitable. A decline in demand at this end is likely to mean declining occupancies that mirror the experience of hospitals in the 1980s.

Many nursing home roles are likely to change. Chronic care services are more readily available in the community, but are in short supply in many places. Consumers pay for much of personal care out-of-pocket. One of the objectives of the community long-term care demonstrations was to show that providing personal care in the community was less expensive than in nursing homes. In order to do this, the policy makers reduced the bias toward nursing homes. Capitated payment systems will encourage use of least cost services. Nursing homes can be a source of expertise and a provider of services within their communities through participation in IDSs. The nursing facility can also offer specialty services on an admission, referral, or community basis [40].

Hospitals generally lack an understanding of and expertise in the rehabilitation and restoration needs of chronic illness. Nursing homes have accumulated considerable experience in the personal and custodial care of persons with Alzheimer's, AIDS, ventilator dependency, and brain injury [40]. There is evidence that a growing number of nursing homes are offering specialty services that are increasingly required within the continuum [44]. The availability of geriatric consultation and health professionals with substantial geriatric experience can decrease length of stay and admissions to expensive inpatient care. Nursing facilities can mobilize this expertise in ways that can be useful to an IDS, such as organizing a geriatric assessment team, offering caregiver training, or creating outreach programs.

SUBACUTE CARE/FUNGIBILITY

Subacute care has received increasing attention in the 1990s as an alternative to acute care for persons who require higher levels of care than most nursing homes provide and lower levels of care than hospitals do [20]. The issue of "subacute" care became more important following the Medicare per discharge payment system for hospitals based on diagnosis related groupings (DRGs). A considerable body of empirical research has confirmed what many knew intuitively—shorter stays and discharges prior to full recuperation (quicker and sicker). Subacute care has been proposed as an intermediate level between acute, inpatient care in a hospital and long-term, chronic care in a nursing facility or personal home.

IDSs based on capitated payment are likely to find the concept has merit. Nursing homes may be a good position to provide subacute care in a cost-effective manner. However, many hospitals have experienced severe stress due to low occupancy. Thus, hospitals are also anxious to utilize slack capacity and may be able to provide higher quality subacute care for persons with complex conditions and comorbidities. Super skilled chronic care or subacute care are likely to go to the physical setting or management structure most able to accommodate long stays cost-effectively [39].

NURSING FACILITIES IN DYNAMIC NETWORKED CHRONIC CARE IDSs

Persons with chronic illnesses require multiple service platforms. Managed care is based partly on uniform service packaging. Nursing homes can play a pivotal role in the organization of IDSs around chronic care needs. However, IDS participation assumes that providers know how to operate under managed care arrangements and capitation [40]. Across the nation, and even in areas of high managed care penetration, nursing facilities have been only minimally involved in managed care. Thus, to participate in an IDS a nursing facility must learn the operational implications of managed care. For example, IDS case managers have authorities regarding patient flow. The director of nurses, social worker, and floor nurses will need to know how to interact with the case manager. The nursing facility needs to know what benefits are covered under managed care contracts, and how to negotiate to provide benefits that may not be explicit but that will be helpful. The nursing facility must have an aggressive orientation toward patient rehabilitation and discharge, including informal or formal arrangements with home health and other community providers who may be essential to facilitate patient discharge.

To maximize their own financial benefit and to know how to participate in an IDS most effectively, nursing facilities must understand how managed care rates are established, how risk pools are constructed, and how incentives differ from fee-for-service payment. For example, the three-day prior hospital stay rule under Medicare does not apply to managed care when the hospitals and physicians receive a capitated payment. Thus, a nursing facility could advocate to admit people who need observation overnight to the nursing facility, at its lower cost, rather than to an acute care hospital. The nursing facility also needs to understand referral differences that are likely to occur if the home and all providers are capitated and share in the risk pool compared to the home having a contract for a per diem rate. The nursing facility also must understand the differences between Medicare HMOs and commercial managed care plans.

PACE—A DYNAMIC NETWORKED ORGANIZATION

The ideal state would allow for the integration of public and private sectors in financing acute and long-term care as part of a continuum. The reality is that little long-term care is capitated, meaning that the integration of long-term care payment depends on providers pulling together fragmented payment mechanisms. PACE provides such an example.[2] The Program of All-Inclusive Care for the Elderly (PACE) is a replication project of the On-Lok Senior Services of San Francisco. On-Lok has had more than twenty years of experience in providing community-based services for the frail elderly. In 1983, On-Lok received its first waivers from Medicare and Medicaid to offer services designed to meet the health and health-related needs of its more than 300 frail participants. Thus, the distinguishing characteristic of On-Lok and its replication projects is that they serve the frail elderly, all of who are certified for nursing home admission. This was a conscious decision to serve this high cost, long-term care population and to bear the financial risk of service delivery.

PACE requires the pooling of funds from Medicare, Medicaid, and member fees. However, there are key distinguishing features. First, since the program is directed specifically at the nursing home eligible population, Medicaid plays a larger part in financing care. The On-Lok site negotiates a Medicaid capitation rate with the California Department of Health Services. Rates are set in accord with the costs of nursing home care. The state Medicaid program then pays On-Lok at the predetermined monthly rate for each Medicaid eligible person participating. On-Lok also receives a Medicare capitation rate that is based on a variation of the standard Medicare methodology that accounts for the population's frailty and utilization experience.

On-Lok uses a consolidated model, in which a multidisciplinary team plans, organizes, and delivers most care, including primary care. Care that is delivered by other organizations, such as hospitals, is closely monitored and managed. Consequently, On-Lok's average hospital length of stay in 1990 was 6.2 days, compared to nine days for all other Medicare beneficiaries in San Francisco [45]. Thus, this model results in a dynamic networked organization of formal and informal arrangements that meet the needs of the consumer group within the limits of pooled, capitated resources available to On-Lok.

---

[2] PACE is one model; others such as Social Health Maintenance Organizations will not be discussed. This is meant to be illustrative only of the potential for network development based on a provider-driven IDS.

PACE is the federally funded and privately endowed attempt to replicate the original On-Lok program at sites throughout the country. The value of PACE is that it provides sponsoring organizations with important lessons in financial risk and health management for a vulnerable and high-risk population. Most of the sponsors are hospitals [46], any organization can be a sponsor. The key to financial and health risk management is to incorporate a network of service providers who are also at risk.

WHAT ROLE WILL PROVIDERS PLAY IN INTEGRATED DELIVERY?

Each provider will need to position their organization for appropriate and fiscally responsible participation in integrated delivery systems. Evashwick and Rundall have defined a multistage approach to understanding the evolution of organized chronic care services [47]. The first stage, emergence, occurs because various factors such as technological change, environmental threats, new market opportunities, or pressure from clients and others lead organizations to seek each other out. Organizations that relate to each other symbiotically are more likely to engage in a continuum, first as a loose network. The emergence of cooperation is based on the need to provide complementary services in response to environmental contingencies.

However, health services organizations are seldom on a level playing field and have divergent cultures. Consequently, if the environmental contingencies are strong enough, they enter a transition period in which the organizations establish mechanisms for coordination, control, and decision making. As the coordination needs increase, trust becomes more critical. At this point, the emerging network enters the third stage, maturity. The common interests drive continued growth and development of linking mechanisms.

As environmental contingencies heat up (competition, managed care penetration, and capitated risk contracts), pressure is placed on participants for even greater commitments to the joint venture. This stage is called the critical crossroads. Networks will solidify in this stage to the extent that they can balance the tendency toward centralization with the need for localized decision making. This is the stage during which the purchaser-driven MCOs are able to influence local service delivery decisions. It is not the intention of this chapter to discuss integration models (alliances, dynamic networks, ownership, etc.). However, suffice it to say here that the integration model selected will determine the relative influence of network participants.

FUTURE DIRECTIONS FOR ORGANIZATIONAL RESEARCH

It is evident that a chapter such as this can only view the tip of the iceberg when assessing financial and organizational dynamics associated with the creation of integrated delivery systems. Our discussion raises far more questions than it answers with respect to the original question raised—organizing chronic care services: are we getting it right? Raising this question in the title of this chapter does not suggest that we can answer it at present. However, there are areas of research that will help us to focus more clearly on an answer.

First, are integrated delivery systems likely to form around populations or targeted constituencies and under what circumstances will this occur? PACE is a dynamic system that forms around a targeted constituency—the frail elderly. HMOs form around targeted constituencies—enrolled populations based on employment, Medicare, or Medicaid status. However, provider sponsored IDSs may form to meet the needs of a community—geographically bound population with common interest. What demographic, economic, and health services resource characteristics will be associated with the development of each type of IDS? Are IDSs that form around populations or constituencies with higher proportions of chronically ill members more likely to include non-health services as benefits to complete the continuum of services? That is, what organizational prototypes are more likely to include traditional chronic care providers in the provider network?

It will also be important to identify who controls the funds and under what circumstances organizational entities are able to capture the capitated revenues. That is, under what circumstances will an integrated chronic care system be provider sponsored or purchaser driven? Provider sponsored IDSs require greater community/ provider based management capability in order to assemble dynamic networks bound together by contracts or common ownership. Does community leadership play a role? Are provider-sponsored or purchaser driven IDSs more likely to include non-health, chronic care service providers in the network? What is likely to be the roles of institutional providers in chronic care provision as the system moves toward IDS formation?

Considering the roles that traditional long-term care providers play and are likely to play, does inclusion of these providers in networked IDSs make a difference in terms of health outcomes or well-being? Some evidence is available from PACE and from the Social Health Maintenance Organization demonstration evaluations, but it is limited.

Finally, it is important to study the linkages between integrated service delivery systems and informal systems of care. Theoretically, an integrated system should provide seamless access. However, persons with chronic illnesses have greater need for personal supportive care. Does an integrated health network provide more or less support to informal support systems? This line of research requires the participation of medical, behavioral, and organizational researchers.

Thus, there is a need for additional research which links organizational and managerial actions to the identification of and efficacious response to chronic care need. It is likely that we will see reduced growth and retrenchment in some areas of health spending. The need for managerial solutions to constrained resources will increase as the system moves toward capitation as a means to shift financial risk onto providers. The question is whether there will be the incentive to create a rational, cost effective system of care for the chronically ill through more effective organization and management. And, will that system be more effective in maintaining and improving the health of the chronically ill? Organization theorists can help to articulate and answer such questions, and thus can contribute to the general body of gerontological literature.

REFERENCES

1. S. Shortell and A. Kaluzny, Organization Theory and Health Services Management, in *Health Care Management: Organization Design and Behavior*, S. Shortell and A. Kaluzny (eds.), Delmar, New York, pp. 3-29, 1994.
2. R. Kane, J. Ouslander, and I. Abrass, *Essentials of Clinical Geriatrics, Second Edition*, McGraw-Hill-Health Professions Division, New York, 1989.
3. T. H. Koff, *New Approaches to Health Care for an Aging Population*, Jossey-Bass, San Francisco, 1988.
4. A. Straus and J. Corbin, *Shaping a New Health Care System*, Jossey-Bass, San Francisco, 1988.
5. W. Aaronson, J. Zinn, and M. Rosko, The Success and Repeal of the Medicare Catastrophic Coverage Act: A Paradoxical Lesson for Health Reform, *Journal of Health Politics, Policy and Law, 19*:4, pp. 753-771, 1994.
6. S. Brody and J. Magel, Long-Term Care: The Long and Short of It, in *Caring for the Elderly: Reshaping Health Policy*, C. Eisdorfer, D. Kessler, and A. Spector (eds.), The Johns Hopkins University Press, Baltimore, pp. 235-258, 1989.
7. C. Evashwick, Definition of the Continuum of Care, in *The Continuum of Care: An Integrated Systems Approach*, C. Evashwick (ed.), Delmar, New York, 1995.
8. W. Aaronson, Financing the Continuum: A Disintegrating Past and an Integrating Future, in *The Continuum of Care: An Integrated Systems Approach*, C. Evashwick (ed.), Delmar, New York, pp. 223-252, 1995.
9. W. Davidow and M. Malone, *The Virtual Corporation*, HarperCollins, New York, 1992.
10. R. C. Coile, Management Teams for the 21st Century, *Healthcare Executive*, pp. 10-13, January/February 1996.
11. J. D. Golenski and M. Cloutier, The Ethics of Managed Care, *Medical Group Management Journal*, pp. 24-28, September-October 1994.
12. F. Porrell and C. Tompkins, Medicare Risk Contracting: Identifying Factors Associated with Market Exit, *Inquiry, 30*:2, pp. 157-169, 1993.
13. C. J. Evashwick, Definition of the Continuum of Care, in *Managing the Continuum of Care*, C. J. Evashwick and L. J. Weiss (eds.), Aspen, Rockville, Maryland, pp. 1-15, 1987.
14. D. Conrad, Coordinating Patient Care Services in Regional Health Systems: The Challenge of Clinical Integration, *Hospitals and Health Services Administration, 38*:4, pp. 509-521, 1993.
15. R. Gillies, S. Shortell, D. Anderson, J. Mitchell, and K. Morgan, Conceptualizing and Measuring Integration: Findings from the Health Systems Integration Study, *Hospital and Health Services Administration, 38*:4, pp. 467-490, 1993.
16. R. Hurley, The Purchaser-Driven Reformation in Health Care: Alternative Approaches to Leveling Our Cathedrals, *Frontiers in Health Services Management, 9*:4, pp. 5-35, 1993.
17. R. Sigmond and J. Seay, In Health Care Reform, Who Cares for the Community? *Journal of Health Administration Education, 12*:3, pp. 259-268, 1994.
18. R. Coffey, J. Richards, C. Remmert, S. LeRoy, R. Schoville, and P. Baldwin, An Introduction to Critical Paths, *Quality Management in Health Care, 1*:1, pp. 45-54, 1992.

19. J. Rakich, B. Longest, and K. Darr, *Managing Health Services Organizations,* Health Professions Press, Baltimore, 1992.
20. W. Aaronson, J. Zinn, and M. Rosko, Subacute Care, Medicare Benefits and Nursing Home Behavior, *Medical Care Research and Review, 52*:3, pp. 364-388, 1995.
21. D. M. Eddy, Variations in Physician Practice, *Health Affairs, 3*:2, pp. 74-89, 1986.
22. J. Falconer, E. Roth, J. Sutin, D. Strassner, and R. Chang, The Critical Path Method in Stroke Rehabilitation: Lessons from an Experiment in Cost Containment and Outcome Improvement, *Quality Review Bulletin,* pp. 8-16, January 1993.
23. S. Shortell, R. Gillies, D. Anderson, J. Mitchell, and K. Morgan, Creating Organized Delivery Systems: The Barriers and Facilitators, *Hospital and Health Services Administration, 38*:4, pp. 447-466, 1993.
24. American Hospital Association, *Transforming Health Care: Toward Community Care Networks,* AHA, Chicago, 1993.
25. W. Fox, Vertical Integration Strategies: More Promising than Diversification, *Health Care Management Review, 14*:3, pp. 49-56, 1989.
26. W. A. Read and J. L. O'Brien, The Involved Hospital, in *Caring for the Elderly: Reshaping Health Policy,* C. Eisdorfer, D. A. Kessler, and A. N. Spector (eds.), The Johns Hopkins University Press, Baltimore, 1989.
27. G. Giardina, M. Fottler, R. Shewchuk, and R. Hill, The Case for Hospital Diversification into Long-Term Care, *Health Care Management Review, 15*:1, pp. 71-82, 1990.
28. J. A. Capitman, J. Prottas, M. MacAdam, W. Leutz, D. Westwater, and D. L. Yee, A Descriptive Framework for New Hospital Roles in Geriatric Care, *Health Care Financing Review,* Annual Supplement, pp. 17-25, 1988.
29. G. R. Wolford, M. Brown, and B. McCool, Getting to Go in Managed Care, *Health Care Management Review 18*:1, pp. 7-19, 1993.
30. P. Kenkel, Filling Up Beds No Longer the Name of the System Game, *Modern Healthcare,* pp. 39-48, September 13, 1993.
31. S. Shortell, E. Morrison, and B. Freidman, *Strategic Choices for America's Hospitals,* Jossey-Bass, San Francisco, 1990.
32. J. P. Clement, Vertical Integration and Diversification of Acute Care Hospitals: Conceptual Definitions, *Hospital and Health Services Administration, 33,* pp. 99-110, Spring 1988.
33. J. B. Christianson, L. H. Warrick, F. E. Netting, F. G. Williams, W. Read, and J. Murphy, Hospital Case Management: Bridging Acute and Long-Term Care, *Health Affairs,* pp. 173-184, Summer 1991.
34. R. Evans and R. Hendricks, Evaluating Hospital Discharge Planning: A Randomized Clinical Trial, *Medical Care, 31*:4, pp. 358-370, 1993.
35. C. A. Coombs, C. Eisdorfer, K. L. Feiden, and D. A. Kessler, Lessons from the Program for Hospital Initiatives for Long-Term Care, in *Caring for the Elderly: Reshaping Health Policy,* C. Eisdorfer, D. A. Kessler, and A. N. Spector (eds.), The Johns Hopkins University Press, Baltimore, 1989.
36. J. C. Robinson, The Changing Boundaries of the American Hospital, *The Milbank Quarterly, 72*:2, pp. 259-275, 1994.
37. J. Griffith, *The Well-Managed Community Hospital,* Health Administration Press, Ann Arbor, Michigan, 1992.
38. C. Evashwick and B. Langdon, Nursing Homes, in *The Continuum of Care: An Integrated Systems Approach,* C. Evashwick, (ed.), Delmar, New York, 1995.
39. K. Wilson and C. Baldwin, Are Nursing Homes Dinosaurs? *Generations,* pp. 69-72, Winter 1996.

40. C. Evashwick, Nursing Facilities in the Emerging Integrated Healthcare Delivery Systems, *Generations*, pp. 36-38, Winter 1996.

41. A. Sirrocco, Nursing Homes and Board and Care Homes, *Advanced Data from Vital and Health Statistics, No. 244*, February 23, 1994.

42. R. Morris, The Evolution of Nursing Homes: An Intermediary Institution, *Generations*, pp. 57-61, Winter 1996.

43. B. Burwell, W. Crown, P. O'Shaughnessy, and B. Price, Financing Long-Term Care, in *The Continuum of Care: An Integrated Systems Approach*, C. Evashwick (ed.), Delmar, New York, pp. 193-221, 1995.

44. V. Mor, J. Banaszak-Holl, and J. Zinn, The Trend Toward Specialization in Nursing Care Facilities, *Generations*, pp. 30-35, Winter 1996.

45. M. Ansak, The On-Lok Model: Consolidating Care and Financing, *Generations, 14*:2, pp. 73-74, 1990.

46. D. Paone, Hospitals, in *The Continuum of Long-Term Care: An Integrated Systems Approach*, C. Evashick (ed.), Delmar, New York, pp. 25-42, 1995.

47. C. Evashwick and T. Rundall, Organizing the Continuum of Long-Term Care, in *The Continuum of Care: An Integrated Systems Approach*, C. Evashwick (ed.), Delmar, New York, 1995.

CHAPTER
9

Nursing Homes and the Long-Term Care Market

Michael A. Morrisey and Fredric D. Wolinsky*

In the 1960s and 1970s, about 4 percent of all Americans aged sixty-five or older could be found in nursing homes [1]. By the early 1990s, that figure had not changed very much. Indeed, the rate has only risen to about 4.5 percent [2]. Thus, it could be said that the demand for nursing homes doesn't seem like much of a issue. After all, the point-prevalence rate is small and rather stable. On the other hand, the total cost of nursing home care in 1993 was about $69.6 billion [3]. The bulk of that was financed by public programs, principally Medicaid (51.7%) or Medicare (8.8%). However, in the year 2020, the number of persons turning age sixty-five will be 76.6 percent greater than in 1990 [4]. In contrast to 1990 when thirty-one million persons were age sixty-five and older and thirteen million where age seventy-five and over, in 2020 there will be fifty-three million persons sixty-five and over and twenty-two million seventy-five and over. These are increases of nearly 70 percent. After extrapolating for the use of and expense associated with nursing homes for these new cohorts, the issue is of considerable national concern.

The purpose of this chapter is threefold. First, to review the empirical literature on nursing home utilization. Next, to review the empirical literature on the economics of the nursing home market. Finally, to suggest areas for further research in these areas. Over the last twenty years the presumption in the literature has been that Medicaid coverage for nursing home care was inadequate. Research has focused on the directions such an expansion might take and the myriad of issues associated with an expanded federal or state role. Given the apparent sea change in Washington, however, research attention needs to focus on the implications of a reduced governmental role and the workings and potential of market forces in the long-term care market.

*Dr. Wolinsky's work is supported, in part, by National Institutes of Health grant AG R37 09692.

Section I deals with the evidence on nursing home utilization. The literature is extensive and has become much more sophisticated over time. However, it is only beginning to include community factors in addition to apparent medical need in analyzing placement, length of stay, and lifetime probability of use. Section II reviews the economic literature on nursing home markets and the fundamental role played by Medicaid. Here the literature is much less extensive, and some key issues have sometimes only been addressed by a single study. The key conclusion, however, is that the nursing home market, including the long-term care insurance market, looks the way it does because of Medicaid. Therefore, changes in Medicaid will likely prompt significant changes in the nursing home market. Section III suggests incremental changes that may occur in Medicaid and identifies an interdisciplinary research agenda that will begin to address the new questions.

I. UTILIZATION OF NURSING HOMES:
NOW AND IN THE FUTURE

The concern over the demand for nursing home care has stimulated a considerable amount of research in recent years (for thoughtful reviews see [5, 6]). This literature has been characterized by several authors for its marked variation in design and analysis [4, 7, 8]. It is perhaps more instructive to characterize that literature, however, as falling into four temporally sequenced categories. The first two focus on episode-based issues, and include the risk of nursing home placement (which has been studied substantially more than the other issues), and the distribution of length of stay (LOS) associated with that placement. In contrast, the second two categories of the literature take a life-course perspective. It is unfortunate that these studies are relatively rare because they have greater relevance for the current discussion. The studies focus on the lifetime risk of nursing home placement, and the proportion of time that will be spent there. Below we use selected studies to briefly illustrate each category of the literature.

A. Risk of Placement

The earliest studies of nursing home utilization were essentially risk factor models. That is, these studies sought to identify the characteristics that made an older adult more likely to be placed in a nursing home. According to Kane and Kane, the motivation for these early studies was the general view that "to prevent unnecessary nursing home admissions without inordinate expenditures, one needs to focus efforts upon that specific group of elderly persons who are most likely both to enter nursing homes and to stay there" [9]. In Kane and Kane's widely cited *Long Term Care,* the frequency of common risk factors for nursing home placement in twelve major studies were graphically displayed [9]. There are three points worth noting. First, no single risk factor has been included in all of the studies. As a result, it is not possible to determine the net (or independent) effect of any of these risk factors. Second, among the risk factors studied most often, the proportion of times that they have been found to be significant is usually about half, with exceptions on the low end for female gender, and on the high end for age. It would seem, therefore, that the risks for nursing home placement do not generalize well across samples. Third, the major risk factors are older age, having debilitating disease, living arrangements (i.e., living alone), physical and cognitive functional deficits, race (i.e., being white), and inadequate social support. This is not entirely surprising, inasmuch as it essentially identifies the ability to maintain one's home (either independently or in consort with one's informal support system) as the common theme underlying the risk of nursing home placement [10].

A common limitation of these early risk factor studies was their reliance on parochial samples, the lack of a unifying theoretical framework, and the absence of multivariate statistical methods [8]. One of the first studies to overcome these limitations was that of Weissert and Cready [6]. Noting that little success had been achieved in the ability to predict nursing home placement, a lament previously made by Kane and Kane [9] among others, Weissert and Cready suggested that a better conceptualization of the risks for nursing home placement was in order. Specifically, they argued that most previous work has focused solely on the characteristics of the population at risk, or patient-level determinants. This ignores community-level factors, such as nursing home bed supply, geographic region, and climate. Weissert and Cready also noted an important anomaly with serious repercussions for risk factor studies: although turnover rates in nursing homes are high (with about half of all lengths of stay [LOSs] being 90 days or less), on any given day, most nursing home residents are long-stayers. Thus, a focus on new admissions to nursing homes might not be as instructive as one that examines ongoing residency.

To address these issues, Weissert and Cready [6] used data from two national surveys: the 1977 National Health Interview Survey (NHIS) and the 1977 National Nursing Home Survey (NNHS). The NHIS is a nationally representative sample of the non-institutionalized civilian population containing detailed data on 11,671 persons aged sixty-five years old or older, while the NNHS is a nationally representative sample of nursing home residents containing detailed data on 6,095 persons aged sixty-five years old or older. Community level data were taken from the Area Resources File, Census tapes, and U.S. Weather Service publications. After recoding the somewhat different data elements in the NHIS and NNHS into equivalent variables, the data were pooled and submitted to multivariate logistic regression analysis to predict the NNHS residents from the NHIS respondents. It is interesting to note that although their results are based on nationally representative samples, are steeped in an explicit conceptual framework, and rely on multivariate techniques, Weissart and Cready's [6] results are essentially the same as those summarized by Kane and Kane [9]. They showed that the major predictors of being a longer-staying nursing home resident vs. living in the community are age, functional and cognitive dependence, disease history, and living arrangements. Not surprisingly, the risk of being a nursing home resident is also higher where there are more nursing home beds available and where the weather is colder.

Another study that sought to overcome the problems of parochial samples, lack of a theoretical framework, and absence of multivariate techniques was that of Wolinsky, Callahan, Fitzgerald, and Johnson [8]. They used data on the 5,151 respondents to the nationally representative Longitudinal Study on Aging (LSOA) obtained at the 1984 baseline interviews to predict which adults aged seventy years old or older would be placed in a nursing home during the next four years. Relying on the behavioral model of health services utilization [11] as the conceptual framework, these authors investigated the sequential roles of sociodemographic and psychosocial characteristics, economic factors, health need, and prior service utilization patterns using multivariate logistic regression. Their results were generally rather similar to those reviewed above. That is, the risk of nursing home placement was higher for older adults, those with fewer social supports (both kin and non-kin), and for those who had difficulty in the ADL activities most directly associated with maintaining a separate residence. In addition, however, the LSOA data revealed that those who worried about their health or had a low sense of control were also more likely to be placed in a nursing home. Nonetheless, once again the major finding is that the ability to maintain one's home (either independently or in consort with one s informal support system) is the common theme underlying the risk of nursing home placement [10].

B. Length of Stay

As alluded to by Weissert and Cready [6], there are two parts to the episode-based approach to the demand for nursing homes: the risk of admission and the length of stay (LOS). Studies focusing on the length of stay have been severely limited by data availability and inadequate conceptualizations of what constitutes an episode of nursing home placement. In terms of data availability, there are a number of issues involved, although they all focus on one theme: simply knowing how long the stay was [12]. If nursing home residents are surveyed, their LOSs are by necessity truncated, because it is not known how long their stay will actually be [13]. This underestimates LOS among long-stayers. At the same time, and as indicated above, the number of short-stayers is underestimated. In contrast, if nursing home discharge records are sampled, more complete LOS data are available. However, using this approach tends to under-represent long-stayers who are discharged outside of the discharge catchment window, at the same time that it captures most of the short-stayers [14].

Perhaps most problematic are conceptual issues involving the definition of a nursing home episode. It has been noted that many nursing home residents have had more than one nursing home stay [15]. At what point are any two of those stays considered to be part of just one episode? Drawing on consensus definitions found in the hospital re-admission literature, Spence and Wiener [13] made an interesting proposal. They argued that LOS from adjacent nursing home stays should be aggregated when any of three conditions were met. The three conditions were: 1) same-day transfers from one nursing home to another; 2) nursing home stays that occurred within 30 days of each other; and 3) nursing home stays separated only by brief hospital stays.

Spence and Wiener applied this aggregation algorithm to data from the 1985 NNHS Discharged Resident Questionnaire in order to estimate nursing home LOS patterns [13]. The 1985 NNHS was based on a sample of 5,329 discharges of older adults aged sixty-five years or older from the 1,079 nursing homes surveyed. In addition to containing the LOS for the index nursing home stay, additional data were obtained concerning up to three previous or subsequent nursing home stays within a thirty-day window of the index stay. After converting the discharges to people, the aggregation algorithm was applied. In order to provide a temporal perspective, Spence and Wiener replicated this approach using comparable data from the 1977 NHHS. They also adjusted the data for the growth in the supply of nursing home beds, so as not to undercount long-stayers who were admitted when fewer nursing home beds were available (and thus fewer people could be long-stayers).

Two important points flow from Spence and Wiener's analysis [13]. First, if one compares their more accurate aggregated LOS distribution with the more simplistic unaggregated LOS distribution there is a substantial difference. The percent of short-stay episodes (i.e., less than 3 months) is reduced by 10.9 percent in 1977, and 6.5 percent in 1985. Similarly, the percent of long-stay episodes (i.e., those lasting 5 or more years) is increased by 5.6 percent in 1977, and 3.9 percent in 1985. This is also reflected in the increase in the mean 1985 LOS from thirteen months for the unaggregated distribution, to nineteen months for the aggregated distribution. Second, whether one looks at the distributions adjusted for the supply of nursing home beds or not, there appears to be little difference in the LOS distributions for 1977 vs. 1985. This suggests that the distribution of nursing home LOS has been relatively stable.

C. Lifetime Risk

Despite the increasing sophistication that has come to studies of the risk of nursing home placement and estimating nursing home LOS, these are fundamentally episode-based approaches. From a policy perspective, it is more important to understand the lifetime risk of nursing home placement [4]. This is true regardless of whether the future growth in the provision of long-term services is going to come from the private long term care insurance market, or from expanded federal financing of long-term care. From the perspective of the private long-term care insurance market, potential purchasers must decide whether to self-insure for the future potential of nursing home expenditures. To do that, they need to have an estimate of their lifetime risk, and how that risk changes across the life-course. And sellers of private long-term care insurance will need the same information to set premium levels and underwrite their markets. From the perspective of expanded federal financing of long-term care (an unlikely event), accurate projections of the incremental costs of such new programs will be needed, as will the identification of those groups most likely to benefit by such subsidization.

Studies estimating the lifetime risk of nursing home use may generally be placed into three categories: place of death studies (by far the largest group), follow-up studies, and life table studies [4]. The place of death studies derive their estimates based on the number of deaths occurring in nursing homes. An important feature of these studies is that regardless of whether local or national data were used, there is marked consistency in the lifetime risk estimates reported. Indeed, Kastenbaum and Candy [1], Ingram and Barry [16], Lesnoff-Caravaglia [17], and Zappolo [18] all estimated the lifetime risk to be about 20 percent. Such consistency, however, is misleading, inasmuch as the place of death studies do not include the nursing home episodes of individuals who did not die in nursing homes.

There have only been two longitudinal follow-up studies used to estimate the lifetime risk of nursing home placement. Both Palmore [19] and Vicente, Wiley, and Carrington [20] relied on relatively small, atypical local samples. This is reflected in the remarkable difference in their estimates. Based on place of residence at their biennial interviews and death certificates, Palmore estimated that prior to their death, 26 percent of the 207 older adults in his sample who died during the study had passed through a nursing home. Using retrospective interviews with caregivers, Vicente, Wiley, and Carrington estimated that prior to their death 46 percent of the 342 older adults in their sample who died had passed through a nursing home. The considerable difference between these two estimates of the lifetime risk of nursing home use reflects Palmore's inability to identify individuals who were admitted to and discharged from nursing homes in-between their biennial interviews [4].

The third category of lifetime risk of nursing home use estimates involves the application of double-decrement life table methods. This represents an important development, because of the considerable power of these methods. However, the data available for the early use of this approach was not up to the task. As [4] note, neither of two of the earliest and more influential life table studies [21, 22] were able to differentiate first-admissions from re-admissions, and both were forced to assume similar death rates for those institutionalized and those who remained in the community. Nonetheless, and despite using different data sources (the 1977 Current Medicare Survey [21] and the 1976 NNHS [22]) and different definitions of nursing home placement (having a physician visit in a nursing home vs. being admitted to a nursing home), the lifetime risk estimates were quite similar (i.e., 34 to 43% under different scenarios vs. 36%, respectively).

Two more studies have been conducted using somewhat more rigorous methods [4, 23]. Murtaugh, Kemper, and Spillman used data from the nationally representative National Long-Term Care Survey (NLTCS) to estimate the lifetime risk of nursing home use among the 2,770 respondents who died between the 1982 baseline and 1984 follow-up interviews. The nursing home data were primarily taken from the location of the baseline interview (i.e., in a nursing home or not), place of death reports, and follow-up interviews with responsible proxies (usually next of kin) that included retrospective questions about any prior nursing home stay. These data were then supplemented by Medicare claims files showing charges from a skilled nursing facility. Using this rather comprehensive approach to data capture, about 37 percent of the decedents were found to have been in a nursing home at some point in their lives. This lifetime risk of nursing home use was highly correlated with age, ranging from a low of 12.3 percent among those dying between the ages of sixty-five to sixty-nine, and a high of 64.2 percent among those dying in their ninth decade or beyond.

Because older adults dying in the 1990s and beyond will be living longer, and thus dying at older ages, Murtaugh, Kemper, and Spillman [4] adjusted the data for increases in life expectancy and population growth over age sixty-five. Then they estimated the size of the population reaching age sixty-five, the percent of those individuals likely to be placed in a nursing home before they die, and the number of those turning sixty-five. They provide these estimates by sex for the years 1990, 2000, 2020, and 2040. There are three points worth noting from their results. First, women are at about 20 percent more risk for nursing home placement upon reaching age sixty-five than are men. This reflects married men pre-deceasing their wives, and leaving them with fewer social supports. Second, there is a temporal increase in the risk of nursing home use for both men and women, but that increased risk is rather modest. Third, the surge in demand for nursing home services will occur when the baby boomers begin to reach age sixty-five, around 2020, and will not dissipate much for at least the next twenty years thereafter.

Kemper and Murtaugh [23] used a very similar method to estimate both the lifetime risk of nursing home use and the lifetime LOS in nursing homes, among the 16,587 persons aged twenty-five years or older who died in 1986 and were included in the National Mortality Followback Survey (NMFS). Despite the fact that the NMFS is a substantially younger cohort of decedents than the NLTCS, Kemper and Murtaugh found a very similar lifetime risk rate of 29 percent (it was an identical 37% among adults aged 65 years or older). This rate was also highly correlated with age (even among older adults), ranging from a low of 17 percent among those aged sixty-five to seventy-four, to a high of 60 percent among those aged eighty-five to ninety-four. More interesting were the lifetime LOS estimates, which they provide by sex, race, education, and marital status for those who were aged sixty-five or older. There are five points worth noting in these results. First, about one-sixth of those with any nursing home stay are long-stayers (i.e., they are there for at least 5 years), and about one-half spend at least a full-year in the nursing home. Second, women have fewer short-stays and more long-stays than men. Third, although whites have significantly greater lifetime risks of nursing home placement, their lifetime LOSs are equivalent. Fourth, education is not associated with lifetime nursing home use risks or LOSs. Finally, those who were never married or were divorced or separated (the fastest growing segments of the population) have the highest lifetime risks of nursing home use, and are most likely to be long-stayers.

D. Time Spent in Nursing Homes

Most recently, Liang, Liu, Tu, and Whitelaw have introduced some innovative expansions of the life table approach [24]. They begin by presenting a four-state increment-decrement model of nursing home use that includes living in the community, being in a hospital, being in a nursing home, and death. In this model they formally recognized only one state, death, as absorbing. That is, only death is viewed as a state from which there is no transition or return. Using data from the 1985 NNHS, the 1985 National Hospital Discharge Survey (NHDS), and the 1987 National Medical Care Expenditure Survey (NMCES), Liang, Liu, Tu, and Whitelaw estimated the nine possible transition rates among the four states for the U.S. population in 1985 at selected ages. There are four important points in their estimates. First, the risks of hospitalization or nursing home placement consistently increase with age. Second, the likelihood of returning to the community from the hospital monotonically decreases with age, and that decrease accelerates dramatically beginning in the seventh decade, when the transition from the hospital to the nursing home or death becomes the norm. Third, the overall mortality pattern is J-shaped, rising steadily after age ten following an initial decline. Fourth, and somewhat surprisingly, the transition to hospitals from nursing homes declines with age, mostly reflecting the increasing transition to death.

Using these transition probabilities, Liang, Liu, Tu, and Whitelaw calculated the expected proportions of life spent beyond certain ages in the community, hospitals, and nursing homes, for the U.S. population as a whole in 1985 [24]. These proportions show that at birth, Americans could expect to spend about 97 percent of their remaining years living in the community. That rate drifts downward ever so slowly until about age fifty-five, when the rate of decline begins to accelerate. It shifts into high gear in the mid-70s, and by age eighty-five less than half of one's remaining life can be expected to be lived out in the community. The lost time in the community, of course, is fundamentally spent in the nursing home.

II. THE NURSING HOME MARKET

The forgoing growth projections imply potentially large changes in the nursing home market. Projections of nursing home utilization based upon the Liang et al. (1996) probabilities raise a number of serious economic and social questions. Nursing home care is not cheap. The American Association of Retired Persons report that in 1993 the average price of a year of nursing home care was $39,000 [3]. How will the nursing home market respond to this increasing demand? How will reductions in Medicaid affect the market? This section lays the groundwork to address these questions by summarizing what we know about that market. It focuses on the role of Medicaid, the nature of the private segment of the market, and the emergence of private long-term care insurance. Two features of this literature are key. First, unlike the utilization literature, the economic literature is sparse. Second, the existing studies do suggest that there is substantial potential for flexibility in the nursing home market.

A. Theory of the Nursing Home Market

The now well-accepted economic model of the nursing home market was provided by Scanlon [25]. Essentially the nursing home is viewed as having some market power and facing two distinct cohorts of service purchasers: private and government (i.e., Medicaid) subsidized purchasers. Private purchasers are characterized as residents who pay what the traffic will bear. They are assumed to have some degree of price sensitivity. Simply put, its is assumed that more of the elderly would use nursing home services if prices were lower. As we note below, the extent of this price sensitivity is both key to understanding this market and largely unknown.

Medicaid sponsored purchasers receive a subsidy in their purchase of care. The program both establishes a price it will pay and determines the amount that a recipient must pay out of pocket. In general, nursing homes price discriminate. The government's established price is below that charged to private residents. The nursing home is viewed as accepting private paying residents as long as the extra revenue from each exceeds both the cost of care and the price offered by Medicaid. Once the private market is satisfied, remaining capacity is sold in the Medicaid market. The nursing home will accept Medicaid residents as long as the Medicaid payment is greater than or equal to the marginal costs of care.

The government can limit the number of eligible Medicaid subsidized residents in a variety of ways. First, it can set its price relatively low, thereby making Medicaid residents less attractive to nursing homes. Second, it can tighten the income/wealth or health status criteria necessary to qualify for the Medicaid subsidy. Third, it can restrict the number of nursing home beds that are available in the market by a more rigorous application of certificate of need (CON) laws.

This characterization of the private and public segments of the market obviously leaves out much important detail. Nonetheless, the model is a powerful tool of analysis. It yields a number of important implications. Among the most important are:

- Private pay residents, willing to pay the going price, will typically be able to find a nursing home bed,
- Any shortages in beds will only be felt in the government cohort, and
- Increased demand by private paying residents will lead to higher prices, a larger share of private residents, and fewer government sponsored residents.

B. Medicaid

It is well known that Medicaid is the major payer of nursing home services in the United States. Indeed, in 1993 Medicaid provided nearly 52 percent of nursing home revenues. Out-of-pocket expenditures were next, contributing about one-third. The remainder came from a variety of other sources.

Medicaid itself is a joint state-federal program. As such, the conditions of eligibility and the extent of coverage vary across the states. Essentially, Medicaid is a means-tested program. Persons qualify either by meeting income and asset tests under the Supplementary Security Income (SSI) program, or by "spending down" income and assets until they meet eligibility criteria. Once qualified, Medicaid eligibles are required to contribute all of their income toward the cost of their care, except for a personal needs allowance that also varies across states, but which is typically about $30 per month.

The only exception to spending all one's income relates to married persons who are allowed to keep additional income to sustain their community-dwelling spouse at some minimum standard of living. One of the few surviving elements of the

Medicare Catastrophic Coverage Act of 1988 (MCCA) was designed to protect more of a couple's income and assets for the benefit of the noninstitutionalized spouse. These provisions allow an institutionalized person to keep enough income to maintain the community spouse at 150 percent of the federal poverty line. This is about two and one-half times the pervious SSI standard. In addition, the community spouse can retain the greater of $12,000 or half of the couple's joint assets, without respect to ownership, up to a maximum of $60,000. These values are indexed to the Consumer Price Index. In addition, the spouse can keep the home in which she/he lives.

Even under Medicaid, the elderly pay a substantial amount for nursing home care. Sloan and Shayne estimate that, in 1991, the average elderly person in the community, admitted to a nursing home, would have had to pay $8,920 in the first year [26]. This was 39 percent of the private charge. Even by the third year of an extended nursing home stay, the Medicaid covered resident would still be paying $8,544 per year, out-of-pocket. These payments are typically made out of the resident's Social Security.

The literature is silent on the effects of this out-of-pocket payment on the decision to enter a nursing home and to stay in a nursing home. The issue is key to Medicaid policy. If Medicaid eligible people are rather price sensitive, then an increase in the out-of-pocket Medicaid price will reduce the number of admissions substantially, and significantly reduce government expenditures. On the other hand, if there is very limited price responsiveness, an increase in the out-of-pocket payment under Medicaid would have very little effect on nursing home utilization. It would simply shift costs from the government to the individual and their families.

Short and Kemper have demonstrated the implications of Medicaid out-of-pocket price sensitivity [27]. They were concerned about the cost implications of various policy proposals to expand Medicaid. They examined policy options of providing: 1) a limited front-end benefit of either three- or six-months of coverage for all with demonstrated need, 2) a back-end benefit of unlimited care after a one- or two-year waiting period, and 3) a full entitlement of nursing home coverage for all medically needy persons. In each scenario they assumed a 30 percent coinsurance rate, somewhat lower than the effective 39 percent rate reported by Sloan and Shayne [26]. Given the absence of hard estimates, they simulate alternative assumptions of price elasticity ranging from .0 to −.8. An elasticity of −.2, for example, says that a 10 percent decrease in price would lead to a 2 percent increase in use. Their simulations, based upon the 1987 National Medical Care Expenditure Survey, are summarized in Table 1. Consider the full entitlement option. With no price response (elasticity equals zero), public Medicaid expenditures would be 21.7 billion dollars. If the elasticity is −.4, the expenditures are $26.1 billion; and if the elasticity is −.8, then public Medicaid expenditures rise to $32.1 billion. This is a swing of over ten billion dollars.

Short and Kemper's elasticity assumptions are just that, assumptions forced because of the dearth of hard estimates. There is potential to obtain real estimates, at least for a portion of the potentially eligible population. The MCCA effectively reduced the price of Medicaid subsidized nursing home care for married persons by

Table 1. Estimated Public Nursing Home Expenditures Under
Alternative Demand Elasticity Assumptions (Billions of 1987 Dollars)

	Elasticity of Demand			
	.0	−.2	−.4	−.8
Front-End Entitlement				
Three-month benefit	$16.7	$17.7	$18.7	$20.6
Six-month benefit	17.2	18.3	19.4	21.7
Back-End Entitlement				
One-year waiting period	19.8	21.1	22.5	25.1
Two-year waiting period	18.7	19.7	20.7	22.8
Full Entitlement	21.7	24.3	26.9	32.1

Source: [27].

excluding more income and assets for the community dwelling spouse. Short and Kemper report that the MCCA effectively reduced the out-of-pocket price of nursing home care for married individuals by two-thirds. Using very different data and methods, Sloan and Shayne found that the net price to these individuals dropped by nearly $4,900 [26]. The spousal impoverishment feature of the MCCA serves as an important natural experiment worthy of evaluation.

In this regard there has been some descriptive work on the effects of the broader, albeit short lived, MCCA which is relevant here. Liu and Kenney analyzed the effects of the reduction of the Medicare copayment associated with the use of skilled nursing facility use [28]. Under pre-MCCA rules there was a maximum copayment of about $5,360 for 100 days of Medicare coverage. During the MCCA period the maximum copayment was $200 for 150 days, and the requirement for a three-day prior hospital stay was removed. Using HCFA data they found a 40.4 percent increase in Medicare patients between 1987 and 1988 and a further 139.7 percent increase between 1988 and 1989. This suggests that there is significant price sensitivity among potential nursing home users.

Analysis of the degree of price responsiveness among Medicaid eligible populations is not a trivial exercise, however. Sloan and Shayne report that while 84 percent of those in need of a nursing home were estimated to be eligible for Medicaid subsidized nursing home care, only 61 percent were actually in a nursing home [26]. While this may relate to the degree of price sensitivity among eligibles, it is also related to CON constraints on nursing home expansion. The theory of the market suggests that these laws have their effect in limiting access by Medicaid eligibles. Empirical work by Scanlon [25] and Nyman [29-32] is consistent with this view and has been nicely summarized by Nyman [33]. However, there have been no rigorous direct tests of the effects of CON on Medicaid subsidized use or expenditures [34].

A related economic issue under Medicaid is the extent to which an individual can become eligible for Medicaid. As noted above, one is eligible for Medicaid only if one's income and/or assets are sufficiently low to qualify. Thus, the conventional wisdom is that people enter a nursing home as private pay residents, rapidly exhaust their resources, and become eligible for Medicaid. Indeed, this scenario has led to widespread concern that the elderly become impoverished by expenditures on nursing home care.

The empirical literature, however, has difficulty establishing this point. Under the spend-down scenario, one should expect to see substantial conversion from private pay to Medicaid among those who enter nursing homes. Work by Burwell, Adams, and Meiners [35], Spence and Wiener [36], and Liu, Doty, and Manton [37] fails to show large numbers of conversions. The estimates suggest that only 10 to 25 percent of residents who enter nursing homes as private payers convert to Medicaid. These authors suggest that the reasons for these unexpected findings are either methodological—resulting from relatively large numbers of short stay residents—or familial—resulting from contributions by relatives for the resident's care.

More recent work suggests that a nursing home stay may not cause impoverishment after all. This is not because the care is not expensive, but because those using the care are already eligible for Medicaid. Sloan and Shayne used the 1989 National Long Term Care Survey to simulate Medicaid spend-down issues [25]. They applied the data on each respondent to the Medicaid eligibility rules applicable in their state at that time. The study focused on the disabled elderly defined as those aged sixty-five and over who had at least one ADL limitation. Table 2 presents their findings. Given asset and income positions, 18.7 percent were already on Medicaid at the time of the survey interview. However, another 64.3 percent were either immediately eligible or would be eligible in less than six months. Notice that nearly 87 percent of the married elderly were eligible or became so within six months. Some of this eligibility is the result of the MCCA. Even before the MCCA, 64.7 percent of the married elderly (with at least one ADL limitation) were eligible for Medicaid within six months.

The Sloan and Shayne work only examines that segment of the elderly population with ADL measured disabilities. It is conceivable that the nursing home destined elderly spend-down their income and assets as their health deteriorates prior to having one ADL and satisfying the Sloan and Shayne definition of being disabled. The lack of conversions upon admission, however, suggests either that the elderly are remarkably adept at reducing their income and assets as their uncertain health status slowly deteriorates, or that they have been very adept at casting off assets and income prior to their need for nursing home care. Sloan and Shayne argue against these interpretations, saying that the wealth positions of their cohort were essentially unchanged between 1984 and 1989, suggesting that there was little casting-off of assets and little need to do so. Although more work is clearly necessary, it does appear that the lack of spend-down activity reflects near-immediate eligibility, and not earlier shedding of assets.

Table 2. Simulated Percentage of the Disabled Elderly Eligible for
Medicaid Coverage Upon Admission to a Nursing Home

When Eligible for Medicaid:	Single	Married	All
Already on	24.0	10.1	18.7
Immediately eligible	48.9	75.3	59.0
Eligible in 1 to 6 months	7.8	1.3	5.3
Eligible in 6 to 30 months	7.5	3.1	5.8
Eligible in 30 to 120 months	4.6	1.6	3.8
Not eligible within 120 months	7.2	7.7	7.4
	100.0	100.0	100.0

Source: [26].

C. The Private Pay Segment of the Market

As we noted above, the salient feature of the private nursing home market is that private residents who are willing to pay the going price can find a bed with little difficulty. Constraints on entry affect only the Medicaid segment of the market. The key issues in this market segment are the degree of price sensitivity, the effect of income, and the degree of substitutability between nursing homes and other forms of care. We also note that there has been a presumption that demanders of nursing home services are unable to make wise decisions about their care. While there is undeniably an element of truth in this point, economically wise decisions are those that follow the laws of economics—responding to price changes and considering substitutes. The slowly growing body of empirical evidence suggests substantial economic rationality on the part of the elderly and/or their families, friends, and caregivers.

There has been little analysis of the private demand for nursing home services. Early work by Scanlon [25] and Chiswick [38] used metropolitan and state level data. Only Scanlon examined private payers distinct from Medicaid subsidized payers. However, both found substantial price sensitivity, −1.1 and −2.3, respectively, implying that a 10 percent reduction in nursing home prices would increase volume by 11 to 23 percent. The work, however, has been criticized for its aggregated units of analysis and the potential that the results are overstated by a failure to account for the spend-down conditions of Medicaid.

The only "recent" study is Nyman's [30] analysis of 1983 Wisconsin facility specific data. In a sophisticated econometric analysis he finds a price elasticity of −1.7 and an income elasticity of 1.2, both significant at the usual levels of confidence. The income result indicates that nursing homes are viewed as normal goods. When incomes are higher, more services are demanded, such that a 1 percent increase was associated with a 1.2 percent increase in private nursing home use. The price effect indicates that a 10 percent reduction in prices would increase use by 17 percent.

The findings, if generalizable, have important implications for the nursing home market. First, they imply that the private segment of the market may not be befuddled or confused when considering their options, as some have assumed. These findings suggest a clear willingness to shop and look for substitutes. One is left to speculate what the market might look like if there were more nursing homes from which to choose. Second, given the current two-tier nature of the nursing home market in which facilities provide care for private patients and "fill-in" with lower paying Medicaid residents, the price and income effects found in this literature suggest that Medicaid patients will increasingly be crowded out of nursing homes as more affluent elders begin to enter the market, assuming that current state CON laws continue in force. Third, the findings suggest a major complication to offering long-term care insurance. Insurance lowers the effective price of care. Given these estimates and even ignoring adverse selection, an insurance policy that provided a 30 percent coinsurance feature for private nursing home care would lead to a 119 percent increase in nursing home use. Fourth, the findings suggest that the aforementioned studies of Medicaid price sensitivities may be based upon overly conservative assumptions of price responsiveness. Lower Medicaid copayments may increase nursing home use more precipitously. Analogously, increases in Medicaid copayments may reduce nursing home use substantially.

C. Substitutes for Nursing Home Care

One of the salient features of a functioning market is that consumers are able to take advantage of a variety of substitute sources of care. In a nursing home market such alternatives obviously include neighboring nursing homes. The Nyman work clearly suggests such alternatives are considered [39]. However, there are other forms of long-term care services ranging from home health care to community-based long-term care to adult foster care. There have been a number of demonstration projects, including the National Long-Term Care Channeling Demonstration (NLTCCD), which have sought to encourage the substitution of less intensive care for nursing home services. Generally speaking, however, the evaluation of those demonstration projects suggested that community-based long-term care was neither a substitute for nursing homes [40-42], nor a cost-effective strategy in and of itself [43, 44].

Even if the demonstration projects like the NLTCCD were shown to be efficacious, they would have limited policy relevance inasmuch as they did not disaggregate the various components of the multidimensional interventions [45]. That is, demonstrations like the NLTCCD used fixed bundles of substituted services, with little or no attempt to optimize the substituted service mix at the individual client level. Greene, Lovely, Miller, and Ondrich published a provocative paper addressing this issue [45]. They used data from the NLTCCD to first estimate multivariate logistic regression models predicting the risk of nursing home placement using a variety of community long-term care services as the predictor variable set. Then, the resulting odds ratios were used to build a mathematical optimization procedure that minimized total nursing home use as a function of community long-term care services within the context of a fixed aggregate budget. This approach effectively simulates a scenario in which a fixed budget is allocated across competing community long-term care services to minimize nursing home use.

Greene, Lovely, Miller, and Ondrich's results are provocative, especially given that they were achieved without any additional expenditures [45]. There are four points worth special mention. First, under the optimal allocation model, the risk of nursing home use falls precipitously from the observed .131 to .045, indicating that a substantial improvement in the efficiency of the NLTCCD could have been obtained. Second, the mean number of in-home nursing service hours increases dramatically from 0.95 to 3.36. Third, personal care services, for which the mean number of monthly hours had been about thirty-two, are completely eliminated. Although this substantially elevates the risk of nursing home placement for those with multiple ADL deficits, it is based on the empirical observation that personal care services are relatively inefficient in reducing the aggregate risk of nursing home placement. Fourth, there is a dramatic increase in the mean number of housekeeping hours, as well as the percentage of respondents receiving such services. This is entirely consistent with the results of the nursing home risk factor models, which identify the inability to maintain one's home as the major risk for nursing home placement [10].

Equally interesting is new work by Nyman, Finch, Kane, Kane, and Illston, which uses real world data to examine the extent to which private long-term care services users substitute adult foster care for nursing home care [46]. The study analyzed 1989 county level data from Oregon. The state had obtained a Medicaid waiver to allow the subsidization of adult foster care. However, the data indicate that two-thirds of the foster care residents were private patients. A simple regression of foster care residents in the county, controlling for other factors, indicated that a nursing home lost .85 residents for every additional foster care resident. In addition, an analysis of the demand for foster care demonstrated substantial price and income responsiveness in the private market. A 1 percent increase in the average adult foster care price was associated with a 5.2 percent decrease in day care residents. A 1 percent increase in per capita income was estimated to increase the number of foster care residents by 2.25 percent. Both results were statistically significant.

The available evidence suggests that there is substantial price responsiveness in both the private nursing home and foster care markets. Further, both types of care are normal goods, implying that higher income is associated with greater use. Finally, while the evidence on substitutability between nursing home and other forms of long-term care certainly lead to a conclusion of limited potential, more recent work on long-term care markets suggest that the elderly paying out of pocket may be very willing to consider substitutes. However, rigorous statistical research on private long-term care markets is very thin—perhaps best characterized as opportunistic studies conducted on very limited populations with less than ideal data. Much more work is needed.

D. Long-Term Care Insurance

The private nursing home market is also characterized by the presence of long-term care insurance. The number of persons with coverage is small but has grown rapidly in the last several years. Coronel and Fulton report that some 3.4 million long-term care polices had been sold in 1993 [47]. This is an increase of 320 percent over 1987. Nonetheless, private insurance continues to play only a minor role in the market, with less than 3 percent of nursing home revenues coming from this source. Premiums vary with the extent of coverage and with the age of the purchaser. Coronel and Fulton report that the best selling plans have an average premium of $1,086 for the basic plan at age sixty-five. The same plan sells for $4,372, on average, for those aged seventy-five. The base plan considered in their analysis paid $100/$50 per day for nursing home/home health coverage. There was a twenty-day waiting period and four years of coverage. Adding inflation protection and a nonforfeiture clause would raise the premiums to $2,525 and $7,713, respectively, at ages sixty-five and seventy-five.

Cohen, Kumar, and Wallack report on a survey of purchasers and nonpurchasers of long-term care insurance policies in 1990 [48, 49]. They find that relative to the over age sixty-five population, active purchasers were wealthier, had higher incomes, were better educated, and disproportionately female. Asset and income differences were most pronounced. Only one-third of the elderly population had assets in excess of $30,000 compared to 75 percent of purchasers; 17 percent of the older population had incomes greater than $25,000 while 52 percent of purchasers did.

As Cohen and colleagues note, there are two general themes in the literature seeking to explain why private long-term care insurance has not been more extensively purchased [49]. The first argument is that the policies are sufficiently expensive that most cannot afford to purchase them. Table 3 summarizes the literature on this point. These studies tend to identify a percentage of disposable income (such as 5%) that an individual or couple might spend on a long-term care policy and then estimate how many could afford the necessary annual premium. The estimates vary but are in the range of roughly 20 to 40 percent of the over age sixty-five population.

Cohen et al., however, suggest that these estimates may be too low. Based upon their survey, they find that 60 to 70 percent of purchasers use at least some assets to purchase the policies. The existing "affordability" studies have assumed that such policies would only be purchased out of current income, not assets. In addition, their survey suggests that the rationale for purchasing long-term care insurance among the elderly is much broader than simply protecting assets. They note a variety of reasons, including, most importantly, the avoidance of dependence upon others and to preserve independence. Thus, Cohen and colleagues conclude that more persons, particularly the younger elderly, are willing to consider purchasing insurance.

The second argument for the lack of the development of the market has been essentially informational. On the one hand, the elderly may be confused about the extent of nursing home coverage provided under Medicare and Medigap plans. The private policies are relatively new in the market and not well understood [49-52]. There is also concern that the policies that are available are sufficiently limiting in

Table 3. Summary of Studies on Potential Size of LTC Insurance Market

Study	Criteria	Estimate
Meiners [55]	Percent greater than Bureau of Labor Statistics hypothetical budgets	About 18% of married couples age 65+ about 37% of single individuals 65+
Cohen et al. [60]	Willing to spend 10% to 25% of discretionary income	10% to 63% of married couples age 65+ 33% to 48% of singles age 65+ 19% to 57% of all elderly age 65+
Rivlin and Wiener [61]	Willing to spend no more than 5% of income on LTC insurance	10% to 21% of individuals 67+ could afford policies
Ball and Bethell [62]	With premiums of $2,000 per couple, only individuals with more than $50,000 income could afford policies	About 11% of elderly couples could afford to purchase LTC insurance
Friedland [63]	Various combinations of willingness to pay, insurance premiums, incomes, and asset levels	Range of affordability of 6% to 20%
Cohen et al. [64]	Subjective purchase criteria based on industry input and accounting for asset levels, presence of Medicaid, level of premiums, and health status	50% of 65-74 age group 38% of 75-84 age group less than 10% of 85+ age group 42% for all groups combined
Zedlowski and McBride [65]	Affordability thresholds of 2.5%, 5%, and 7.5% of income excluding assets	By 2010, 2.3% to 18.9% could afford insurance depending on affordability threshold used. At a threshold of 5% of income, 12% of married couples and 11% of those age 65 to 69 could afford insurance

Source: [49].

their benefits that many of the elderly who purchase coverage may not obtain much in the way of benefits paid out [53, 54]. On the other hand, insurers have been characterized as being fearful of entering a market in which they have little knowledge of claims costs, particularly in light of unknown degrees of adverse selection and moral hazard [55].

There is a third reason, however, for the non-purchase of long-term care insurance. The reason is at the heart of Pauly's [56] conceptual analysis of the market, and is mentioned by Norton and Newhouse [57] among others, typically in passing while making other points. One straightforward explanation for the lack of private insurance is the presence of Medicaid. People don't buy private coverage because they already have public coverage. In the majority of states Medicaid provides insurance to everyone, but with deductibles that vary with the size of one's nonhousing assets.

The new research by Sloan and Shayne reviewed above indicates that 83 percent of the disabled elderly are eligible for Medicaid coverage in their state at the time they are admitted or within six months [26]. Given this, there is little economic reason for one to purchase expensive long-term care insurance.

To our knowledge there is no empirical evidence of the broad effects of Medicaid on the development of the private long-term care insurance market. Indeed, it would be difficult to imagine a study that would yield such a relationship in the absence of either international comparisons or large scale demonstration projects. To our knowledge Kumar, Cohen, Bishop and Wallack are the only ones to attempt to rigorously relate Medicaid program characteristics to the purchase of long-term care insurance [58]. Using the previously described survey of purchasers of long-term care policies, Kumar et al. used a two-stage selection model to analyze both the decision to purchase coverage and the amount of coverage. The results of this study largely confirm the earlier work by these authors. However, here they also include three measures of the relevant state Medicaid program: the Medicaid reimbursement rate, the presence of an estate recovery program whereby the state can recover nursing home costs from the estate of a deceased Medicaid recipient, and Medicaid income limits on eligibility. They find that the income threshold does not affect either the purchase decision or the amount of coverage. The estate recovery provision is associated with a greater likelihood of purchase and a more generous plan. The Medicaid reimbursement level is associated with a greater likelihood of purchase and adoption of a more generous plan, but the result is probably related as much to higher private prices in the state as to higher Medicaid reimbursement levels.

The rational non-purchase argument does not diminish the importance of non-financial motives. Research on participation in all manner of public programs suggests that there are psychological or "taste" factors that matter in use (see McGarry [59] and references therein). Nor does it refute the importance to both buyers and sellers of information on the product and expected use. However, the point here is that the presence of the current Medicaid program has severely limited the growth of the private long-term care insurance market. The hypothesis from this theory is straightforward: given a stable Medicaid program, the market will grow only to the extent that more of the elderly have substantially more assets to protect than has been the case heretofore. This point is critical for a consideration of future long-term care policy in which Medicaid coverage may be significantly scaled back.

III. POLICY CHANGES AND FUTURE RESEARCH PRIORITIES

One of the conclusions that emerges from any study of the U.S. nursing home market is that it looks the way it does because Medicaid looks the way it does. Essentially, everyone has a public long-term care insurance policy called Medicaid. It provides unlimited days of care subject to a health status constraint, an availability of beds constraint, and a deductible that is virtually all of one's non-housing assets and income. The presence of Medicaid has constrained the supply of nursing home beds. It's coverage provisions have arguably limited the development of the private long-term care insurance market and have tilted the mix of services considered by those in need of long-term care services.

Policy recommendations made as recently as two or three years ago focused on expansions of Medicaid and the creation of Medicaid—private sector partnerships to expand both Medicaid eligibility and access to an expanded array of long-term care services. The political landscape with respect to health care reform, welfare reform, and the willingness of the electorate to support current federal programs, much less expanded programs, suggests a different future for the nursing home market and a different research agenda.

It's clear that Medicaid will not expand for the elderly. Indeed, it is likely that the program will be scaled back, and perhaps completely overhauled. This will happen regardless of whether the program is shifted back to the states. The growth of the elderly population, the cost of the program to governments at both the federal and state levels, and the reluctance of the taxpaying population assure this.

Several incremental changes are likely. The first is simply a continuation of the current policies of restricting the number of nursing home beds in the market. Because these constraints tend to affect only the Medicaid population, they have a particular appeal. Over time, of course, such policies will likely severely reduce the Medicaid subsidized segment of the market. The second incremental change is to restrict eligibility either by increasing the level of physical or mental infirmity that is necessary to qualify for benefits. A related approach would be to lower the bar with respect to the amounts of income or assets that are exempt from a calculation of eligibility. As we saw with the spousal impoverishment features of the MCCA, such provisions would lead to reduced expenditures for Medicaid programs.

More fundamental changes to the program could take many forms. The program could be converted to a voucher program. Tax incentives for the purchase of private insurance or for expenditures on long-term care services could be put in place. There could be efforts to increase the use of managed care in this market and to increase the extent of price competition in both the nursing home market and other segments of the long-term care field. Each of these possibilities suggest their own unique research questions. However, our review of the existing literature and our sense of the changing future of Medicaid suggest four major areas for new research:

- Price sensitivity in the use of long-term care services,
- Substitutability among types of care,
- The effects of bed limitations, and
- The market distortions resulting from the Medicaid program.

First, the changing world of long-term care puts a greater emphasis on the *price sensitivity* of the elderly to nursing homes, and other forms of long-term care services, including adult foster care, home health services, retirement housing, light-care, and check-ins. The very limited evidence suggests that there is substantial willingness to use more at lower prices. There is also some evidence, albeit very limited, that there may be significant willingness to consider alternative care scenarios under real world prices. Information on price response is key to understanding how people will respond to reduced Medicaid coverage. It is essential to determining the cost of long-term care insurance. It is also key to being able to develop viable private alternatives to nursing home care.

Second, we need to know much more about the willingness of the elderly to *substitute* one form of care for another. This implies better information of the services, quality, and price of alternative sources of care, as well as their effects on health outcomes. We need to examine the reasons for the development or lack of development of such markets as adult foster care, and the conditions under which people are willing to buy it rather than nursing home care. It is particularly important that we understand differences that may exist among income and racial groups with respect to the willingness and ability to substitute one form of care for another.

Third, we need to know much more about the effects of *bed limitations* in the nursing home market. In particular, what have been the effects of CON repeals on Medicaid access, and on private nursing home prices? Have the repeals affected the development of adult foster care and other alternatives to nursing homes? If the answers to these questions indicate that greater numbers of nursing homes lead to enhanced price and quality competition, then it would mitigate the effects of reduced availability of Medicaid.

Finally, we need much more hard evidence of the *market distortions* associated with Medicaid. This work must include both the long-term care service and insurance markets. One of the more amazing things in our review of the literature has been the pervasive effect that Medicaid has had on long-term care markets, and the almost complete lack of research on how changes in Medicaid have or could affect these markets. Fundamentally, policy analysis of long-term care markets must take a much stronger market perspective. As the role of public programs shrinks, these factors will take on a much more important role than they have to date.

This research agenda bodes well for interdisciplinary research. Gerontologists in general and medical sociologists in particular know much about the feasibility of substituting alternative forms of long-term care. They know much about the people and types of conditions that can benefit and could be harmed by changes in the nature of care. They understand the familial and social consequences of alternatives. Just as importantly, they know how to analyze these sorts of issues. Health economists and gerontologists specializing in financial issues understand price incentives, the functioning of health care and insurance markets, and the effects of regulation—and they know how to address these issues empirically. Together they will be better able to answer the policy questions raised by price sensitivity, the extent of use of feasible substitutes, and the benefits and risks associated with changing incentives.

REFERENCES

1. R. S. Kastenbaum and S. Candy, The 4% Fallacy: A Methodological and Empirical Critique of Extended Care Facility Program Statistics, *International Journal of Aging and Human Development, 4,* pp. 15-23, 1973.

2. H. C. Lazenby and S. W. Letsch, National Health Expenditures, 1989, *Health Care Financing Review, 12,* pp. 1-26, 1990.
3. American Association of Retired Persons, *Long Term Care,* AARP, Washington, D.C., 1995.
4. C. M. Murtaugh, P. Kemper, and B. C. Spillman, The Risk of Nursing Home Use in Later Life, *Medical Care, 28,* pp. 952-962, 1990.
5. V. L. Greene and J. I. Ondrich, Risk Factors for Nursing Home Admissions and Exits: A Discrete-Time Hazard Function Approach, *Journal of Gerontology: Social Sciences, 45,* pp. S250-S258, 1990.
6. W. G. Weissert and C. M. Cready, Toward a Model for Improved Targeting of Aged at Risk of Institutionalization, *Health Services Research, 24,* pp. 485-510, 1989.
7. D. L. Wingard, D. Williams-Jones, J. McPhillips, R. M. Kaplan, and E. Barrett-Connor, Nursing Home Utilization in Adults: A Prospective Population-Based Study, *Journal of Aging and Health, 2,* pp. 179-193, 1990.
8. F. D. Wolinsky, C. M. Callahan, J. F. Fitzgerald, and R. J. Johnson, The Risk of Nursing Home Placement and Subsequent Death Among Older Adults, *Journal of Gerontology: Social Sciences, 47,* pp. S173-S182, 1992.
9. R. A. Kane and R. L. Kane, *Long Term Care: Principles, Programs, and Policies,* Springer, New York, 1987.
10. B. Soldo and K. G. Manton, Health Status and Service Needs of the Oldest Old: Current Patterns and Future Trends, *Milbank Memorial Fund Quarterly, 63,* pp. 286-319, 1985.
11. R. M. Andersen, *A Behavioral Model of Families' Use of Health Services,* Center for Health Administration Studies, Chicago, 1968.
12. K. Liu and K. G. Manton, The Length of Stay Pattern of Nursing Home Admissions, *Medical Care, 21,* pp. 1211-1222, 1983.
13. D. A. Spence and J. M. Wiener, Nursing Home Length of Stay Patterns: Results From the 1985 National Nursing Home Survey, *The Gerontologist, 30,* pp. 16-20, 1990.
14. K. Liu and Y. Palesch, The Nursing Home Population: Different Perspectives and Implications for Policy Research, *Health Care Financing Review, 3,* pp. 15-23, 1981.
15. M. A. Lewis, S. Cretin, and R. L. Kane, The Natural History of Nursing Home Patients, *The Gerontologist, 25,* pp. 382-388, 1985.
16. D. Ingram and J. Barry, National Statistics on Deaths in Nursing Homes, *The Gerontologist, 17,* pp. 303-316, 1977.
17. G. Lesnoff-Caravaglia, The Five Per Cent Fallacy, *International Journal of Aging and Human Development, 9,* pp. 187-193, 1978.
18. A. Zappolo, Discharges From Nursing Homes, *Vital and Health Statistics,* Series 13 Number 54, DHHS Publication 81-1715, National Center for Health Statistics, Hyattsville, Maryland, 1981.
19. E. Palmore, Total Chance of Institutionalization Among the Aged, *The Gerontologist, 16,* pp. 504-510, 1976.
20. L. Vicente, J. Wiley, and R. A. Carrington, The Risk of Institutionalization Before Death, *The Gerontologist, 19,* pp. 361-369, 1979.
21. M. Cohen, E. J. Tell, and S. S. Wallack, Client Related Risk Factors of Nursing Home Entry Among Elderly Adults, *Journal of Gerontology, 41,* pp. 785-792, 1986.
22. J. Liang and E. J. Tu, Estimating Life Time Risk of Nursing Home Residency: A Further Note, *The Gerontologist, 26,* pp. 560-563, 1986.
23. P. Kemper and C. M. Murtaugh, Lifetime Use of Nursing Home Care, *New England Journal of Medicine, 324,* pp. 595-601, 1991.

24. J. Liang, X. Liu, E. Tu, and N. Whitelaw, Probabilities and Lifetime Durations of Short-Stay Hospital and Nursing Home Utilization in the U.S., 1985, *Medical Care, 34,* pp. 1018-1036, 1996.
25. W. Scanlon, A Theory of the Nursing Home Market, *Inquiry, 17,* pp. 25-41, 1980.
26. F. A. Sloan and M. W. Shayne, Long-Term Care, Medicaid, and Impoverishment of the Elderly, *Milbank Quarterly, 71,* pp. 575-599, 1993.
27. P. F. Short and P. Kemper, Nursing Home Financing Reform: How Would It Affect Expenditures for Nursing Home Care? *Inquiry, 31,* pp. 141-152, 1994.
28. K. Liu and G. Kenney, Impact of the Catastrophic Coverage Act and New Coverage Guidelines on Medicare Skilled Nursing Facility Use, *Inquiry, 30,* pp. 41-53, 1993.
29. J. A. Nyman, Excess Demand, the Percentage of Medicaid Patients, and the Quality of Nursing Home Care, *Journal of Human Resources, 23,* pp. 76-92, 1988.
30. J. A. Nyman, Analysis of Nursing Home Use and Bed Supply in Wisconsin, 1983, *Health Services Research, 24,* pp. 511-538, 1989.
31. J. A. Nyman, Excess Demand, Consumer Rationality, and the Quality of Care in Regulated Nursing Homes, *Health Services Research, 24,* pp. 105-128, 1989.
32. J. A. Nyman, Testing for Excess Demand in Nursing Home Care Markets, *Medical Care, 31,* pp. 680-693, 1993.
33. J. A. Nyman, The Private Demand for Nursing Home Care, *Journal of Health Economics, 8,* pp. 209-232, 1990.
34. M. A. Morrisey, R. L. Ohsfeldt, and E. Asper, *The Effects of CON Repeal on Medicaid Nursing Home Expenditures,* Final Report, UAB Lister Hill Center for Health Policy, Birmingham, Alabama, 1992.
35. B. Burwell, K. E. Adams, and M. M. Meiners, Spend-down of Assets before Medicaid Eligibility among Elderly Nursing-Home Residents in Michigan, *Medical Care, 28,* pp. 349-363, 1989.
36. M. A. Spence and J. M. Wiener, Estimating the Extent of Medicaid Spend-Down in Nursing Homes, *Journal of Health Politics, Policy and Law, 15,* pp. 607-626, 1990.
37. K. Liu, P. Doty, and K. Monton, Medicaid Spenddown in Nursing Homes, *The Gerontologist, 30,* pp. 7-15, 1990.
38. B. R. Chiswick, The Demand for Nursing Home Care: An Analysis of the Substitution Between Institutional and Noninstitutional Care, *Journal of Human Resources, 9,* pp. 293-316, 1976.
39. J. A. Nyman, The Future of Nursing Home Policy: Should Policy be Based on an Excess Demand Paradigm? *Advances in Health Economics and Health Services Research, 11,* pp. 229-250, 1990.
40. S. Hughes, Apples and Oranges: A Review of Community Based Long Term Care, *Health Services Research, 20,* pp. 461-487, 1985.
41. P. Kemper, R. A. Applebaum, and M. Harrigan, Community Care Demonstrations: What Have We Learned? *Health Care Financing Review, 8,* pp. 87-100, 1987.
42. W. G. Weissert, C. M. Cready, and J. Pawelak, The Past and Future of Home- and Community-Based Long-Term Care, *The Milbank Quarterly, 66,* pp. 309-388, 1988.
43. V. L. Greene, M. E. Lovely, and J. I. Ondrich, The Cost-Effectiveness of Community Services in a Frail Elderly Population, *The Gerontologist, 33,* pp. 177-189, 1993.
44. C. Thornton, S. M. Dunstan, and P. Kemper, The Effect of Channeling on Health and Long-Term Costs, *Health Services Research, 23,* pp. 129-142, 1988.
45. V. L. Greene, M. E. Lovely, M. D. Miller, and J. I. Ondrich, Reducing Nursing Home Use Through Community Long-Term Care: An Optimization Process, *Journal of Gerontology: Social Sciences, 50B,* pp. S259-S268, 1995.

46. J. A. Nyman, M. Finch, R. A. Kane, R. L. Kane, and L. H. Illston, *The Substitutability Between Adult Foster Care and Nursing Home Care in Oregon,* working paper, University of Minnesota, 1996.
47. S. Coronel and D. Fulton, Long-Term Care Insurance in 1993, *Managed Care & Insurance Operations Report,* Health Insurance Association of America, Washington, D.C., 1995.
48. M. A. Cohen, N. Kumar, and S. S. Wallack, Who Buys Long-Term Care Insurance? *Health Affairs, 11,* pp. 208-223, 1992.
49. M. A. Cohen, N. Kumar, and S. S. Wallack, New Perspectives on the Affordability of Long-Term Care Insurance and Potential Market Size, *The Gerontologist, 33,* pp. 105-113, 1993.
50. Z. V. Lambert, Elderly Consumers Knowledge Related to Medigap Protection Needs, *Journal of Consumer Affairs, 2,* p. 434, 1980.
51. J. W. Reinke and M. Michol, Commercial Insurance—A Regulator's Analysis, *American Health Care Association Journal, 5,* p. 10, 1982.
52. C. M. Murtaugh, P. Kemper, and B. C. Spillman, Risky Business: Long-Term Care Insurance Underwriting, *Inquiry, 32,* pp. 271-284, 1995.
53. C. E. Wilson and W. G. Weissert, Private Long-Term Care Insurance: After Coverage Restrictions Is There Anything Left? *Inquiry, 26,* pp. 493-507, 1989.
54. T. Rice, K. Thomas, and W. Weissart, The Effect of Owning Private Long-Term Care Insurance Policies on Out-of-Pocket Costs, *Health Services Research, 25,* pp. 907-933, 1991.
55. M. R. Meiners, The Case for Long-Term Care Insurance, *Health Affairs, 12,* pp. 55-79, 1983.
56. M. V. Pauly, The Rational Nonpurchase of Long Term Care Insurance, *Journal of Political Economy, 98,* pp. 153-168, 1990.
57. E. C. Norton and J. Newhouse, Policy Options for Public Long-Term Care Insurance, *Journal of the American Medical Association, 271,* pp. 1520-1524, 1994.
58. N. Kumar, M. A. Cohen, C. E. Bishop, and S. S. Wallack, Understanding the Factors Behind the Decision to Purchase Varying Coverage Amounts of Long Term Care Insurance, *Health Services Research, 29,* pp. 653-678, 1995.
59. K. McGarry, *Factors Determining Participation of the Elderly in SSI,* working paper 5250, National Bureau of Economic Research, New York, 1995.
60. M. Cohen, E. Tell, J. Greenberg, and S. S. Wallack, The Financial Capacity of the Elderly to Insure for Long-Term Care, *The Gerontologist, 27,* pp. 495-502, 1987.
61. A. Rivlin and J. Wiener, *Caring for the Disabled Elderly: Who Will Pay?* The Brookings Institution, Washington, D.C., 1988.
62. R. Ball and T. Bethell, *Because We're All in this Together,* Families USA Foundation, Washington, D.C., 1989.
63. R. Friedland, *Facing the Costs of Long-Term Care,* Employee Benefit Research Institute, Washington, D.C., 1990.
64. M. Cohen, N. Kumar, T. McGuire, and S. S. Wallack, *Long Term Care Financing Proposals: Their Costs, Benefits and Impact on Private Insurance,* Research Bulletin, Health Insurance Association of America, Washington, D.C., 1991.
65. S. Zedlowski and T. McBride, The Changing Profile of the Elderly: Effects on Future Long-Term Care Needs and Financing, *Milbank Quarterly, 70,* pp. 247-275, Hyattsville, Maryland, 1992.

SECTION III

Patient Care Concerns

CHAPTER
10

Perspectives on Aging: Progress and Priorities for Age-Related Cancers*

Harvey Jay Cohen

Cancer is the second leading cause of death in people over the age of sixty-five. Over half of all cancer occurs in this age group. Moreover, the incidence of and mortality from cancer rises successively throughout the lifespan [1]. With the well documented increase in the number of people over the age of sixty-five, and indeed over the age of eighty-five, that has already occurred in this country and is projected to continue over the next five decades, it is clear that we will be seeing an increasing number of older people with cancer. Thus, this is a critically important issue for us to address from the standpoint of research priorities.

What are the age-related cancers? They are virtually most of the common malignancies occurring in humans. This includes cancer of the breast, prostate, GU tract in females, bladder, lung, colon, rectum, and hematologic malignancies. These all basically increase in incidence throughout the life span, although in some instances, such as breast and gynecologic malignancies, there is a plateau in the post-menopausal period.

I will address this topic using the paradigm of the biopsychosocial model. Figure 1 shows what we have previously described as the Comprehensive Geriatric Model, which places the occurrence of a new cancer in the context of the bio-psychosocial model [2]. The components of the hierarchy are the biological, psychological, and social facets, as Engle described many years ago and applied in this context to the older individual, as you envision the functional reserve and the decrease in homeostatic reserve being the inner part of this box [3]. Conceptually, what we are dealing with is a patient with cancer for whom interventions might be considered, in whom one has to consider the interactions of all the aspects of the

*This work was supported in part by the National Institutes of Health, National Institute on Aging, Claude D. Pepper Older Americans Independence Centers, Grant #5 P60 AG11268.

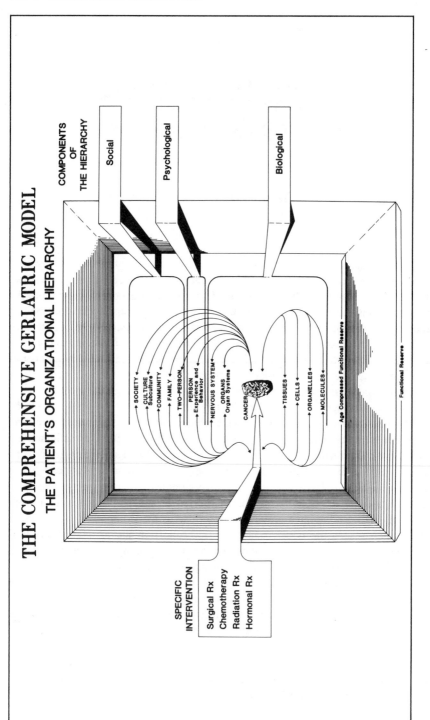

Figure 1. The Comprehensive Geriatric Model for Cancer in Older Persons. **Source:** [2].

hierarchy with both the disease and the patient, and the potential interventions that we see. So, in a sense, this is a conceptual checklist of the various areas in the biopsycho-social and clinical interactions that we must consider when dealing with cancer in the older patient.

I will address each of these in turn, starting with the biological, then psycho-social, then clinical aspects of the interaction and try to give you a sense, predominantly using some examples, of some progress I think we have made in each of these areas, and then the priorities I see for future investigations in these areas.

PROGRESS IN BIOLOGIC RESEARCH

Previous chapters have already commented on progress in areas of basic biology. But progress has also been made at the interface [4]. When we think about the incidence of cancer rising with increasing age, we must ask the question, "Why would cancer rise throughout the age span?" There are a number of possibilities. Probably none of them as a single entity explains it; perhaps all of them together might get closer to explaining it; and perhaps there are factors that we haven't thought about yet that play in this interaction. Let us briefly consider the possibilities wherein we have made some progress. First, as already discussed, there is a decrease in immune surveillance with age. However, it is clear that while this may play a role, it is not the whole story since the pattern of age-related cancers is not what is seen when clear cut severe immune deficiency states are present.

Second, we have potential of longer duration of carcinogenic exposure. If one lives longer, with many carcinogens in the environment, one is exposed to them longer. It is clear also that this is not enough to explain the increase. One simply has to look at species comparisons to see that short lived species, as in longer lived species, have an incidence of cancer that occurs at about the same percentage of their lifespan as in humans. So while it takes humans somewhere around fifty years to start seeing that increase, it takes mice about twelve months to start seeing that increase; presumably they are exposed to the same carcinogenic bath that we are, yet there are these dramatic differences.

That may have to do with the next possibility: differences of susceptibility of cells to carcinogens. As cells age, it is possible that they obtain a higher level of susceptibility to any given level of carcinogen they may experience. We know that there is somewhat decreased ability to repair DNA as we age. This may play a role in allowing initial damage to proceed to full neoplasia. More recently, as we learn more about oncogenes (genes that control the emergence of neoplasia), some evidence suggests that activation of such oncogenes or amplification of them with increasing age may play a role. More attractive potentially, are defects in tumor suppressor genes, genes whose job appears to be to suppress the emergence of uncontrolled proliferation or cancer. Defects in such genes as we age may play a role in this emergence. It is very interesting that a number of tumor suppressor genes have properties that are very similar to genes that have been labeled as "aging" genes, so that for these functions which work on the one hand perhaps to suppress cancer, we may actually pay the price for that down the line by having aging occur as a process emerging from the same physiological biochemical mechanisms.

Most recently, there has been a lot of excitement in the area previously discussed in the chapter by Ershler, shortening of telomeres, which appears to be at least some degree of a controlling process in senescence, and the emergence of telomerase, an enzyme which maintains these telomeres, and seems to create immortality for cells. That area of work suggests, once again, that there are two sides of the coin here in terms of neoplasia and senescence. It is likely that work in this area will produce results that will aid our understanding of both processes, neoplasia and senescence.

Another area of biology that we have learned a lot about has to do with physiology of aging and its relationship to cancer in a number of ways. What is shown in Table 1 are areas in which what we've learned about aging physiology we have now been able to increasingly successfully apply to thinking about the older cancer patient.

Again, I am using these as examples. So, for example, our knowledge about cardiopulmonary changes in terms of decreases in cardiac output and pulmonary elasticity have come into play increasingly in our recognition of the potential importance of surgery for cancer and the use of cardiopulmonary toxic drugs and how we need to modify those. Changes in wound healing are of great importance in our approach to surgery. CNS changes are important in patient communications in dealing with cancer patients, and for CNS toxic drugs. Changes in the special senses like taste and salivary flow turn out to be extremely important considerations in nutrition for the elderly cancer patient and, for example, in using modalities such as radiation therapy especially for the upper half of the body. Our increasing knowledge about changes in the erythropoietic system (production of red cells, white cells, etc.) is beginning to aid our approaches to chemotherapy and radiation therapy for the older patient. Knowledge about immune system responses is very important in control for infection in the older patient. Knowledge of changes in such areas as body

Table 1. Aging Physiology and Cancer

Aging Physiology	Cancer Relevance
*Hematopoiesis — ↓ response under stress	Chemo and Radiation Therapy
*Immune System — ↓ response	Infection
*Body Composition — ↓ lean ↑ fat	Drug Distribution
*Liver — ↓ mass and flow ↓ oxidative metabolism	Hepatic Drug Metabolism
*Kidney — ↓ GFR	Renal Drug Excretion
Cardiopulmonary —	
↓ Max CO, VO2 Max	Surgery
↓ Elasticity	C/P toxic drugs
*Skin — ↓ wound healing	Surgery
*CNS — ↓ brain wt, cerebral blood flow	Patient interactions, CNS toxic drugs
*Special Senses — ↓ taste, smell ↓ salivary flow	Nutrition, Radiation Therapy

composition and changes in the liver and kidney have become very important for considerations of drug treatments of a variety of types, both direct chemotherapy as well as adjunct drug treatment, for problems like pain control and others. This is another area we have begun to make progress in, but there is still a lot to do.

PRIORITIES FOR BIOLOGIC RESEARCH

That brings me to the area of suggesting priorities for research in the future in the area of biological interfaces (Table 2). Priorities in this and other areas have recently been considered by the Task Force on Aging Research and indicated in the recent publication, "The Threshold of Discovery" [5]. They include a need for more work in the area of cell growth and differentiation to learn the basic processes that may link the neoplasia process and the senescence process and control factors that may relate to such. The area of genetics, i.e., longevity genes and cancer genes, is going to be extremely important for defining these relationships. We need to know more about the processes of DNA repair and how it may be different in this situation. A lot more needs to be done assessing free radicals and antioxidants, as described in previous chapters, because both of these seem to play a role in both the aging and neoplasia process. Finally, we need to learn a lot more about the interface of environmental factors with genetic factors and the aging process as a multifactorial approach to how those integrate to greatly increase the incidence of cancer in the older person.

PROGRESS IN PSYCHOSOCIAL RESEARCH

I would like to turn to what I see as some progress in the psychosocial areas. There are a number of issues in which we have made some progress. These are shown in Table 3, and I will discuss several in more detail here. We have learned quite a bit about these issues [6]. In the area of early diagnosis, we have learned that there are clearly lower levels of participation of older people in screening programs. It is not entirely clear what the reasons for this are, but we are starting to learn a few of them. Some have to do with economics, access, attitudes, and knowledge. We are learning how we may be able to apply psychosocial principles to correcting some of these areas. In the area of response to signs and symptoms by patients as well as physicians,

Table 2. Age-Related Cancers:
Biology Priorities

- Cell growth and differentiation
- Control factors
- Genetics
- DNA repair
- Free radicals and antioxidants
- Environmental factors

we are learning that many older patients have a lack of knowledge, many have a fear of diagnosis and treatments, or attribute changes to simply "age" and do not follow up on it. Perhaps, with diminishing social networks, they have less support to follow up on these areas. Also, with respect to the physician, ageism still clearly exists with the attribution of changes to "age" and not following up on them, something we must continually strive to improve.

There are a number of fears that older people have that impact on this area. Fear of death and dying; in many cases older people do not fear death *per se* but do fear the dying process and the things they associate with that process. This can be a tremendous barrier to people seeking care, because they associate this with what is going to happen when and if something is diagnosed and something is found. There is somewhat of a denial process and avoidance leading to failure to seek care. There are many misconceptions and fears of hospitalizations, fear of helplessness and being a burden, and certainly fear of desertion which both families and the medical establishment need to be aware of.

We are learning about communications issues that may certainly be complicated by cognitive dysfunction in the older persons. We have learned that we need caregiver involvement because there are issues of how much we need to tell. The entire area of informed consent and advanced directives, and the communication relating to them, become particularly pointed when dealing with the older cancer patient.

Quality of life issues have begun to be recognized as extremely important. Physicians dealing with cancer patients have always recognized this to some extent, but it has become much more explicit lately, and I think that it is a good sign recognizing the multidimensional constructs involved here. When dealing with family and health providers who make poor proxies much of the time, and do not very accurately reflect the desires of the patients, we have to be very careful of how we interpret interactions with other than the patients themselves. Previous chapters have described about how the older patient often rates their health and general feeling state as much better than anyone else seems to think they are doing. The older patient is the final common pathway, but there continues to be a tendency to doubt them.

There are a number of psychosocial impacts on treatment that are important. Some of these have been discussed previously, but it is very interesting that in the

Table 3. Psychosocial Issues

1. Approach to prevention
2. Response to symptoms and signs
3. Fears
4. Communications
5. Response to diagnosis
6. Approach to treatment decisions
7. Response to treatment; coping
8. Response in remission

care and treatment of the older cancer patient it is now well described that older patients adapt and cope much better, with much less emotional distress, than do younger cancer patients. It would appear that they have different coping mechanisms and more effective coping mechanisms. This may be consistent with the concept of enhanced wisdom with older age discussed previously, but it has certainly been well described, and this also seems to translate to the caregiver, where-in studies at our institution evaluated caregiver distress in the caregivers of cancer patients [7]. They demonstrated that the older caregivers of older cancer patients had less caregiver stress than did younger caregivers of younger cancer patients. Again, perhaps indicating more effective coping mechanisms. Thus, there is a paradox that, despite greater comorbidity and more physical frailty, older persons in fact appear to have fewer psychosocial consequences of cancer.

PSYCHOSOCIAL RESEARCH PRIORITIES

What are some of the priorities that we still need to pursue (Table 4)? We need to do much more work on the barriers for prevention and early protection. We need to work on improved communications. We have to look at improving supportive measures that would enhance quality of life for older patients in a number of aspects of the provision of treatment and prevention. We desperately need more studies on the barriers to care and the barriers to research. One of the real problems in talking about the clinical interface, is that, really up until recently, older people have not participated in the research looking at how to treat cancer better. So, if we do not have older people in the studies designed to improve cancer care, we are never going to know what the appropriate cancer care is for that population. We will always be destined to be doing studies on fifty-year-olds and trying to translate them to seventy-year-olds. We have already seen that this does not work. We need ways to enhance the ability to get older people involved directly in research trials in this area. Over the years this has partly been laid at the feet of the patient, but it can very much be laid at the feet of the establishment in not wanting to get those people involved. I think we can do a lot better.

We have to look at the impact of changing delivery systems on psychosocial activities and the impact of managed care on the care of the older cancer patient. What will happen when Medicare becomes Managed Medicare? This is going to be a very important issue for future care of the elderly cancer patient.

Table 4. Age-Related Cancers:
Psychosocial Priorities

• Barriers to prevention and early detection
• Improved communications
• Improved supportive measures/QOL
• Barriers to care/research
• Impact of changing delivery systems

PROGRESS IN CLINICAL RESEARCH

In the clinical arena, I believe we have made strides in several areas [1, 4]. First I will address aging and the clinical course of cancer. One example is breast cancer, where we have learned in recent years that in women with breast cancer, older women present with more distant spread of disease than do younger women and proportionately less localized disease than younger women. That is, older women are in a worse situation from that perspective than younger women. On the other hand, when one looks at the two-year doubling time of breast cancer by age, one finds that younger women have a shorter doubling time, older women a much longer doubling time. This would suggest a better prognosis for older women. Thus, younger women appear to have tumors that are biologically behaving much more aggressively, older women less aggressively. Despite this, the older women have more widespread disease at presentation. This is another one of the paradoxes for which we do not fully have the answer yet. It suggests one possibility, which is that there are two phenomenon here that we have to take into account: the tumor aspect and the host aspect. It is the complex interface of the tumor-related phenomena and the host-related phenomena that ultimately will determine the clinical course of disease, and this will vary for different tumors. As an example of the variation, when one studies lung cancer there is exactly the opposite situation of what was just described for breast cancer. In the case of lung cancer, younger people have a greater proportion of distant disease than do older people. In fact, some years ago Dr. Ershler described the analog of this in animal tumor models where it turns out that there are some animal tumor models in which you see the lung cancer situation and others in which you see the breast cancer situation. We still have some work to do to determine why these differences occur and how we can potentially take advantage of them in designing approaches to therapy.

Finally, I would like to discuss management issues. We have already alluded to the age and physiology interactions that we have learned about, but we have also learned about a number of the treatment modalities which we use for cancer [1, 4]. One is surgery, which is a very prominent part of the cancer treatment armamentarium. We have learned that surgery for older people is something that can be done safely and effectively as long as one takes careful account of comorbidities in that situation. Radiation therapy has been studied much less, but we have learned a bit about it in that it has about a 10 to 15 percent increased toxicity in older people. Chemotherapy has now been addressed as well. We have learned that there are a number of potential causes of treatment failure in older people. These include comorbid disease, resistant neoplasia, altered drug handling, increased treatment toxicity, and potentially decreased responses to toxicity. This is a complex array of interactions that will require careful investigation as we try to learn more about this. One can establish some general principles with regard to chemotherapy from synthesizing a lot of work that has been done in the past ten years or so, i.e., if one is using mild to moderate intensity of chemotherapy, it appears that the otherwise healthy older person can be treated with the expectation of about the equivalent response and toxicity as the younger person. If you escalate the complexity and toxicity of these regimens, you start seeing increased toxicity, but frequently the responses may remain about equivalent. An example of that is small cell carcinoma of the lung. With the most aggressive forms of therapy, for example that used for non-Hodgkins lymphoma or acute leukemias, toxicities then start generally becoming excessive and the outcomes are poor.

PRIORITIES FOR CLINICAL RESEARCH

This again suggests some areas for future research and research priorities (Table 5), among which I would include the following. We have already discussed the need for improved modalities and applications of screening. We need more work on defining disease behavior, the impact and interface of comorbidity and disease, the host tumor interface. We need more work on the responses to treatment, what can be expected, what can we plan, how can we design treatment that will be improved, especially for those areas where we see increased toxicities and decreased responses. We really need biomarkers for treatment vulnerability. Earlier chapters have discussed biomarkers for aging, but here what we need are biomarkers for treatment vulnerability so one could have a sense of which patient is at risk for toxicity of treatment modalities. Now, we take guesses. We try to assemble as much physiologic, biologic, and social information, and try to determine whether this is someone who might be at risk. We do not have really good formulas for risk, and we do not have markers for it. It would be a tremendous advancement if we did. We need new approaches for pharmacotherapeutics and even new approaches for therapeutics in general. For example, the area of bone marrow transplantation and its use in the treatment of malignancy is one that has always been reserved for the young, for many good reasons because of tremendous toxicity. That envelope is being pushed progressively, so now there are people in their early seventies receiving bone marrow transplantation in certain controlled circumstances. I think we are starting to see changes in attitude as well as exploration of new approaches, and we always will need continued work on appropriate supportive care.

CONCLUSION

I believe that there is tremendous potential for discovery if we pursue the research priorities in the biologic, psychosocial, and clinical aspects of the age-related

Table 5. Age-Related Cancers: Clinical Priorities

- Improved modalities and applications of screening
- Disease behavior—comorbidity
- Responses to treatment
- Biomarkers for treatment vulnerability
- Pharmacotherapeutics—new approaches
- Symptom control—supportive care

cancers. Moreover, as indicated by the Comprehensive Geriatric Model, these aspects of research are intricately connected, and the potential for success is greatest if we proceed with interdisciplinary interactions and awareness in pursuit of these goals. Thus, for example, the basic biologists must interact with the clinicians to be aware of the needs for development of toxicity sparing agents in order to target research on drug action, and the clinical scientist must be involved in the generation of new information regarding cancer biology to appropriately target new therapy. The psychosocial scientists' interactions with clinical scientists will target their work to the issues described above which clearly impact on patient care, and the clinicians will benefit from interactions with the psychosocial scientists by better understanding the basis for these problems. While each of the disciplines must conduct research in their area at the highest level, interdisciplinary collaboration will produce a whole greater than the sum of its parts.

In the context of proposing priorities for work on cancer and aging, interdisciplinary takes on an additional meaning. Thus not only must there be interactions among the basic disciplines noted above, but there must be interactions among the disciplines of oncology and geriatrics as a whole. In my view, this is actually what should happen in many of our clinical disciplines, but oncology and geriatrics are certainly appropriate examples. Thus, both at an investigative and a clinical level, combining the perspectives of oncologists and geriatricians, allowing for sharing and pooling of experiences and seeking areas where the disciplines may be complementary is essential if we are to make further progress. This need has now been recognized at a number of levels.

Perhaps the most striking was the convening of a geratric education retreat (GER) under the auspices of the American Geriatrics Society and supported by the Hartford Foundation. This retreat brought together leaders in the fields of oncology and geratrics to share information from both disciplines regarding needs for training and research. An immediate product from that meeting was the publication of many of the discussions from it as part of a special issue of the journal, *Cancer*, in October 1997 [8-11]. An additional outcome was the creation of a joint task force of the American Geriatrics Society and the American Society for Clinical Oncology to address these issues. Through these and other efforts, the NIH has now recognized the need for targeted studies in this area, and there have been joint program announcements from the NIA and NCI on topics such as cancer pharmacology and treatment in the elderly, breast cancer in the elderly, prostate cancer in the elderly, and psychosocial and behavioral aspects of cancer in the elderly, reflecting interdisciplinary attention to many of the priorities noted above.

The ultimate response to calls for interdisciplinary activities would be to have actual joint training among the disciplines. Just such a program has now been proposed and, with the support of the Hartford Foundation, a pilot program of joint fellowship training in geriatrics and oncology will be initiated at several medical centers with strengths in both disciplines. Hopefully, this will produce individuals who can lead the way in interdisciplinary studies and treatment of cancer in the elderly, and can serve as a model for other disciplines to do the same.

REFERENCES

1. H. J. Cohen, Oncology and Aging: General Principles of Cancer in the Elderly, in *Principles of Geriatric Medicine and Gerontology* (3rd Edition), W. Hazzard, E. Bierman, J. Blass, W. Ettinger, and J. Halter (eds.), McGraw-Hill, New York, pp. 77-89, 1994.
2. H. J. Cohen and L. DeMaria, Comprehensive Cancer Care: Special Problems of the Elderly, in *Physician's Guide to Cancer Care Complications,* J. Laszlo (ed.), Dekker, New York, pp. 237-275, 1986.
3. G. L. Engel, The Clinical Application of the Biosychosocial Model, *American Journal of Psychiatry, 137*, pp. 535-544, 1980.
4. H. J. Cohen, Biology of Aging as Related to Cancer, *Cancer, 74*:7, pp. 2092-2100, 1994.
5. The Threshold of Discovery: Future Directions for Research on Aging, *Report of the Task Force on Aging Research,* Administrative Document, 1995.
6. V. Mor, S. Allen, and M. Malin, The Psychosocial Impact of Cancer on Older Versus Younger Patients and Their Families, *Cancer (Suppl), 74*:7, pp. 2118-2127, 1994.
7. E. C. Clipp and L. K. George, Dementia and Cancer: A Comparison of Spouse Caregivers, *The Gerontologist, 33*:4, pp. 534-541, 1993.
8. J. M. Bennet, D. M. Sahasrabudhe, and W. J. Hall, Medical Oncology and Geriatric Medicine: Is It Time for Fellowship Integration? *Cancer, 80*:7, pp. 1351-1353, 1997.
9. H. J. Cohen, The Oncology Geriatric Education Retreat: Commentary and Conclusions, *Cancer, 80*:7, pp. 1354-1356, 1997.
10. R. Yancik, Cancer Burden in the Aged: An Epidemiologic and Demographic Overview, *Cancer, 80*:7, pp. 1267-1356, 1997.
11. Special Section—Aging and Cancer, *Cancer, 80*:7, pp. 1267-1356, 1997.

CHAPTER
11

Caring for Alzheimer's Disease Patients: Issues of Verbal Communication and Social Interaction

Louis Burgio, Rebecca Allen-Burge,
Alan Stevens, Linda Davis, and Daniel Marson

Humans are, by nature, social animals. The research literature is replete with reports showing that social contact is a predictor for decreased morbidity and mortality. Verbal communication and social interaction is no less important for individuals with declining cognitive abilities. Indeed, because of the Alzheimer's patients' progressive difficulty in communicating needs and forming and maintaining social contacts, it is all the more important for caregivers to both understand the impact of these impairments and to develop skills for compensating for this loss.

A review and discussion of all the topics relevant to the focus of this chapter would require a manuscript of considerable length. We have chosen three topics that are of particular current interest to Alzheimer's researchers: problems and interventions for community residing patients; problems and interventions in the nursing home; and the assessment of Alzheimer's patients' abilities to communicate medical consent and advance directives. The authors chose these topics to show the breadth of pertinent issues. Not coincidentally, these are also areas wherein the authors are conducting ongoing research. Consequently, wherever possible, we have provided more detailed descriptions of recently completed and ongoing research.

PATIENTS AND CAREGIVERS IN THE COMMUNITY

Caring for individuals with progressive dementia constitutes an impressive set of challenges. In the early stages of the illness, caregivers must learn to guide an increasingly forgetful and confused person through instrumental activities of daily living (ADLs) such as managing finances, social, and work responsibilities. As the illness progresses, caregivers must learn to monitor and structure the patient's environment in order to avoid, reduce, or control catastrophic behavioral responses. In the later stages of the illness, caregivers must provide basic ADL care (feeding, bathing, toileting) as well as intercede with others on behalf of an incapacitated, bed-bound loved one who has become a stranger. Finally, caregivers also must find a personal sense of meaning in caregiving for an illness that typically lasts four to seven years after diagnosis [1, 2]. While some families are able to cope with the caregiving stressors that characterize progressive dementia, many are not. A major, contributory factor in family caregiver decisions to terminate home care and seek long-term care placement for their impaired family member is embedded in the progressively altered communications between dementia patients and their caregivers.

Dementia and Communication

Dementia of the Alzheimer's type (DAT) has a profound effect on communication. Word finding, object naming, syntactical fluency, inappropriate responses, "empty" or meaningless sentences, perseveration, and difficulty with topic maintenance and conversational turn-taking, all become more problematic as the illness progresses [3, 4]. The importance of therapeutic communication intervention with a DAT patient as a method for cognitive stimulation and retraining, as well as cuing appropriate social and behavioral responses, is documented in an increasing number of studies.

Cognitive Deficits and Communication

Cognitive decline is believed to be a major contributor to poor quality DAT patient-caregiver relationships [5-7]. While numerous studies have documented communication difficulties associated with cognitive decline, few have explored alterations in communication patterns and behaviors between DAT patients and their caregivers. Further, studies of altered communication in DAT have focused largely on the patient's speech and language difficulties, with little attention given to the ability of the conversational partner to improve or direct interactions. However, those few studies that have utilized interactions as the unit of analysis suggest that as cognitive decline begins to impede patient communication, caregivers begin to make alterations in their own listening and speech behaviors.

Although DAT results in deficits in thinking, ordering, and expressing ideas, syntactic fluency (word grouping according to commonly-accepted rules) and phonologic fluency (rules for sound combinations) are retained until late in the illness. Through attentive listening, a conversational partner may be able to identify patterns of incorrect or missing words as well as shifts in the patient's conversational frame of reference (i.e., shifts in time, place, or affective feeling) and better interpret the essential meaning of what the patient is saying. Bohling analyzed videotaped conversational interactions between eleven DAT patients and unimpaired conversational partners in an adult day care center [8]. Bohling noted that more attentive listening on the part of the conversational partner enabled them to edit and organize the often-garbled expressions of DAT patients. By listening for missing word patterns and implied meanings, attentive partners were able to substitute correct for incorrect words and identify likely missing words, as well as provide conversational cues to the patient that were helpful in establishing and maintaining the conversational frame of reference. These adaptations on the part of the conversational partner improved both the quantity as well as the quality of interaction with the patient.

Speech accommodation by caregivers also can be assistive. Kemper compared the speech patterns of DAT patients in describing and cuing their normal spouse on a picture description task with the speech accommodations made by the spouses in describing pictures to the DAT-impaired individual [3]. As expected, picture descriptions made by the DAT-impaired person did not vary, regardless of whether they were describing the picture to a trained interviewer or to their spouse in a barrier task. However, the spouses made speech accommodations that resulted in more frequent use of conversational modifiers than enhanced picture descriptions through the use of qualifiers, quantifiers, and connective expressions. Normal spouses used more semantic redundancy, simpler syntax, and restriction of picture descriptions to only highly salient picture elements. Investigators hypothesized that these spouses had made speech adjustments to enhance communication as a response to the cognitive and affective losses of communicating with the impaired spouse. The findings of this study substantiate the benefits of speech accommodation in interactions with a DAT patient.

Conversational coaching is an often-unnoted aspect of effective interaction with a DAT patient. Cavanaugh and colleagues noted the benefits of caregiver cuing on problem solving by DAT patients [9]. Caregiver-DAT patient dyads were compared to normal elderly dyads on completion of the Block Design part of the WAIS-R. Caregiver cuing consisted of *location cues* (indicating where the block should be placed), *task reminders, goal direction* (reminding the elder of the end state design to be achieved), *strategies for placing the block, problem solving rationale* (answers to questions from the elder as to "why" the block should be so placed), *motivation, restriction* (saying "no" or physically restraining the elder in incorrect block placement), *reinforcing feedback, and help requests* to the elder for "more assistance."

Normal dyads were more interactive in the problem solving around block placement, and normal elders used more self-direction and interactions with others for problem solving. Caregivers of DAT patients used location, strategy, motivation, and feedback more often than caregivers in the normal dyads. Replications of this caregiver-DAT patient problem solving study [10] continue to demonstrate that family caregivers can enhance DAT patients' daily problem solving through coaching and cuing procedures.

Conversational cuing is believed to be most effective at early stages in the illness, when automatic cognitive processes are still accessible. However, Bourgeois [11, 12] reported that both mid-stage and early-stage dementia patients' verbal and behavioral responses could be improved by teaching caregivers to use prosthetic memory aids. These memory aids (collections of familiar pictures in a special wallet or purse), in conjunction with conversational phrases, were used as stimuli to improve the focus and quality of interactions with DAT patients. Positive patient outcomes included improved memory orientation, more on-topic conversation, fewer inappropriate utterances, more appropriate conversational turn-taking, and, in general, more purposive, focused, and satisfying interactions. Improvements in DAT patient conversational encounters with others were observed for as long as thirty months post-intervention.

In one of the earliest efforts to improve home care for DAT patients through family caregiver skill training, Green, Linsk, and Pinkston reported successfully teaching two spouses to ignore negative verbal interactions with their spouse and instead reinforce only positive verbal responses [13]. In one of the few in-home interventions to teach caregivers cognitive remediation skills, Quayhagen and colleagues compared DAT patient outcomes from three treatment conditions [14]. Seventy-eight care recipient-caregiver dyads stratified by severity of care recipient cognitive impairment were assigned to experimental, placebo, or control groups. The experimental group received twelve weeks (60 minutes daily) of active cognitive stimulation around improving memory, problem solving, and conversational activities. Placebo subjects were exposed to a program of passive stimulation (e.g., television viewing), and the remaining subjects were those in a wait-list control group. Although both experimental and placebo patients improved over time, the experimental group showed significantly greater improvements in overall cognitive functioning, word recall, and general memory. However, nine months after termination of the intervention all groups had declined toward baseline. Such findings underscore the need for formal treatment maintenance programs when employing caregiver interventions.

Behavioral Deficits and Communication

Communication difficulties are believed to trigger disruptive behavior in DAT patients. More than 50 percent of dementia patients will demonstrate behavior problems such as agitation, aggressiveness toward self or others, repetitive actions, paranoid delusions, hallucinations, and wandering during the course of the illness [15]. Kinney and Stephens reported that DAT caregivers' sense of well-being and relational loss were influenced even more strongly by disruptive patient behaviors than by cognitive decline in their relative [16]. Chenoweth and Spencer reported over half of the caregivers they interviewed cited behavior problems as the major factor in early institutional placement of their DAT-impaired relative [17].

Some studies indicate that disruptive behaviors may be triggered by specific patterns of communication. The reinforcing characteristics of elder and caregiver communication are demonstrated in the work of Baltes and Wahl [18], who compared elder-caregiver interactions in institutional and home settings. A major focus of the study was to determine whether home-residing elders demonstrated and received reinforcement for more independent behaviors.

Elder behaviors were classified as independent self-care, constructive engagement (reading, conversing, watching television), and destructive engagement (quarreling, screaming, hitting, throwing food). Social partner (family members, home health nurses, residential facility staff members) behaviors were classified according to whether they encouraged/discouraged independent and dependent behaviors. All of the one hundred elders observed (78 in institutions; 22 in homes) were over sixty-five, and not bedridden, confused, or suffering from acute illness. Data obtained from observers who independently rated morning self-care activities of elders indicated that independent self-care behaviors ranged from 25 percent (in chronic illness settings) to 46 percent in nursing homes. Dependent self-care behaviors ranged from 4 percent in the nursing home to 41 percent in home-health visits. Elders in the two institutional groups showed *fewer* dependent self-care behaviors and the two community groups (family member or home health nurse as social partner) showed more. However, regardless of the setting dependent self-care behaviors in these elders were significant predictors of more dependence-supportive responses from their social partners. Although the confounding effects of the preexisting relationships between these elders and their social partners were controlled for, these findings do demonstrate the reciprocal nature of elder and caregiver behaviors.

Caregiver affect also appears to influence DAT patient functioning. Vitaliano and colleagues concluded that negative expressed emotions (i.e., expressions of criticism and anger) in DAT caregivers were correlated with a higher incidence of disruptive behaviors in their DAT-impaired relative [19]. However, those negative emotions were not predictors of cognitive or ADL decline.

Family Conflicts and Communication

The psychological impact of dementing illness is particularly difficult for families because, unlike physical death with its tangible and final termination, the psychological death of progressive dementia denies families the distance and time to come to terms with the loss of a member. Although most of the care for DAT patients is provided within the family, there is little theoretical or empirical information about the effects of dementia on family dynamics. Family members experience frustration, depression, loneliness, and social isolation around dementing illness, much like the patient and primary caregiver. Orange compared perceptions among family members of demented elders ($n = 15$) with those of family members of healthy elders ($n = 13$) on the home care experience [20]. The majority of family members of healthy elders reported few communication problems with their elders. In fourteen of the fifteen DAT family situations, family members stated that friends and family members had become the primary communication partners for the impaired elder whose social circle had shrunk to only a few primary contacts. Family members of the DAT patients reported they managed their impaired relative's communication problems by ignoring them, acting as translators and talking for the care recipient, supplying missing or incorrect words, using distraction with the care recipient, trying to remain calm and not showing frustration, and controlling conversations to avoid topics upsetting to the elder. These DAT caregivers reported that showing frustration, impatience, giving or guessing the wrong word, and pointing out or correcting the impaired elder's communication errors made the situation worse.

The commonly held assumption is that families provide caregiving assistance, affective support, and respite for both the DAT patient and the primary caregiver. Yet, the literature indicates ongoing family caregiving conflicts: expressed, unresolved disagreements among family members around caregiving issues are common when an elder has a progressive, dementing illness [21-26].

In many caregiving situations, family conflicts prevent members from sharing caregiving tasks with the primary caregiver [27]. More than 50 percent of DAT family caregivers complain that other family members refuse to help with care [21]. Family conflicts around DAT care are also believed to increase the primary caregiver's burden. Shields concluded that depressive symptomology in the primary caregiver is directly related to the amount of anger and sadness expressed toward them by other family members [28]. George hypothesized that such conflicts will arise within caregiving families of frail and impaired ill elders because of declining family reciprocity (a growing imbalance in giving and receiving affective support and assistance between the impaired elder and other family members) coupled with declining family solidarity (loss of the belief that family members must always help each other without regard for reciprocal aid and assistance) [29].

Semple [24] attempted to categorize family conflicts in dementia caregiving families by using cross-sectional data from a longitudinal study of caregiver stress [24]. Family caregiving conflicts could be classified as 1) diagnosis-focused, conflicts between members around differences in diagnosis, prognosis, and treatment of the dementing illness; 2) elder-focused, conflicts around family members' actions and attitudes toward the demented individual; or 3) caregiver-focused, conflicts around family members' actions, and attitudes toward the primary caregiver. According to Semple, these family caregiving conflicts increased depressive symptoms and angry feelings in the primary caregiver.

Based on analysis of intensive interviews with thirty-eight multigenerational families about home caregiving during the early stages of dementia, Garwick and colleagues reported family conflict from 1) uncertainties of the disease, 2) difficulty among members in accepting that something was "wrong" with a family member, 3) the actions by some family members to exclude the elder from daily family life, and 4) pervasive ambiguity in family relationships as a function of the disease [30]. Garwick and colleagues concluded that families will exclude a cognitively impaired member from family life in an effort to reduce relational ambiguity and increase family stability. However, such exclusion can distress the primary caregiver whose anger and depressive responses then results in family exclusion of the primary caregiver.

In an effort to determine whether certain dementia caregiving activities are more conflictual, Davis [31] interviewed family members of thirty-nine dementia patients seen in a memory disorders clinic. At the time of an initial clinic intake interview, these caregiver respondents had scored their family high on a self-report measure of conflict. Content analysis of audiotaped interviews with these family members indicated family conflicts were pervasive in both indirect caregiving tasks (e.g., financial management, household chores) as well as direct caregiving tasks (e.g., feeding, bathing, toileting, monitoring symptoms). However, conflicts were highest in caregiving activities that required family members to cooperate and collaborate with each other.

Caregiving issues can have differential effects related to the identity of family members. Based on data collected from ninety-seven caregiving families, Fisher and Lieberman concluded that the health and emotional well-being of spousal caregivers was least influenced by family functioning, while the well-being of adult child caregivers was most affected [32].

From their comparison of 100 primary and secondary family caregivers of DAT patients about their perceptions of their caregiving situation, Bourgeois, Beach, Schulz, and Burgio reported substantial differences in perceptions of the two caregivers [33]. Primary and secondary caregivers differed most on perceptions of the primary caregiver's coping efficacy. They were more congruent in defining patient problems and assessing the primary caregiver's caregiving strain. However, the long-term effects of those differences on DAT patient and family outcomes were not explored.

In one of the few family-focused programs of caregiver research, Mittelman and colleagues reported findings from a longitudinal investigation of DAT caregiving [34, 35]. Although the intervention (counseling, support group participation, and ad hoc telephone consultation) was aimed at the primary caregiver, these investigators noted that family involvement in counseling sessions increased the likelihood that families would provide support and respite for the primary family caregiver. Further, when families provided that support, institutionalization of the AD-afflicted family member was significantly delayed. While this program of research has been critiqued [36] for potential sampling biases and incomplete descriptions of the multi-component intervention, these study findings do suggest that, when combined with primary caregiver interventions, family-level involvement can delay early placement of DAT patients.

Based on a series of interviews with 192 primary caregivers of DAT patients, Aneshensel, Pearlin, and Schuler concluded that the precipitating factors for caregivers who subsequently institutionalized their impaired elder were constriction of coexisting social roles, intrapsychic discomforts, and family conflicts [37]. However, institutionalization does not terminate involvement with a DAT-impaired family member.

Gold, Reis, Markiewicz, and Andres studied 157 caregivers of dementia patients for two years and reported that those who institutionalized a cognitively-impaired elder cited the decline in the elder's condition and their own exhaustion as the two primary reasons for placement [38]. These caregivers reported that they did not regret their placement decision and described varying degrees of continued involvement in the care of their impaired elder, usually through some form of ADL assistance to the elder at the time of visits to the long-term care facility. In one of the few post-institutionalization studies of DAT patient problems, Shulman and Mandel reported that workshops with speech pathologists were assistive in enabling family members to improve their communication and maintain involvement with a relative in the long-term care facility [39].

COMMUNICATION AND SOCIAL INTERACTIONS IN THE NURSING HOME

Recent demographic trends showing increased numbers of older individuals, many exhibiting physical and mental deficits, translate into higher demands for nursing home services. An estimated 1.4 million older adults are living in nursing homes; and the lifetime risk in 1990 for those age sixty-five or older of spending some time in a nursing home setting before they die is 20 to 40 percent [40-42]. This number is expected to increase as greater numbers of individuals reach older ages.

In general, nursing home residents are predominantly women (75%) over the age of seventy-five (82%). These individuals are severely impaired in both activities of daily living (ADL) and instrumental activities of daily living (IADL), with 97 percent of residents exhibiting impairment in at least one activity. Ninety-six percent of the older adults in nursing homes require skilled or intermediate nursing services, suggesting the need for twenty-four-hour health care supervision.

With increasing numbers of older adults requiring nursing home care, greater attention has been focused on the quality of life nursing home residents experience. Clinical experience, as well as a growing number of empirical studies, suggest higher quality of life in the nursing home can be achieved with a therapeutic model of service delivery. Therapeutic caregiving resulting in improved quality of life is an essential goal of the sweeping changes in nursing homes mandated by OBRA 1987 [43]. An overall goal is to create a community that promotes the physical, mental, and psychosocial health of each resident [44]. The importance of social engagement as a factor involved in resident quality of life was underscored by Mor and colleagues using data from the Minimum Data Set (MDS) [45]. Confirmatory factor analyses indicated that the item data was well represented by the following four factors: social engagement, mood problems, conflicted relationships, and behavior problems. The authors interpreted these four factors to represent dimensions of the higher order construct quality of life for residents with varying levels of physical and cognitive functioning.

Due to the large numbers of nursing home residents with physical, cognitive, and emotional disabilities [46], attempts to improve quality of life must focus necessarily on the environment. Environmental manipulations that focus on optimizing interactions are one such example of attempts to improve quality of life. One manifestation of this shifting model of care is the impetus to train the nursing staff in behavioral interventions, with emphasis on communication skills.

In the typical nursing home, the nursing staff, i.e., 1) registered nurses (RN), 2) licensed practical nurses (LPN), and 3) nursing assistants (NA), comprise over 60 percent of total nursing home personnel. The nursing aide has the highest frequency of contact with the resident, providing 90 percent of direct care in the nursing home. Thus, specialized NA training that promotes therapeutic caregiving has the potential of dramatically changing the care received by nursing home residents; however, NA's training has focused typically on physical care rather than psychosocial care [47]. Typical certification programs designed to train individuals as certified nursing assistants (CNA) are composed of an initial training course and twelve hours per year of continuing education in the form of inservices. The content of the certification program is dominated by issues related to the physical care of the resident [48]. Indeed, the lack of training in the psychosocial needs of older adults in the nursing home may inhibit the nursing staff's ability to identify these needs in their residents, and in implementing therapeutic interventions to redress these needs.

Research has demonstrated that custodial models of care may encourage over-dependence and passive behavior on the part of residents [49-51]. Thus, regardless of new guidelines requiring training in resident's psychosocial needs, NAs are poorly trained to meet these needs, thus adversely affecting resident quality of life.

Social Ecology of the Nursing Home

The risk of social isolation is great in nursing homes, and the paucity of social interactions results in a social environment that appears bleak and sterile [8, 52-55]. The lack of social stimulation was clearly demonstrated in a study by Burgio, Scilley, Hardin, Janosky, Bonino, Cadman, and Engberg in which residents were reported displaying "no activity" during 87 percent of the total time observed [56]. Burgio, Engel, Hawkins, McCormick, Scheve, and Jones found twice as much staff-staff than staff-resident interaction [57]. Also disconcerting is the extremely low rate of verbal exchange between staff and residents during a caregiving episode [57, 58]. Forty-eight percent of the verbal exchange between staff and residents involved instruction-giving by staff.

Regarding resident-resident interactions, staff report indicates that 65 percent of residents spend time with at least one other resident during meals, social visits, or recreational and leisure periods [59]. In general, residents spend time with others who live on the same unit and are of a similar age. In this study, individuals who did not spend time with other residents were typically impaired in cognition, sensory functioning, and communication. These findings were supported by Kaakinen who transcribed conversations occurring during role-play situations between cognitively intact nursing home residents and the investigator [60]. These conversations centered on nursing home residents' verbal report of the social rules of nursing home life. Kaakinen found that residents did not interact with other residents perceived as senile or hearing impaired.

Thus, the social ecology in most long-term care settings can be characterized by a low rate of social interaction between residents and staff, and between residents and other residents. It also appears that low rate social interaction, in itself, can produce negative clinical sequelae for elderly individuals. Lawton and others assert that elderly individuals are more vulnerable to their environmental context than younger adults. Each environment exerts a "press" on the individual's resources, and each individual displays a certain level of competence to deal with this press. According to Lawton, maximum performance potential is achieved when press is either slightly above or below the individual's ability to adapt to environmental demands [61, 62]. As the resident's competence to master the constant environmental press decreases as a result of disease processes, the clinical sequelae for residents become more negative. A small absolute amount of change in press strength, however, may make a major difference in the quality of outcome for a person with low competence. Thus, demented nursing home residents (60 to 80% of the nursing home population) are increasingly sensitive to noxious or even less than optimal environments.

A growing body of literature suggests that environmental interventions designed to address the social atmosphere of the nursing home have the potential of impacting the resident's life. A key environmental factor is the nursing staff. Nursing staff's awareness of their impact on the resident's psychological/psychiatric well being has been the target of training programs for both professional nurses and nursing assistants. For example, the "train-the-trainer" education model has a positive impact on the level of mental health knowledge and improved attitudes toward these issues in both professional and paraprofessional nursing staff [63]. Additionally, training programs on behavior management techniques appropriate for nursing home residents have been used to educate nursing assistants in the nursing home. Cohn, Horgas, and Marsiske conducted five, 1.5-hour inservice sessions covering behavioral management techniques and the application of these techniques to specific problem behaviors in the nursing home [47]. Their results showed that NAs' knowledge of behavioral interventions improved after treatment; unfortunately no direct measure of caregiving performance was included.

The lack of a performance-based measure of the influence of staff training programs is not atypical. Staff training programs seldom document actual changes in staff performance due to the educational efforts of the training program. Therefore, actual impact on the residents' life is unknown. Intervention programs designed to document actual changes in resident characteristics, such as fewer disruptive behaviors or improved psychological well-being, are more typically conducted by research staff. For example, Rovner and colleagues implemented a comprehensive intervention aimed at reducing problem behaviors among demented nursing home residents [64]. Their intervention program consisted of 1) an activities program conducted by a creative arts therapist and two nursing aides trained and employed by research staff, 2) psychiatric control of medication prescriptions, and 3) educational rounds conducted weekly by research staff. Residents participating in this intervention were compared to a group of no-treatment controls. Results indicated that intervention residents were less likely than controls to exhibit problem behaviors, more likely to participate in structured activities, and less likely to be restrained six months post-intervention. Although the intervention appeared to have positive and lasting effects on the residents, the heavy involvement of the research staff in the implementation of the study limits the generalizability of the intervention to other settings.

Studies conducted by Burgio and colleagues have also demonstrated positive resident outcomes following research of staff-conducted behavioral interventions [65]. Intervention consisted of "environmental white noise" (e.g., a running brook) audiotapes delivered by headphones worn by nine residents with dementia. Although nursing staff were responsible for the implementation of the treatment, prompting of the staff was conducted by research staff to increase intervention usage. Behavioral observations of this individualized treatment strategy indicated an average 23 percent reduction in verbal agitation across the nine participants. Using this intervention delivery strategy, however, residents were observed to wear headphones during only 51 percent of the observations.

While these studies demonstrate the feasibility of conducting interventions that impact resident behavior and well-being, it is clear that the complex and often deprived environment of the nursing home requires multicomponent interventions targeting both resident and staff behaviors. Such interventions should involve the provision of materials to enrich the environment as well as comprehensive in-service and on-the-job staff training targeting social interaction.

Examining the Influence of Therapeutic Activities on Social Interaction

Although various types of activity programs can be found in the nursing home, most share a common theme of providing some form of social stimulation to the resident. According to the research literature, socialization activities are necessary to encourage social interaction among individuals who cannot or do not visit with others on their own; however, the benefits of participating in activity programs have not been established empirically due to the dearth of methodologically sound evaluative studies.

In order to systematically investigate the role of activities programs in general and the specific role of external memory aides, Stevens and Burgio are currently implementing an intervention research project to examine the influence of therapeutic activities on the level of social interaction and activity engagement displayed by residents [66]. The experimental design requires two nursing units of a nursing home to be randomly selected as experimental and matched untreated control units. Residents from these nursing units who currently attend activity programs offered by the nursing home compose the two condition design. Residents in the experimental condition participate in three types of activity programs, each conducted by indigenous nursing home staff. The three activity programs are conducted across separate six-week phases of the study. Baseline observations are conducted in the first phase to provide information on the amount of social interaction during usual structured activities prior to intervention. A Traditional Reading group phase follows Baseline assessment and examines the effects of a traditional reading group activity. Following the Traditional Reading phase, a Question Asking Reading (QAR) activity is conducted (phase 3). Residents in the untreated control condition experience the Baseline phase condition (usual nursing home activity program) for the entire length of the study (18 weeks). Controlling the number of residents participating in the group activity is the only manipulation of the untreated control condition activities. This manipulation ensures equivalent group size across the experimental and untreated control conditions.

Traditional Reading Group Activity

The Traditional Reading activity used in the second phase of this study is similar in format to those typically used in long-term care facilities. An activity leader leads a group reading and discussion of a short reading passage. Each reading group utilizes a short, two paragraph passage. The group leader reads the passage to the residents. Reading group participants are encouraged to read along silently as the passage is read by the group leader and to look for designated "Key Words" in the text. "Key Words" are listed on a sheet of paper given to the participants with the reading passage. Although traditional reading groups sometimes exist in nursing homes, we provided specific training to activity group leaders so that Traditional Reading groups activities were applied in standardized fashion across the four nursing homes included in this study. Immediately following the inservice, group leaders practice implementing the procedure with actual participants.

QAR Group Activity

The QAR procedure is a group activity wherein a series of external informational cues is provided during a structured group activity so that the task of reading is socially distributed. The Question Asking Reading (QAR) group activity is guided by the QAR script (Figure 1). The script is present during the group activity to serve as an external memory aid of each step of the activity. As shown on the QAR script, the activity begins with general orienting information such as date, location, and the theme of the day's reading. Following this discussion, reading group participants are given that day's text to be read and a card containing a "Support Activities" question. The "Support Activities" are six questions that focus the group members on the reading passage and encourage social interaction. Following the oral reading of the text by the group leader, each support activity question is "asked" and "answered" by the group participants. These questions are discussed in the same order as listed on the script. Therefore, the group member holding the "Ask about a word that is hard to

---

Question-Asking-Reading Script

- General Orienting Information and Introduction to Theme of Reading
- Distribute Cards
- Distribute Text
- Group Reading
- Support Activities
  - Ask about a word that is hard to say
  - Ask about a word that is hard to understand
  - Ask about the main idea
  - Ask about what happens next
  - Ask about a specific detail in the story
  - Ask if anyone knows additional information on this topic
- Content Test

*The distribution of the text and cards, and the "support activities" are repeated for each paragraph.

Figure 1.

say" card would be prompted by the group leader to read the question from the card. This process continues until all six "Support Activities" questions are presented and discussed by the group. The "support activities" are repeated for each paragraph of the two paragraph passages. They are identified as "Support Activities" to emphasize their role of reducing or alleviating the cognitive demands of the reading comprehension and retention.

To encourage generalization of QAR effects to situations outside of the reading group activity, the QAR reading materials, as well as information related to the reading text, are available to the participants throughout the day. By seeding the environment with stimulus material related to the theme of the QAR group activity, such as additional readings, picture books, and figurines, it was the researcher's intention to encourage continued discussion of the reading group theme. The items are chosen to accommodate the varying levels of cognitive impairment expected among the participants.

Staff training is also conducted in the QAR procedure to ensure consistent application of the QAR group activity across different group leaders (indigenous nursing home personnel). Training consists of a one-hour inservice plus hands-on training and supervisory feedback in the actual implementation of the procedure. Both nursing and activities staff members are trained in specific procedures for encouraging generalization of any increase in social interaction to situations outside of the formal reading group. This special training is a component of our program intended to promote the generalization of social interaction outside of the group activity.

Preliminary Findings

Computer-assisted, real time behavioral observations are completed to assess the effects of the activity programs on resident's social interactions and engagement in activity related materials. Residents participating in the group activities are observed during two time periods, during the group activity and during the afternoon hours immediately following the group activity. Observations conducted during the group activity provide data on the frequency and duration of social interactions among residents and between staff and residents. Residents are also observed in the afternoon hours immediately following the group activity. Afternoon observations are conducted to measure generalized or "carry-over" effects from the group activity. Data are similar to those collected during the group activity, providing detailed measurement of the level of social interaction and engagement with materials in the nursing home environment.

Preliminary findings show very low rates of social interaction during baseline activities [67]. Baseline observations collected across three nursing homes suggest that these nursing homes typically conducted large group activities that did not promote social interaction among residents or between staff and residents, nor did these activities promote engagement with materials related to the group activity (suggesting a lack of stimuli in the environment). Observations conducted on residents in the experimental group during the Traditional and QAR phases indicate a large increase in the duration of time residents spent verbalizing with each other and with the indigenous staff. Comparing observations during these phases to the baseline phase, the data suggest that the smaller group size (approximately 8 to 10 residents per group) and the more structured nature of the activity promoted social interaction and engagement with materials related to the group activity. Similar increases in social interaction were also noted in the untreated control residents when the group size was reduced from approximately twenty to eight residents.

Observations conducted in the afternoon hours following the group activities show little variation in the level of social interaction across the three phases of the experimental condition. Not unexpectedly, no reliable variation is found in the afternoon observations conducted with residents serving in the untreated control condition. However, afternoon observations conducted after the QAR activity do suggest an increase in the percentage of time residents are engaged with reading group materials. These data suggest that efforts to program for generalization following the QAR activity resulted in higher levels of engagement in the afternoon hours. These generalized effects may serve to ameliorate the significant sensory deprivation that is common in most nursing homes.

The Influence of Communication Aids on the Rate and Quality of Staff-Resident and Resident-Resident Interactions

As suggested by the Stevens and Burgio study, the provision of context relevant stimuli in nursing home residents' environment can produce enriched opportunities for cognitive and social stimulation [66]. Such stimuli can function to enrich communication, and interventions can be designed specifically using such aids to improve staff-resident and resident-resident interactions. One such intervention that has shown promise in a variety of settings uses a type of prosthetic memory aid termed a "memory book" to enhance the social engagement of older individuals with communication impairments [11, 12, 68, 69]. Prosthetic memory aids use the preserved automatic processing abilities of even moderately demented adults to improve the structure and quality of communication with others, making interactions more pleasant for both the impaired individual and their partner in communication. Dementia patients with a wide range of cognitive deficits have been shown to increase the informativeness and accuracy and to decrease the ambiguity and repetiveness of their conversations. These treatment effects have been shown to maintain over thirty-six months post treatment [68-70]. Additionally, use of these aids has decreased disruptive verbal behaviors such as repetitive questioning and verbal abuse [71]. These treatment effects have been found primarily in community settings, although such interventions have been piloted in nursing homes [72, 73].

Burgio and Allen-Burge are currently involved in an ongoing investigation designed to increase nursing home residents' social engagement by providing prosthetic communication aids, specifically memory books, in combination with staff training in use of these aids, general communication skills, and staff management procedures. As used in this study, memory books consist of 5 inch by 5 inch laminated pages containing pictures and information about the resident's past and current life situation. They are tailored to each individual but are uniform in size and general topics covered. Clear pictures are paired with simple declarative statements (less that 10 words) about the content of the picture. Thus, preserved automatic processing abilities are utilized in reading the text and scanning the pictures on these pages. These stimuli typically evoke verbal elaborations about the person's prior life and lead to more positive interactions with others [68-70]. Additionally, memory books contain orientation information pertinent to the individual resident. Each resident is provided with a daily schedule and simple instructions regarding the autonomous performance of one activity of daily living (i.e., eating meals, grooming, transfer from bed to wheelchair, transfer to tub). Individualized problem behaviors such as wandering, physical aggression, and inappropriate public sexual behaviors are also addressed. The content of the memory book is updated monthly, with input from the nursing staff, to maintain the currency of resident present-life and problem behavior information and to provide novel information regarding the resident's past. This helps maintain staff interest in the aids.

In this ongoing investigation, resident selection occurs after a period of data gathering designed to provide descriptive information about the residents and staff on the treatment and control units of the nursing home. Residents from two nursing units are selected such that cognitive status, communication ability, and functional impairment do not differ between the two groups. One unit is randomly assigned to receive the combined memory book and staff management intervention; the other serves as a no-treatment control group. The communication patterns of residents and staff on both units are observed for four weeks. A five-week period follows in which the staff on the intervention unit receive three to four hours of didactic inservice training (week 1) and four weeks of on-the-job training in the use of the memory books, general communication skills, and staff management procedures. The direct involvement of research staff in the intervention is then gradually decreased so that the intervention is maintained solely by indigenous nursing home staff. This occurs over an eight-week period during which the interaction patterns of residents and staff are again monitored on both the intervention and control units.

Direct observational assessments using computer-assisted real-time recording of behavior serve as the primary measure of treatment efficacy. These observations are conducted during peak interaction periods of the day, care routines, and a structured, five-minute conversation between the resident and their primary staff caregiver. It is predicted that after the implementation of this combined intervention, residents in the intervention group will show increases in their rate of interactions with staff and with other residents without memory books when compared with their rate of interaction prior to the introduction of the memory books and the staff management system. The interactions of residents in the intervention group are also predicted to improve in quality, with the frequency of positive interactions increasing after implementation of the combined intervention. As intervention residents become more interactive with staff and other residents and the quality of interactions improve, disruptive behaviors exhibited by residents with memory books under the care of trained staff are expected to decrease. It is hypothesized that residents in the control group will show no such changes in their interaction patterns.

ASSESSING THE MEDICAL DECISION MAKING CAPACITY
OF ALZHEIMER'S PATIENTS

The capacity to make decisions about the care of one's body and mind (hereafter *consent capacity* or *competency*) is a fundamental aspect of personal autonomy [74]. From a functional standpoint, consent capacity may be viewed as an "advanced activity of daily life" (ADL) [75], an important aspect of functional health and independent living skills in older adults [76, 77]. Consent capacity is also the cornerstone of the medical-legal doctrine of informed consent, which requires that a valid consent to treatment be informed, voluntary, and *competent* [78, 79]. For purposes of the present chapter, consent capacity refers to a patient's cognitive and emotional capacity to make medical treatment decisions (treatment consent capacity), and to make advance care decisions about health care proxies and end of life treatment (advance directive capacity).

Consent capacity is a topic with particular relevance to Alzheimer's disease (AD) patients. Loss of consent capacity is an inevitable consequence of AD, and can occur fairly early in the disease course [79]. Treatment of AD patients thus raises special concerns regarding the adequate assessment of consent capacity and securing of informed consent, and the possible need for surrogate consent [80]. AD patients also represent a useful population for studying pathological cognitive changes which mediate loss of consent capacity [81, 82]. Communication deficits are among the most significant of these cognitive changes.

Communication Deficits and Medical
Decision Making Capacity

Formal medical decision making usually occurs in a context of oral dialogue between a patient and a physician (or other healthcare professional), or in some cases between a client and an attorney. Intact communication abilities are obviously integrally related to intact medical decision making. Marson and colleagues have developed a conceptual cognitive model of consent capacity which illustrates this point [74].

Consent capacity may be conceptualized as consisting of three core cognitive tasks: 1) comprehension and encoding of medical information, 2) information processing and making a medical decision, and 3) communication of the medical decision [74, 83]. The comprehension/encoding task involves oral and written comprehension and subsequent encoding of novel and often complex medical information verbally presented to the patient by the treating physician. It is apparent that disturbances of receptive language characteristics of moderate AD can significantly limit the quantity and quality of treatment or advance care related information received by these patients [82]. Expressive language deficits related to declining semantic memory [84] can also limit the AD patient's ability to direct meaningful questions to the physician about medical treatment or advance directives [82].

The information processing/decision making task involves the patient processing (at different levels depending on the complexity of the information and treatment options) the consent and other information presented, integrating this information with established declarative and episodic knowledge (including values and risk preferences), and arriving at a treatment or advance care decision [74]. Although this mental processing task is internal and does not depend explicitly on communication abilities, the quality of decision making obviously will relate in part to the quantity and quality of information received.

The decision communication task involves the patient communicating his/her treatment decision to the physician in some understandable form (e.g., oral, written, and/or gestural expression of consent/non-consent) [74]. Such communication often includes, beyond the treatment choice itself, some form of explanation or justification for the treatment choice made. Here again, expressive language deficits related to declining semantic memory [84] can contribute to impairments of comprehension, reasoning, and presentation which adversely affect consent capacity [82].

It is apparent that the language disturbances characteristic of AD will over time significantly impact medical decision-making capacity in these patients. The next two subsections address the phenomenon of declining decision making capacity in AD in more detail. Specifically, an examination of recent research on empirical assessment of treatment consent capacity in AD patients will be presented, followed by an examination of cognitive issues and the existing research related to capacity of AD patients to execute advance directives.

Assessing Capacity to Consent to Medical Treatment in AD Patients

Marson and colleagues have recently used a psychometric competency instrument and neuropsychological test measures to assess consent capacity in AD patients. Specifically, an instrument was developed consisting of two specialized clinical vignettes (A-neoplasm and B-cardiac) designed to test the AD patients capacity to consent to treatment under five differentially stringent legal standards (Capacity to Consent to Treatment Instrument) (CCTI) [79]. Each vignette presents a hypothetical medical problem and symptoms and two treatment alternatives with associated risks and benefits. After simultaneously reading and listening to oral presentation of a vignette, subjects answer questions designed to test consent capacity under five well-established [85, 86] and increasingly stringent legal thresholds or standards (LSs). These LSs are:

LS1: *the capacity simply to "evidence" a treatment choice;*
LS2: *the capacity to make the "reasonable" treatment choice (Vignette A only);*
LS3: *the capacity to "appreciate" the consequences of a treatment choice;*
LS4: *the capacity to provide "rational reasons" for a treatment choice;*
LS5: *the capacity to "understand" the treatment situation and treatment choices.*

The CCTI has been used to assess consent capacity in a sample of older controls ($n = 15$) and AD patients ($n = 29$). Using Mini-Mental State Examination (MMSE) scores [87], AD subjects were divided into groups of mild dementia (MMSE ≥ 20) ($n = 15$) and moderate dementia (MMSE ≥ 10 and < 20) ($n = 14$). Performance on the five LSs was compared across groups. As shown below in Table 1, the CCTI discriminated the performance of the normal control, mild AD, and moderate AD subgroups on three of the five LSs. While the three groups performed equivalently on minimal standards requiring merely a treatment choice (LS1) or the reasonable treatment choice (LS2), mild AD patients had difficulty with more difficult standards requiring rational reasons (LS4) and understanding treatment information (LS5). Moderate AD patients had difficulty with appreciation of consequences (LS3), rational reasons (LS4), and understanding treatment (LS5) [79].

Capacity status of AD patients on the LSs was classified (competent, marginally competent, incompetent) using psychometric cut-off scores referenced to control group performance on each LS. As shown in Table 2, assignment of capacity status resulted in a consistent pattern of compromise (marginal competency and incompetency) among AD patients which related both to dementia stage and stringency of LS. Mild AD patients demonstrated significant competency compromise on the two most stringent LSs (LS4 [53%] and LS5 [100%]). Moderate AD patients demonstrated significant competency compromise on both moderate and stringent LSs (LS3 [64%], LS4 [93%], and LS5 [100%]). The results raised the concern that, depending on circumstances and the standard to be applied, many mild AD patients may lack consent capacity [79, 88].

Instruments like the CCTI represent an important first step toward standardized evaluation of consent capacity in dementia patients. Recent studies have used these instruments to explore important related areas, such as the cognitive correlates and neurological substrates of competency function in AD patients [81, 82, 89], the factor structure of the competency construct in AD [90], and the competency judgments of physicians in patients with AD [91]. Future studies should test the value of such objective competency assessment measures in other populations of patients with neurodegenerative disease.

Table 1. Performance on CCTI Legal Standards by Diagnostic Group

	N	LS1 0-4		LS2[a] 0-1		LS3 0-10		LS4 0-12		LS5 0-70
Older Controls[c,e] (6.6)	15	4.0	(0.0)	.93		8.7[b]	(1.2)	10.3[c,d]	(3.8)	58.3
Mild AD[e] (9.6)	15	3.9	(0.4)	1.00		7.1	(2.0)	6.1[f]	(3.4)	27.3
Moderate AD (10.6)	14	3.6	(0.9)	.79		5.9	(2.7)	2.3	(2.4)	17.9

[a]No group differences emerged on LS2 ($\chi^2 = 4.2$, $p = .12$)
[b]Normal mean differs significantly from moderate AD mean ($p < .001$)
[c]($p < .0001$)
[d]Normal mean differs significantly from mild AD mean ($p < .01$)
[e]($p < .0001$)
[f]Mild AD mean differs significantly from moderate AD mean ($p < .01$)
Source: [79]

Table 2. Competency Outcomes by Legal Standard (LS) and Group

LS/Group[a]	Competent		Incompetent		Marginally Competent	
LS1 Evidencing Choice						
Controls	15	(100%)	0	(0%)	0	(0%)
Mild AD	13	(87%)	2	(13%)	0	(0%)
Moderate AD	11	(79%)	1	(7%)	2	(14%)
LS2 Reasonable Choice						
Controls	14	(93%)			1	(7%)
Mild AD	15	(100%)			0	(0%)
Moderate AD	11	(79%)			3	(21%)
LS3 Appreciate Consequences						
Controls	14	(93%)	1	(7%)	0	(0%)
Mild AD	10	(67%)	2	(14%)	3	(20%)
Moderate AD	5	(36%)	2	(14%)	7	(50%)
LS4 Rational Reasons						
Controls	14	(93%)	1	(7%)	0	(0%)
Mild AD	7	(47%)	5	(33%)	3	(20%)
Moderate AD	1	(7%)	3	(22%)	10	(71%)
LS5 Understand Treatment						
Controls	15	(100%)	0	(0%)	0	(0%)
Mild AD	0	(0%)	1	(7%)	14	(93%)
Moderate AD	0	(0%)	0	(0%)	14	(100%)

[a]Control = (N = 15); Mild AD = (N = 15); Moderate AD = (N = 14)

Assessing AD Patients' Capacity to Execute Advance Directives

The capacity of AD patients to execute advance directives for health care is a topic which is receiving increasing attention. An advance directive is a written or oral statement by a competent individual identifying: 1) The forms of end of life medical care that the individual would accept or refuse in specific medical circumstances (called a *living will*), and/or 2) the proxy decision maker who should make medical care decisions when the individual is no longer capable of making his/her own decisions (called a *durable power of attorney for health care [DPOA]* [92]. Advance directives are useful insofar as they can provide healthcare professionals, families, and the legal system with important information about an individual's healthcare preferences, values, and proxy designations while he/she is still mentally competent.

The execution of an advance directive refers to the behaviors that an individual performs to formally state his or her wishes regarding end-of-life care. The Patient Self-Determination Act (PSDA) [93], which took effect on December 1, 1991, was passed with the intention of increasing the execution of such advance care documents. The PSDA requires most hospitals, healthcare organizations, and nursing homes (all those who receive Medicare or Medicaid funds) to provide patients with a written statement of their rights under state law to accept or refuse treatment and to prepare advance directives for health care. The Act also requires that hospital staff inquire as to whether patients have executed an advance directive [92].

In general, citizens, healthcare professionals, and public policy makers agree with the main tenets of advance directives and advance care planning [94]. Surveys indicate that the vast majority of physicians and patients endorse the use of advance directives and would like to see more advance care planning take place [95, 96]. Most studies, however, find only a 15 to 20 percent prevalence rate of advance directive execution [94]. Additionally, intervention studies to increase execution of directives have shown only modest effects [97-99]. In nursing home settings, the prevalence of documented advance directives in medical charts has been estimated from 14 to 54 percent [100, 101]. Thus, the utilization of living wills and DPOAs is currently low.

Although it was hoped that the passage of the PSDA would increase advance directive execution [102], studies of the implementation of the PSDA in hospital settings have shown little increase in the number of people choosing to execute such formal advance care plans [103-105]. Interventions designed to increase the use of advance directive documents instead often increase informal advance care planning in the form of discussions with potential surrogate decision makers [97] (informal discussions increased from 44 to 61% post-intervention). Research focusing on the individual differences of people who choose to execute advance directives has shown that these individuals are typically older [103, 106, 107], Caucasian [108], sicker [94], and more likely to engage in preventive health practices [109]. The influence of individual differences and the societal emphasis on individual autonomy have spurred professional groups such as the American Geriatrics Society (AGS) to develop position statements to guide health care professionals' treatment of these issues in practice [110]. Accordingly, accurate and reliable assessment of decisional capacity for advance directives is crucial so that individuals can participate in treatment decisions regarding their care as fully as possible.

The execution of advance directives, however, presents particularly challenging capacity assessment issues. From a conceptual neuropsychological standpoint, the cognitive abilities underlying advance directive capacity appear to be more complex than those required for treatment consent capacity. An advance directive is a contingent, future-oriented document which anticipates healthcare circumstances that have not yet arisen. In deciding about an advance directive, therefore, a patient must have the abstractive and projective abilities to move beyond present real circumstances and consider possible future health care situations requiring decisions about care and surrogates. Certainly higher order executive functions, as well as attention, auditory verbal comprehension and episodic memory, appear to be required [82, 111]. In the case of AD patients, who demonstrate characteristic early deficits in episodic memory and executive function [84, 111], and whose grasp of current personal circumstances is steadily eroding, such projective abilities are likely to be compromised relatively early in the disease course.

Research on the topic of advance directive capacity is currently very limited. Most of the work to date has been conducted in inpatient and nursing home settings. Frank tested a decision making model in a hospitalized sample of older adults using two different decisional contexts: medical treatment decisions involving heart disease and decisions regarding the execution of advance directives [112]. Using Applebaum and Grisso's methodology, this study investigated the impact of both "state" variables (e.g., cognitive status, depressive symptomatology, medication use) and "trait" variables (e.g., education level, verbal ability) on two outcome variables: the ability to understand treatment or advance directive information and the ability to rationally manipulate that information [113]. These outcome variables correspond to LS5 and LS4, respectively, of the Capacity to Consent to Treatment Instrument [79]. Interestingly, Frank found few quantitative differences on these outcome variables across the two decisional contexts. This finding suggests that advance directive capacity may not be a more stringent competency than treatment consent capacity. Frank, however, suggested that while there were no differences in this study in the mean level of performance in medical treatment versus advance directive decisions, the absolute level of difficulty of these two types of tasks needs further empirical investigation [112].

There are similarly few investigations of nursing home residents' capacity to execute advance directives. This group is of particular importance because residents frequently do not have advance directives, are at great risk for medical crises requiring end of life decision making by surrogates, and very often have AD or a related dementia. Pruchno and colleagues compared a clinician's assessment of residents' capacity with predictions developed from a composite psychometric assessment score [114]. They found that scores on the Mini-Mental Status Examination (MMSE) [87] and an information recognition score based on procedures developed by Appelbaum and Grisso [86] were the best predictors of the clinician's assessment of resident capacity.

In a similar study, Molloy and colleagues compared five different measures of capacity to assess the competency of those residents judged by their nurses to be capable of participating in medical decision making [115]. Measures included the judgments of a geriatrician, judgments of a nurse in collaboration with an interdisciplinary treatment team, resident understanding of either generic or specific advance directive forms, and scores on the Mini-Mental State Examination (MMSE) [87]. Results indicated that a MMSE cut-off of twenty best differentiated residents with capacity to execute an advance directive from those without capacity. This finding would suggest that residents with only mild dementia may still have the capacity to understand and execute advance directives.

FUTURE DIRECTIONS

At UAB our research group has recently commenced a pilot study of demented nursing home residents' capacity to execute advance directives using an instrument adapted from that of Marson and colleagues [79]. Although data collection is not complete, initial impressions suggest that demented residents are generally not capable of providing rational reasons for executing an advance directive, or of understanding the context for seeking advance directives and the options available. However, most residents appear to have capacity under a more minimal standard— the simple ability to state a treatment choice in advance.

In summary, the capacity to execute an advance directive is an increasingly important issue for AD patients and for older adults generally. At the present time research work on advance directive capacity remains limited. Areas for further research include instrument development, studies of normal older adult capacity to execute advance directives, identification of neuropsychological predictors of this capacity, and individual differences differentiating those people who choose to execute advance directives from those who do not. Such research will lead to the development of interventions to support the advance directive capacity of AD and other dementia patients with decisional impairment. For those individuals without full autonomous decisional capacity and for those choosing not to formally execute advance directives, the roll of surrogate decision makers in the process of medical decision making must be better understood [116].

REFERENCES

1. E. Larson, W. Kukull, and R. Katzman, Cognitive Impairment: Dementia and Alzheimer's Disease, *Annual Review of Public Health, 13,* pp. 431-449, 1992.
2. Y. Stern, M. Tang, M. Albert, D. Jacobs, K. Bell, M. Sano, D. Devanand, S. Albert, F. F. Byslama, and W. Tsai, Predicting Time to Nursing Home Care or Death in Individuals with Alzheimer's Disease, *Journal of the American Medical Association, 227,* pp. 806-812, 1997.
3. S. Kemper, C. Anagnopoulos, K. Lyons, and W. Heberlein, Speech Accommodations in Dementia, *Journal of Gerontology: Psychological Sciences, 49,* pp. 223-229, 1994.
4. B. Murdoch, H. Chenery, V. Wilks, and R. Boyle, Language Disorders in Dementia of the Alzheimer's Type, *Brain and Language, 31,* pp. 122-137, 1987.
5. T. Hadjistavropoulos, S. Taylor, H. Tuokko, and L. Beattie, Neurological Deficits, Caregiver Perceptions of Deficits and Caregiver Burden, *Journal of the American Geriatric Society, 42,* pp. 308-314, 1994.
6. R. Pruchno, E. Michaels, and S. Potashnik, Predictors of Institutionalization Among Alzheimer's Disease Victims with Caregiving Spouses, *Journal of the American Geriatrics Society, 45*:6, pp. S259-266, 1990.
7. M. Severson, G. Smith, E. Tangalos, R. Petersen, E. Kokmen, R. Ivnik, E. Atkinson, and L. Kurland, Patterns and Predictors of Institutionalization in Community-Based Dementia Patients, *Journal of the American Geriatric Society, 42*:2, pp. 181-185, 1994.
8. H. R. Bohling, Communication with Alzheimer's Patients: An Analysis of Caregiver Listening Patterns, *International Journal on Aging and Human Development, 33*:4, pp. 249-267, 1991.

9. J. C. Cavanaugh, N. J. Dunn, D. Mowery, C. Feller, G. Niederehe, E. Fruge, and D. Volpendesta, Problem-Solving Strategies in Caregiver-Patient Dyads, *The Gerontologist, 29,* pp. 156-158, 1989.

10. J. C. Cavanaugh, J. M. Kinney, N. J. Dunn, L. C. McGuire, and R. Nocera, Caregiver-Patient Dyads: Documenting the Verbal Instructions Caregivers Provide in Joint Cognitive Tasks, *Journal of Adult Development, 1,* pp. 27-36, 1994.

11. M. Bourgeois, Evaluating Memory Wallets in Conversations with Persons with Dementia, *Journal of Speech and Hearing Research, 35,* pp. 1344-1357, 1992.

12. M. Bourgeois, Effects of Memory Aids on the Dyadic Conversations of Individuals with Dementia, *Journal of Applied Behavior Analysis, 26,* pp.77-87,1993.

13. G. R. Green, N. L. Linsk, and E. M. Pinkston, Modification of Verbal Behavior of the Mentally Impaired Elderly by their Spouses, *Journal of Applied Behavior Analysis, 19*:4, pp. 329-336, 1986.

14. M. Quayhagen, M. Quayhagen, P. Corbeil, P. Roth, and J. Rodgers, A Dyadic Remediation Program for Care Recipients with Dementia, *Nursing Research, 44,* pp. 153-159, 1995.

15. J. Cummings, B. Miller, M. Hill, and R. Neshkes, Neuropsychiatric Aspects of Multi-Infarct Dementia and Dementias of the Alzheimer's Type, *Archives of Neurology, 44,* pp. 389-393, 1987.

16. J. Kinney and M. Stephens, Hassles and Uplifts of Giving Care to a Family Member with Dementia, *Psychology and Aging, 4,* pp. 402-408, 1989.

17. B. Chenoweth and B. Spencer, Dementia: The Experience of Family Caregivers, *The Gerontologist, 26,* pp. 267-272, 1986.

18. M. Baltes and H. Wahl, The Dependency-Support Script in Institutions: Generalization to Community Settings, *Psychology and Aging, 7,* pp. 409-418, 1992.

19. P. Vitaliano, H. Young, J. Romano, and A. Magna-Amato, Does Expressed Emotion in Spouses Predict Significant Problems among Care Recipients with Alzheimer's Disease? *Journal of Gerontology: Psychological Sciences, 48,* pp. P202-P209, 1993.

20. J. C. Orange, Perspectives of Family Members Regarding Communication Changes, in *Dementia and Communication,* R. Lubinski (ed.), B. C. Decker, Philadelphia, Pennsylvania, pp. 168-186, 1991.

21. E. M. Brody, The Family at Risk, in *Alzheimer's Disease Treatment and Family Stress: Directions for Research,* E. Light and B. Lebowitz (eds.), National Institute of Mental Health, Washington, D.C., pp. 2-49, 1989.

22. L. Davis, Dementia Caregiving Studies: A Typology for Family Interventions, *Journal of Family Nursing, 2*:1, pp. 30-56, 1996.

23. L. Gwyther, When "The Family" Is Not One Voice: Conflict in Caregiving Families, *Journal of Case Management, 4,* pp. 150-155, 1995.

24. S. Semple, Conflict in Alzheimer's Caregiving Families: Its Dimensions and Consequences, *The Gerontologist, 32,* pp. 648-655, 1992.

25. G. Smith, F. Smith, and R. Toseland, Problems Identified by Family Caregivers in Counseling, *The Gerontologist, 31,* pp. 15-22, 1991.

26. W. Strawbridge and M. Wallhagen, Impact of Family Conflict on Adult Caregivers, *The Gerontologist, 31,* pp. 770-778, 1991.

27. S. Mathews and T. Rosner, Shared Filial Responsibility: The Family as the Primary Caregiver, *Journal of Marriage and the Family, 50,* pp. 185-195, 1988.

28. C. Shields, Family Interaction and Caregivers of Alzheimer's Disease Patients: Correlates of Depression, *Family Process, 31,* pp. 19-33, 1992.

29. L. George, Caregiving Burden: Conflicts Between Norms of Reciprocity and Solidarity, in *Elder Abuse: Conflict in the Family*, K. Pillemer and R. Wolf (eds.), Auburn House, Dover, Massachusetts, pp. 67-92, 1986.

30. A. Garwick, D. Detzner, and P. Boss, Family Perceptions of Living with Alzheimer's Disease, *Family Process, 33*, pp. 327-340, 1994.

31. L. Davis, Family Conflicts Around Dementia Home Care, *Families, Systems and Health, 15*, pp. 85-98, 1997.

32. L. Fisher and M. Lieberman, Alzheimer's Disease: The Impact of the Family on Spouses, Offspring and In-Laws, *Family Process, 33*, pp. 305-325, 1994.

33. M. Bourgeois, S. Beach, R. Schultz, and L. Burgio, When Primary and Secondary Caregivers Disagree: Predictors and Psychosocial Consequences, *Psychology and Aging, 11*:3, pp. 527-537, 1996.

34. M. Mittelman, S. Ferris, M. Steinberg, E. Shulman, J. Mackell, A. Ambinder, and J. Cohen, An Intervention That Delays Institutionalization of Alzheimer's Disease Patients: Treatment of Spouse-Caregivers, *The Gerontologist, 33*, pp. 730-740, 1993.

35. M. Mittelman, S. Ferris, E. Shulman, M. Steinberg, and B. Levin, A Family Intervention to Delay Nursing Home Placement of Patients with Alzheimer's Disease: A Randomized, Controlled Study, *Journal of the American Medical Association, 276*:21, pp. 1725-1731, 1996.

36. J. Beck and A. Struck, Preventing Disability: Beyond the Black Box [Editorial response], *Journal of the American Medical Association, 276*:21, pp. 1756-1757, 1996.

37. C. Aneshensel, L. Pearlin, and R. Schuler, Stress, Role Captivity and the Cessation of Caregiving, *Journal of Health and Social Behavior, 34*, pp. 54-70, 1993.

38. D. Gold, M. Reis, D. Markiewicz, and D. Andres, When Home Caregiving Ends: A Longitudinal Study of Outcomes for Caregivers of Relatives with Dementia, *Journal of the American Geriatric Society, 43*:1, pp. 10-16, 1995.

39. M. Shulman and E. Mandel, Communication Training of Relatives and Friends of Institutionalized Elderly Persons, *The Gerontologist, 28,* pp. 797-799, 1988.

40. N. Foner, *The Caregiving Dilemma: Work in an American Nursing Home,* University of California Press, Berkeley, California, 1994.

41. E. Hing, *Nursing Home Utilization by Current Residents: United States, 1985,* National Center for Health Statistics, Hyattsville, Maryland, 1989.

42. P. Kemper and C. Murtaugh, Lifetime Use of Nursing Home Care, *New England Journal of Medicine, 324,* pp. 595-600, 1991.

43. American Health Care Association, *The Long-Term Care Survey: Regulations, Forms, Procedures, Guidelines,* CAT# 4697/UBP/2.5k/7/90, Washington, D.C., 1990.

44. M. A. Smyer, Nursing Homes as a Setting for Psychological Practice, *American Psychologist, 44,* pp. 1307-1314, 1989.

45. V. Mor, K. Branco, J. Fleishman, C. Hawes, C. Phillips, J. Morris, and B. Fries, The Structure of Social Engagement among Nursing Home Residents, *Journal of Gerontology: Psychological Sciences, 50,* pp. 1-8, 1995.

46. A. N. Dey, Characteristics of Elderly Nursing Home Residents: Data from the 1995 National Nursing Home Survey, *Advance Data, 289,* pp. 1-8, 1997.

47. M. D. Cohn, A. L. Horgas, and M. Marsiske, Behavior Management Training for Nurse Aides: Is it Effective? *Journal of Gerontological Nursing, 16*:11, pp. 21-25, 1990.

48. J. M. Stolley, K. C. Buckwalter, and M. D. Shannon, Caring for Patients with Alzheimer's Disease: Recommendations for Nursing Education, *Journal of Gerontological Nursing, 17*:6, pp. 34-38, 1991.

49. M. M. Baltes, The Etiology and Maintenance of Dependency in the Elderly: Three Phases of Operant Research, *Behavior Therapy, 19,* pp. 301-319, 1988.
50. M. M. Baltes and R. Reisenzein, The Social World in Long-Term Care Institutions: Psychosocial Control Toward Dependency? in *The Psychology of Control and Aging,* M. M. Baltes and P. B. Baltes (eds.), Lawrence Erlbaum, Hillsdale, New Jersey, pp. 315-343, 1986.
51. H. W. Wahl, Dependence in the Elderly from an Interactional Point of View: Verbal and Observational Data, *Psychology and Aging, 6,* pp. 238-246, 1991.
52. L. R. Caporael and G. H. Culbertson, Verbal Response Modes of Baby Talk and Other Speech at Institutions for the Aged, *Language and Communication, 6,* pp. 99-112, 1986.
53. J. Nussbaum, J. Robinson, and D. Grew, Communicative Behavior of the Long-Term Care Employee: Implications for the Elderly Resident, *Communication Research Reports, 2,* pp. 16-22, 1985.
54. H. R. Quilitch, Purposeful Activity Increased on a Geriatric Ward Through Programmed Recreation, *Journal of the American Geriatrics Society, 22,* pp. 226-229, 1974.
55. C. Seers, Talking to the Elderly and its Relevance to Care, *Nursing Times, 82:2,* pp. 51-54, 1986.
56. L. D. Burgio, K. Scilley, J. M. Hardin, J. Janosky, P. Bonino, S. Cadman, and R. Engberg, Studying Disruptive Vocalization and Contextual Factors in the Nursing Home Using Computer-Assisted Real-Time Observation, *Journal of Gerontology: Psychological Sciences, 49,* pp. 230-239, 1994.
57. L. D. Burgio, B. T. Engel, A. Hawkins, K. McCormick, A. Scheve, and L. T. Jones, A Staff Management System for Maintaining Improvements in Continence with Elderly Nursing Home Residents, *Journal of Applied Behavior Analysis, 23,* pp. 111-118, 1990.
58. E. Kahana and A. Kiyak, Attitudes and Behavior of Staff in Facilities for the Aged, *Research on Aging, 6,* pp. 395-416, 1984.
59. J. Retsinas and P. Garrity, Nursing Home Friendships, *The Gerontologist, 25,* pp. 376-381, 1985.
60. J. R. Kaakinen, Living with Silence, *The Gerontologist, 32,* pp. 258-264, 1992.
61. M. Lawton, Sensory Deprivation and the Effects of the Environment on Management of the Patient with Senile Dementia, in *Clinical Aspects of Alzheimer's Disease and Senile Dementia,* N. Miller and G. Cohen (eds.), Raven Press, New York, pp. 227-251, 1981.
62. M. P. Lawton, Behavior-Relevant Ecological Factors, in *Social Structure and Aging: Psychological Processes,* K. W. Schaie and C. Schooler (eds.), Lawrence Erlbaum, Hillsdale, New Jersey, pp. 57-58, 1989.
63. M. Smith, K. C. Buckwalter, L. Garand, S. Mitchell, M. Albanese, and C. Kreiter, Evaluation of a Geriatric Mental Health Training Program for Nursing Personnel in Rural Long-term Care Facilities, *Issues in Mental Health Nursing, 15,* pp. 149-168, 1994.
64. B. W. Rovner, C. D. Steele, Y. Shmuely, and M. F. Folstein, A Randomized Trial of Dementia Care in Nursing Homes, *Journal of the American Geriatrics Society, 44,* pp. 7-13, 1996.
65. L. D. Burgio, K. Scilley, J. M. Hardin, J. Hsu, and J. Yancey, Environmental White Noise: An Intervention for Verbally Agitated Nursing Home Residents, *Journal of Gerontology: Psychological Sciences, 51B,* pp. 364-373, 1996.
66. A. B. Stevens and L. D. Burgio, *Social and Behavioral Effects of a Nursing Home Activity Program,* grant proposal submitted to and subsequently funded by the Retirement Research Foundation, 1995.

67. A. B. Stevens, N. B. Marshall, T. Wessel-Blaski, J. Baldwin, and L. D. Burgio, *Influence of Group Structure on Verbal Interaction in Nursing Home Activity Programs,* paper presented at the annual meeting of the American Geriatrics Society, Washington, D.C., 1996.

68. M. S. Bourgeois, Enhancing Conversation Skills in Patients With Alzheimer's Disease Using a Prosthetic Memory Aid, *Journal of Applied Behavior Analysis, 23,* pp. 29-42, 1990.

69. M. Bourgeois, *Conversing with Memory Impaired Individuals Using Memory Aids,* Northern Speech Services, Inc., Gaylord, Michigan, 1992b.

70. M. Bourgeois and L. Mason, Memory Wallet Intervention in an Adult Day Care Setting, *Behavioral Interventions, 11,* pp. 3-18, 1996.

71. M. Bourgeois, L. Burgio, R. Schulz, S. Beach, and B. Palmer, Modifying Repetitive Verbalization of Community Dwelling Patients with AD, *The Gerontologist, 37,* pp. 30-39, 1997.

72. R. Allen-Burge, L. D. Burgio, M. S. Bourgeois, R. Sims, and J. Nunnikhoven, *Increasing Communication among Nursing Home Residents,* manuscript submitted for publication, 1999.

73. L. Hoerster, E. Hickey, and M. Bourgeois, *Effects of Personalized Memory Aids on the Conversational Content and Attitudes of Nursing Home Assistants Toward Patients with Dementia,* in preparation, Master's Thesis.

74. D. Marson and L. Harrell, Neurocognitive Changes Associated with Loss of Capacity to Consent to Medical Treatment in Patients with Alzheimer's Disease, in *Processing of Medical Information in Aging Patients: Cognitive and Human Factors Perspective,* D. Park, R. Morrell, and K. Shifren (eds.), Lawrence Erlbaum, New York, in press.

75. F. D. Wolinsky and R. J. Johnson, The Use of Health Services by Older Adults, *Journal of Gerontology: Social Sciences, 46,* pp. S345-S357, 1991.

76. D. Park, Applied Cognitive Aging Research, in *The Handbook of Aging and Cognition,* F. Craik and T. Salthouse (eds.) Lawrence Erlbaum, Hillsdale, New Jersey, pp. 449-493, 1992.

77. S. Willis, Everyday Cognitive Competence in Elderly Persons: Conceptual Issues and Empirical Findings, *The Gerontologist, 36,* pp. 595-601, 1996.

78. M. B. Kapp, *Geriatrics and the Law: Patient Rights and Professional Responsibilities* (2nd Edition), Springer, New York, 1992.

79. D. Marson, K. Ingram, H. Cody, and L. Harrell, Assessing the Competency of Alzheimer's Disease Patients under Different Legal Standards, *Archives of Neurology, 52,* pp. 949-954, 1995.

80. D. Marson, M. Dymek, and J. Geyer, Neurodegenerative Dementia: Ethical and Legal Issues of Clinical Care and Research, in *Neurodegenerative Dementias,* J. Trojanowski and C. Clark (eds.), McGraw Hill, New York, in press.

81. D. Marson, H. Cody, K. Ingram, and L. Harrell, Neuropsychological Correlates of Declining Competency in Alzheimer's Disease Using a Rational Reasons Standard, *Archives of Neurology, 52,* pp. 955-959, 1995.

82. D. Marson, A. Chatterjee, K. Ingram, and L. Harrell, Toward a Neurologic Model of Competency: Cognitive Predictors of Capacity to Consent in Alzheimer's Disease Using Three Different Legal Standards, *Neurology, 46:3,* pp. 666-672, 1996.

83. M. Alexander, Clinical Determination of Mental Competence, A Theory and a Retrospective Study, *Archives of Neurology, 45,* pp. 23-26, 1988.

84. M. Butters, D. Salmon, and N. Butters, Neuropsychological Assessment of Dementia, in *Neuropsychological Assessment of Dementia and Depression in Older Adults: A*

Clinician's Guide, M. Storandt and G. VandenBos (eds.), American Psychological Association, Washington, D.C., pp. 33-59, 1994.

85. L. Roth, A. Meisel, and C. Lidz, Tests of Competency to Consent to Treatment, *American Journal of Psychiatry, 134,* pp. 279-284, 1977.

86. P. Appelbaum and T. Grisso, Assessing Patients' Capacities to Consent to Treatment, *New England Journal of Medicine, 319,* pp. 1635-1638, 1988.

87. M. Folstein, S. Folstein, and P. McHugh, Mini-Mental State, *Journal of Psychiatric Research, 12,* pp. 189-198, 1975.

88. D. High, Research with Alzheimer's Disease Subjects: Informed Consent and Proxy Decision Making, *Journal of the American Geriatrics Society, 40,* pp. 950-957, 1992.

89. D. Marson, L. Hawkins, B. McInturff, and L. Harrell, Cognitive Models That Predict Physician Judgments of Capacity to Consent in Mild Alzheimer's Disease, *Journal of the American Geriatrics Society,45,* pp. 458-464, 1997b.

90. M. Dymek, D. Marson, and L. Harrell, Factor Structure of Competency to Consent to Medical Treatment Patients with Alzheimer's Disease, *Journal of Forensic Neuropsychology,* pp. 27-48, 1999.

91. D. Marson, B. McInturff, L. Hawkins, A. Bartolucci, and L. Harrell, Consistency of Physician Judgments of Capacity to Consent in Mild Alzheimer's Disease, *Journal of the American Geriatrics Society,45,* pp. 453-457, 1997.

92. D. Doukas and W. Reichel, *Planning for Uncertainty: A Guide to Living Wills and Other Advance Directives for Health Care,* Johns Hopkins University Press, Baltimore, Maryland, 1993.

93. Patient Self-Determination Act, Section 4206, Omnibus Budget Reconciliation Act of 1990 (Public Law 101-508), 42 U.S.C. Sec. 1395cc(a)(1).

94. G. Sachs, Advance Consent for Dementia Research, *Alzheimer's Disease and Associated Disorders,* 8(supplement 4), pp. 19-27, 1994.

95. K. Davidson, C. Hackler, D. Caradine, and R. McCord, Physicians' Attitudes on Advance Directives, *Journal of the American Medical Association, 262,* pp. 2415-2419, 1994.

96. L. L. Emmanuel, M. J. Barry, J. D. Stoeckle, L. M. Ettleson, and E. J. Emmanuel, Advance Directives for Medical Care: a Case for Greater Use, *New England Journal of Medicine, 324,* pp. 889-895, 1992.

97. J. Hare and C. Nelson, Will Outpatients Complete Living Wills? A Comparison of Two Interventions, *Journal of General Internal Medicine, 6,* pp. 41-46, 1991.

98. D. High, Advance Directives and the Elderly: A Study of Intervention Strategies to Increase Use, *The Gerontologist 33,* pp. 342-344, 1993.

99. G. A. Sachs, C. B. Stocking, and S. H. Miles, Empowerment of the Older Patient? A Randomized, Controlled Trial to Increase Discussion and Use of Advance Directives, *Journal of the American Geriatrics Society, 40,* pp. 269-273, 1992.

100. N. Lurie, A. M. Pheley, S. H. Miles, and S. Bannick-Mohrland, Attitudes Toward Discussing Life-Sustaining Treatments in Extended Care Facility Patients, *Journal of the American Geriatrics Society, 40,* pp. 1205-1208, 1992.

101. N. B. Palker and B. Nettles-Carlson, The Prevalence of Advance Directives: Lessons from a Nursing Home, *Nurse Practitioner, 20:*2, pp. 7-19, 1995.

102. D. Park, T. Eaton, E. Larson, and H. Palmer, Implementation and Impact of the Patient Self-Determination Act, *Southern Medical Journal, 87,* pp. 971-977, 1994.

103. E. J. Emanuel, D. S. Weinberg, R. Gonin, L. R. Hummel, and L. L. Emanuel, How Well Is the Patient Self-Determination Act Working?: An Early Assessment, *The American Journal of Medicine, 95*, pp. 619-628, 1993.

104. M. K. Robinson, M. J. DeHaven, and K. A. Koch, Effects of the Patient Self-Determination Act on Patient Knowledge and Behavior, *The Journal of Family Practice, 37*, pp. 363-368, 1993.

105. S. M. Wolf, P. Boyle, D. Callahan, J. J. Fins, B. Jennings, J. L. Nelson, J. A. Barondess, D. W. Brock, R. Dresser, and L. Emanuel et al., Sources of Concern about the Patient Self-Determination Act, *New England Journal of Medicine, 325*, pp. 1666-1671, 1991.

106. T. R. Fried, R. R. Rosenberg, and L. A. Lipsitz, Older Community-Dwelling Adults' Attitudes Toward and Practices of Health Promotion and Advance Planning Activities, *Journal of the American Geriatrics Society, 43*, pp. 645-649, 1995.

107. R. S. Schonwetter, R. M. Walker, M. Solomon, A. Zndurkhya, and B. E. Robinson, Life Values, Resuscitation Preferences, and the Applicability of Living Wills on an Older Population, *Journal of the American Geriatrics Society, 44*:8, pp. 954-958, 1996.

108. G. P. Eleazer, C. A. Hornung, C. B. Egbert, C. Eng, J. Hedgepeth, R. McCann, H. Strothers, M. Sapir, M. Wei, and M. Wilson, The Relationship Between Ethnicity and Advance Directives in a Frail Older Population, *Journal of the American Geriatric Society, 44*, pp. 938-943, 1996.

109. M. D. Zwahr, R. Allen-Burge, S. L. Willis, and K. W. Schaie, *Individual Differences in Possession of Living Wills: Relationships with Preventive Health Behaviors*, manuscript in preparation, 1999.

110. American Geriatrics Society Ethics Committee, Making Treatment Decisions for Incapacitated Older Adults Without Advance Directives, *Journal of the American Geriatrics Society, 44*, pp. 986-987, 1996.

111. G. LaFleche and M. S. Albert, Executive Function Deficits in Mild Alzheimer's Disease, *Neuropsychology, 9*, pp. 313-320, 1995.

112. L. B. Frank, *Psychological and Legal Considerations in the Assessment of Decision-Making Capacity of Older Adults*, The Pennsylvania State University, University Park, Pennsylvania, unpublished doctoral dissertation, 1995.

113. P. S. Appelbaum and T. Grisso, The Macarthur Treatment Competence Study I: Mental Illness and Competence to Consent to Treatment, *Law and Human Behavior, 19*:2, pp. 105-126, 1995.

114. R. Pruchno, M. Smyer, M. Rose, P. Hartman-Stein, and D. Henderson-Laribee, Competence of Long-Term Care Residents to Participate in Decisions about Their Medical Care: A Brief, Objective Assessment, *The Gerontologist, 35*, pp. 622-629, 1995.

115. D. W. Molloy, M. Silberfeld, P. Darzins, G. H. Guyatt, P. A. Singer, B. Rush, M. Bédard, and D. Strang, Measuring Capacity to Complete an Advance Directive, *Journal of the American Geriatrics Society, 44*, pp. 660-664, 1996.

116. R. Allen-Burge and W. E. Haley, Individual Differences and Surrogate Medical Decisions: Differing Preferences for Life-Sustaining Treatments, *Aging and Mental Health, 1*:2, pp. 121-131, 1997.

CHAPTER
12

The Geriatric Medical Encounter

Patricia S. Baker, Jeffrey Michael Clair,
William C. Yoels, and Richard M. Allman

The practice of healing begins with the exchange of information between patient and physician during the medical encounter. Communication goals of the medical interview have been conceptualized from the physician's perspective as gathering information, providing emotional support and building rapport, and educating and motivating [1]. Specific studies confirm the effect of communication on patient outcomes such as satisfaction, compliance, and enhanced health outcomes [2, 3]. These studies highlight the delineation of older patient-physician interaction as a problem and have generated an impetus to investigate the uniqueness of geriatric encounters. In this chapter we consider properties of older patient-physician encounters in terms of the medical system and patients' and physicians' expectations. We focus on the content and context of communication during geriatric encounters. Since an increasing number of older persons are accompanied by others when they visit physicians, we then present transcripts illustrating situations in which patients are accompanied.

REVIEW OF LITERATURE

Demographics

It is well accepted that demographic data predict an increased number of health care visits by older patients as a consequence of an older population that is not only growing in number and proportion, but living longer. Older patients are known to have a higher average utilization of healthcare services than the general population (9 physician visits per year compared to 5 visits per year) [4]. The number of community dwelling persons aged sixty-five and older living with disability defined as limitations in the capacity to perform normal activities of daily living, is projected to increase threefold by the middle of the twenty-first century [5]. Complicating these demographic shifts is the reality that the average period a person lives with disability may be lengthening [6, 7]. Another demographic factor is the increased proportion of women who are likely to be patients [8].

One result of the increasing proportion of older people is that physicians will have more interaction with geriatric patients, who by the age of seventy-five have generally accumulated multiple, co-morbid health problems [9] (also see Allman, Baker, and Maisiak this volume). General problems of communication inherent in medical interviewing can be expected in these encounters. Unique situations also may arise with older patients, reflecting both issues of aging and cultural diversity [see also Stanford, Chapter 6, this book]. Studies have noted that between 20 percent to 57 percent of older patients may be accompanied by another person [10, 11], adding an additional participant to the traditionally dyadic interaction. Moreover, a guidebook for helping older patients "communicate successfully with their doctors" recommends that older persons bring someone with them [12].

Geriatric Medicine as a Specialty

One response to the increasing older population has been the medical specialty of geriatrics, with a focus on maintaining functional independence in the presence of chronic and age-related diseases. Geriatric medicine in the United States typically targets persons over the age of sixty-five. It should be noted, however, that a cut-off age of seventy-five is used in European countries where geriatric medicine is more established, with variation based on the age and needs of individual patients [9]. For instance, a chronically ill person under the age of sixty-five may be treated by a geriatrician.

Guidelines for the practice of geriatric medicine (from the Greek root "geras-", old age) identify potential problems of older adults that should be integrated into clinical assessment for the optimal practice of medicine. Williams notes that a different perspective is needed for the medical evaluation of older patients [13]. Geriatricians are alerted to possible problems both with communication and medical concerns [14]. The goal of the geriatric-trained physician is to improve the health status and maintain independence of the older patient through the assessment of function and prevention of functional disability. Consequently, geriatric medicine encompasses preventive, remedial, and research aspects of aging related diseases which require the physician to understand physiological and psychological changes of normal aging as well as clinical and social aspects of caring for their older patients [4].

The nature of clinical assessment differs for older patients in that disease is likely to be chronic and progressive, with specific problem complexes emphasized rather than diagnostic categories [9]. Acute problems may occur in the context of one or more chronic diseases [4]. Geriatricians are trained to recognize special characteristics of older patients and to distinguish disease states from normal physiological changes associated with aging [4]. Care plans should be age and need appropriate, directed toward the prevention of further decline and more expensive outcomes such as nursing home placement and/or emergency care [4]. Hazzard identifies four areas that represent the difference in addressing the older patient [9]. There is an expectation of multiple disabilities, some of which may be covert, assessed by *the five I's:* *I*atrogenic disease, mental *I*ncompetence, *I*ncontinence, *I*mmobility, *I*mpaired homeostasis. Limited physiologic reserves may make a diagnosis that is without consequences in younger patients, a serious concern for the elderly; diseases may present in atypical ways; and most significantly, management rather than cure is the aim.

Guidelines indicate that, while not every older person needs the attention of a geriatrician, there is a need for a different approach with older patients, particularly the oldest and frailest [4]. A recent study that screened community dwelling elderly found that 68 percent had difficulty in at least one of four geriatric conditions (depression, urinary incontinence, falling, and functional impairment) [15, 16]. The comprehensive geriatric assessment (CGA) is a formalized interdisciplinary approach to the screening and diagnosis of physical and psychosocial impairments and functional disabilities in frail older adults in which the traditional medical examination is supplemented with specific assessments to detect impairments likely among frail elderly. These include assessments of cognition, depression, mobility problems, problems of nutrition, sensory (vision and hearing) impairment, and functional status [16]. A simplified version has been shown to detect potential problems when used in an opportunistic way in general practice [17].

Physicians

Focusing on the physician, the Alliance for Aging Research, "Will You Still Treat Me When I'm 65?" presents a pessimistic prognosis of a "severe shortage of doctors trained to manage the special health care needs of older people" [4, p. 4]. "Working with Your Older Patient: A Clinician's Handbook," emphasizes anticipated problems with diagnosis, adherence, efficient time usage, and both patient and physician satisfaction when the patient is an older adult [18].

Among medical residents there is a common belief that elderly patients will be unreliable "historians," creating an interviewing burden on the physician [19]. Physicians identify patient attributes as the cause of communication problems. These include having multiple problems, feeling distressed, inability to understand, and lack of adherence [20]. In a review of the literature, Hall, Roter, Milburn, and Daltroy [21] note that health status may be a critical factor in physician assessment of "liking" a patient [21]. In their research, the impact of patients' health status on communication was somewhat paradoxical. Although engaging in many positive communication behaviors, physicians' voice tone and lack of social conversation may have conveyed dislike such that patients reported being less satisfied with the encounter. In part then, elderly persons may be suspect before they even speak, predefined as having multiple chronic health problems that are difficult to manage. Another possibility is that older patients may be seen as responsible for their own poor health, having rejected lifestyle practices in middle age that could have significantly prevented or attenuated chronic diseases of old age, particularly for hypertension, atherosclerotic cardiovascular disease, some cancers, chronic obstructive pulmonary disease, diabetes mellitus, osteoporosis, and osteoarthritis [7]. Both possibilities point toward stereotyping by physicians that clearly place the elderly patient at a disadvantage in the interaction.

One factor that has been addressed is whether or not medical encounters with older patients take more time than those with younger patients. Even when accompanied by others, results have been inconclusive; confounding factors appear to be the sickness of the patient and the type of visit, whether initial or return [22-24]. It is unclear if physicians, anticipating communication difficulties, consciously control the duration of the encounter. Recent work by Baker, Yoels, Clair, and Allman indicate that when elderly patients are accompanied by a third party the exam time is no different than when elderly patients are unaccompanied [25]. They suggest that physicians may operate with a mental baseline for what constitutes an "appropriate" length of a medical encounter modeled on the standard dyadic situation. Participation by caregivers may replace communication between physician and patient.

Older Patients

One basis for classifying persons as older is chronological age. However, in the research literature the starting age for "older adults" ranges from fifty to seventy years [26]. Chronologic criteria are problematic due to varying rates of aging and disease accumulation [9]. An alternative perspective is to classify persons by functional age, which, although having some intuitive appeal, also has no clear demarcations. One problem in studying communication in older patient-physician medical encounters is that age inclusion criteria are not comparable across studies and only rarely is health status addressed as a controlling variable. Additionally, it is often not specified whether the patient has been designated as a geriatric patient or if the visit is a general interview with a patient who happens to be older.

Non-compliance may be a particular problem for older patients, since older adults are prescribed three times as many prescription medications than younger patients [27]. For all ages, poor adherence is common, contributing significantly to treatment failures in medical care [28, 29]. Estimates of non-adherence range from 30 to 75 percent [3, 30-34]. Inappropriate drug use accounts for 6 to 10 percent of hospital admissions in the United States [35-37], and it is estimated that 23 percent of nursing home placements result from the inability to manage therapy adequately [38]. Salzman reports that the elderly who take three or more drugs a day are more likely to be at risk for poor compliance, yet as many as 25 percent of elderly take at least three drugs a day [33]. (Average drug use among elderly hospitalized patients suggest that eight drugs may be typical.)

Communicating risks and benefits of therapy to patients may become increasingly important when dealing with older adults. For instance, elderly hypertensive patients adhered to therapeutic regimens even in the presence of adverse side effects [39]. Contrary to stereotypes of older people as hypochondriacs and a drain on the healthcare system, often presenting with trivial complaints, older persons may, in fact, *underreport* significant symptoms of illness [13]. One reason may be that family members, caregivers, and society dismiss health complaints of older people because of age [4]. Another possible reason is the perception of an unresponsive system of care which may, in part, be related to communication problems within the encounter [13].

In contrast to expected problems in interviewing the elderly [40, 41], caution that the healthy sixty-five year old has no reason to be treated differently from middle-aged patients. Along the same line, it should be noted that 85 percent of persons over the age of sixty-five *have no disability* [42]. In the absence of disease, normal aging is a benign process. However, clinically relevant implications of age-related physiologic changes that may affect medical care include the increasing differentiation among persons, accumulated biologic effects of lifestyle circumstances such as tobacco usage, physical activity, and nutrition, and a decreased functional reserve with which to meet life events [13]. Maddox notes the importance of including contextual factors, such as material and social resources available to individuals, to explain the diversity of aging processes and outcomes [43].

COMMUNICATION AND MEDICAL PRACTICE

The general medical encounter can be viewed as an opportunity to create a good interpersonal relationship, exchange information, and negotiate treatment [44, 45]. The conversational verbal component of such encounters cannot be underestimated: 60 to 80 percent of medical diagnosis and treatment decisions may originate from the interview before the physical exam or performance of medical tests [19, 46]. The techniques of conversation or discourse analysis have been applied to talk in medical encounters and powerfully illustrate issues of authority, control, and power in doctor patient communications [47]. Drew and Heritage argue that micro-level analyses of talk in institutional settings are pathways to connect talk to the broader social context [48]. Extracts of talk have been used to show how conversation establishes relationships between patients and physicians while reflecting larger, macro-level societal considerations [see especially 49-54].

The basic function of conversation within medical interviews regardless of age is to enable the physician to formulate an evaluation, diagnosis, and treatment plan for the patient. The therapeutic aspect of the physician-patient relationship also is strongly influenced by communication ability [55]. Positive aspects of communication have been shown to be associated with health outcomes such as patient satisfaction, compliance to treatment, recall and understanding of information, health status, and decreased malpractice claims [3, 20, 44]. Several studies have noted that elderly patients are among the least likely to file claims [56-58], or even to report unmet expectations [59].

Financial implications of successful communication are suggested by patients' improved health status, such as shorter hospital stays and reduced pain medication usage [60]. For elderly patients, the duration of the physician-patient relationship also is associated with decreased likelihood of hospitalization and lower health care costs [61]. Since "doctor-shopping" often results from patient dissatisfaction [19], sustained relationships may, in part, be due to successful communication between the patient and the physician.

Physicians frequently report problems with adherence as a source of frustration in communicating with patients [62]. Noncompliance has been related to the complexity of the medical regimen and poor communication. Communication and collaboration of patient and physician occurring in the clinical setting are of prime importance in determining patient adherence [32]. Donovan noted that patients failed to recall one-third to one-half of statements made by physicians, and that elderly patients may have more problems with memory [63]. Poor physician-patient communication is the single most important factor determining compliance with treatment [39]. Less time spent with the physician correlated with higher noncompliance rates [64]. When and whether to use medications are among the most common decisions regarding health care that patients will make, yet physicians tend to overestimate the extent to which they discussed patients' ability to follow treatment plans, elicited patients' opinions, or discussed risks of medication [65, 66]. The importance of the medical encounter in establishing understanding and priority for the treatment plan is underscored by a study of inadequate health literacy correlated independently with age and education [67]. They reported that 48 percent to 81 percent of persons aged sixty or older in their sample were unable to understand written healthcare information.

One indication of changing dynamics of physician-patient relationship is the current differentiation of compliance and adherence in which adherence involves clinicians' responsibility to form a therapeutic alliance with the patient [68]. "Enhanced autonomy," in which the physician uses open dialogue, informs patients and possible surrogates about therapeutic possibilities and odds of success, explores patient values, and makes recommendations, has been recommended to replace the traditional medical model [69]. Desired outcomes are associated with a communication style that provides a high level of information and opportunities for participation in decision making [70, 71]. Although previous studies have shown the importance of involving family members in health education [72], the role of persons who come with elderly patients to medical encounters has not been specified in terms of adherence [73]. Perhaps "medication management" [35], a participatory model that acknowledges the decision making responsibility and power of both the patient and the healthcare provider, should be expanded to include potential caregivers.

CLINICAL PRESENTATION OF ELDERLY PATIENTS

In a clinical vignette, Kavesh illustrates the difference in the way a complaint of a sore knee resulting from a fall will be treated for an eighty-five-year-old woman accompanied by her daughter in contrast to her forty-five-year-old unaccompanied counterpart [74]. All phases of the encounter, collecting information, judging, and weighing the evidence to reach a treatment plan are subtly different. For the younger patient, the focus is on the knee pain only, whereas this is only the beginning of the assessment for the physician treating the older woman. The cause of the fall becomes significant. Did medications, environment, or housing contribute? Was it accompanied by symptoms such as dizziness or weakness associated with a more serious medical sequelae such as a heart problem or a transient neurological deficit? Were there neurologic consequences of the fall such as confusion? Why is the patient accompanied by the daughter? For the elderly patient, evaluation proceeds in a dramatically different way that encompasses far more of patients' lives. A detailed examination of mental status, functional status, and social support may be critical to maintenance of independence in the elderly patient. This can be a time consuming task that is particularly problematic for primary care physicians [74, 75].

Beisecker summarizes studies about older patients indicating that physicians may show an age bias [2]. Treatment options offered may differ for older patients, with the physician making decisions unilaterally rather than striving for mutual understanding. The content of medical interviews with older patients is mostly medical [76] and little preventive counseling may be given [77]. Patient themselves may influence differential treatment. Older patients tend to be more passive than younger adults, verbally disagree with physicians less, and seem more content to let physicians make decisions for them. Older patients are less likely to ask for information from their physicians [11]. Although Greene et al. [10] found that psychosocial concerns are rarely addressed, issues of bereavement, retirement from work, financial insecurity, gender roles and sexuality, isolation and loneliness, dependency in activities of daily living are more likely to arise in interviews with older patients [78]. Perhaps because of the minimal participation by elderly patients, physicians may underestimate their interest in having surgical interventions [79]. Physicians often assume that patients who do not ask questions understand what is being said [80], but as many as 47 percent of general practice patients may not understand what they are told [44]. This may be especially true for elderly patients with cognitive deficits [74]. It has been noted that it is necessary to assess older patients' cognitive and functional capacities to comply with medication regimens [81].

One recommendation to older people for improving communication is to bring a family member or friend with them [12]. In recognition of the growing proportion of medical encounters in which patients are accompanied by caregivers, the American Medical Association created a model of partnership in which caregivers are acknowledged as both observers and participants [82]. Research suggests that the resulting interaction differs significantly from the dyad of patient and physician. Such family centered medical care encompasses the provision of information, planning and implementing decisions for medical care, and personal assistance [83]. Physicians face additional challenges dealing with two people having different and possibly conflicting needs [2, 11, 24].

COMMUNICATION IN
OLDER PATIENT-PHYSICIAN TRIADS

Empirical studies of elderly patient-physician triads remain limited. In one of the first analyses of coalition development in medical triads, Coe and Prendergast found that coalition formation varied by the topics discussed and each party's agenda [84]. Adelman, Greene, and Charon note that third persons may inhibit or facilitate the physician-patient relationship [85]. The former effect is found in studies of elderly cancer patients [86, 87] in which the presence of family members led to more physician-provided information but less emotional support for patients than when patients were unaccompanied.

In one of the few studies comparing dyads and triads, fifteen triadic geriatric medical encounters were matched to fifteen dyads on the basis of patient and physician race and gender [24]. While the specific content and quality of physician-patient interactions were not affected by the presence of a third person, in triads older patients raised fewer topics in all content areas than they did in dyads. Patients in triads were less assertive and expressive, and, more importantly, were often excluded when physicians talked with caregivers.

An analogy can be found in the practice of pediatric medicine, in which discourse between doctors and patients objectify the child by the way questions are composed and directed [88]. This potential also exists for elderly patients as can be inferred from Beisecker's [11] finding that companions participated in 83 percent of twenty-one older patient encounters. Older patients may be overlooked as the companion becomes the principal conveyor of information to the doctor concerning topics such as the patient's symptoms, medications, and compliance. Recently, Baker et al. showed how laughter patterns in triadic geriatric medical encounters reflected coalitions between third parties and physicians which had the effect of excluding patients from participation in the encounters [25]. Another potential is that the topical content of the encounter may change, the presence of an additional person acting as a signal to the physician that the patient may differ mentally or physically from unaccompanied patients. In view of physician's concerns about controlling time [89, 90], physicians may view the presence of a third person as a way to quickly gain accurate information as well as to guarantee adherence to treatment regimens [84].

CONTEXTUAL EXAMPLES OF TRIADIC INTERACTIONS

Content analysis of a subset of tapes collected during a research project of doctor-patient communication in out-patient clinics of an urban university's medical center over a four-year period[1] reveal differing patterns between dyadic and triadic encounters. These patients were first time visitors to the clinic. In this study of thirty-nine triadic older (over 60 years) patient-physician encounters, none of the patients were asked if they wanted the third person to be present; in almost all encounters with third persons, the third person and the patient were waiting in the examining room for the doctor [91].

Comparison of a set of sixteen dyads and triads matched for age, race, gender, severity of illness as rated by the physician, and clinic status (either a transfer to a new physician or a first time clinic user) showed subtle differences in topics

[1] The data used in this study was collected in part from grants from the University of Alabama at Birmingham Hospital Continuous Innovations in Patient Care Program (Richard Allman, M.D., and Jeffrey M. Clair, Ph.D., Co-PIs) and the AARP Andrus Gerontology Foundation (Jeffrey M. Clair, PI).

discussed [91]. Only in triads were issues of memory problems, incontinence, and falling likely to be discussed, clearly issues that are discrediting in terms of persons' ability to function independently. The omission of topics directed to patients who were accompanied provided another indication of differential treatment by physicians. In contrast to dyadic encounters, patients in triads were never asked if they provided care for someone else (as in a grandmother who comes with a daughter but who herself cares for the children while the daughter works), nor was prior or current occupation as likely to be discussed. In contrast, patients appearing by themselves were not asked if they needed help to live independently; in some cases these patients were accompanied to the clinic but the third person remained in the waiting room. Patients' competence was not overtly questioned, but the initial acceptance by the physician that a third person is necessary was not negotiated or re-evaluated. Accompanied patients were seldom given the opportunity to present themselves as competent adults. It should be noted that in this sample of patients ($N = 32$), there was only minimal discussion of the four geriatric conditions targeted by Maly, Hirsch, and Reuben [15] as potential screening measures for frailty, whether or not patients were accompanied. Patients' depression was a topic in six encounters; incontinence was discussed in five encounters; falling in seven encounters; and functional impairments other than difficulty walking were discussed in one to six of the thirty-two interviews.

We present excerpts from transcriptions of the audio taped medical encounters from the above mentioned study that show ways in which elderly patients may be marginalized by the presence of a third party (see Appendix 1 for transcript notations).

Excerpt 1

(Discourse 304: African-American male, age 69, accompanied by his spouse, age 67; female physician; time is 1.2 minutes into the encounter)

D: And in your past medical history, you've got hypertension, high blood pressure? (2)

P: *That's (word)

D: High blood pressure.

P: Yes'm.

D: And how long have you had high blood pressure? (2)

P: That was way back, in um (words) (1)

T: He been on that medicine for about=

D: =the Betatec?=

T: =been about (1) (word) put you on that last year.

D: But was he on anything before that? Or was this, was that the first [time he was medicated] for high blood pressure?=

P: [(word) first time]

T: =That was the first, the first time, he was, that they put him on that medicine.

D: So he's been on, he's had high blood pressure, for about [two years?]

T: [He was eighty] eight.

D: It was three years?
P: [No I was on (word)]
T: [Eighty nine] I think they put him on that eighty nine.

This excerpt, from the beginning of the encounter, begins with the physician directing a question about the patient's blood pressure to the patient. Asked about how long he has had high blood pressure the patient hesitates 2 seconds, then begins to say that was "way back" and hesitates 1 second at which point the wife takes over telling the physician about medication usage. The wife directs a comment to the patient about his own medication. The physician next redirects the original question of when the first diagnosis of high blood pressure was made, but *this time the question is directed to the wife*. The patient begins to answer the physician before the physician finishes the question, and the wife essentially repeats the patient's answer. The physician continues to direct the conversation to the wife. When the physician requests confirmation of the wife's response, the patient's voice is overlapped by the wife. In this sequence, the wife answers a question directed to the patient after which the physician orients the next question to her. The physician may be assuming that directing questions to the wife will result in more accurate and quicker information based on the patient's initial hesitancy to respond. A similar situation is presented in excerpt 2.

Excerpt 2

(Discourse 509: African-American male, age 72, accompanied by sister, age 70; male physician; time .3 minutes)

D: How are you feeling today? (3)
P: *I don't know.
D: You don't know?
D: Are you hurting anywhere? (3)
P: I don't know, just hurts.
D: Huh? ((laughs)) Ok.
D: How's he been doing? (1)
T: We'll, I tell you he [has]
D: [how old] is he now, let me get that str=
T: Nineteen-twenty*(word)=
D: =you're eight-nineteen twenty. Okay.
T: I don't know nineteen, nineteen, ummp.
P: I'm nineteen nineteen.
T: No. (1)
P: I don't know.
D: Okay.
D: Umm, he- how's he been doing? (1)

In this sequence, the patient's uncertainty and hesitation seem to prompt the physician to focus on the sister. In answering a question, asked just after the physician has introduced himself, the patient hesitates 3 seconds before giving a soft and indefinite response. The physician turns to the sister who speaks loudly, but doesn't even get to finish answering the question before the physician interrupts to direct a question about the patient's age to her. After the sister answers the physician he directs acknowledgment of the birth date to the patient, but the sister corrects what she has previously said. Disagreement between the patient and sister follows, with the sister negating the patient's contribution, at which point the patient reverts back to "I don't know." The physician continues talking to the sister.

These two examples show how quickly the physician utilizes the third party as the source of information. It may be that the third party is the better informant; what is significant here is that the physician evidently makes this assumption based on the wife's contribution in the first sequence, and by the presence of the sister in the second excerpt. In both cases, the patient's hesitancy seems to instigate the physician turning to the third party rather than an assessment of the patients' ability to express themselves. There is even evidence that both of these patients are more capable of answering than the physician has initially assumed, yet the physician continues to direct questions to the third party. In both cases the patient attempts to regain the conversational floor after the physician directs a question to the third person.

The next selection is from an encounter in which the physician has been talking to the patient while the son was parking the car. The patient has had breast cancer and recently lost the sight of his one good eye. He is in a wheelchair. He is a widow, and now lives by himself near his son. He has been in a nursing home in another part of the state before coming here to live. The following occurs shortly after the son enters the room.

Excerpt 3

(Discourse 213: white male, age 75, accompanied by son, age 53; male physician)

    D: Were you having troubles emptying your bladder? Things like that?
    T: Yeah.
    P: Like, no, I wasn't
    D: You weren't, no?
    T: No. He had a lot of infections back in those days, he did.
    D: Okay . . .

Later in this encounter (time: 25 minutes).

    D: Are you diabetic?
    P: Oh no, no sir.
    D: Anybody else in the family have problems [like that]?
    T: [no]
    P: No. (2)
    T: It's real funny. Cause they said he's got diabetic eyes.
    D: *Yeah, he does (1)
    D: Okay. (3)
    P: (Words) (1)
    D: But he's not a diabetic?

T: No. They've run glucose [tolerance and everything else]
P: [(word) they've done everything to me on that]
D: Okay.
D: Umm, anybody else in your family have diabetes?
T: [nope]
P: [no]

After the son enters the room, there is competition for the physician's attention. The physician begins by directing a question to the patient which the son answers. This answer is contradicted by the patient, and when the physician seeks confirmation from the patient, the third negates the patient's response, reiterating his assertion that the patient was having troubles in the form of infections. Later in the conversation, the son and patient both answer a question directed to the patient. After a brief pause, the son introduces information. The patient says something, not intelligible on the tape, and the physician directs the next question to the son. Apparently not wanting to be *talked about,* the patient speaks up. Verbally, the next question is ambiguously directed and both the patient and the son answer simultaneously. This pattern continues throughout the exam.

The next excerpt occurs during the physical examination. The patient's daughter has been sitting quietly throughout the examination to this point. The physician has acknowledged her presence at the beginning of the encounter, and since has directed questions only to the patient.

Excerpt 4

(Discourse 211: New to clinic; African American female, age 73, accompanied by daughter, age 24; female physician)

P: We had uh, grandbaby in Germany. I didn't even know that B ((first name)) was going to have another one.
D: Yeah?
P: And uh, my son, called and told me that.
D: Umm hmm.
P: And uh, they's got a girl, this time.
D: Really.
P: And I want to see her so bad [(((laughs))]
D: [yeah]
D: He's over in Germany?
P: They're not now.
D: They're not now. But they've been, really. Okay. Okay.
D: Umm. (1). Anything else been going on, or is, that pretty much it? Hadn't been having=
T: =Bathroom. (1)
D: Huh?
T: Going to the bathroom . . .

This doctor has been using the physical examination to talk about social aspects of the patient's life. What is significant here is that the daughter's interruption is so unexpected the physician has to refocus. The daughter successfully introduces a possible problem, but it is unclear whether or not the patient would have brought this up *on her own*. By her presence the daughter retains the right to participate when she chooses, even if not specifically addressed by the physician.

These examples of triadic interaction show attributes of coalition formation. While the physician directs the encounter, the role of the patient is in question by the presence of the third person. Although the first examples show the physician choosing to direct questions to the third person, third persons often answer questions specifically directed to patients. The final example shows how the third person retains the right to intercede, even when not specifically invited to participate. This conversational *privilege* is an indication of patients' possible loss of autonomy occurring when a third person is present.

In an early taxonomy of the potential coalitions that could be formed between patients, physicians, and accompanying persons [84], there is noted a range of possibilities with the caregiver aligned completely with the physician or with the patient. While it is often assumed that third persons are caregivers and while it could be argued that any accompanying person is somehow involved as a caregiver, the situation is much more complex. Relationships of third persons and patients are varied, ranging from a caregiver spouse to someone only peripherally involved with the patient, perhaps a neighbor or friend of a primary or secondary caregiver [91]. This relationship is another variable to be considered in studying triadic patient-physician communication. Silliman notes that while the physician-caregiver alliance may be critical for diagnosis and therapy, the goal of the physician should be to maximize patient well-being while preserving autonomy [83]. Physicians of elderly patients may have yet another task, namely, *to determine the role of the third person in medical care.* They need to assess the extent to which a third person may facilitate the exchange of information and balance possible conflicting goals and priorities. The cognitive status of the patient may necessitate a change in the interaction dynamics within the patient-physician relationship.

It has been noted that both cancer and Alzheimer's disease provide unique situations in which the caregiver may become a "hidden patient" [2]. The notion of the third person as "hidden patient" has been explored by Haug [8] who notes that physicians have been encouraged to become partners of caregivers and to look after the physical and mental health of caregivers as well as patients. This situation can further complicate communication by aligning the physician with the caregiver in care of the patient, at the same time placing the physician in a support role in which the caregiver is the patient. The balance of the relationship between members of medical triads may be influenced by both patients' stage of illness and the source and acuity of active problems [83].

Caregivers report dissatisfaction with physician communication in terms of the amount of information given, emotional support, and assistance in referrals to services [92]. Beiseker notes that reports of caregiver dissatisfaction when patients are satisfied with the communication may be due to physicians' competing demands of serving the disparate needs of patients and caregivers [2]. She offers two alternative explanations, that patients who come with caregivers are too sick to care about communication, or that general unhappiness at being in a caregiving situation may be responsible for caregiver dissatisfaction.

CONCLUSION

While age seems to be the single most important focus of problematic older patient-physician interaction, it might be more valuable to look at concomitant factors such as mental and physical health status. Factors other than age *in and of itself* are responsible for differences in the interaction dynamics. Care and treatment of chronic disease is more likely than cure. The older persons who seek medical attention are often seen as suffering from declining health resulting from multiple comorbid conditions.

Communication with older patients and physicians must include the expansion of the healing relationship to a triad. Physicians will have the burden of assessing the extent to which third persons should be involved in medical interviewing while considering the conflicting goals and priorities of participants [83]. Greene et al. suggest that in most cases it is unnecessary for the third person to remain in the room for the entire encounter, and that physicians utilize the formal structure of the encounter to set limits on when the third person is present [24]. In terms of preserving the patient-physician relationship and respecting patient autonomy, Silliman proposes that seeing the patient alone provides the opportunity to seek the patient's permission for speaking with family members [83]. This permission should be explicitly obtained from all but the most paranoid or impaired patients, and, once given, caregivers should also be seen alone. We also suggest that seeing the patient alone would allow the physician to assess patients' competence in deciding how much to involve accompanying persons.

The presence of a third party in the medical encounter poses serious challenges for the physician in terms of how to allocate attention; more specifically, how long should physicians speak to each party, and about what topics. In effect, physicians must decide how they are going to "use" the third party during the encounter. In the first empirical paper on triads in medical encounters, Coe and Prendergast noted:

> . . . the physician also has goals such as gaining accurate information and obtaining adherence to a therapeutic regimen. Therefore, despite the more powerful status, the physician is dependent upon others in the triad and may have a need to enter such a coalition [84, p. 245].

The likelihood of physician-third party coalitions is enhanced by the possibility that third parties enter the encounter with a "hidden agenda," so to speak, of wanting attention for their own life problems and stresses associated with caregiving. Not only do caregivers bring their own personal experience to the encounter, but they also provide their own perspectives about the patient's medical history and current health problems.

As we have suggested elsewhere [25], the medical encounter can become a kind of miniature *attention contest* in which caregivers compete with patients for a sympathetic hearing by physicians. The mere presence of a caregiver may lead physicians to doubt the patient's competency, an example of a stigmatizing label [93]. When caregivers answer for patients, without allowing them the opportunity to respond first, there is a greater likelihood that physicians "will view competent older patients as impaired or incapable of speaking for themselves" [24, p. 418] or as "unreliable historians" [86].

In view of physicians' concerns about controlling the time agenda of medical encounters [see 89, 90], they may respond to the presence of caregivers by allowing them to speak, *but at the expense of patients' participation.* Findings from Greene et al. [24] lead us to suggest that physicians may operate with a mental baseline for what constitutes an "appropriate" length of a medical encounter which is modeled on the standard dyadic situation of doctor-patient. They may try to orchestrate a time line for a triadic encounter which approximates that of the dyad. Thus, Greene et al. note that

> Since *the visit is not longer in triads than in dyads* and third persons use some time to raise topics . . . patients "lose" time in which they might have raised their own particular agenda items (emphasis added) [24, p. 417].

Ironically, it is assumed that bringing someone to the encounter will improve medical care and patient satisfaction, but patients' contributions to the process are diminished by the appearance of another. The mere presence of a third party may immediately orient the doctor to assume patient incompetence. It would appear that physicians bypass patients and that third persons retain the right to intercede, placing the patient in a subordinate position. Coalitions may be formed, but the process seems to be at the discretion of the physician and the third person, leaving the patient as a bystander in their own medical care.

The study of communication in medicine is inherently interdisciplinary. The medical encounter represents the meeting of physicians, for whom dealing with sickness is an everyday occurrence, and persons individually motivated to seek medical care. This meeting involves the social, psychological, and physical worlds of patient, physician, and potential caregivers. Older patients are defined as presenting *problems* rather than *challenges* to physicians, the very choice of language revealing social connotations. Medicine's goal should be for these encounters to enhance the well-being of patients, not only through mitigation of physical symptoms but through the benefits of the therapeutic relationship. Applying micro-level conversational analysis to the broader patterns that may be unique in interactions with older patients will improve healthcare outcomes, patient satisfaction, and caregiver satisfaction.

Finally, we feel a few comments on the role of the social scientist in the geriatric clinical setting highlight the potential for interdisciplinary research. Social scientists are traditionally researchers, yet in these settings also may serve simultaneously as teacher and consultant. Research activities in which, for instance, a medical sociologist can participate include: 1) clinical efficacy/patient satisfaction;

2) communication patterns; and 3) compliance/adherence. Such issues are basic to sociological research and, in addition, have practical implications for medical practitioners, educators, and researchers.

As previously mentioned, the basic objectives of geriatric assessment are to promote healthy aging and to prevent or minimize morbidity and disability. Most geriatric outpatient clinics are staffed with interdisciplinary providers, including all or some of the following: board-certified general internists with specialization in geriatrics, geriatric fellows, residents and acting interns, a clinical nurse specialist in geriatrics, a registered nurse, a social worker, a pharmacist, an optometrist, an audiologist, a dietitian, and a clinical psychologist. The team approach to geriatric patient care does not usually include the services of medical sociologists, although the function that a medical sociologist can serve working "with-in" geriatric assessment is multifaceted, including the roles of researcher, teacher, and consultant.

As a researcher, the medical sociologist brings quantitative and qualitative skills to the data available from clinic participation. Many medical sociologists have developed research skills allowing them to integrate field observations, interviews, and quantitative assessment of medical records. Medical sociologists can develop research agendas that contribute to social, medical, and clinical knowledge. For instance, in addition to collecting basic socio-demographic data on the patient and primary caregivers, the medical sociologist can adopt a strategy that includes collection of data on depression, locus of control, social activity and support, strain, life events, complete ADL and IADL information, baseline morbidity, data on hospital admission, stays, days confined to bed because of illness, and physical, social, and indicators of psychological well-being. Although much of this information seems of obvious importance, most is not gathered, even in specialized geriatric assessment units. Post-encounter assessments of physician, patient, and caregiver given by the medical sociologist can be used to assess the larger social context of illness. The patient can be followed to obtain outcome measures related to health and adherence issues, at one- and six-month intervals, for example. This data can be useful to both clinic personnel and the researcher.

The social scientist's role as consultant involves assisting other healthcare and service providers in aspects of work for which the he/she has special knowledge. Consultative contributions are periodically requested when medical sociologists participate in the study of individual cases with medical practitioners. Sociologists are invited to participate in medical "rounds" and the discussion of cases with the interdisciplinary team.

The teaching component of the medical sociologist is one of systematic instruction, providing both practical and theoretical aspects. For instance, paralleling the role of the clinical psychologist in training healthcare providers to recognize and intervene with dementia, the sociologist can train providers in the skills to improve interaction with patients and with each other. In general, such instruction will sensitize physicians and other health professionals to ways the values of biomedicine affect patients' life-worlds.

Balancing these three roles is a dynamic process that generates hypotheses and leads to theory building. The research-oriented medical sociologist obtains data that similar practitioners, even social workers and psychologists, may not collect as part of an initial interview. Operating from this research perspective, sociologists can provide a needed interdisciplinarly component to the diagnostic work-up. This type of collaboration between social, behavioral, and medical scientist illustrates how working together can ultimately benefit healthcare providers, patients, and caregivers. Although it is possible for useful intergrative dialog and collaboration to take place in geriatric settings, members of these interdisciplinary teams must make a significant commitment of time and energy in order to generate the strength and synergy that can come from interdisciplinary interaction.

APPENDIX I. TRANSCRIPT CONVENTIONS

D: P:T: Speaker, D for doctor, P for patient, T for person accompanying patient.
(( ))   Double enclosure "descriptive," not transcribed utterances
[ ]   Bracket used to indicate overlapping speech
(0)   Silences representing 1.0 second intervals
=   No time elapses between speakers utterances
-        Used when a word or sentence is broken off in the middle
(word)   When a word is heard but remains unclear
(....)   Speaking sounds that are unintelligible
:   Used when a word is stretched (as in wel:l)
word   Underlined for marked increase in loudness or emphasis
*   Softness or decreased amplitude
(x)   Hitch or stutter
hh   Alone stands for exhalation
hh.   Followed by period denotes inhalation

Names of persons and places are indicated by number or initial. Titles reflecting patient gender are used, e.g. "Ms." "Mr."

REFERENCES

1. A. Lazare, M. Putnam, and M. Lipkin, Jr., Three Functions of the Medical Interview, in *The Medical Interview,* Springer-Verlag, New York, 1994.
2. A. Beisecker, Older Person's Medical Encounters and Their Outcomes, *Research on Aging, 18,* pp. 9-31, 1996.
3. D. L. Roter and J. A. Hall, *Doctors Talking with Patients/Patients with Doctors,* Auburn House, Westport, Connecticut, 1992.
4. Alliance for Aging Research, *Will You Still Treat Me When I'm 65?* The National Shortage of Geriatricians, Washington D.C., 1996.
5. S. R. Kunkel and R. A. Applebaum, Estimating the Prevalence of Long-Term Disability for an Aging Society, *Journal of Gerontology, 47,* pp. S253-60, 1992.
6. K. G. Manton and B. J. Soldo, Disability and Mortality among the Oldest-Old: Implications for Current and Future Health and Long-Term-Care Service Needs, in *The Oldest Old,* R. M. Suzman, D. P. Willis, and K. G. Manton (eds.), Oxford University Press, New York, pp. 199-250, 1992.

7. E. L. Bierman and W. R. Hazzard, Preventive Gerontology: Strategies for Attenuation of the Chronic Diseases of Aging, in *Principles of Geriatric Medicine and Gerontology*, W. R. Hazzard, E. L. Bierman, J. P. Blass, W. H. Ettinger, Jr., and J. B. Halter (eds.), McGraw Hill, New York, pp. 187-194, 1994.

8. M. R. Haug, Elements in Physician/Patient Interactions in Late Life, *Research on Aging*, *18*, pp. 32-51, 1996.

9. W. R. Hazzard, Introduction. The Practice of Geriatric Medicine, in *Principles of Geriatric Medicine and Gerontology*, W. R. Hazzard, E. L. Bierman, J. P. Blass, W. H. Ettinger, Jr., and J. B. Halter (eds.), McGraw Hill, New York, pp. 23-24, 1994.

10. M. R. Greene, S. Hoffman, R. Charon, and R. D. Adelman, Psychosocial Concerns in the Medical Encounter: A Comparison of the Interactions of Doctors with Their Old and Young Patients, *The Gerontologist, 27*, pp. 164-168, 1987.

11. A. Beisecker, Aging and the Desire for Information and Input in Medical Decisions: Patient Consumerism in Medical Encounters, *The Gerontologist 28*, pp. 330-335, 1988.

12. U. S. Department of Health and Human Services, *Public Health Service, National Institutes of Health*, National Institute on Aging, NIH Publication No. 94-3452, 1994.

13. M. E. Williams, Clinical Management of the Elderly Patient, in *Principles of Geriatric Medicine and Gerontology*, W. R. Hazzard, E. L. Bierman, J. P. Blass, W. H. Ettinger, Jr., and J. B. Halter (eds.), McGraw Hill, New York, pp. 195-202, 1994.

14. F. Beland and B. Maheux, Medical Care for the Elderly: Attitudes of Medical Caregivers, *Journal of Aging and Health 2*, pp. 194-214, 1990.

15. R. C. Maly, S. H. Hirsh, and D. B. Reuben, The Performance of Simple Instruments in Detecting Geriatric Conditions and Selecting Community-Dwelling Older People for Geriatric Assessment, *Age and Aging, 26*, pp. 223-231, 1997.

16. A. L. Siu, D. B. Reuben, and A. A. Moore, Comprehensive Geriatric Assessment, in *Principles of Geriatric Medicine and Gerontology*, W. R. Hazzard, E. L. Bierman, J. P. Blass, W. H. Ettinger, Jr. and J. B. Halter (eds.), McGraw Hill, New York, pp. 203-212, 1994.

17. S. Shah, M. F. Harris, D. Conforti, H. Dickson, and R. Fisher, Elderly Care. A Pilot Project on Opportunistic Geriatric Assessments in General Practice, *Australian Family Physician, 26*, pp. 275-279, 1997.

18. B. Gastel, *Working with Your Older Patient: A Clinician's Handbook,* National Institute on Aging, National Institutes of Health, Bethesda, Maryland, 1994.

19. G. P. Schecter, L. L. Blank, H. A. Godwin, M. A. LaCombe, D. H. Novack, and W. F. Rosse, Refocusing on History-Taking Skills during Internal Medicine Training, *American Journal of Medicine, 101*, pp. 210-216, 1996.

20. R. J. Kravitz, E. J. Callahan, D. Paterniti, D. Antonius, M. Dunham, and C. E. Lewis, Prevalence and Sources of Patients' Unmet Expectations for Care, *Annals of Internal Medicine, 125*, pp. 730-737, 1996.

21. J. A. Hall, D. L. Roter, M. A. Milburn, and L. H. Daltroy, Patient's Health as a Predictor of Physician and Patient Behavior in Medical Visits. A Synthesis of Four Studies, *Medical Care, 34*, pp. 1205-1218, 1996.

22. K. D. Bertakis, L. J. Helms, E. J. Callahan, R. Azari, and J. A. Robbins, The Influence of Gender on Physician Practice Style, *Medical Care, 33*, pp. 407-416, 1995.

23. S. E. Radecki, R. Kane, D. H. Solomon, R. Mendenhall, and J. C. Beck, Do Physicians Spend Less Time with Older Patients? *Journal of the American Geriatrics Society, 36*, pp. 713-718, 1988.

24. M. G. Greene, D. Majerovitz, R. D. Adelman, and C. Rizzo, The Effects of the Presence of a Third Person on the Physician-Older Patient Medical Interview, *Journal of the American Geriatrics Society, 42,* pp. 413-419, 1994.
25. P. S. Baker, W. C. Yoels, J. M. Clair, and R. M. Allman, Laughter in Triadic Geriatric Medical Encounters: A Transcript-based Analysis, *Social Perspectives on Emotion, 4,* pp. 179-207, 1997.
26. R. C. Atchley, *Social Forces and Aging,* Wadsworth, Belmont, California, 1997.
27. P. A. Rochon and J. H. Gurwitz, Drug Therapy, *Lancet, 346,* pp. 32-36, 1995.
28. J. Dunbar-Jacob, Contributions to Patient Adherence: Is it Time to Share the Blame? *Health Psychology, 12,* pp. 91-92, 1993.
29. C. K. Tebbi, Treatment Compliance in Childhood and Adolescence, *Cancer, 71,* pp. 3441-3449, 1993.
30. R. J. Botelho and R. Dudrak 2nd, Home Assessment of Adherence to Long-Term Medication in the Elderly, *Journal of Family Practice, 35,* pp. 61-65, 1992.
31. C. S. Rand and R. A. Wise, Measuring Adherence to Asthma Medication Regimens, *American Journal of Respiratory and Critical Care Medicine, 149,* pp. S69-76, 1994.
32. K. I. Kjellgren, J. Ahlner, and R. Saljo, Taking Antihypertensive Medication—Controlling or Co-Operating with Patients? *International Journal of Cardiology, 47,* pp. 257-268, 1995.
33. C. Salzman, Medication Compliance in the Elderly, *Journal of Clinical Psychiatry, 56* (Suppl. 1), pp. 18-22, 1995.
34. M. L. Stockwell and R. M. Schulz, Patient Compliance: An Overview, *Journal of Clinical Pharmacy and Therapeutics, 17,* pp. 283-295, 1992.
35. B. Chewning and B. Sleath, Medication Decision-making and Management: A Client-Centered Model, *Social Science and Medicine, 42,* pp. 389-398, 1996.
36. P. P. Gerbino, Forward, *Annals of Pharmacotherapy, 27,* pp. S3-4, 1993.
37. S. Sullivan, D. H. Kerling, and T. K. Hazlet, Noncompliance with Medication Regiments and Subsequent Hospitalizations: A Literature Analysis and Cost of Hospitalization Estimate, *Journal of Research Pharmacological Economics, 2,* p. 12, 1990.
38. Annals of Pharmacotherapy (editorial), Patient Compliance, *Annals of Pharmacotherapy, 27,* pp. S5-24, 1993.
39. L. T. Clark, Improving Compliance and Increasing Control of Hypertension: Needs of Special Hypertensive Populations, *American Heart Journal, 121,* pp. L664-668, 1991.
40. S. M. Putnam, Nature of the Medical Encounter, *Research on Aging, 18,* pp. 70-83, 1996.
41. T. H. Goldberg and S. I. Chavin, Preventive Medicine and Screening in Older Adults, *Journal of the American Geriatric Society, 45,* pp. 344-354, 1997.
42. U.S. Senate Committee on Aging, *Aging America—Trends and Projections,* DHHS Publication No. PcoA 91-28001, U.S. Department of Health and Human Services, Washington, D.C., 1991.
43. G. H. Maddox, Sociology of Aging, in *Principles of Geriatric Medicine and Gerontology,* W. R. Hazzard, E. L. Bierman, J. P. Blass, W. H. Ettinger, Jr., and J. B. Halter (eds.), pp. 125-134, McGraw Hill, New York, 1994.
44. L. M. L. Ong, J. C. J. M. de Haes, A. M. Hoos, and F. B. Lammes, Doctor Patient Communication: A Review of the Literature, *Social Science and Medicine, 40,* pp. 903-918, 1995.
45. R. L. J. Street, Analyzing Communication in Medical Consultations. Do Behavioral Measures Correspond to Patient's Perceptions, *Medical Care, 30,* pp. 976-988, 1992.
46. L. G. Frederickson, Exploring Information-Exchange in Consultation: The Patient's View of Performance and Outcomes, *Patient Education and Counseling, 25,* pp. 237-246, 1995.

47. P. Atkinson, *Medical Talk and Medical Work: The Liturgy of the Clinic,* Sage, London, 1995.
48. P. Drew and J. Heritage, Analyzing Talk at Work: An Introduction, in *Talk at Work: Interaction in Institutional Settings,* P. Drew and J. Heritage (eds), Cambridge University Press, New York, pp. 3-65, 1992.
49. R. M. Frankel, From Sentence to Sequence: Understanding the Medical Encounter Through Microinteractional Analysis, *Discourse Processes, 7,* pp. 135-170, 1984.
50. S. Fisher and A. D.Todd, *The Social Organization of Doctor-Patient Communication,* Center for Applied Linguistics, Washington, D.C., 1983.
51. E. G. Mishler, *The Discourse of Medicine: Dialectics of Medical Interviews,* Ablex, Norwood, New Jersey, 1984.
52. D. Silverman, *Communication and Medical Practice: Social Relations in the Clinic,* Sage, London, 1987.
53. H. B. Waitzkin, *The Politics of Medical Encounters: How Patients and Doctors Deal with Social Problems,* Yale University Press, New Haven, 1991.
54. C. West, Medical Misfires: Mishearings, Misgivings, and Misunderstandings in Physician-Patient Dialogues, *Discourse Processes, 7,* pp. 107-134, 1984.
55. A. Suchman and D. Matthews, What Makes the Patient-Doctor Relationship Therapeutic? Exploring the Connexional Dimension of Medical Care, *Annals of Internal Medicine, 108,* pp. 125-130, 1988.
56. R. Penchansky and C. Macnee, Initiation of Medical Malpractice Suits: A Conceptualization and Test, *Medical Care, 32,* pp. 813-831, 1994.
57. H. R. Burstin, W. G. Johnson, S. R. Lipsitz, and T. A. Brennan, Do the Poor Sue More? A Case-Study Control of Malpractice Claims and Socioeconomic Status, *Journal of the American Medical Association, 270,* pp. 1697-1701, 1993.
58. M. Sager, S. Voeks, P. Drinka, E. Langer, and P. Grimstad, Do the Elderly Sue Physicians? *Archives of Internal Medicine, 150,* pp. 1091-1093, 1990.
59. W. Levinson, D. L. Roter, J. P. Mullooly, V. T. Dull, and R. M. Frankel, Physician-Patient Communication. The Relationship with Malpractice Claims among Primary Care Physicians and Surgeons, *Journal of the American Medical Association, 277,* pp. 553-559, 1997.
60. I. Press, R. Graney, and M. P. Malone, Satisfied Patients Can Spell Financial Well-Being, *Healthcare Financial Management, 45,* pp. 34-36, 38, 42, 1990.
61. L. J. Weiss and J. Blustein, Faithful Patients: The Effect of Long-Term Physician-Patient Relationships on the Costs and Use of Health Care by Older Americans, *American Journal of Public Health, 86,* pp. 1742-1747, 1996.
62. W. Levinson,W. B. Stiles, T. Inui, and R. Engle, Physician Frustration in Communicating with Patients, *Medical Care, 31,* pp. 285-295, 1993.
63. J. L. Donovan, Patient Decision Making. The Missing Ingredient in Compliance Research, *International Journal of Technology Assessment in Health Care, 11,* pp. 443-455, 1995.
64. C. G. McLane, S. J. Zyzanski, and S. Flock, Factors Associated with Medication Noncompliance in Rural Elderly Hypertensive Patients, *American Journal of Hypertension, 8,* pp. 206-209, 1995.
65. G. Makoul, P. Arntson, and T. Schofield, Health Promotion in Primary Care: Physician-Patient Communication and Decision Making About Prescription Medications, *Social Science and Medicine, 41,* pp. 1241-1254, 1995.
66. D. R. Calkins, R. B. Davis, P. Reiley, R. S. Phillips, K. L. C. Pineo, T. L. Delbano, and L. I. Iezzoni, Patient-Physician Communication at Hospital Discharge and Patients Understanding of the Postdischarge Treatment Plan, *Archives of Internal Medicine 157,* pp. 1026-1030, 1997.

67. M. V. Williams, R. M. Parker, D. W. Baker, N. S. Parikh, K. Pitkin, W. C. Coates, and J. R. Nurss, Inadequate Functional Health Literacy among Patients at Two Public Hospitals, *Journal of the American Medical Association, 274,* pp. 1677-1682, 1995.
68. J. Fawcett, Compliance: Definitions and Key Issues, *Journal of Clinical Psychiatry, 56* (Suppl 1), pp. 4-8, 1995.
69. T. E. Quill and H. Brody, Physician Recommendations and Patient Autonomy: Finding a Balance Between Physician Power and Patient Choice, *Annals of Internal Medicine, 125,* pp. 763-771, 1996.
70. J. M. Clair, The Application of Social Science to Medical Practice, in *Sociomedical Perspectives on Patient Care,* J. M. Clair and R. M. Allman (eds.), University Press, Kentucky, pp. 12-28 1993.
71. N. Leopold, J. Cooper, and C. Clancy, Sustained Partnership in Primary Care, *Journal of Family Practice, 42,* pp. 129-137, 1996.
72. D. E. Morisky, N. M. DeMuth, M. Field-Fass, L. W. Green, and D. M. Levine, Evaluation of Family Health Education to Build Social Support for Long-Term Control of High Blood Pressure, *Health Education Quarterly, 12,* pp. 35-50, 1985.
73. M. R. Greene, R. D. Adelman, R. Charon, and S. Hoffman, Ageism in the Medical Encounter: An Exploratory Study of the Doctor-Elderly Patient Relationship, *Language and Communication, 6,* pp. 113-124, 1986.
74. W. Kavesh, The Practice of Geriatric Medicine: How Geriatricians Think, *Generations,* pp. 54-59, Winter 1996.
75. R. C. Maly, A. F. Abrahams, S. H. Hirsh, J. C. Frank, and D. B. Reuben, What Influences Physician Practice Behavior? An Interview Study of Physicians Who Received Consultative Geriatric Assessment Recommendations, *Archives of Family Medicine, 5,* pp. 448-454, 1996.
76. R. D. Adelman, M. G. Greene, R. Charon, and E. Friedmann, The Content of Physician and Elderly Patient Interaction in the Medical Primary Care Encounter, *Communication Research, 19,* pp. 370-380, 1992.
77. R. D. Adelman, M. G. Greene, and R. Charon, Issues in Physician-Elderly Patient Interaction, *Aging and Society, 2,* pp. 127-148, 1991.
78. H. B. Waitzkin, T. Britt, and C. Williams, Incomplete Narratives of Aging and Social Problems in Routine Medical Encounters, in *Sociomedical Perspectives on Patient Care,* J. M. Clair and R. M. Allman (eds.), University Press, Kentucky, pp. 140-161, 1994.
79. J. G. Ouslander, A. J. Tymchuk, and B. Rahbat, Health Care Decisions Among Elderly Long-Term Care Residents and Their Potential Proxies, *Archives of Internal Medicine, 149,* pp. 1367-1372, 1989.
80. F. W. Platt, P. K. Tippy, and D. C. Turk, Helping Patients Adhere to the Regimen, *Patient Care, 28,* pp. 43-52, 1994.
81. L. J. Fitten, L. Coleman, D. W. Siemieda, M. Yu, and S. Ganzell, Assessment of Capacity to Comply with Medication Regimens in Older Patients, *Journal of the American Geriatrics Society, 43,* pp. 361-367, 1995.
82. Council on Scientific Affairs, American Medical Association, Physicians and Family Care-Givers: A Model for Partnership, *Journal of the American Medical Association, 269,* pp. 1282-1284, 1993.
83. R. Silliman, Family-Centered Geriatric Care, in *Sociomedical Perspectives on Patient Care,* J. M. Clair and R. M. Allman (eds.), University Press, Kentucky, pp. 162-173, 1993.
84. R. Coe and C. Prendergast, Research Note: The Formation of Coalitions; Interaction Strategies in Triads, *Sociology of Health and Illness, 7,* pp. 236-247, 1985.

85. R. D. Adelman, M. G. Greene, and R. Charon The Physician-Elderly Patient-Companion Triad in the Medical Encounter: The Development of a Conceptual Framework and Research Agenda, *The Gerontologist, 27,* pp. 729-734, 1987.
86. J. M. Clair, Regressive Intervention: The Discourse of Medicine during Terminal Encounters, *Advances in Medical Sociology, 1,* pp. 57-97, 1990.
87. M. S. LaBrecque, C. G. Blanchard, J. C. Ruckdeschel, and E. B. Blanchard, The Impact of Family Presence on the Physician-Cancer Patient Interaction, *Social Science and Medicine, 33,* pp. 1253-1261, 1991.
88. D. W. Maynard, Interaction and Asymmetry in Clinical Discourse, *American Journal of Sociology, 97,* pp. 448-495, 1991.
89. W. Yoels and J. M. Clair, Never Enough Time: How Medical Residents Manage a Scarce Resource, *Journal of Contemporary Ethnography, 23,* pp. 185-213, 1994.
90. T. Mizrahi, *Getting Rid of Patients,* Rutgers University Press, New Brunswick, 1986.
91. P. S. Baker, *Discourse Analysis of Elderly Patient Medical Encounters,* doctoral dissertation, UMI Dissertation Services, 1996.
92. W. E. Haley, J. M. Clair, and K. Saulsberry, Family Caregiver Satisfaction with Medical Care of Their Demented Relatives, *The Gerontologist, 32,* pp. 219-226, 1992.
93. E. Goffman, *Stigma: Notes on the Management of Spoiled Identitities,* Prentice-Hall, Englewood Cliffs, New Jersey, 1963.

CHAPTER
13

Treatment of Urinary Incontinence: Current Status and Future Directions

Kathryn L. Burgio, Patricia S. Goode,
R. Edward Varner, L. Keith Lloyd,
Donald A. Urban, and Mary G. Umlauf

INTRODUCTION

Urinary incontinence is the involuntary loss of urine. It is a common condition that affects individuals of every age but is most prevalent among older adults. Incontinence is estimated to affect 30 percent of community dwelling older adults [1] and more than 50 percent of those elders who reside in nursing homes [2]. Although it is not considered to be a serious medical condition, urinary incontinence is known to have important emotional, social, and economic sequelae. Incontinence is a significant source of dependence among the elderly and a widely cited factor in nursing home admissions. It also predisposes patients to other health problems such as skin breakdown and urinary tract infections. Incontinence often restricts daily activities and interpersonal relationships and can contribute to depression and anxiety in some people [3]. In addition, the costs of incontinence are significant, accounting for more that $10 billion per year in medical care, wetness management products, and caregiver time in the United States alone [4].

Because incontinence is so common among older adults, it is frequently misattributed to age. Older adults are more likely to have medical conditions or functional problems that predispose them to incontinence. However, incontinence is not a normal facet of aging and in most cases can be reduced or eliminated with treatment. In general, older patients can be managed with the same therapies that are used for younger patients, although special attention should be directed toward age-related deficits such as sensory impairment and decreased mobility as well as toward common co-morbidities such as dementia.

Older patients with incontinence can be divided into two general categories: those who are essentially intact functionally, living independently in the community and able to participate in their own treatment; and those with significant cognitive or physical impairments which make them dependent on caregivers at home or in an institutional setting. This chapter will address the first group of individuals because their numbers are larger and the treatment modalities are oriented to patients themselves rather than a caregiver or an institutional environment.

Urinary incontinence is a multi-faceted condition with many causes, presentations, and treatments. As a result, a variety of treatments have been developed to address behavioral, physiological, environmental, medical, and surgical aspects of the problem. This chapter will describe the current status of the major approaches to incontinence including behavioral treatments, pharmacologic treatments, electrical stimulation, surgical treatments, periurethral injection, and artificial sphincter devices.

TYPES OF INCONTINENCE

Rational decisions about treatment need to include a basic understanding of the type or types of incontinence and thus an understanding of the mechanism of urine loss. In community-dwelling older adults, the most common types of incontinence are stress incontinence, urge incontinence, and mixed symptomology of stress and urge incontinence. Together these three types account for more than 80 percent of incontinence [1].

Stress incontinence is the involuntary loss of urine associated with an increase in intra-abdominal pressure produced by physical activities such as coughing, sneezing, lifting, or straining. Increased intra-abdominal pressure causes a rise in bladder pressure and results in urine loss when bladder pressure exceeds urethral resistance. Urine escapes because the bladder outlet is inadequate and does not stay closed tightly during the rise in bladder pressure. Stress incontinence is caused by weakness of or damage to the bladder outlet or urethra, or to the pelvic floor which surrounds and supports these structures. Treatments for stress incontinence focus on the bladder outlet and aim to prevent urine loss by keeping the urethra closed tightly during increases in intra-abdominal pressure.

Urge incontinence is the involuntary loss of urine associated with the urge to void. Urine loss occurs when the detrusor muscle of the bladder wall contracts, forcing urine through the urethra. Ordinarily, when an individual feels the urge to urinate, detrusor contraction can be inhibited through cortical control or contraction of pelvic muscles. The person with urge incontinence is unable either to inhibit detrusor contraction or prevent loss of urine by adequate closure of the outlet. Treatments for urge incontinence focus primarily on inhibiting bladder contraction but also include procedures to strengthen the bladder outlet.

BEHAVIORAL TREATMENTS

Behavioral treatments are a diverse group of therapies that modify stress, urge, or mixed urinary incontinence either by changing the patient's bladder habits or teaching new skills. There are a number of approaches, each of which involves multiple behavioral components. For the purpose of this chapter they are grouped into three broad categories. The behavioral approaches have evolved over a considerable period of time and are supported by a body of scientific literature demonstrating their effectiveness. The literature in each of these areas is summarized below, focusing on the most recent scientific findings.

Pelvic Muscle Exercise

Pelvic muscle exercise is a learned skill of muscle contraction and relaxation. It is thought to reduce urinary incontinence by producing urethral closure with a contraction of the peri-urethral and other pelvic floor muscles. Voluntary contraction of these muscles can keep the urethra closed during sudden increases in intra-abdominal pressure such as a cough or sneeze, thus preventing stress leakage. Traditionally, it was used almost exclusively for the treatment of stress incontinence. However, because voluntary pelvic muscle contraction can also inhibit detrusor contractions, this technique is now frequently used as a component in the treatment of urge incontinence [5].

The literature on pelvic muscle exercise is based primarily on studies of incontinent women. In most of these studies, pelvic muscle exercise was implemented alone, although biofeedback was used in some cases to teach the proper control of pelvic muscles, and in a small number of studies pelvic muscle exercise was combined with estrogen or electrical stimulation. In these studies 27 percent to 73 percent of patients were cured. Rates of improvement or cure ranged from 38 percent to 100 percent [5-16]. It is difficult to summarize the studies because investigators used different combinations of techniques, different teaching methods, different methods of assessing outcome, and different definitions of cure and improvement.

Only two randomized clinical trials appear in the literature. In one, pelvic muscle exercise was compared to medication (phenylpropanolamine) for stress incontinence in older women [16]. Phenylpropanolamine is a medication that tightens the sphincter and increases pressure in the bladder outlet. Although the site of action of the two treatments is different (one modifies striated muscle, the other modifies smooth muscle), they produced similar results as measured by patients' subjective report of improvement (77% vs. 84%) as well as by bladder diary. In addition, this study demonstrated that improvements in stress incontinence were accompanied by changes in objectively measurable parameters such as muscle strength. Measurement of physiological changes accompanying behavioral treatments has become more important in recent studies and allows the testing of hypotheses about mechanisms of change. As Wells has noted, it should not be assumed without actual testing that pelvic muscle control is learned, practiced, or in fact increases muscle strength. Among the possible mechanisms are increased resting tone, improved resting pressure in the urethra, increased bulk around the urethra, and improved muscle strength. It is also possible that these physiological parameters are not as important as simple acquisition of the skill of contracting peri-urethral muscles during a cough or sneeze.

The other clinical trial compared groups treated with pelvic muscle exercises to an untreated control group [17]. Pelvic muscle exercise yielded a mean 61 percent reduction of incontinence when taught with biofeedback and a mean 54 percent reduction of urinary incontinence when taught without biofeedback, both significantly more effective than the no treatment control condition which produced an average 6 percent improvement. These studies show clearly that pelvic muscle exercise is effective for the treatment of stress incontinence in older women.

Although the effectiveness of pelvic muscle exercise is established, several questions remain to be addressed in future research. It is not known, for example, what is the best method of teaching pelvic muscle exercise. There is evidence that biofeedback improves the likelihood of successful outcomes; however, findings on this issue are inconsistent. Although many clinicians advocate the use of a resistive device to improve the effects of exercise on the pelvic muscles, there has been no research to support this modality. There is also little information on how to configure the optimal exercise regimen [16]. In addition, some investigators are applying principles of athletic conditioning and testing the efficacy of using sub-maximal muscle contractions for stress incontinence. It is widely accepted that the effectiveness of behavioral intervention relies on the patients' adherence to the regimen. Indeed, behavioral treatment of incontinence *requires* the active participation of the patient. However, we actually know very little about how compliant most women are with pelvic muscle exercise. Research is needed to explore how compliance can be improved and whether this would yield better clinical results.

Future research might also address the issue of combining pelvic muscle exercise with other therapies to enhance outcomes. Wells et al. showed that pelvic muscle exercise and phenylpropanolamine had similar effects [16]. Because they have different mechanisms, there is potential for effectiveness to be improved by combining them into one treatment package.

Finally, little attention has been paid to long-term effectiveness of behavioral therapies. Understanding the reasons for regression might provide clues for improving behavioral intervention in the long term. For example, if results are not durable because compliance declined, future studies could address ways to improve long-term adherence to the behavioral program.

Biofeedback

Biofeedback is not a treatment in and of itself. It is a teaching technique based on operant conditioning that facilitates learning by providing patients with immediate and observable information about their physical performance. It is used to modify bladder function, sphincter function, or both. Biofeedback is most often used to teach patients to contract and relax pelvic muscles selectively while keeping other muscle groups such as abdominal muscles relaxed. This helps to assure the patient is using the muscles properly to prevent stress incontinence. It has also been demonstrated that a strong pelvic muscle contraction can abort bladder contractions in the treatment of urge incontinence. Thus, biofeedback can be an important component of a comprehensive behavioral program for treatment of stress or urge incontinence.

Several studies have investigated the use of biofeedback to modify physiological responses in the treatment of urinary incontinence. These include studies of bladder biofeedback, pelvic muscle biofeedback, and combined bladder and pelvic muscle biofeedback. Studies included men and women, many of whom were older. Several etiologies were studied, including urinary incontinence following stroke, prostatectomy, Parkinson's disease, and incontinence of unknown etiology. In studies that measured the rates of cure or improvement of incontinence, the figures ranged from 68 percent to 92 percent. In those that measured frequency of incontinent episodes before and after treatment, the mean reductions ranged from 61 percent to 85 percent [5-10, 14, 15, 18-20]. Most studies have used clinical series design but one clinical trial has been reported [10]. This study demonstrated that pelvic muscle exercise taught with biofeedback resulted in 61 percent reduction of stress incontinence, which overall was not significantly better than results achieved without biofeedback (54% reduction). However, biofeedback did appear to produce better outcomes in patients with moderate and severe incontinence. In addition, three smaller controlled studies have demonstrated an advantage for patients trained with biofeedback [7, 15, 21].

Although the effectiveness of biofeedback-assisted behavioral treatment has been established, several questions remain. We know little about the optimal techniques for performing biofeedback. For example, it is not known whether anal sphincter training differs in effectiveness from circumvaginal training, or how many biofeedback sessions are necessary for cost effective treatment. Further, there is great potential for testing the combination of biofeedback with other therapies. For example, would electrical stimulation further enhance the effects of biofeedback training? Would combining biofeedback with drug therapy such as estrogen yield better outcomes? Well-designed clinical trials of combined therapies for incontinence are needed to address these issues.

Bladder Training

In bladder training, the focus of treatment is on changing the patient's bladder habits. The goal of bladder training is to reduce urinary incontinence by increasing bladder capacity and restoring normal bladder function. This is accomplished by placing the patient on a voiding schedule and increasing the intervals between voids gradually over time.

Traditionally used for urge incontinence, some of the early studies involved what was then called bladder drill [22, 23]. Treatment was conducted in an intensive way on an inpatient basis after employing sedatives to ease anxiety. In more recent studies, similar results were achieved on an outpatient basis, and some studies mixed inpatient and outpatient treatment. Cure rates ranged from 44 percent to 90 percent [22-33].

There is one randomized clinical trial of bladder training in older women conducted by Fantl and colleagues [33]. The data show clearly the significant reduction of urinary incontinence that occurred in the bladder training group (mean = 57% reduction) while minimal change occurred under no treatment control conditions. An interesting aspect of the findings is that bladder training, a therapy intended to modify bladder function and urge incontinence produced similar results when applied to stress incontinence. Further, while early studies of bladder training documented a return to normal bladder function in patients with detrusor instability, this study showed that reduction of incontinence occurred in the absence of physiological improvement. Thus, the mechanism of improvement in bladder training needs to be investigated further in future research.

Another issue for future study is how best to implement this treatment, especially with regard to expanding the voiding schedule. In the original studies, subjects were forced to postpone urination even when the urge to void caused physical distress. Now, the trend is more moderate to keep patients more comfortable during the bladder training. Bladder training also needs to be compared to other behavioral and non-behavioral therapies, as well as combined with these therapies to see if increased efficacy would result.

PHARMACOLOGIC TREATMENT

Medications to treat incontinence are selected to alter specific physiologic parameters such as bladder outlet resistance in stress urinary incontinence or bladder contractions in urge incontinence. To date, pharmacotherapy has been much more effective in treatment of urge incontinence than other types. Also, the usefulness of pharmacotherapy is often limited by the side effects, many of which are sufficient to cause discontinuation of therapy despite a positive outcome with the incontinence.

Before medications are prescribed for incontinence, a careful medication history, including non-prescription medications, is essential. The goal is to discover medications, prescribed for other conditions, that may be having an adverse effect on continence. These drugs can often be discontinued or changed to other agents with resultant improvement or elimination of incontinence. Examples of this include alpha adrenergic blockers for hypertension, worsening stress incontinence in older women; diuretics for hypertension worsening urge incontinence in elderly persons with mobility impairment; sedatives causing confusion about the location of the bathroom for persons with early dementia; or antidepressants with anticholinergic effects causing urinary retention and overflow incontinence in older diabetics.

Medications to treat incontinence can be used alone or in combination with other therapies. Since many of the medications used for incontinence were developed for other conditions, clinical trial data specific to their use for incontinence are limited. The variability in design across studies also makes it difficult to base clinical decisions on the published clinical pharmacotherapeutic trials. Problematic design variations include inconsistency in defining outcome criteria, failure to isolate the effect of the drug from other therapies such as behavioral treatment, lack of systematic methodology for assessing side effects, lack of long-term follow-up, and protocols that have limited comparability to actual clinical practice such as setting a fixed dose of a medication without any adjustment during the clinical trial.

Pharmacotherapy for Urge Incontinence

Pharmacotherapy for urge incontinence is directed at increasing bladder capacity or inhibiting detrusor contractions. Anticholinergic medications (e.g., oxybutynin, propantheline, hyoscyamine) are the most commonly used agents to treat urge incontinence. Antimuscarinic agents inhibit detrusor contractions by interfering with the major neurohumoral stimulus for bladder contraction, acetylcholine acting on postganglionic parasympathetic cholinergic receptor sites on the bladder smooth muscle [34]. Some anticholinergic agents also have direct smooth muscle relaxant properties (oxybutynin, flavoxate, and dicyclomine) and act at a site that is metabolically distal to the cholinergic receptor mechanism in the bladder [35]. Additionally, some may possess local anesthetic activity [35]. Tricyclic antidepressants have anticholinergic effects, but, in addition, block the re-uptake of norepinephrine, which is thought to stimulate the alpha receptors in the bladder neck as well as the beta receptors in the detrusor, resulting in contraction of the bladder neck and relaxation of the detrusor [34].

Controlled studies with adequate sample sizes exist for oxybutynin, propantheline, dicyclomine, imipramine, desipramine, nortriptyline, doxepine, and flavoxate. These studies have demonstrated decreases in the frequency of incontinence ranging from 15 percent to 58 percent [36-41] and up to 67 percent of subjects became subjectively continent [37, 38]. Flavoxate, however, did not demonstrate any significant difference over placebo in several trials [41-44]. The tricyclic antidepressants have demonstrated effectiveness in reducing nocturnal incontinence only [45-47]. Side effects (dry mouth, constipation, nausea, blurred vision, altered mental status) were common, significant, and affected most patients who took anticholinergic medications.

Transdermal scopolamine, a belladonna alkaloid with prominent anticholinergic effects, administered at the standard dose of one patch every three days, resulted in clinical and urodynamic improvement in a randomized, placebo patch controlled trial of twenty women with detrusor instability [48]. Dry mouth and dizziness were common, but were insufficient to cause discontinuation of the drug. However, in another small study [49], eight of ten patients discontinued therapy due to severe side effects. Use of a smaller dose, such as 1/4 or 1/2 of a patch, should be tested to see if efficacy could be maintained with fewer side effects, especially in a geriatric population.

Nonsteroidal anti-inflammatory drugs inhibit prostaglandin synthesis, and are thought to interfere with prostaglandin-mediated bladder contractions. However, despite evidence of effectiveness of indomethacin and flurbiprofen in urge incontinence [50, 51], the short duration and limited follow-up of most trials have provided little data on potentially serious long-term side effects for older persons, such as gastrointestinal bleeding and renal insufficiency.

Calcium channel blockers interfere with calcium flow into the muscle fibers of the detrusor. If the inflow is blocked, detrusor contractility should be decreased because calcium is essential in excitation-contraction coupling in muscle fibers [34]. The one agent (terodiline) that demonstrated effectiveness in decreasing detrusor contraction, was associated with serious ventricular arrhythmias and U.S. clinical trials were stopped [4].

Beta-adrenergic agonists are thought to increase bladder capacity by stimulating beta receptors in the detrusor. In a small clinical trial, terbutaline (5 mg BID) was effective in both detrusor hyperactivity and sensory urge incontinence, with twelve of fifteen women becoming subjectively continent, and a demonstrable increase in first desire to void on cystometrogram (200 to 300 ml) [52].

Desmopressin (desmopressin diacetate arginine vasopressin [DDAVP] or anti-diuretic hormone) has been used successfully to treat nocturnal enuresis in children, and nocturia in adults. Since it decreases urine output, DDAVP could be potentially useful as an adjunct to other treatments for urge incontinence and warrants further study. The effect of vasopressin on fluid and electrolyte balance, particularly in the elderly, needs further examination in clinical trials.

Pharmacotherapy for Stress Incontinence

Pharmacotherapy for stress urinary incontinence is directed toward increasing muscular tone in the bladder neck and proximal urethra. A high concentration of alpha adrenergic receptors allows alpha agonists to selectively stimulate muscles in this area, increasing outlet resistance. Seven prospective randomized controlled studies of phenylpropanolamine or pseudoephedrine in women with stress incontinence showed a 19 percent to 60 percent reduction in incontinence with 0 percent to 14 percent becoming dry [16, 53-58]. In normotensive women, there was no problem with hypertension, but this remains to be determined in hypertensive women. This is especially important in elderly patients, over 50 percent of whom have hypertension.

Theoretically, beta blockers may increase urethral and bladder outlet resistance by potentiating the alpha-adrenergic response to adrenergic stimuli. However, there are no controlled clinical trials of beta blockers for treatment of stress urinary incontinence.

Another pharmacological agent for stress incontinence in post-menopausal women is estrogen, which is believed to improve urethral mucosal coaptation by increasing vascularity and thickening the submucosal layer. In addition, estrogen is believed to increase the alpha-adrenergic responsiveness of the urethra and bladder neck, further increasing outlet resistance. Anecdotally, estrogen is also effective in decreasing bladder irritability and urge incontinence. As with other pharmacotherapy for stress incontinence, clinical trials of estrogen alone have demonstrated modest but significant improvement with 0 percent to 14 percent becoming dry and 29 percent to 89 percent improved [59, 60]. Fantl and colleagues, in a randomized, controlled three-month trial of combined estrogen and progesterone in hypoestrogenic women with urge, stress, or mixed incontinence, failed to show any objective or subjective improvement in incontinence [61].

Combination Pharmacotherapy

Combinations of pharmacologic agents are useful for urge, stress, or mixed incontinence, especially if their mechanisms of action are different and their side effects are not synergistic. Pharmacotherapy may also be combined with electrical stimulation or behavioral therapy. In some cases medications are useful for an additive effect, and in other cases they can be used temporarily until sufficient muscle strength and control can be achieved.

For stress incontinence, estrogen and alpha agonists together have been more effective than either alone [57, 58, 62]. It is possible that estrogen could also be an additive to the effect of tricyclic agents on alpha adrenergic receptors and improve efficacy in stress incontinence. The similarity of the side effect profiles of most drugs for urge incontinence makes combination therapy more difficult, but estrogen combined with oxybutynin, propantheline, or another similar agent could have an additive effect and should be studied.

Future of Pharmacotherapy for Incontinence

More research is needed on the physiology of urine storage and voiding to uncover keys to new pharmacologic agents. Also, more randomized, placebo-controlled, double-blinded clinical trials are needed comparing various pharmacologic agents and combinations as well as comparing pharmacotherapy with other forms of treatment. These trials need to closely duplicate clinical practice, include outcomes that are meaningful to the patients (e.g., satisfaction and quality of life), and to include long-term follow-up since virtually all published trials have been short-term. Long-term follow-up studies also should monitor for adverse events related to side effects. For example, tricyclic agents have side effects especially worrisome in the elderly, such as weakness, fatigue, and postural hypotension, and are associated with an increased incidence of falls, which can increase the risk of morbidity and mortality. Lastly, little is known about the sensory mechanisms in the bladder and its outlet, and very few drugs have been developed to treat sensory urgency. Sensory urgency may occur in the presence or absence of detrusor contraction and is a common cause of voiding dysfunction and incontinence. As the physiology of continence becomes better defined through research, more effective medications should become available.

ELECTRICAL STIMULATION THERAPY FOR URINARY INCONTINENCE

A variety of methods for using electrical stimulation to treat urinary incontinence have been reported over the past four decades. All of the methods use electrical current to stimulate contraction of the muscular pelvic floor. This is thought to improve incontinence through several mechanisms. Since the electrical current stimulates pudendal nerve afferents, causing activation of pudendal and hypogastric nerve efferents and contraction of smooth and striated peri-urethral muscles and striated pelvic floor muscles, electrical stimulation results in a more effective contraction than can be obtained with voluntary pelvic muscle exercises [63]. Indeed, electrical stimulation has been shown to improve urethral closure pressure [64]. Also, this stronger contraction of the pelvic floor can increase sensory awareness and help patients learn to contract the pelvic floor more effectively and target their voluntary exercises to the correct muscle groups [65-67]. Electrical stimulation is very helpful for teaching voluntary pelvic muscle exercises to patients with limited sensory awareness of the pelvic floor, or who lack sufficient motor strength to achieve a measurable contraction.

Electrical stimulation also is useful for reducing detrusor instability. Stimulation of pudendal nerve afferents by electrical stimulation has been shown to induce detrusor relaxation due to the pudendal-to-hypogastric and pudendal-to-pelvic spinal reflexes [63, 68]. Electrical stimulation has been shown to dramatically increase bladder capacity in some patients, and the effects may be prolonged for many months [68]. In addition, since electrical stimulation enhances the effectiveness of voluntary pelvic floor contraction, it may be useful initially for patients with weak musculature who are learning to inhibit detrusor contractions by contracting pelvic muscles.

The final postulated mechanism of electrical stimulation is a reorganization of the complex motor patterns involved in maintaining continence, including local neuronal circuits, spinal reflex arcs, the pontine micturition center, and other brainstem and cortical pathways. The rapid and lasting improvement in some persons as a result of a single electrical stimulation session is hypothesized to be the result of reprogramming of reflex neuronal pathways, with the reestablishment of functionally lost motor patterns [69]. Indeed, reemergence of voluntary recruitment of motor units in the urethral sphincter following electrical stimulation has been demonstrated. Thus, the normal reflex arcs which mediate bladder inhibition may be restored or enhanced by electrical stimulation treatment.

The earliest reported study by Huffman and colleagues in 1952 [65] used a combination of short-term, intermittent electrical stimulation applied via vaginal probe combined with pelvic muscle exercise to treat a group of seventeen women with intractable stress urinary incontinence. Despite Huffman's initial success using acute or short-term electrical stimulation (usually referred to as maximal electrical stimulation or MES), all other early research involving non-implanted electrical stimulation for urinary incontinence used chronic stimulation (i.e., stimulation applied for many hours a day for 3 to 12 months or more). It was not until 1967, when Moore and Schofield revisited Huffman's technique of short-term electrical stimulation, that this more convenient and practical technique (MES) became more widely used [70]. Scott in 1979 first described an MES unit for home use, and subsequent clinical trials of home MES have been promising [71].

The electrical stimulation parameters used for MES vary. In more recent clinical trials, MES is most often applied via vaginal and/or rectal plug, for fifteen to thirty minutes per session, with frequencies of 5-50 Hz, current adjusted to maximal tolerated intensity up to 100 mA. Some studies used anesthesia to increase patient tolerance of higher current, but their success rates were not improved. Gradually, it was found that frequencies of 20 Hz achieved both detrusor inhibition and improved sphincter closure [64]. MES current is usually applied intermittently with a 1:3 ratio of a pulse train/rest period which has been shown to be most effective without excess muscle fatigue [72].

The length and frequency of treatment sessions and the total duration of treatment vary from study to study, with ranges from a single treatment to multiple sessions given over six to twelve months [64, 73, 74]. Most trials provided treatments one to three times per week for two to three months. Duration of individual MES sessions was usually fifteen to twenty minutes. Some studies suggested that it was sufficient to use electrical stimulation only until the patient was able to perform voluntary pelvic contractions, as Huffman did in his original report [65, 75].

There have been no reports of complications associated with MES. Reversible local mucosal irritation, transient pelvic discomfort, and constipation have been the only side effects described. Some have suggested that vaginal stimulation is less irritating than anal stimulation. Cardiac pacemakers are believed to be the only contraindication for MES, but this contraindication is theoretical.

MES has been tested on varied populations of incontinent patients with generally promising results. However, methodologies vary widely, and success rates (patients significantly improved as well as cured) range from 0 percent to 100 percent [76-78]. In reviewing the literature, it is clear that more well-designed clinical trials are needed to further test this promising modality to treat urinary incontinence. Among the issues that remain to be determined are the optimal stimulation parameters, including electrical current type and amount, duty cycles, methods of delivery (e.g., vaginal probe, anal probe, implanted units, skin electrodes), duration and frequency of sessions, total duration of treatment, need for booster sessions, as well as patient selection criteria, long-term efficacy, and synergistic combinations of therapies (e.g., behavioral and electrical stimulation or medications and electrical stimulation). As more questions are answered concerning optimal application of a pelvic floor electrical stimulation for patients with incontinence, its use should become more widespread.

SURGICAL TREATMENTS FOR STRESS INCONTINENCE IN WOMEN

Since 1910, hundreds of papers describing numerous surgical procedures for stress incontinence and modifications thereof have been written. However, as with other incontinence therapies, there are relatively few data on long-term results, patient satisfaction, and quality of life after surgery.

Patients with stress incontinence have varying degrees of defects in extrinsic support and in intrinsic sphincter function. When considering surgical therapy, it is convenient to characterize patients with stress incontinence into three basic categories: 1) those with bladder neck or urethral detachment without severe intrinsic urethral defects, 2) those with significant intrinsic sphincter deficiency but apparently normal bladder neck support, and 3) those with both bladder neck or urethral detachment and significant intrinsic sphincter deficiency.

Surgical Procedures

Most surgical procedures for stress incontinence either fixate or elevate the extrinsic connective tissue around the urethra and bladder neck to other pelvic support structures, thereby allowing for physical forces to apply external pressure to the proximal urethra as well as the bladder. These procedures, when performed correctly, work well when the primary defect is one of extrinsic urethral support. A few procedures utilize urethral wall plication or apply bands or slings to increase intrinsic urethral pressure at rest as well.

Surgical procedures for stress incontinence can be divided into four categories:

1. Transvaginal procedures such as the anterior colporrhaphy plicate the inferior aspect of the urethral wall and, by appropriate suture placement, may re-establish the integrity of the pubourethral connective tissue. These procedures generally include a correction of a cystocele which accompanies stress incontinence in at least 20 percent of the cases.

2. Retropubic urethral or bladder neck suspensions (the prototypes being the Marshall-Marchetti-Krantz procedure [79] and the Burch procedure [80]) utilize an abdominal incision through which the space of Retzius is dissected and sutures are placed into the connective tissue on each side of the urethra or bladder neck. The sutures are then secured to the periosteum or cartilage of the symphysis pubis or to the iliopectineal ligaments, thereby elevating and stabilizing the bladder neck area. This allows either mechanical compression or kinking of the proximal urethral when abdominal pressure increases.

3. Long needle suspension procedures, first described by Pereyra (with prototypes being the Stamey procedure, Raz procedure, and the Gittes procedure [81]) are performed by placing periurethral sutures through a transvaginal route, making a smaller suprapubic incision, and passing a long needle through the space of Retzius which is used to carry the supportive sutures to the rectus fascia. There, the sutures are secured and serve functions similar to the supportive sutures of the retropubic procedures.

4. Sling procedures utilize a strip of autologous fascia or heterologous material which is passed through the space of Retzius, around the proximal urethra. Both ends of the strip are anchored to either rectus fascia or to the bony-ligamentous pelvis, thereby creating a sling or hammock on which the bladder neck sits.

Results of Surgery for Stress Incontinence

Surgical success depends in part on patient satisfaction and includes not only whether the patient is cured of stress urinary incontinence, but whether or not she develops or retains other lower urinary symptoms or other problems that can be attributed directly or indirectly to the surgery. "Success" for a young patient who leaks only during aerobics is qualitatively different from that for the obese seventy-five year old who leaks continuously. The latter patient is going to be more tolerant of some voiding dysfunction or occasional urge incontinence occurring after surgery than is the former.

There are several clinical factors that appear to affect success of these procedures. Patient age, general health, and estrogen status all appear to affect the quality of the pelvic tissues. It appears that weaker connective tissue with poor vascular and neural supply is less likely to be held securely by suture material or to adhere to adjacent structures. Other lower urinary tract disorders such as difficulty voiding, recurrent urinary tract infections, or detrusor instability (motor urge incontinence) may occur concurrently with stress incontinence and are frequently not helped, and occasionally worsened, by surgical procedures. Obesity, chronic coughing, and other physical factors which increase intra-abdominal pressure appear to diminish the success of the operations due to physical stress on the suspended area. Previous surgery for incontinence may predispose the patient to other urinary problems or to scarring and adhesions around the bladder neck making a repeat procedure more technically difficult. Any of these factors, which affect tissue quality, may adversely affect intrinsic sphincter function and thus increase the chance of surgical failure. The continence function of a urethra that is scarred and fixed in place with a defective intrinsic sphincter mechanism is unlikely to be improved by any of the described surgeries, with the exception of an occlusive sling procedure.

Published data on the correction of leakage with stress may be summarized as follows. All of the above-mentioned procedures performed by capable surgeons will temporarily cure stress incontinence in the patient with primarily a bladder neck support defect. However, some of these procedures are more likely to fail with time. Although a few surgeons would disagree, the transvaginal procedures show the most rapid decline in success, with as many as 40 percent of patients having significant recurrence within one year. Because there are differences in individual modifications and surgical expertise, the true success rates with needle procedures are difficult to ascertain. One-to-five-year cure rates range from 43 percent to 95 percent, with both objective and subjective data showing the lowest cure rates in those studies with longer follow-up [82]. Overall success rates with needle procedures appear to be lower than those with retropubic procedures when comparable follow-up methods are used prospectively.

More data are available on the effectiveness of retropubic procedures. Reports show that cure rates for stress incontinence are between 80 percent and 95 percent with Marshall-Marchetti-Krantz procedures [82], and between 63 percent and 87 percent with Burch procedures when patients are followed for five to ten years postoperatively [83, 84]. Exclusion of patients with severe intrinsic sphincter deficiency improves the success of Burch procedures to 87 percent to 98 percent [83]. Recently, numerous surgeons have begun to perform retropubic procedures with laparoscopic techniques, thereby decreasing hospital stay and postoperative pain. Although initial results appear to be comparable to those obtained with open procedures, longer term success rates are not yet available. Laparoscopic procedures have obvious limitations in patients who have had previous lower abdominal surgery, especially when there is retropubic scarring.

Sling procedures have generally been considered separately from the other procedures because most surgeons choose slings only for patients who have evidence of intrinsic sphincter deficiency and are at high risk for failing the other procedures [85]. Cure or significant improvement of stress incontinence is obtained in greater than 80 percent of these types of patients having sling procedures. Slings have not generally been recommended in patients with primarily bladder neck support defects without intrinsic sphincter deficiency because of a presumed higher incidence of obstructive voiding after the sling procedure and the fact that retropubic procedures produce good success rates. When heterologous sling materials such as Marlex, Mersalene, or Silastic are employed, the incidences of graft infection or erosion appear to occur in at least 5 percent of the individuals; however, this has not been a problem when autologous fascia is used.

Of the patients who have recurrence of leakage after any of the procedures for incontinence, typically one-half to two-thirds report that their stress incontinence is much improved as compared to prior to the operation.

Complications

Acute and subacute complications of surgical procedures for stress incontinence include blood loss, wound infection, urinary tract injury, urinary tract infection, and associated complications such as thrombosis, emboli, and pneumonia [86]. Postoperative urinary tract infection is unfortunately common, occurring in between 10 percent and 30 percent of patients, and is probably related to voiding dysfunction (inability to empty) and the need for either continuous or intermittent catheterization. The other complications mentioned have been noted in less than 5 percent of patients in most series.

Other problems which may be associated with surgery for stress incontinence include prolonging voiding dysfunction, detrusor instability, the development of posterior/superior vaginal prolapse, and various symptoms including pain, dysuria, dyspareunia, and anorgasmia [86]. Most reports fail to address the latter symptoms, so their true incidence and significance are uncertain. Voiding dysfunction is clearly related to the degree of urethral or bladder neck suspension. For example, a Marshall-Marchetti-Krantz procedure which suspends the urethra directly to the symphysis pubis may be more likely to cause subsequent voiding dysfunction than a procedure that simply stabilizes the pubourethral connective tissue [82].

Symptomatic detrusor instability or motor urge incontinence has been reported to occur de novo in 5 percent to 10 percent of patients having retropubic suspension procedures. Although definitive data is lacking, some of the abnormal bladder contractions may be attributed to urinary tract infections, some to outflow obstruction, and some to interference with the nerve supply to the bladder by the surgery. In addition, many of the patients who develop these symptoms after surgery may have had unrecognized detrusor instability prior to the surgery that persisted and became more apparent when the bladder was allowed to fill to a greater extent.

Lastly, some reports have indicated that vaginal cuff prolapse, enterocele, and rectocele may be exacerbated when the vagina is displaced anteriorly as occurs in some surgical procedures. This may permit more pronounced gravitational effects posteriorly which may be conducive to prolapse in patients who have weak support tissues. Pelvic prolapse and incontinence frequently coexist.

Many questions remain regarding stress incontinence and the limits and optimal combinations of therapy. Can we better standardize decision making about which patients will benefit from surgical therapy and how long that benefit can be maintained? Which patients should have which surgical procedure? Will those surgeons who have additional training and expertise in incontinence surgery obtain better results than other competent surgeons who do not have a primary interest in incontinence? Are there specific connective tissue defects or neuromuscular defects that directly cause stress incontinence? Can these conditions be prevented or be better treated, yielding more acceptable results?

PERIURETHRAL COLLAGEN INJECTION

Periurethral injections are a new treatment innovation for severe stress urinary incontinence due to urethral insufficiency. This treatment is performed in an out-patient setting and involves injecting bulking agents around the urethra. The added bulk in the submucosa of the proximal urethra is thought to improve coaptation and possibly compression in the urethra. Prior to periurethral injections, options for patients with severe intrinsic urethral sphincter deficiency, characterized by leakage of urine with only minimal exertion, consisted of more invasive procedures, the pubovaginal sling or artificial urinary sphincter.

Since 1993, collagen has become the preferred substance for periurethral injections. Commercially available collagen (Contingen®) is a highly purified suspension of glutaraldehyde cross-linked bovine collagen suspended in normal saline and containing approximately 95 percent Type 1 collagen and 1 percent to 5 percent Type 3 collagen. It is biocompatiable and biodegradable and elicits minimal or no inflammatory or foreign body reaction. It has been reported that 1 percent to 3 percent of patients will demonstrate skin test hypersensitivity to collagen and therefore cannot receive this bulking agent. To determine sensitivity to the material, a skin test must be performed and observed over a four-week interval prior to treatment.

The procedure itself is fairly straightforward. In women, paraurethral needle placement can be guided with endoscopic control or, as in men, a transendoscopic needle can be positioned at the bladder neck region for collagen injection. The goal of collagen injection is to produce coaptation at the bladder neck level. This is usually easily obtained in female patients but more difficult in males. Typically, men with incompetent sphincters after prostatectomy have required multiple injections to obtain satisfactory results. As a post-treatment precaution, patients are required to void prior to dismissal and, if unable to do so, are taught intermittent self-catheterization. Indwelling catheters should not be left in place following the periurethral collagen injection procedure.

Because collagen injection is a relatively new treatment, experience with its results are limited. However, the existing literature has demonstrated the effectiveness of collagen injection for both men and women [87-91]. Cure rates in these studies ranged from 16 percent in men to 42 percent to 46 percent in women. Combined improvement and cure rates were reported in 69 percent of men and from 80 percent to 82 percent of women. A retrospective analysis of the first sixty-six patients (41 women, 25 men) treated at our site indicated that 86 percent of the women and 53 percent of the men were improved following treatment. The average number of injections was 1.75 for women and 2.25 for men, although some of the men were still in the process of treatment at the time of analysis.

This treatment offers both economic and personal advantages to patients. Patients are spared extensive surgical procedures, anesthesia, hospitalization, and prolonged recovery periods because they are treated in the outpatient setting where they are premedicated and only topical, local, or combinations of local anesthetic agents are utilized. In addition, the results of the procedure are evident to patients and physicians fairly quickly—within the first hours after recovery from the local anesthetics.

One limitation of this treatment is that implanted collagen begins to degrade in approximately twelve weeks and is completely degraded between nine and nineteen months after injection. The maintenance of continence even after the injected collagen has been completely degraded is thought to result from replacement by naturally occurring collagen.

Periurethral implantation of collagen has produced a valuable new option for treatment of patients with intrinsic urethral sphincter deficiency. It is anticipated that future research will refine instrumentation for delivery of the collagen and focus on development of newer, more stable injectable substances. With the current emphasis on cost containment and optimal clinical pathways, studies will also be needed to compare the efficacy of collagen to that of other forms of treatment for intrinsic urethral insufficiency.

ARTIFICIAL URINARY SPHINCTER

The artificial sphincter is an implantable prosthetic device for severe stress incontinence due to intrinsic urethral deficiency. Several different devices have been developed over the past two decades. The current model (AMS 800 [American Medical Systems, Minnetonka, MN]) consists of three components all made of silicon: the pressure cuff, the fluid reservoir, and the pump. The circular cuff is placed around the urethra or bladder neck. It is filled with liquid and provides occlusive pressure to keep the urethra closed. The key to success of the device's occlusive mechanism is the continuous closure pressure surrounding the urethra. If this pressure is insufficient, the patient's incontinence will persist. If the pressure is excessive, then ischemia will result, leading to erosion of the urethral tissue. The reservoir is an elastic pressure balloon which is filled with liquid and maintains a predetermined pressure within the hydraulic system of the sphincter. The reservoir is placed under the rectus muscle. The pump mechanism is about the size of the tip of one's smallest finger and contains unidirectional valves, a flow reservoir, an "on and off" button, and the deflation pump. The pump mechanism is positioned in the male scrotum or the female labia for easy patient access. The components are connected by nonkinking tubing that provides constant hydraulic pressure within the sphincter system determined by the balloon reservoir specifications. The reservoirs of the AMS 800 model are manufactured to deliver a range of pressures (51-60, 61-70, 71-80, 81-90 cm H_2O).

The operative procedure takes one to two hours and is done with extreme care to avoid bacterial contamination of the device. When the sphincter system is implanted, the cuff is deflated and turned off to keep the cuff in a non-occlusive position while postoperative healing takes place. The artificial sphincter is then activated four to six weeks after surgery. To empty the bladder, the pump is activated and the fluid moves from the cuff to the reservoir, relieving pressure on the urethra and allowing the patient to void. After voiding, the process is reversed. It is recommended that the sphincter be deactivated in the non-occlusive open position at night to prevent urethral ischemia at the cuff site. The aim is to prevent erosion or atrophy of the urethra and improve the urethral tolerance of the implanted sphincter.

Due to the inherent risks of implantation and the potential for device failure, the artificial sphincter is generally reserved for cases of severe incontinence for which other surgical options are not advised or have been unsuccessful. The ideal patient for the artificial sphincter is the individual with intrinsic sphincteric deficiency who has normal detrusor function. The post-prostatectomy patient with urinary incontinence who has not responded to behavioral or medical therapies and has not responded to (or cannot undergo) a collagen implant can be offered the artificial sphincter. However, patients who have undergone previous pelvic irradiation are at high risk for poor healing and wound infection after implantation.

Research on the artificial sphincter indicates that 65 percent to 75 percent of patients can be cured with this procedure and 80 percent to 85 percenet are cured or improved [92-99]. Patients can expect an excellent level of urinary continence after the placement of an artificial sphincter if they have normal bladder capacity and compliance. Candidates for the device need a reasonable level of dexterity to manipulate the deflation pump. A basic understanding of the workings of the implanted device is also necessary. Time spent screening and educating the patient, demonstrating the model of the device, and answering questions is an invaluable element in this treatment option.

New developments in the design of a narrow backed cuff and more precise volumes in the reservoir balloon used to exert pressure have produced more successful prosthetic implants. Presently, further research to refine the techniques and reduce complications would be more beneficial than comparative studies.

CONCLUSION

It is widely accepted that 80 percent to 90 percent of cases of incontinence can be either cured or significantly improved with the treatments currently available. However, fewer than half of the individuals with this problem are evaluated or treated [100, 101]. Even as treatments for incontinence are improved and made more available, barriers to treatment exist within the attitudes held by patients and health care providers. Because incontinence is embarrassing and socially unacceptable, many people go to great lengths to conceal the problem rather than seeking help. The prevalent view that incontinence is an inevitable feature of growing older, or that it is untreatable, can further deter patients from seeking treatment. Studies to further explore the barriers to treatment as well as strategies for overcoming these barriers would be an invaluable contribution to this field.

A major limitation of much of the research on treatment of incontinence is the scarcity of data on long-term outcomes. Studies with long follow-up periods, extending for example to five years after treatment, are difficult to conduct and susceptible to problems with attrition. However they are essential to understanding the durability of the various therapies especially behavioral and surgical interventions.

Finally, most studies have examined the results of treatment in terms of physiological change or reduction in the size or frequency of incontinent episodes. Few have considered the psychosocial impact of incontinence or the effects of treatment or the quality of the patient's life. Often incontinence can be cured, but treatments may introduce new problems such as intolerable side-effects or new voiding difficulties. A satisfactory outcome for one patient might be considered a treatment failure to another. A reduction of incontinence that gives one person a renewed sense of freedom may have little impact on the restricted lifestyle of another. Therefore, future studies could be improved by measuring not only the reduction of urine loss but the patient's satisfaction with treatment and the impact of that treatment on quality of life.

REFERENCES

1. A. C. Diokno, B. M. Brock, H. B. Brown, and A. R. Herzog, Prevalence of Urinary Incontinence and Other Urologic Symptoms in the Non-institutionalized Elderly, *Journal of Urology, 136,* pp. 1022-1025, 1986.
2. J. G. Ouslander, R. L. Kane, and I. B. Abrass, Urinary Incontinence in Elderly Nursing Home Patients, *Journal of the American Medical Association, 248,* pp 1194-1198, 1982.
3. J. F. Wyman, S. W. Harkins, and J. A. Fantl, Psychosocial Impact of Urinary Incontinence in the Community-Dwelling Population, *Journal of the American Geriatrics Society, 38,* pp. 282-288, 1990.
4. J. A. Fantl, D. K. Newman, and J. Colling, J. O. L. DeLancy, C. Keeys, R. M. Loughery, and B. J. McDowell, Urinary Incontinence in Adults: Acute and Chronic Management, *Clinical Practice Guideline, No. 2 Update:* AHCPR Publication No. 96-0682, U.S. Department of Health and Human Services, Public Health Service, Agency for Health Care Policy and Research, Rockville, MD, 1996.
5. K. L. Burgio, W. E. Whitehead, and B. T. Engel, Urinary Incontinence in the Elderly: Bladder-sphincter Biofeedback and Toileting Skills Training, *Annals of Internal Medicine, 104,* pp. 507-515, 1985.
6. J. Baigis-Smith, D. A. J. Smith, M. Rose, and D. K. Newman, Managing Urinary Incontinence in Community-Residing Elderly Persons, *Gerontologist, 29,* pp. 229-233, 1989.
7. K. L. Burgio, J. C. Robinson, and B. T. Engel, The Role of Biofeedback in Kegel Exercise Training for Stress Urinary Incontinence, *American Journal of Obstetrics and Gynecology, 157,* pp. 58-64, 1986.
8. K. L. Burgio, R. E. Stutzman, and B. T. Engel, Behavioral Training for Post-Prostatectomy Urinary Incontinence, *Journal of Urology, 141,* pp. 303-306, 1989.
9. P. A. Burns, K. Pranikoff, T. H. Nochajski, E. C. Hadley, K. J. Levy, and M. G. Ory, A Comparison of Effectiveness of Biofeedback and Pelvic Muscle Exercise Treatment of Stress Incontinence in Older Community-Dwelling Women, *Journal of Gerontology, 48,* pp. 167-174, 1993.
10. J. R. Burton, K. L. Pearce, K. L. Burgio, B. T. Engel, and W. E. Whitehead, Behavioral Training for Urinary Incontinence in Elderly Ambulatory Patients, *Journal of the American Geriatrics Society, 36,* pp. 693-698, 1988.

11. M. Dougherty, K. Bishop, R. Mooney, P. Gimotty, and B. Williams, Graded Pelvic Muscle Exercise. Effect on Stress Urinary Incontinence, *Journal of Reproductive Medicine, 39,* pp. 684-691, 1993.

12. A. H. Kegel, Progressive Resistance Exercise in the Functional Restoration of the Perineal Muscles, *American Journal of Obstetrics and Gynecology, 56,* pp. 238-248, 1948.

13. A. H. Kegel, Stress Incontinence of Urine in Women: Physiologic Treatment, *Journal of the International College of Surgeons, 25,* pp. 487-499, 1956.

14. B. J. McDowell, K. L. Burgio, M. Dombrowski, J. L. Locher, and E. Rodriguez, Interdisciplinary Approach to the Assessment and Behavioral Treatment of Urinary Incontinence in Geriatric Outpatients, *Journal of the American Geriatric Society, 40,* pp. 370-374, 1992.

15. A. M. Shepherd, E. Montgomery, and R. S. Anderson, Treatment of Genuine Stress Incontinence with a New Perineometer, *Physiotherapy, 69,* p. 113, 1983.

16. T. J. Wells, C. A. Brink, A. D. Diokno, R. Wolfe, and G. L. Gillis, Pelvic Muscle Exercise for Stress Urinary Incontinence in Elderly Women, *Journal of the American Geriatrics Society, 39,* pp. 785-791, 1991.

17. P. A. Burns, K. Pranikoff, T. Nochajski, P. Desotelle, and M. K. Harwood, Treatment of Stress Incontinence with Pelvic Floor Exercises and Biofeedback, *Journal of the American Geriatrics Society, 38,* pp. 341-344, 1990.

18. S. J. Middaugh, W. E. Whitehead, K. L. Burgio, and B. T. Engel, Biofeedback in Treatment of Urinary Incontinence in Stroke Patients, *Biofeedback and Self Regulation, 14,* pp. 44-51, 1989.

19. L. D. Cardozo, P. D. Abrams, S. L. Stanton, and R. C. L. Feneley, Idiopathic Bladder Instability Treated by Biofeedback, *British Journal of Urology, 50,* pp. 27-30, 1978.

20. L. D. Cardozo, S. L. Stanton, J. Hafner, and V. Allan, Biofeedback in the Treatment of Detrusor Instability, *British Journal of Urology, 50,* pp. 250-254, 1978.

21. K. Glavind, S. B. Nohr, and S. Walter, Biofeedback and Physiotherapy Versus Physiotherapy Versus Physiotherapy Alone in the Treatment of Genuine Stress Urinary Incontinence, *International Urogynecology Journal, 7,* pp. 339-343, 1996.

22. W. K. Frewen, An Objective Assessment of the Unstable Bladder of Psychosomatic Origin, *British Journal of Urology, 50,* pp. 246-249, 1978.

23. W. K. Frewen, Role of Bladder Training in the Treatment of the Unstable Bladder in the Female, *Urologic Clinics of North America, 6,* pp. 273-277, 1979.

24. W. K. Frewen, A Reassessment of Bladder Training in Detrusor Dysfunction in the Female, *British Journal of Urology, 54,* pp. 372-373, 1982.

25. G. J. Jarvis, A Controlled Trial of Bladder Drill and Drug Therapy in the Management of Detrusor Instability, *Journal of Urology, 53,* pp. 565-566, 1981.

26. G. J. Jarvis, The Management of Urinary Incontinence Due to Primary Vesical Sensory Urgency by Bladder Drill, *British Journal of Urology, 54,* pp. 374-376, 1982.

27. G. J. Jarvis and D. R. Millar, Controlled Trial of Bladder Drill for Detrusor Instability, *British Medical Journal, 281,* pp. 1322-1323, 1980.

28. D. D. Elder and T. P. Stephenson, An Assessment of the Frewen Regime in the Treatment of Detrusor Dysfunction in Females, *British Journal of Urology, 52,* pp. 467-471, 1980.

29. J. A. Fantl, W. G. Hurt, and L. J. Dunn, Detrusor Instability Syndrome: The Use of Bladder Retraining Drills and With and Without Anticholinergics, *American Journal of Obstetrics and Gynecology, 140,* pp. 885-890, 1981.

30. A. W. Pengelly and C. M. Booth, A Prospective Trial of Bladder Training as Treatment for Detrusor Instability, *British Journal of Urology, 52,* pp. 463-466, 1980.

31. J. M. Svigos and C. D. Matthews, Assessment and Treatment of Female Urinary Incontinence by Cystometrogram and Bladder Retraining Programs, *Obstetrics and Gynecology, 50,* pp. 9-12, 1977.
32. T. N. A. Jeffcoate and W. J. Francis, Urgency Incontinence in the Female, *American Journal of Obstetrics and Gynecology, 94,* pp. 604-618, 1966.
33. J. A. Fantl, J. F. Wyman, D. K. McClish, S. W. Harkins, R. K. Elswick, J. R. Taylor, and E. Hadley, Efficacy of Bladder Training in Older Women with Urinary Incontinence, *Journal of the American Medical Association, 265:5,* pp. 609-613, 1991.
34. A. J. Wein, Pharmocologic Treatment of Incontinence, *Journal of the American Geriatric Society, 38:3,* pp. 317-325, 1990.
35. A. Finkbeiner, L. Welch, and N. Bissada, Urophramacology IX: Direct Acting Smooth Muscle Stimulant and Depressants, *Urology, 12,* p. 231, 1978.
36. D. M. Holmes, F. J. Montz, and S. L. Stanton, Oxybutynin Versus Propantheline in the Management of Detrusor Instability: A Patient-Regulated Variable Dose Trial, *British Journal of Obstetrics and Gynaecology, 96,* pp. 607-612, 1989.
37. K. H. Moore, D. M. Hay, A. E. Imrie, A. Watson, and M. Goldstein, Oxybutynin Hydrochloride (3 Mg) in the Treatment of Women with Idiopathic Detrusor Instability, *British Journal of Urology, 66,* pp. 479-485, 1990.
38. D. Riva and E. Casolati, Oxybutynin Chloride in the Treatment of Female Idiopathic Bladder Instability, *Clinical and Experimental Obstetrics and Gynecology, 11:1-2,* pp. 37-42, 1984.
39. A. J. Tapp, L. D. Cardozo, E. Versi, and D. Cooper, The Treatment of Detrusor Instability in Postmenopausal Women with Oxybutynin Chloride: A Double-Blind Placebo Controlled Study, *British Journal of Obstetrics and Gynaecology, 97,* pp. 521-526, 1990.
40. J. W. Thuroff, B. Bunke, A. Ebner, P. Faber, P. de Geeter, J. Hannappel, H. Heidler, H. Madersbacher, H. Melchior, and W. Schafer, Randomized, Double-Blind, Multicenter Trial on Treatment of Frequency, Urgency and Incontinence Related to Detrusor Hyperactivity: Oxybutynin Versus Propantheline Versus Placebo, *Journal of Urology, 145,* pp. 813-817, 1991.
41. A. G. M. Zeegers, H. Kiesswetter, A. E. J. L. Kramer, and U. Jonas, Conservative Therapy of Frequency, Urgency and Urge Incontinence: A Double-Blind Clinical Trial of Flavoxate Hydrochloride, Oxybutynin Chloride, Emepronium Bromide and Placebo, *World Journal of Urology, 5,* pp. 57-61, 1987.
42. H. H. Meyhoff, T. C. Gerstenberg, and J. Nordling, Placebo—The Drug of Choice in Female Motor Urge Incontinence? *British Journal of Urology, 55,* pp. 34-37, 1983.
43. J. M. Robinson and J. C. Brocklehurst, Emepronium Bromide and Flavoxate Hydrochloride in the Treatment of Urinary Incontinence Associated with Detrusor Instability in Elderly Women, *British Journal of Urology, 55,* pp. 371-376, 1983.
44. C. R. Chapple, H. Parkhouse, C. Gardener, and E. J. Milroy, Double-Blind, Placebo-Controlled, Crossover Study of Flavoxate in the Treatment of Idiopathic Detrusor Instability, *British Journal of Urology, 66,* pp. 491-494, 1990.
45. G. Milner and N. F Hills, A Double-Blind Assessment of Antidepressants in the Treatment of 212 Enuretic Patients, *Medical Journal of Australia, 1,* pp. 943-947, 1968.
46. G. Lose, L. Jorgensen, and P. Thunedborg, Doxepin in the Treatment of Female Detrusor Over-Activity: A Randomized Double-Blind Crossover Study, *Journal of Urology, 142,* pp. 1024-1026, 1989.
47. C. M. Castleden, H. M. Duffin, and R. S. Gulati, Double-Blind Study of Imipramine and Placebo for Incontinence Due to Bladder Instability, *Age and Ageing, 15,* pp. 299-303, 1986.

48. Y. Muskat, I. Bukovsky, D. Schneider, and R. Langer, The Use of Scopolamine in the Treatment of Detrusor Instability, *Journal of Urology, 156,* pp. 1989-1990, 1996.

49. J. L. Cornella, A. E. Bent, D. R. Ostergard, and N. S. Horbach, Prospective Study Utilizing Transdermal Scopolamine in Detrusor Instability, *Urology, 35,* p. 96, 1990.

50. L. D. Cardozo and S. L. Stanton, An Objective Comparison of the Effects of Parenterally Administered Drugs in Patients Suffering from Detrusor Instability, *Journal of Urology, 122,* p. 58, 1979.

51. L. D. Cardozo, S. L. Stanton, H. Robinson, and D. Holer, Evaluation of Flurbiprofen in Detrusor Instability, *British Medical Journal, 280,* pp. 281-282, 1980.

52. P. Lindholm and G. Lose, Terbutaline (Bricanyl) in the Treatment of Female Urge Incontinence, *Urologia Internationalis, 41,* pp. 158-160, 1986.

53. L. Collste and M. Lindskog, Phenylpropanolamine in Treatment of Female Stress Urinary Incontinence: A Double-Blind Placebo Controlled Study in 24 Patients, *Urodynamics, 30,* pp. 398-403, 1987.

54. E. Fossberg, H. O. Beisland, and R. A. Lundgren, Stress Incontinence in Females: Treatment with Phenylpropanolamine: A Urodynamic and Pharmacological Evaluation, *Urologia Internationalis, 38,* pp. 293-299, 1983.

55. T. Lehtonen, S. Rannikko, O. Lindell, M. Talja, E. Wuokko, and M. Lindskog, The Effect of Phenylpropanolamine on Female Stress Urinary Incontinence, *Annales Chirurgiae et Gynaecologiae, 75,* pp. 236-241, 1986.

56. A. Ek, K. E. Andersson, B. Gullberg, and U. Ulmsten, The Effects of Long-Term Treatment with Norephedrine on Stress Incontinence and Urethral Closure Pressure Profile, *Scandinavian Journal of Urology and Nephrology, 12*:2, pp. 105-110, 1978.

57. P. Hilton, A. L. Tweddell, and C. Mayne, Oral and Intravaginal Estrogens Alone and in Combination with Alpha-Adrenergic Stimulation in Genuine Stress Incontinence, *International Urogynecology Journal, 1,* pp. 80-86, 1990.

58. S. Walter, B. Kjaergaard, G. Lose, J. T. Andersen, L. Heisterberg, H. Jakobsen, P. Klarskov, K. Moller-Hansen, and M. Lindskog, Stress Urinary Incontinence in Post-menopausal Women Treated with Oral Estrogen (Estriol) and an Alpha-Adrenoceptor-Stimulating Agent (Phenylpropanolamine): A Randomized Double-Blind Placebo-Controlled Study, *International Urogynecologic Journal, 1,* pp. 74-79, 1990.

59. G. Samsioe, I. Jansson, D. Mellstrom, and A. Svanborg, Occurrence, Nature and Treatment of Urinary Incontinence in a 70-Year-Old Female Population, *Maturitas, 7,* pp. 335-342, 1985.

60. T. G. Judge, The Use of Quinestradol in Elderly Incontinent Women, A Preliminary Report, *Gerontologia Clinica, 11,* pp. 159-164, 1969.

61. J. A. Fantl, R. C. Bump, D. Robinson, D. K. McClish, and J. F. Wyman, Efficacy of Estrogen Supplementation in the Treatment of Urinary Incontinence, *Obstetrics and Gynecology, 88,* pp. 745-749, 1996.

62. A. Ek, K. E. Andersson, B. Gullberg, and U. Ulmsten, Effects of Oestradiol and Combined Norephedrine and Oestradiol Treatment on Female Stress Incontinence, *Zentralblatt für Gynakologie, 102,* pp. 839-844, 1980.

63. B. C. Eriksen, M. Fall, C. A. Carlsson, and L. E. Linder, Effect of Anal Electrostimulation with the Incontan Device in Women with Urinary Incontinence, *British Journal of Obstetrics and Gynaecology, 94,* pp. 147-156, 1987.

64. B. Kralj, The Treatment of Female Urinary Incontinence by Functional Electrical Stimulation, in *Urogynecology and Urodynamics, Theory and Practice,* D. R. Ostergard and A. E. Bent (eds.), Williams and Wilkins, Baltimore, pp. 508-517, 1991.

65. J. W. Huffman, S. L. Osborne, and J. K. Sokol, Electrical Stimulation in Treatment of Intractable Stress Incontinence, *Archives of Physical Medicine, 33,* p. 674, 1952.
66. G. D. Stoddard, Research Project into the Effect of Pelvic Floor Exercises on Genuine Stress Incontinence, *Physiotherapy, 148*:69, p. 149, 1983.
67. K. S. Olah, N. Bridges, and D. Farar, The Conservative Management of Genuine Stress Incontinence, *International Urogynecologic Journal, 2,* pp. 161-167, 1991.
68. S. Lindstrom M. Fall, C. A. Carlsson, and B. E. Erlandson, The Neurophysiological Basis of Bladder Inhibition in Response to Intravaginal Electrical Stimulation, *Journal of Urology, 129,* pp. 405-410, 1983.
69. M. Fall, Does Electrostimulation Cure Urinary Incontinence? *Journal of Urology, 131,* pp. 664-667, 1984.
70. T. Moore and P. F. Schofield, Treatment of Stress Incontinence by Maximum Perineal Electrical Stimulation, *British Medical Journal, 3,* pp. 150, 1967.
71. R. S. Scott and G. S. Hsueh, A Clinical Study of the Effects of Galvanic Vaginal Muscle Stimulation in Urinary Stress Incontinence and Sexual Dysfunction, *American Journal of Obstetrics and Gynecology, 135,* p. 663, 1979.
72. S. Racovec, Reflex Electrical Stimulation for Urinary Incontinence, *European Urology, 1,* pp. 24-25, 1975.
73. A. E. Bent, P. K. Sand, D. R. Ostergard, and L. T. Brubaker, Transvaginal Electrical Stimulation in the Treatment of Genuine Stress Incontinence and Detrusor Instability, *International Urogynecology Journal, 4,* pp. 9-13, 1993.
74. A. Jonasson, B. Larsson, H. Psehera, and L. Lylund, Short-Term Maximal Electrical Stimulation—A Conservative Treatment of Urinary Incontinence, *Gynecologic and Obstetric Investigations, 30,* pp. 120-123, 1990.
75. E. Montgomery and A. M. Shepherd, Electrical Stimulation and Graded Pelvic Exercises for Genuine Stress Urinary Incontinence, *British Journal of Urology, 69,* p. 112, 1983.
76. E. S. Glen, B. M. Samuels, I. M. MacKenzie, and D. Rowan, Maximum Perineal Stimulation for Urinary Incontinence, *Urologia Internationalis, 31,* p. 134, 1976.
77. A. G. Turner, An Appraisal of Maximal Faradic Stimulation Muscles in the Management of Female Urinary Incontinence, *Annals of the Royal College of Surgeons of England, 61,* p. 441, 1979.
78. C. Godec and A. Cass, Acute Electrical Stimulation for Urinary Incontinence, *Urology, 12,* p. 340, 1978.
79. V. F. Marshall, A. A. Marchetti, and K. E. Krantz, The Correction of Stress Incontinence by Simple Vesicourethral Suspension, *Surgery, Gynecology and Obstetrics, 88,* p. 509, 1949.
80. J. C. Burch, Urethrovaginal Fixation to Cooper's Ligament for Correction of Stress Incontinence, Cystocele, and Prolapse, *American Journal of Obstetrics and Gynecology, 81,* p. 281, 1961.
81. M. M. Karram and N. A. Bhatia, Transvaginal Needle Bladder Neck Suspension Procedures for Stress Urinary Incontinence: A Comprehensive Review, *Obstetrics and Gynecology, 73,* pp. 906-914, 1989.
82. T. C. Mainprize and H. P. Drutz, The Marshall-Marchetti-Krantz Procedure: A Critical Review, *Obstetrics and Gynecological Survey, 43,* p. 724, 1988.
83. M. Colombo, S. Scalambrino, A. Maggioni, and R. Milani, Burch Colposuspension Versus Modified Marshall-Marchetti-Krantz Urethropexy for Primary Genuine Stress Urinary Incontinence: A Prospective, Randomized Trial, *American Journal of Obstetrics and Gynecology, 171,* pp. 1573-1579, 1994.

84. A. Bergman and G. Elia, Three Surgical Procedures for Genuine Stress Incontinence: Five-Year Follow-Up of a Prospective Randomized Study, *American Journal of Obstetrics and Gynecology, 173*, pp. 66-71, 1995.

85. E. J. McGuire and J. Wan, Pubovaginal Slings, in *Urogynecologic Surgery*, G. Hurt (ed.), Aspen Publishers, Inc., Gaithersburg, Maryland, 1992.

86. I. E. Nygaard and K. J. Kreder, Complications of Incontience Surgery, *International Urogynecologic Journal, 5*, pp. 353-360, 1994.

87. R. A. Appell, Collagen Injection Therapy for Urinary Incontinence, *Urological Clinics of North America, 21*, pp. 177-182, 1994.

88. S. D. Eckford and P. Abrams, Para-Urethral Collagen Implantation for Female Stress Incontinence, *British Journal of Urology, 68*, pp. 586-589, 1991.

89. E. J. McGuire and R. A. Appell, Transurethral Collagen Injection for Urinary Incontinence, *Urology, 43*, pp. 413-415, 1994.

90. H. E. O'Connell, E. J. McGuire, S. Aboseif, and A. Usui, Transurethral Collagen Therapy in Women, *Journal of Urology, 154*, pp. 1463-1465, 1995.

91. P. Stricker and B. Haylen, Injectable Collagen for Type 3 Female Stress Incontinence: The First 50 Australian Patients, *Medical Journal of Australia, 158*, pp. 89-91, 1993.

92. M. M. Karram, B. A. Rosenzweig, and N. N. Bhatia, Artifical Urinary Sphincter for Recurrent/Severe Stress Incontinence in Women, *Journal of Reproductive Medicine, 38*, pp. 791-794, 1993.

93. H. J. Duncan, D. E. Nurse, and A. R. Mundy, Role of the Artificial Urinary Sphincter in the Treatment of Stress Incontinence in Women, *British Journal of Urology, 69*, pp. 141-143, 1992.

94. A. C. Diokno, J. B. Hollander, and T. P. Alderson, Artificial Urinary Sphincter for Recurrent Female Urinary Incontinence: Indications and Results, *Journal of Urology, 138*, p. 778, 1987.

95. R. A. Appell, Techniques and Results in the Implantation of the Artificial Urinary Sphincter in Women with Type III Stress Urinary Incontinence by a Vaginal Approach, *Neurourological Urodynamics, 134*, p. 476, 1988.

96. D. J. Warwick and P. Abrams, The Perineal Artificial Sphincter for Acquired Incontinence: A Cut and Dried Solution? *British Journal of Urology, 66*, pp. 495-499, 1990.

97. Y. Wang and H. R. Hadley, Management of Persistent or Recurrent Urinary Incontinence after Placement of Artificial Urinary Sphincter, *Journal of Urology, 146*, pp. 1005-1006, 1991.

98. J. C. Gundian, D. M, Barrett, and B. G. Parulkar, Mayo Clinic Experience with Use of the AMS 800 Artificial Urinary Spincter for Urinary Incontinence Following Radical Prostatectomy, *Journal of Urology, 142*, p. 1459, 1989.

99. C. G. Brito, J. J. Mulcahy, M. E. Mitchell, and M. C. Adams, Use of a Double Cuff Ams800 Urinary Sphincter for Severe Stress Incontinence, *Journal of Urology, 149*, pp. 283-285, 1993.

100. Consensus Conference, Urinary Incontinence in Adults, *Journal of the American Medical Association, 261*, pp. 2685-2690, 1989.

101. K. L. Burgio, D. G. Ives, J. L. Locher, V. C. Arena, and L. H. Kuller, Treatment Seeking for Urinary Incontinence in Older Adults, *Journal of the American Geriatrics Society, 42*, pp. 208-212, 1994.

CHAPTER
14

Mobility Impairment and Its Consequences in the Elderly

Cynthia Owsley, Richard M. Allman,
Marilyn Gossman, Sherron Kell, Richard V. Sims,
and Patricia S. Baker

This chapter represents initial steps toward building a new framework for research on the causes and treatments of mobility impairment in older adults. A major tradition in the mobility field has been to conduct research on a problem-specific basis (e.g., falls, vehicle crashes, hip fractures, public transportation use, pressure ulcers) where the theoretical framework is focused uniquely on that problem, rather than within a more general context of mobility and its complications. One aim of this chapter is to underscore the similarities in the causes of different mobility problems and to propose that it is useful to approach them, at least on occasion, from a single conceptual framework.

It is most appropriate to begin building our conceptual framework with a definition of what we mean by "mobility." For the purposes of our discussion, mobility is defined as a person's purposeful movement through the environment from one place to another. It typically involves moving through space to accomplish some task or achieve some goal that cannot be reached where one already resides. Mobility is linked to a person's physical and psychological well-being. Limitation in mobility is associated with problems in quality of life, basic physiological functions, independent living, and personal autonomy, and increases the need for both formal and informal care [1, 2]. In fact, studies have identified mobility problems, especially difficulty with ambulation, as one of the most common types of disability in both older men and women [3]. Assessment of whether one can independently leave the home and use transportation have served as markers of older adults in need of assistance with the activities of daily living (ADLs). In short, not being able to go where one wants or needs to go takes a toll unless effective coping strategies are developed and implemented. Thus, mobility impairment, and the diseases and health conditions which cause it, can have serious ramifications for the affected individual and his/her family support system. In addition, mobility impairment is a challenge for the society in which affected individuals live, since those who have impaired mobility, like everyone else, have daily needs to move around in their immediate and more distant environment. It is within this broad context that mobility problems in the elderly should be considered.

Mobility in the older adult population can be measured in research studies in several different ways. One approach is to assess the performance of specific maneuvers, such as walking, stair climbing, and transferring from a seated to a standing position [1, 4]. Performance is typically evaluated in terms of speed, success, and/or the integrity of component movements. Another approach to mobility measurement is to assess a person's ability to carry out those instrumental activities of daily living (IADLs) that involve movement through the environment, such as bathing, dressing, toileting, and meal preparation. The focus is not actually on mobility per se but rather on performance of a task that embodies multiple domains including physical and cognitive functioning, general health, psychological status, and social and environmental factors. A third approach is to assess adverse mobility outcomes, as discussed previously. Each of these measurement approaches taps into a unique aspect of the mobility process, and can serve as outcome measures in intervention evaluation studies.

Mobility can be conceptualized as a functional continuum from bed bound on one extreme (i.e., no mobility), to distant excursions outside the home on the other. The continuum should be based on function or performance rather than defined by traditional disease-oriented concepts. As Tinetti pointed out, impaired mobility is not merely the sum of distinct disease processes and is not consistently related to anatomic or biochemical abnormalities [4]. Points along the functional continuum can be characterized with respect to many cross-cutting dimensions, such as frequency and duration of excursions, purpose, medical and psychological predispositions and implications, satisfaction, and the use of adaptive strategies and their effectiveness, be they devices, services, or technologies.

Fried and colleagues document that "task modification" represents an intermediate step in the disablement process between elders who report difficulty or inability to do a task and high functioning older cohorts (i.e., those reporting no difficulty or no required task modification) [5]. This relationship is particularly valid for mobility tasks, as illustrated in the work by Guralnick and colleagues [6], which demonstrated that non-disabled older adults with impaired lower extremity function were at risk for disability, institutionalization, and death.

The concept of "life-space" as introduced by May, Nayak, and Isaacs may be useful in characterizing the magnitude or extent of an older person's mobility, and could be a useful research tool in intervention evaluation studies as well as in epidemiological research [7]. In their study, May et al. defined it as the area in which a person moves in a given time period (e.g., within a day). Research participants were asked to complete a "life-space" diary each day for one month. The daily entries consisted of checking off boxes as to whether the person had moved into a particular "zone" on a given day. Zones consisted successively of concentric areas beginning with the bedroom at the center, and including increasingly wider areas, such as the rest of the home, the yard or grounds surrounding the dwelling where they lived, the block in which the dwelling was located, and the area across a traffic-bearing street. Additional items pertaining to specific trips outside the home also could be checked off, such as stores, clinics, churches, places of entertainment, restaurants, and so on. The diary entries then were converted to a life-space diameter score, which summarized a person's mobility over a month's time.

A quantitative measure of mobility in terms of life-space allows one to compare the extent of a person's mobility before and after an intervention. An interview format of the life-space diary was recently developed in order to assess the impact of cataracts on mobility in older adults [8]. Findings were that cataract restricts life-space, even when adjusted for co-morbid medical conditions, depressive symptoms, and mental status impairment. This cohort is being followed to see if cataract surgery and intraocular lens insertion will expand life-space over pre-intervention baseline. A life-space outcome measure may also be useful in evaluating the impact of other mobility enhancing interventions, such as exercise, new drugs, environmental modifications in the home, and public transportation systems targeted to benefit senior citizens.

Measuring life space also assists in determining how laboratory measures of mobility, often used in intervention evaluation studies, relate to mobility in everyday life, and thus can serve as an important step in validation. For example, laboratory measurements of mobility and component maneuvers are correlated with mobility indices and life-space diameter scores. Those who had a larger life-space had a faster gait speed and larger sway path, suggesting that laboratory measures are predictive of everyday mobility functioning [7]. Along similar lines, a larger life-space is associated with a longer functional reach, a dynamic balance measure defined as the maximal distance an individual can reach beyond an arm's length while standing [9, 10].

Earlier research on mobility impairment has primarily focused on adverse outcomes or complications of mobility (e.g., falls, hip fractures, vehicle crashes, traffic violations, pressure ulcers) and their risk factors [e.g., 2, 11-13]. Studies on all these adverse outcomes have stressed the multifactorial nature of their causes. What is also noteworthy is that many of these outcomes share risk factors. For example, falls, hip fractures following falls, vehicle crashes, and driver's license suspensions appear to have several common risk factors, such as vision impairment, cognitive impairment, lower extremity problems, and medication usage [11-19]. Thus, the presence of any or a combination of these risk factors may lead to several types of mobility impairment, or an "impaired mobility syndrome."

In support of this notion, Sims and colleagues present preliminary evidence that a history of at-fault crash involvement is significantly associated with a history of falling in older adults, even when adjusted for visual processing impairment and medication usage [20]. Koepsell and colleagues have also reported an association between crashing and falling in older adults, although the finding did not reach statistical significance [21]. Interventions to reduce risk targeted at one type of mobility impairment may in fact reduce risk for other types of mobility impairment. This approach of evaluating interventions in terms of their impact on multiple mobility outcomes may be more fruitful than a "single problem" approach. Tinetti and colleagues found that falls, incontinence, and functional dependence also share risk factors [2]. Thus, the finding that crashing and falling are associated contributes to the position that a unified approach to solving geriatric syndromes is more fruitful than addressing each problem in isolation.

Slowed information processing speed has emerged as a promising key in understanding older adults' everyday functional problems, yet it has not received a great deal of attention in the mobility literature. A slowing of visual and cognitive processing speed is a common problem in the elderly [for example, 22, 23], and has been linked to older adults' increased risk for vehicle crashes [12, 15, 24] and decreased performance of everyday tasks such as managing one's finances, using the telephone, and transporting oneself to locations outside walking distance [25]. Laboratory studies have indicated that visual processing speed in some older adults can be made more rapid through training interventions [26, 27], and thus it would be useful to examine whether increased processing speed leads to a reduction in adverse outcomes related to impaired mobility and expansion of the life-space.

Another area in need of focused investigation is ethnic differences in mobility impairment. Jette, Crawford, and Tennstedt [28] have reported that the prevalence of mobility impairment in older African Americans is higher (13.6%) than in whites (8.7%), where mobility is defined as walking or going outside. This impairment was linked to deficits in physical performance. A recent study found that inner city African Americans had particular problems with lower extremity impairment and visual problems [29], both of which can lead to mobility impairment. Early studies of disability in older adults suggest that although this ethnic difference in mobility impairment exists before age seventy-five years, the difference may decline or "cross-over" with increasing age [30]. Older African Americans have a higher prevalence of certain health problems (e.g., hypertension, kidney disease, glaucoma), and historically have had reduced access to educational and health services [31, 32]. Both of these factors could directly or indirectly elevate risk for mobility impairment, an area worthy of further study, especially from the standpoint of developing interventions.

There are other areas in need of research. Studies on adverse mobility outcomes such as falling and crashing have been largely targeted at risk factor identification. This approach is important for the initial stages of a research program, but a pragmatic issue from the standpoint of clinical care is to determine functional thresholds beyond which serious complications ensue, i.e., at what impairment levels do mobility problems emerge such that quality of life is seriously hampered and adverse outcomes apt to result? For example, vision and cognitive impairment, especially mild forms, are common in the elderly. They have been identified as risk factors for falling and crashing, yet one wonders how severe these impairments must be before the risk of falling and/or crashing reaches some criterion high level of risk. Even if cutpoints for a screening test could be identified which result in high sensitivity and specificity, we are still left with the challenge of determining who will benefit most from which interventions, and of determining how practical and cost-effective those interventions are. A unified approach to studying impaired mobility syndromes may be the most useful way to approach these research issues, given the conceptual and empirical similarities among the risk factors for different mobility problems.

REFERENCES

1. W. H. Ettinger, Jr., Immobility, in *Principles of Geriatric Medicine and Gerontology, Third Edition*, W. R. Hazzard, E. L. Bieman, J. P. Blass, W. H. Ettinger, Jr., J. B. Halter (eds.), McGraw-Hill, New York, pp. 1307-1311, 1994.
2. M. E. Tinetti, S. K. Inouye, T. M. Gill, and J. T. Doucette, Shared Risk Factors for Falls, Incontinence, and Functional Dependence: Unifying the Approach to Geriatric Syndromes, *Journal of the American Medical Association, 273*, pp. 1348-1353, 1995.
3. W. H. Ettinger, L. P. Fried, T. Harris, L. Shemanski, R. Schulz, and J. Robbins, Self-Reported Causes of Physical Disability in Older People: The Cardiovascular Health Study, *Journal of the American Geriatrics Society, 42*, pp. 1035-1044, 1994.
4. M. E. Tinetti, Performance-Oriented Assessment of Mobility Problems in Elderly Patients, *Journal of the American Geriatrics Society, 34*, pp. 119-126, 1986.
5. L. P. Fried, K. Bandeen-Roche, J. D. Williamson, P. Prasada-Rao, E. Chee, S. Tepper, and G. S. Rubin, Functional Decline in Older Adults. Expanding Methods of Ascertainment, *Journal of Gerontology: Medical Sciences, 51A*, pp. M206-M214, 1996.
6. J. M. Guralnick, L. Ferrucci, E. M. Simonsick, M. E. Salive, and R. B. Wallace, Lower Extremity Function in Persons Over Age 70 Years as a Predictor of Subsequent Disability, *New England Journal of Medicine, 332*, pp. 556-561, 1995.
7. D. May, U. S. L. Nayak, and B. Isaacs, The Life-Space Diary: A Measure of Mobility in Old People at Home, *International Rehabilitation Medicine, 7*, pp. 182-186, 1985.
8. B. T. Stalvey, C. Owsley, M. E. Sloane, and K. Ball, The Life Space Questionnaire: A Measure of the Extent of Mobility of Older Adults, *Journal of Applied Gerontology*, in press.
9. D. K. Weiner, P. W. Duncan, J. Chandler, and S. A. Studenski, Functional Reach: A Marker of Physical Frailty, *Journal of the American Geriatrics Society, 40*, pp. 203-207, 1992.
10. C. C. Hogue, S. Studenski, and P. Duncan, Assessing Mobility: The First Step in Falls Prevention, in *Key Aspects of Recovery: Improving Nutrition, Rest and Mobility*, S. G. Funk, E. M. Tornquist, and M. P. Champagne (eds.), Springer, New York, pp. 275-280, 1990.
11. S. R. Cummings, M. C. Nevitt, W. S. Browner, K. Stone, K. M. Fox, K. E. Ensrud, J. Cauley, D. Black, and T. M. Vogt, Risk Factors for Hip Fractures in White Women, *New England Journal of Medicine, 332*, pp. 767-773, 1995.
12. K. Ball, C. Owsley, M. E. Sloane, D. L. Roenker, and J. R. Bruni, Visual Attention Problems as a Predictor of Vehicle Crashes in Older Drivers, *Investigative Ophthalmology and Visual Science, 34*, pp. 3110-3123, 1993.
13. R. A. Marottoli, L. M. Cooney, Jr., D. R. Wagner, J. Doucetter, and M. E. Tinetti, Predictors of Automobile Crashes and Moving Violations among Elderly Drivers, *Annals of Internal Medicine, 121*, pp. 842-846, 1994.
14. R. M. Allman, P. S. Goode, M. M. Patrick, N. Burst, and A. A. Bartolucci, Pressure Ulcer Risk Factors among Hospitalized Patients with Activity Limitation, *Journal of the American Medical Association, 273*, pp. 865-870, 1995.
15. C. Owsley, K. Ball, M. E. Sloane, D. L. Roenker, and J. R. Bruni, Visual/Cognitive Correlates of Vehicle Accidents in Older Drivers, *Psychology and Aging, 6*, pp. 403-415, 1991.

16. M. E. Tinetti, M. Speechley, and S. F. Ginter, Risk Factors for Falls among Elderly Persons Living in the Community, *New England Journal of Medicine, 319,* pp. 1701-1707, 1988.
17. D. Heitman, M. R. Gossman, S. A. Shaddeau, and J. R. Jackson, Balance Performance and Step within Non-Institutionalized Elderly Women, *Physical Therapy, 69,* pp. 923-931, 1989.
18. B. D. Iverson, M. R. Gossman, S. A. Shaddeau, and M. E. Turner, Balance Performance, Force Production, and Activity Levels in Non-Institutionalized Men 60-90 Years of Age, *Physical Therapy, 70,* pp. 348-355, 1990.
19. W. A. Ray, R. L. Fought, and M. D. Decker, Psychoactive Drugs and the Risk of Injurious Motor Vehicle Crashes in Elderly Drivers, *American Journal of Epidemiology, 136,* pp. 873-883, 1992.
20. R. V. Sims, C. Owsley, R. Allman, K. Ball, and T. Smoot, Medical and Functional Correlates of Vehicle Crashes in Older Adults, *Journal of the American Geriatrics Society, 46,* pp. 556-561, 1998.
21. T. D. Koepsell, M. E. Wolf, L. McCloskey, D. M. Buchner, D. Louie, E. H. Wagner, and R. S. Thompson, Medical Conditions and Motor Vehicle Collision Injuries in Older Adults, *Journal of the American Geriatrics Society, 42,* pp. 695-700, 1994.
22. K. Ball, D. L. Roenker, and J. R. Bruni, Developmental Changes in Attention and Visual Search Throughout Adulthood, in *Advances in Psychology,* Vol. 23, J. Enns (ed.), Elsevier Scientific Publishers, North Holland, pp. 489-508, 1990.
23. K. W. Schaie, Perceptual Speed in Adulthood: Cross-Sectional and Longitudinal Studies, *Psychology and Aging, 4,* pp. 443-453, 1989.
24. C. Owsley, K. Ball, G. McGwin, Jr., M. E. Sloane, D. L. Roenker, M. F. White, and E. T. Overley, Visual Processing Impairment and Risk of Motor Vehicle Crash among Older Adults, *Journal of the American Medical Association, 279,* pp. 1083-1088, 1998.
25. S. L. Willis, Cognition and Everyday Competence, in *Annual Review of Gerontology and Geriatrics,* Vol. 11, K. W. Schaie and M. P. Lawton (eds.), Springer, New York, pp. 80-109, 1991.
26. K. K. Ball, B. L. Beard, D. L. Roenker, R. L. Miller, and D. S. Griggs, Age and Visual Search: Expanding the Useful Field of View, *Journal of the Optical Society of America, 5,* pp. 2210-2219, 1988.
27. D. Walsh, The Development of Visual Information Processes in Adulthood and Old Age, in *Aging and Human Visual Function,* R. Sekuler, D. Kline, and K. Dismukes (eds.), Alan R. Liss, New York, pp. 185-202, 1982.
28. A. M. Jette, S. L. Crawford, and S. L. Tennstedt, Toward Understanding Ethnic Differences in Late-Life Disability, *Research on Aging, 18,* pp. 292-309, 1996.
29. D. K. Miller, M. E. Carter, J. P. Miller, J. E. Fornoff, J. A. Bentley, S. D. Boyd, J. H. Rogers, N. M. Cox, J. E. Morley, L. Y. L. Lui, and R. M. Coe, Inner-City Older Blacks have High Levels of Functional Disability, *Journal of the American Geriatrics Society, 44,* pp. 1166-1173, 1996.
30. R. C. Gibson and J. S. Jackson, The Health, Physical Functioning, and Informal Supports of the Black Elderly, *The Milbank Quarterly, 65*(Supplement 2), pp. 421-453, 1987.
31. W. C. Cockerham, *Medical Sociology,* Prentice-Hall, New York, 1995.
32. K. F. Ferraro and M. N. Farmer, Double Jeopardy, Aging as Leveler, or Persistent Health Inequality? A Longitudinal Analysis of White and Black Americans, *Journal of Gerontology: Social Sciences, 51B,* pp. S319-S328, 1996.

CHAPTER
15

Closing Comment: Barriers To and Potential For An Interdisciplinary Research Agenda In Aging

Richard M. Allman and Jeffrey M. Clair

The Institute of Medicine's recommendations for a national research agenda on aging were published in 1991 in the book, *Extending Life, Enhancing Life* [1]. This report was developed by a committee of eighteen national authorities on health care, and outlined research priorities on age-related research that should be addressed and provided cost estimates for the work needed to address these research priorities.

In 1990, the United States Congress authorized the formation of a thirty-eight-member Task Force on Aging Research to assess progress in the scientific understanding of aging, to advise where the search for these answers should be concentrated, and to make recommendations for allocation of resources in the support of research. The members of the Task Force on Aging Research included four members of Congress, representatives from the Office of the Surgeon General, the Department of Veterans Affairs, the National Institute on Aging, other NIH Institutes and federal agencies with responsibilities relevant to aging, and three members of the general public. The recommendations of this Task Force were published in 1995 in a monograph entitled *The Threshold of Discovery: Future Directions for Research in Aging* [2].

The reports of both the Institute of Medicine (IOM) and the Task Force on Aging Research identified research priorities, and both benefitted from the advise of multiple scientific expert consultants. These reports also provided cost estimates needed to fully implement the recommendations. The estimated incremental annual cost for pursuing the research agendas proposed by the two reports was between $200 and $300 million per year.

Unfortunately, since the reports of the IOM and the Task Force on Aging Research were published, the recommended increases in funding for research in aging have not occurred, and the questions related to most of the research priorities in aging remain to be answered. Even if the resources committed to aging research had been increased as recommended, the total annual federal expenditure for research in aging would have represented less than 0.5 percent of the costs of the care associated with age-associated disability, morbidity, and mortality among Medicare beneficiaries in the United States. Research offers the best hope that our Nation has for optimizing quality of care while reducing these tremendous healthcare costs.

An interdisciplinary approach would be required to fully address the questions pertinent to many, if not most, of the research priorities identified by the Institute of Medicine and the Task Force on Aging Research. The Institute of Medicine (IOM) report specifically noted that there are a number of cross-cutting issues related to aging that require an interdisciplinary approach to research training and scientific investigation, especially questions related to gender, ethnicity, cultural background, ethics, and race. In addition, the IOM noted that clinical research on aging engages many disciplines. Basic molecular and cell biology provides insights that frequently lead to specific clinical research questions, while behavioral, social, and healthcare delivery research also inform the clinical investigation of the response of older people to disease and of the effect of interventions designed to prevent or reduce age-associated disability and morbidity.

The underlying premise of this book is that interdisciplinary research will ultimately lead to the greatest discoveries and to the most important advances in the field of aging. Unfortunately, there are a great number of barriers inhibiting truly interdisciplinary research in gerontology and geriatrics. Even among those of us who are gerontologists and geriatricians, we frequently find that psychologists only work with other psychologists; biologists only speak with other biologists; health policy and healthcare organizational experts mingle solely with other such experts; while clinicians frequently focus on the service needs of the increasingly large number of geriatric patients, and never even get to the research that needs to be done—they are spending time talking to patients, families, and trying to convince healthcare systems to make the changes required to develop the programs needed to address the specific needs of an aging population.

Thus, this book grew out of an effort to bring together gerontologists and geriatricians from multiple disciplinary perspectives at one place and at one time to review what progress has been made in the field of aging over the past decade, and to define the research questions that remain to be answered. The resulting presentations and book chapters provide a diverse perspective on gerontological research as we close the twentieth century and a look at issues that remain to be addressed during the future millennium. In a conference setting, these presentations provided an opportunity for gerontologists and geriatricians from multiple disciplines to interact with and to learn from each other, perhaps laying the foundation for truly interdisciplinary research in the future. At a minimum, conference participants went away informed about discipline-specific contributions gerontology, cross-cutting issues, and the degree to which interdisciplinary research has already advanced clinical geriatrics and research in some specific areas, namely in regard to the care of persons with Alzheimer's disease, incontinence, and mobility problems. Moreover, the conference participants were provided some insights into the potential of interdisciplinary approaches to high priority research issues related to aging. The conference facilitated communication and understanding, the first step toward a truly interdisciplinary research agenda for gerontology that perhaps also can be encouraged by the publication of this book.

While this book may be a first step in addressing communication barriers inhibiting a truly interdisciplinary research agenda in aging, a number of other barriers remain. The barriers to a truly interdisciplinary gerontology and geriatric research agenda in the United States include those external to the institutions and professionals directly involved in aging-related research. Examples of these external barriers include public policies that have discouraged the development of strong academic programs in gerontology and geriatric medicine. In addition to inadequate funding for specific research priorities in aging, similar funding shortages exist in terms of support for the research infrastructure needed to ensure a strong program of aging research in the country. The IOM identified the need for an investment of $110 million for construction of facilities to support the research priorities in aging. Medicare payment policy does not provide coverage for interdisciplinary approaches to geriatric care, such as geriatric assessment programs, despite evidence that these programs improve care greatly. Such policies impede the development of clinical sites required for training healthcare professionals to work together as interdisciplinary teams, not only to carry out patient care activities, but to pursue patient-oriented geriatric research. Medical, nursing, and health related professional schools accrediting bodies have failed to mandate interdisciplinary geriatric training for their students. Geriatric content is insufficiently covered in certification examinations for medical and other health professionals. Interdisciplinary educational programs such as Geriatric Education Centers also remain inadequately funded, with many states and regions of the country without the availability of such a resource.

Another barrier has been the increase in specialization and the strength of discipline-specific societies with their own professional meetings and journals. This has led to decreased participation of researchers in interdisciplinary research societies. This diminishes the opportunities for interdisciplinary communication and collaboration. Communication is also impeded by the use of discipline-specific technical terms and language.

The fragmentation of the healthcare system itself is encouraged by the multiple payers for healthcare services, with hospital, physician, and long-term care payments predominantly coming from different sources, i.e., Medicare Part A, Part B, and Medicaid, respectively. Thus, there remains little incentive for integrating and coordinating care for geriatric patients or for developing healthcare systems that would foster interdisciplinary collaboration. Opportunities for enhanced integration and coordination of geriatric services may exist with Medicare managed care and within the VA Health Care System, but developing novel programs in an era of cost-containment can be very difficult.

The lack of sufficient numbers of physicians trained as geriatricians and with the ability to carry out patient-oriented research also is a major barrier to interdisciplinary research in aging. Such clinicians are needed to facilitate interdisciplinary research focusing on the issues identified during the course of geriatric patient care activities. The lack of a sufficient number of such physician leaders is a major limiting factor in developing linkages between clinical medicine, basic, and social-behavioral scientists. It is estimated that there is a need for more than 2000 geriatric medical faculty in the Nation right now, and current estimates suggest that we only have 500 such faculty among the medical schools in the United States.

In addition to these barriers to an interdisciplinary research agency in aging, there remain institutional barriers even where research in aging is being pursued. Many institutional leaders question the value or importance of geriatrics and gerontology. This leads to inadequate support for the development of programs in geriatrics and decisions that delay the exposure of medical and other health professional students to the principles of geriatrics. Thus, these students often receive experience in geriatrics late in the course of their training, after they have already made decisions about specialty or other training.

Unfortunately, many programs in aging also experience fragmentation that impedes interdisciplinary research, as well as clinical and educational efforts. This may be a problem when programs in aging are scattered among many different schools and departments, without any coordination through an interdisciplinary aging program, center, or department. For example, many institutions have geriatric programs in psychiatry, family medicine, neurology, and medicine with little coordination or integration. Such fragmentation may be exacerbated when increased patient care activities are required to maintain clinical revenues or meet clinical demand, and research and educational activities no longer remain integrated within the clinical activities of a patient care program. Such fragmentation harms the prospect for interdisciplinary research in gerontology.

Despite the external and internal institutional barriers to the implementation of an interdisciplinary agenda for aging research, there are a number of promising developments that bode well for efforts to implement such an agenda. Professional societies are encouraging interdisciplinary collaboration. The American Geriatrics Society is expanding outreach efforts to all disciplines involved in providing geriatric patient care services, as well as to the public sector. Medicare managed care provides opportunities for integration and coordination of health care systems, and the implementation of interdisciplinary approaches to geriatric patient care, teaching, and research. The burgeoning number of older adults, as well as the increasing numbers of Baby Boomers being faced with responsibilities as caregivers for older parents, will put increasing pressure on the healthcare system and will likely prompt policy changes that will encourage interdisciplinary approaches to geriatrics. Recent evidence of more Congressional support for increased funding of NIH and reductions in the federal deficit offer hope that funding increases needed to support research in high priority areas may become reality, especially to address the need for investigators pursuing patient-oriented research. Finally, we trust that this edited volume will contribute to the development of an interdisciplinary research agenda in aging by fostering communication among researchers, policy experts, and students interested in the field of aging.

Much has been accomplished already despite the barriers to interdisciplinary research in aging, and the potential is great for greater advances in the future. In the next decade, we trust that the "gerontological prism" will permit researchers to focus their efforts together to address the high priority research issues in aging from an interdisciplinary perspective, and do much to improve the health and well-being of older adults.

REFERENCES

1. Institute of Medicine, Committee on a National Research Agenda on Aging, E. T. Lonergan (ed.), *Extending Life, Enhancing Life: A National Research Agenda on Aging,* National Academy Press, Washington, D.C., 1991
2. Task Force on Aging Research, *The Threshold of Discovery: Future Directions for Research in Aging. Report of the Task Force on Aging Research,* U.S. Department of Health and Human Services, 1995.

Contributors

William E. Aaronson is an Associate Professor and Chair of Health Administration at Temple University. He received his Ph.D. in business administration from Temple and has held faculty positions at Widener University and the Medical University of South Carolina. He has been a Robert Wood Johnson Faculty Fellow in Long-Term Care Administration and the recipient of two Gerontological Society of America Technical Assistance Program research awards. He has published a number of studies on organization, quality, and financial incentives in long-term care. Dr. Aaronson is a fellow of the American College of Health Care Administrators, and is an active member of several professional and research organizations. His current interests have taken him to the New Independent States of Eastern Europe, where he has taught health management to healthcare executives.

Rebecca Allen-Burge, Ph.D. (1994), Washington University in St. Louis, Dr. Allen-Burge is the Associate Director of the Applied Gerontology Program in the School of Social Work and Department of Psychology at The University of Alabama. Her primary research interests include advance care planning among older adults, their personal caregivers, and health care professionals regarding life-sustaining medical treatments. Her intervention research focuses on improving communication between care-recipients and their caregivers. Dr. Allen-Burge has published numerous journal articles and book chapters and teachers Introductory Statistics in the Department of Psychology.

Richard M. Allman, MD, is Professor of Medicine and Director of the Center for Aging and the Division of Gerontology and Geriatric Medicine at the University of Alabama at Birmingham (UAB). He also serves as Chief of Geriatrics at the Birmingham VA Medical Center, and as the Principal Clinical Coordinator of the Alabama Quality Assurance Foundation (AQAF). AQAF is the Health Care Financing Administration's peer review organization for Medicare beneficiaries in Alabama. He is co-editor of the John A. Hartford Foundation Southeast Center of Excellence in Geriatric Medicine, a joint program of UAB and Emory University. Dr. Allman completed his MD and residency in internal medicine at West Virginia University and then served as a fellow in general internal medicine at Johns Hopkins University. His current research interests include mobility disorders and improving health care processes and outcomes for geriatric patients.

Patricia S. Baker, Ph.D., is Assistant Professor of Sociology at the University of Alabama at Birmingham where she is Director of UAB's Gerontology Education

317

Program. She has been Project Coordinator for the UAB Study of Aging, a longitudinal study of community-dwelling older adults for the last two years. Her research interests include medical sociology, gerontology, and doctor-patient communication.

Vern L. Bengtson is AARP/University Professor of Gerontology and Professor of Sociology at the University of Southern California, and is past President of the Gerontological Society of America. He received his BA at North Park College, and his MA and Ph.D. from the University of Chicago. For over twenty-five years he has directed the Longitudinal Study of Four Generation Families at USC, doing research on the sociology of the life course, socialization, ethnicity, and aging. He has published ten books, the most recent is *Adulthood and Aging: Research on Continuities and Discontinuities* (1996). He has also produced over 170 papers in professional journals and books. He has been awarded a MERIT award from the National Institute on Aging and has twice won the Reuben Hill Award for outstanding research and theory on the family. He won the 1991 University of Southern California Associates Award for Creativity in Research, in 1995 was given the Distinguished Scholar Award of the American Sociological Association's Section on Aging for his Longitudinal Study of Four-Generation Families research program and in 1996 he was awarded the prestigious Robert W. Kleemeier Award for outstanding research in the field of gerontology by the Gerontological Society of America. He spent his Spring 1997 sabbatical as the Benjamin Meaker Visiting Professor at the University of Bristol in England.

Timothy J. Biblarz, is an Assistant Professor of Sociology and Research Associate in the Andrus Gerontology Center at the University of Southern California. He received his MA and Ph.D. from the University of Washington. His research focuses on the consequences for children of recent changes in the American family. He has published his findings in the *American Sociological Review, American Journal of Sociology, Social Forces, Journal of Marriage and the Family,* and other journals.

Kathryn Burgio is a behavioral psychologist with sixteen years of experience in the field of urinary incontinence. She completed her doctoral training at the University of Notre Dame and a fellowship in behavioral medicine at the National Institute on Aging. Currently, she is Professor of Medicine at UAB. She is co-editor of the Behavioral Sciences Section in the Division of Gerontology and Geriatric Medicine, Director of the UAB Continence Program, and Research Director, Genitourinary Disorders Center. He research agenda in incontinence has included investigations of its prevalence and risk factors and clinical studies of the effectiveness of behavioral treatment with a variety of populations.

Louis D. Burgio, Ph.D., is Professor in the Division of Gerontology and Geriatric Medicine, University of Alabama School of Medicine at Birmingham (UAB). His administrative positions include Co-Director of the Section of Behavioral Sciences and Director of the Behavioral Gerontology Program. Within the Center for Aging, Dr. Burgio is the Director of the Behavioral and Social Science Aspects of Alzheimer's Disease through which he has mentored several UAB investigators. He is also Adjunct Professor of Psychology and Nursing. Dr. Burgio is a funded researcher, having received funding from the National Institute on Aging and the National Institute for Nursing Research, and private foundations. Dr. Burgio received a Special Emphasis Research Career Award in Behavioral Gerontology from NIA in 1990. Dr. Burgio is on the editorial boards of five major gerontological journals. He has published extensively and has presented numerous papers at scientific meetings, particularly in the areas of conducting dementia management interventions in the nursing home and developing the staff management systems that are needed for successful adoption of intervention programs.

Laura L. Carstensen is Associate Professor of Psychology at Stanford University. She is Director of the Institute for Research on Women and Gender and Vice-chair of the Psychology Department. Carstensen received her B.S. from the University of Rochester and her Ph.D. from West Virginia University. She is a Fellow of the American Psychological Association, the Gerontological Society of America and the American Psychological Society. She is past-president of the Society for a Science of Clinical Psychology and 1997 Chair of the Behavioral Sciences Section of the Gerontological Society of America. In 1993, she received the Richard Kalish Award for her research from the Gerontological Society of America. Dr. Carstensen currently serves on the scientific editorial boards of *Psychology and Aging, Journal of Gerontology: Psychological Sciences,* and *Journal of Gender, Culture and Health.* She co-edited with Barry A. Edelstein, Ph.D. and Laurie Dornbrand, M.D., *The Practical Handbook of Clinical Gerontology* and, with John Neale, Ph.D., *Mechanisms of Psychological Influence on Physical Health, With Special Attention to the Elderly.* Her clinical practice is devoted to the assessment and treatment of older adults. Her research, supported by the National Institute on Aging, focuses on life-span development, gender and emotion.

Jeffrey M. Clair, Ph.D., is an Associate Professor of Sociology and Medicine at the University of Alabama at Birmingham. He completed an N.I.A. Postdoctoral Research Fellowship in Health and Aging at the Andrus Gerontology Center, University of Southern California, after completing his Ph.D. in Sociology at Louisiana State University, with a National Science Foundation Dissertation Research Award for a study on doctor-patient-family communication. His substantive areas of specialization are medical sociology, social gerontology, social psychology, and triangulated research techniques.

Ed Clarke earned his Ph.D. at the University of Southern California in 1996. His areas of specialization include Deviance, Delinquency, and Marriage and the Family. Dr. Clarke teaches a wide range of sociology courses at California State University, Los Angeles. Current research includes conflict and support in later-life families and support system utilization of young custodial parents.

Harvey Jay Cohen is Professor of Medicine; Director, Center for the Study of Aging and Human Development; and Chief, Division of Geriatric Medicine at Duke University Medical Center; and Associate Chief of Staff for Geriatrics and Extended Care; and Director of the Geriatric Research, Education and Clinical Center (GRECC) of the Veterans Administration Medical Center in Durham, North Carolina. He trained in internal medicine and in hematology/oncology at Duke University Medical Center. Following a Staff Associateship at the National Institutes of Health, he returned to Duke as a faculty member of the Department of Medicine in 1971. He served as Chief of the Hematology/Oncology Division and, later, Chief of the Department of Medicine of the Duke affiliated Durham VA Medical Center from 1976-82. Dr. Cohen has published extensively with over 200 articles and book chapters on topics in geriatrics and hematology/oncology, with special emphasis on aspects of cancer and immunologic disorders in the elderly, and geriatric assessment. He serves on several editorial boards and is past Editor of the *Journal of Gerontology: Medical Sciences,* the major clinical research journal in geriatrics and gerontology. Dr. Cohen is a Fellow of The Gerontological Society of America and was Program Chairman for the 1994 annual meeting and was Chairman of the Publications Committee. He has been named as the winner of the Freeman Award for 1998 by GSA. He was a member of the Board of Directors of The American Geriatrics Society from 1987; served as president from 1994-95; and Chairman of the Board from 1995-96. He serves on numerous national committees and advisory boards. He participated in writing the first Geriatrics board exam and in formulating the guidelines for accreditation of Geriatrics fellowship programs. He has been a pioneer in the establishment of programs to train physician-scientists in geriatric medicine and is recognized as one of the leading U.S. academic clinical investigators in geriatrics. In March 1996, he was recognized as one of The Best Doctors in America in AMERICAN HEALTH. In 1997, he was elected to membership in the American Association of Physicians, one of few geriatricians so honored.

Stephen J. Cutler is Professor of Sociology and the Bishop Robert F. Joyce Distinguished University Professor of Gerontology at the University of Vermont. Prior to joining the UVM faculty in 1984, he taught at Oberlin College from 1969-1984. He received his M.A. and Ph.D. from the University of Michigan and his B.A. from Dartmouth College, all in sociology. Dr. Cutler is co-author of *Middle Start: An Experiment in the Educational Enrichment of Young Adolescents* (New York: Cambridge University Press, 1977), co-editor of *Major Social Issues: A Multidisciplinary View* (New York: The Free Press, 1978), and co-editor of *Promoting Successful and Productive Aging* (Thousand Oaks, CA: Sage Publications, 1995). His principal gerontological research interests are in the areas of caregiving, transportation, household composition, social and political attitude change, voluntary association participation, cognition, and ethics. He is the past Editor of the *Journal of Gerontology: Social Sciences;* he has served as Chair of the Behavioral and Social Sciences Section of the Gerontological Society of America and as Chair of the Sociology of Aging Section of the American Sociological Association; and he is a member of the Executive Committee of the Association for Gerontology in Higher Education.

Linda Lindsey Davis, RN, Ph.D., is Professor, School of Nursing and a Scientist in the Center for Aging and the Alzheimer's Disease Center at the University of Alabama at Birmingham. She currently is principal investigator for a clinical trial (KO1 1 NR00095) funded by the National Institute of Nursing Research, to compare the outcomes from telephone-based with home visit-based skill training of family caregivers of dementia patients. She is the author of numerous papers on family theory, measurement and family care in various chronic disease situations. Dr. Davis received the doctorate in Nursing from the University of Maryland at Baltimore.

Theresa Drinka, Ph.D., President of River's Edge Consulting® received her masters degree in Social Work and her Ph.D. in Continuing Education from the University of Wisconsin-Madison. She had over twenty years of experience in developing, managing, and evaluating work teams before establishing a consulting and training business in 1996. Dr. Drinka trains teams in health care, education, information technology, and other service settings. Dr. Drinka has given lectures and teambuilding workshops and provided consultation on interdisciplinary team development and self-directed work teams throughout the United States, as well as in Canada, and England. She focuses on assisting teams and organizations that want to create positive change and she specializes in assisting teams that are experiencing difficulty. She is author of "Case Studies from Purgatory" and over thirty other publications on self-directed work teams, health care teams, and assessment instruments, e.g., the Assessment of Living Skills and Resources (ALSAR) and Team Signatures® to help teams survive and increase their efficiency and effectiveness. Dr. Drinka serves on the editorial board for the *Journal of Interprofessional Care* and is a clinical faculty member in the Department of Medicine at the University of Wisconsin Medical School. She was awarded the Association of Gerontology in Higher Education Master Teacher Award in 1997.

Connie Evashwick, Ph.D., is the Archstone Foundation Endowed Chair and Director of the Center for Health Care Innovation at California State University, Long Beach. Her expertise is in the continuum of care and long-term care delivery systems. Dr. Evashwick holds a bachelor's and master's degree from Stanford University and a master's and doctoral degree from the Harvard School of Public Health. She is a Fellow of the American College of Healthcare Executives. Dr. Evashwick's multifaceted career has included positions in academia, consulting, and direct operations management. She has been vice president of long-term care for two major healthcare systems and consulted with health systems, hospitals, and long-term care organizations across the nation. Dr. Evashwick has authored over eighty-five publications, including five books.

Roseann Giarrusso received her Ph.D. in sociology at the University of California, Los Angeles. She is a Research Assistant Professor of Gerontology and Sociology at the University of Southern California, and the Project Director of the Longitudinal Study of Generations. Her research interests include intergenerational family relations, social psychology, and the sociology of aging and the life-course. Her most recent publications include an examination of the stresses and rewards of grandparents raising grandchildren, and an investigation of how changes in the occupation and performance of family roles across the life cycle are associated with changes in self-esteem twenty years later.

Patricia S. Goode, M.D., is a board certified internist and geriatrician. She received her BSN degree from Temple University, Philadelphia; Master of Science in Nursing from the University of Alabama at Birmingham; Enterostomal Therapy certificate from Emory University, Atlanta, Georgia; and Doctor of Medicine from the University of Alabama at Birmingham. She is currently Assistant Professor of Medicine at the University of Alabama School of Medicine, Birmingham, Alabama; as well as Medical Director of the UAB Continence Program, Assistant Clinical

Director of the Geriatric Medicine Primary Care Clinic at The Kirklin Clinic, and Medical Director of the Visiting Nursing Association. She is actively involved in research to improve the diagnosis and treatment of urinary incontinence, and educational programs for health care professionals managing patients with this disorder.

Marilyn Gossman, Ph.D., was Professor and Director, Division of Physical Therapy at the University of Alabama at Birmingham, until her death on January 12, 1998. She was a licensed Physical Therapist. Dr. Gossman received her Ph.D. in Anatomy from the Union Institute, Cincinnati, Ohio in 1984. Her research interests included muscle performance and gait characteristics in women with osteoarthritis, balance performance as a function of age, musculoskeletal profile of fallers in the elderly, and length associated changes in muscle.

Jeremy Graff is currently a medical student at the University of Chicago. He received his MA in psychology from Stanford University in 1996. At Stanford, he studied social and emotional aspects of aging, and co-authored a book chapter "Affect in Intimate Relationships, the Developmental Course of Marriage," in the *Handbook of Emotion, Adult Development, and Aging* (1996), with Laura Carstensen, Robert Levenson, and John Gottman.

David A. Karp, Ph.D., Professor of Sociology at Boston College, has coauthored: *Sociology in Everyday Life* (1993, 1986); *Being Urban: A Sociology of City Life* (1991, 1977); *The Research Craft* (1982); *Experiencing the Life Cycle: A Social Psychology of Aging* (1982; 1993). His most recent book, *Speaking of Sadness: Depression, Disconnection and the Meanings of Illness* (1996) won the best book of the year award from the Society for the Study of Symbolic Interaction. He has published numerous articles in *The Gerontologist, Qualitative Sociology, Symbolic Interaction, The Journal of Contemporary Ethnography,* and *Qualitative Health Research.*

Sherron H. Kell, MD, MPH, graduated from the University of Alabama School of Medicine in 1987. She is board certified in internal medicine and is a fellowship trained geriatrician with her Certificate of Added Qualifications in geriatric medicine. She was an Assistant Professor of Medicine at the University of Alabama at Birmingham (UAB) from 1993 until 1998. As part of her responsibilities at UAB, she was the Medical Director of the Mobility Assessment Clinic and was the Assistant Principle Coordinator for Alabama's Medicare quality improvement organization. Currently she is the Regional Scientific Director for the Mountain States Region at Novartis Pharmaceuticals Corporation.

Frieder R. Lang is working as an assistant professor of Social Psychology and Education at the Humboldt University of Berlin. He received his MA at the Technical University of Berlin in 1990, and his Ph.D. in Psychology at the Free University of Berlin and the Max-Planck-Institute of Human Development in 1993. In 1996 he spent one term as a visiting scholar at the Stanford University. His research interests are Social Motivation and Personality across the life span, Family and Social Relationships, and Successful Aging. His mailing address is Humboldt University of Berlin, Department of Sociology, Social Psychology and Education, Geschwister-Scholl-Str. 7, 10099 Berlin, Germany or e-mail to flang@rz.hu-berlin.de.

L. Keith Lloyd, MD, is Professor and Director of the Division of Urology at the University of Alabama at Birmingham. He has been on faculty there for twenty-three years and has developed the programs in Neurourology and Urinary Incontinence. He serves as Director of the Urological Rehabilitation and Research Center and of the Urodynamics Laboratory. His scholarly contributions have been primarily in the area of Spinal Cord Injury Urology and Outcomes Research. Dr. Lloyd along with Drs. Burgio, Goode, and Varner helped establish the Continence Center of Alabama, a multidisciplinary clinic for the treatment and research into the causes and management of disorders of urinary control.

Richard Maisiak, Ph.D., MSPH, is currently Professor, Education in Medicine, at the UAB School of Medicine with a secondary appointment in the Department of Biostatistics and Biomathematics, UAB School of Public Health and is a Scientist at the UAB Center for Aging, UAB Arthritis Center, UAB Center for Health Promotion, and the UAB Injury Control Research Center. He earned a Ph.D. (1975) in Psychology from Northwestern University and a MSPH in Epidemiology and Biostatistics (1989) from the University of Alabama at Birmingham. He is the author of over fifty scientific publications.

Daniel Marson, JD, Ph.D., has received training in law, clinical psychology, and neuropsychology. He earned his JD at the University of Chicago Law School in 1981, and is a member of the bar in Illinois (1981) and in Alabama (1992). He has practiced law in both private and governmental settings. Dr. Marson earned his Ph.D. in Chicago in 1990, where he specialized in geropsychology and neuropsychology. Dr. Marson is currently Associate Professor and Director of the Division of Neuropsychology in the Department of Neurology at the University of Alabama at Birmingham. He is Associate Director of the Alzheimer's Disease Research Center at UAB funded by the National Institute of Aging. He is also an Associate Scientist and member of the Executive Committee of the UAB Center for Aging. He is currently the Chair of the Internal Ethics Committee of the Alzheimer's Disease Cooperative Study, a National Institute of Aging research project involving all Alzheimer's Disease Centers nationwide.

Michael A. Morrisey, Ph.D., is Professor in the Department of Health Care Organization and Policy of the UAB School of Public Health, and Director of the UAB Lister Hill Center for Health Policy. His research interests are in the workings of health care markets and the effects of health insurance and managed care on health care organization, financing, and delivery. Current research focuses on the effects of managed care market penetration on the financial and organizational linkages between physicians and hospitals, and the health insurance choices made by small employers.

Cynthia Owsley is Professor of Ophthalmology, School of Medicine, at the University of Alabama at Birmingham where she is also Director of the Clinical Research Unit in the Department of Ophthalmology and Co-Director of the Roybal Center for Applied Gerontology. She received her Ph.D. in Psychology at Cornell University and underwent post-doctoral training in vision and aging at Northwestern University. Her research, funded by the National Institute on Aging since 1979, is focused on vision impairment and eye disease in the elderly, and their implications for the performance of everyday tasks and health-related quality of life.

Judith Richlin-Klonsky is currently a Senior Researcher at UCLA. She has also been a lecturer for many years, developing an innovative course in the sociology of aging. She holds a master's degree in family therapy and received her Ph.D. in sociology from UCLA, specializing in qualitative research and an interpretive theoretical framework. Her research publications include an analysis of the history of the marriage and family therapy license in California and a longitudinal case study of a five-generation family. Other recent professional activities include working with the Playwrights' Project in the development and presentation of *Spotlight on Six Angelinos: Illuminating History Through Ordinary Lives,* nonfictional dramatic monologues representing the lives of older people of different racial and ethnic backgrounds.

Robert E. L. Roberts is Associate Professor of Sociology at California State University, San Marcos, and research associate in U.S.C.'s Andrus Gerontology Center. He also directs the Human Development program at CSUSM. He received his Ph.D. from the University of Southern California. For ten years he has been a co-investigator in the Longitudinal Study of Generations, conducting research on the influence of intergenerational relationships on individual psychological and social development over the life course. He has published his findings in *Social Psychology Quarterly, Journals of Gerontology, Journal of Marriage and the Family, The Gerontologist, The Sociological Quarterly, Marriage and Family Review,* and several edited volumes.

Richard Shewchuk, Ph.D., received his Ph.D. from the University of Oregon and is an associate professor in the Department of Health Administration at the University of Alabama at Birmingham where he teaches courses in long-term-care administration and quantitative methods. He is the associate editor of the gerontology education program at UAB, has appointments in the Lister Hill Center for Health Policy, the Center for Aging, and is co-director of Project Focus, a community-based family caregiver training program. His research addresses the role of family care-givers in community-based long-term care. His studies have been published in journals such as *Health Psychology, Rehabilitation Psychology,* and *Health Care Management Review.*

Merril Silverstein, Ph.D., is Assistant Professor of Gerontology and Sociology at the Andrus Gerontology Center of the University of Southern California. Dr. Silverstein's research is concerned with understanding how individuals age within the context of family life, including such issues as social support across generations and return migration in later life. Dr. Silverstein has published widely in the fields of sociology, gerontology, and demography. He is a fellow of the Brookdale Foundation, the Gerontological Society of America, and the Fulbright international program. He is also the recipient of a FIRST award from the National Institute of Aging to study grandparenting over the life-course.

Richard V. Sims, MD, is a graduate of Amherst College, Harvard Medical School and the internal medicine residency program at Harlem Hospital in New York City. After five years in medical practice, he completed fellowships in general internal medicine and geriatrics at the University of Pennsylvania in 1986. Thereafter, Dr. Sims served as a clinician-educator at Penn until 1994, when he joined the Division of Gerontology and Geriatric Medicine at the University of Alabama at Birmingham (UAB). Currently an assistant professor, Dr. Sims is developing a research career devoted to the study of older driver safety, falling and geriatric mobility. His clinical activities are based at the Birmingham Department of Veterans Affairs Medical Center and The Kirklin Clinic. Dr. Sims is the director of the Geriatric Medicine Fellowship and is also the UAB Research Training Director for the Southeast Center for Excellence in Geriatric Medicine, a joint UAB-Emory University program funded by the Hartford Foundation.

E. Percil Stanford, Ph.D., is professor and director of the University Center on Aging in the College of Health and Human Services at San Diego State University. He is also the Director of the National Institute on Minority Aging and has served as the Director of the National Resource Center for Minority Aging Populations. Other involvements include: Co-Director of the San Diego Geriatric Education Center; Co-Director National Resource Center on Diversity and Long-Term Care; Assistant to the Director of the Administration on Aging Title V Training Program in the U.S. Department of Health Education and Welfare; Co-Director of the San Diego Geriatric Education Center and Regional operations officer, office of the Secretary, Department of Health Education and Welfare. Previously authored subject matter includes: *Suburban Block Elderly, Health and Functional Life Styles, Service Utilization and Access, Elder Abuse, Retirement in Modern Society,* and *Director for Education and Training.*

Gwendolyn E. Stanford, M.S., is Extension Advisor for Nutrition, Family and Consumer Sciences, and the Expanded Food and Nutrition Education Program, in San Diego, California. She has been with the University of California Cooperative Extension Division of Agriculture and Natural Resources since 1983. Her consumer education outreach programs, research activities and publications have focused on nutrition and health, food safety, family issues, and financial management. Professional involvements include the American Association of Family and Consumer Services, the National Extension Association of Family and Consumer Services, the Society for Nutrition Education, and the Institute of Food Technology.

Alan Stevens is an Assistant Professor and Director of the Dementia Care Research Program in the Division of Gerontology and Geriatric Medicine at UAB. Dr. Stevens received his doctorate in Applied Developmental Psychology from the University of New Orleans. Following the completion of his graduate education in 1993, Dr. Stevens began development of his current research program focused on interventions to assist Alzheimer's patients and their caregivers. Dr. Stevens conducts research in both community and long-term care settings. Dr. Stevens' research program is supported currently by a Mentored Research Scientist Development Award (MRSDA) from the National Institutes of Health. In addition to his work at UAB, Dr. Stevens is currently President of the Board of Directors of Alzheimer's of Central Alabama, a nonprofit organization providing educational and support services to Alzheimer's caregivers.

Mary Umlauf, RN, Ph.D., is an Associate Professor at the University of Alabama School of Nursing and is an active member of the UAB Continence Program research team. She is a Fulbright Scholar and a graduate of the University of Texas at Austin and Texas Woman's University. Her specialty is bladder control in older adults and currently has two NIH grants underway: "Mechanisms of Nocturia in Older Adults" and "Paracrine Regulation of Urine Production."

Donald A. Urban, MD, is a graduate of the University of Cincinnati College of Medicine 1982, a graduate of the surgery and urology residency program at the University of Pennsylvania 1988, board certified by the American Board of Urology 1990, and a fellow in the American College of Surgeons 1991. After four years in private practice, he joined the faculty at the University of Alabama at Birmingham School of Medicine in 1992 as an assistant professor in the Department of Surgery, Division of Urology. He serves as the chief of the urology service at the Birmingham Veterans Medical Center. He is a research scientist at the Wallace Comprehensive Cancer Center. He is active in patient care at the Kirklin Clinic and the University of Alabama at Birmingham Medical Center. Dr. Urban's research interests are focused in the areas of prostate cancer chemoprevention, treatment outcomes, and quality of life.

R. Edward Varner, MD, is Professor and Division Director of Medical/Surgical Gynecology in the Department of Obstetrics and Gynecology at the University of Alabama at Birmingham School of Medicine. He received his medical degree from UAB in 1980 and received training in Urogynecology in Bristol, United Kingdom. Dr. Varner serves as a scientist with the UAB Center for Aging and an Associate Professor in General Surgery, and a Co-Director of the Center for Genitourinary Disorders at UAB. He is a member of numerous professional societies, serves on various councils and committees, and was recently appointed to a term on the Board of Directors of the Jefferson County Medical Society. Dr. Varner is the principal investigator, co-principal investigator, and/or gynecologic investigator on several NIH and privately funded research studies on women's health care issues.

Fredric D. Wolinsky is Professor of Health Services Research and Geriatric Medicine at Saint Louis University, and Editor of the *Journal of Gerontology: Social Sciences*. His principal interests are secondary analyses of large, national surveys to examine the health and illness behavior of older adults. Most recently he has concentrated on the development, refinement, and replication of structural models of health status using the Longitudinal Study on Aging, the National Long-Term Care Survey, the Survey on Assets and Health Dynamics, and the Health and Retirement Survey. Dr. Wolinsky is also evaluating different approaches for establishing clinically meaningful change in the measurement of functional health status over time.

William C. Yoels, Ph.D., Professor of Sociology at UAB, has co-authored Sociology in Everyday Life (1993, 1986); *Experiencing the Life Cycle: A Social Psychology of Aging* (1993; 1982); *Being Urban: A Sociology of City Life* (1991, 1977). He has published thirty articles in journals such as *The American Journal of Sociology, The Sociology of Health and Illness, Qualitative Sociology, The Sociological Quarterly, Sociology of Education, Symbolic Interaction,* and *The Archives of Physical Medicine and Rehabilitation.*

Index

Other Books of Interest in the Society and Aging Series
Series Editor: Jon Hendricks

Older Adults with Developmental Disabilities
By Claire Lavin and Kenneth J. Doka

Rural Health and Aging Research:
Theory, Methods and Practical Applications
*Editors: Wilbert M. Gesler, Donna J. Rabiner
and Gordon H. DeFriese*

Staying Put:
Adapting the Places Instead of the People
Editors: Susan Lanspery and Joan Hyde

Surviving Dependence:
Voices of African American Elders
By Mary M. Ball and Frank J. Whittington

The Old Age Challenge to the Biomedical Model:
Paradigm Strain and Health Policy
By Charles F. Longino, Jr. and John W. Murphy

Aging Public Policy:
Bonding the Generations
By Theodore H. Koff and Richard W. Park

Special Research Methods for Gerontology
Editors: M. Powell Lawton and A. Regula Herzog

Health and Economic Status of Older Women:
Research Issues and Data Sources
*Editors: A. Regula Herzog, Karen C. Holden,
and Mildred M. Seltzer*

DATE DUE

APR 0 8 2002		
MAY 1 5 2003		
DEC 0 7 2005		